POLICING FROM BOW STREET

Principal Officers, Runners and The Patroles

Peter Kennison and Alan Cook

BLUE LAMP
BOOKS

First edition published 2019

Dust jacket:
'A Duel Prevented – The Arrival of the Peace Officers' (1834) © Alan Cook

ISBN: 978-1-911273-38-7 (hardcover)
ISBN: 978-1-911273-39-4 (ebook)

Published by Blue Lamp Books

An Imprint of
Mango Books
18 Soho Square
London W1D 3QL
www.MangoBooks.co.uk

POLICING
FROM
BOW STREET

Principal Officers,
Runners and The Patroles

Print by Rowlandson Pugin: 'Bow Street Office' (1808)

Bow Street patrol routes © Chris Hilman

Policing From Bow Street

Acknowledgements

Alan Moss; David Swinden; Phill Barnes-Warden; Neil Paterson; Simon Littlejohn; James McColl; Alastair McColl, illustrator; Andrew Lott (Senior Information Officer LMA); Louise Hurlow; Greg Ruthven; Frederick Wilkinson; Phil Anderson; Justine Taylor (Archivist Honourable Artillery Company); Chris Hillman; Gary Powell; Sid Mackay; John Bearchell; Dr David J. Cox; Chris Forrester; Louise Kennison; Nicola Minney; Edward Conant; Sue Fincham; David Green. Thanks are also due to Adam Wood, who as publisher has generously helped, guided and encouraged us in our journey to print.

Lastly, to our wives Julie and Rowena, whose encouragement and unwavering support has helped to make this book happen.

Preface

This book represents the merging of two similar but different sets of starting points. For Peter Kennison, this occurred through his interest in police history especially in the metropolis after he joined the London Police in 1970. The project that developed into this book arose following his publishing (with David Swinden and Alan Moss) of the *Behind the Blue Lamp* series of London police station histories printed in 2003, 2011 and 2014. The underlying idea behind that trilogy of publications focussed on looking "Behind the Blue Lamp" to reveal the private domain of the police station, a world that most people never see. *Policing from Bow Street* seeks to do the same thing and reveal to the reader the challenges, secrets and functions faced by the early Constables of Georgian London.

For Alan Cook, this project came about because of his love of police history - more precisely, his passion for finding, collecting and preserving police artefacts, equipment and accoutrements from times gone by. His particular interest in London and its early Public or Police Offices has resulted in the acquisition of equipment, correspondence and publications particularly relating to Georgian Bow Street. Alan published his book on truncheons and tipstaves, *Truncheons – An Unequal Match*, in 2014. It is through these artefacts, perhaps for the first time, that the story of Bow Street can be better understood.

Peter Kennison and Alan Cook share other common factors as well, namely both have satisfied the selection process of becoming a police officer and held the office of Constable. Both recognised similar patterns in procedures and established practice from the historical past echoed today in policing – its perceptual blueprint.

What surprised them was the fact that even the early Bow Street officers of the 1760s had gathered a range of practical experience, advice and knowledge on policemanship which predated their previous understanding. The conception that this perceptual blueprint was commenced and developed during the formative years of Peel's New Police in 1829 needed to be re-thought. In this way, both authors have identified with the Bow Street Patroles (including the erroneously-named Runners) as being the very roots of the job they recognised and understood, and in writing this book want to ensure the reputation of the Patroles are given their rightful place in the history of policing.

*

Authors' note: Because this book has been written from individual stand points, the reader will naturally encounter repetition in some pen portraits of the Bow Street Patroles, Runners and Principal Officers since many shared the same particular experiences.

In the period covered in this book, British currency was divided into pounds, shillings and pence. One pound was made up of 20 shillings, and there were 12 pence to the shilling. £1 in 1740 was the equivalent of around £120 in 2018.

Introduction

This book covers the 100 years between 1740 and 1840, including over eighty years before the advent of the New London Police established by Sir Robert Peel in 1829. Crime and criminality in Georgian England was rising, unchecked against a backdrop of public corruption, drunkenness, gambling, sexual promiscuity and vagrancy, combined with an over-severity of justice administration. Despite a bankrupt Treasury, and social and political upheaval, advances were made in reconciling and combating the high levels of violent criminality.

The name of Bow Street became revered by the honest citizens and feared by the dishonest. Number 4 Bow Street was a three-storey family house and Court of Justice. The court was presided over by Henry Fielding, a Justice of the Peace who, in a few short years, established a forward-thinking plan for policing based on strong principles and methods – the details we can understand today. As Lucy Inglis (2014) rightly asserts, "Less has changed than you might think".

We will commence with a look at the gradual development of the early crime control administration and practice commenced by Sir Thomas de Veil, further developed by Henry Fielding and enhanced by his half–brother and successor John Fielding. We acknowledge the contribution made by Saunders Welch, the High Constable of Holborn who seems to have been conveniently airbrushed out of Bow Street's history, and who importantly wrote one of the very first police instruction books that gave crucial advice on the office of Constable and how to avoid its pitfalls. There are certain established rules in policing practice which every person who holds the office of Constable learns from the start – the "fundamentals of policing" as we have named them, as part of their perceptual blueprint. For example, these "fundamentals" include the searching of a suspect at the start not only to preserve any evidence and stolen artefacts found, but also to ensure the officer's own safety by removing any weapons, knives or sharp instruments which could be used to do harm. These "fundamentals" predate our original understanding and can be found in Welch's 1754 book of Instructions for Constables (see Appendix 1 for further details).

Sir Robert Peel has been credited with creating the first professional uniformed police in 1829, but in doing so he not only copied and developed these instructions to Constables but also many of the lessons learned by Bow Street. These included its features of organisation, crime recording methods, discipline, instructions and recruiting techniques, even introducing some of the same clothing and accoutrements of the patroles. Whilst much innovation can be attributed to Peel, many of these systems predate our original perception.

Henry Fielding, with the help of Saunders Welch, brought together like-minded public-spirited individuals to combat street crime, initially called "Thief Takers". Bow Street's gradual success took on something akin to a mythical status. The myth acquired in retrospect was of a group of active individuals who uncovered law-breaking and arrested felons. There was no hiding place for offenders and Bow Street always got their man, even though they were a small group of no more than eight investigators.

There were other patroles at Bow Street who supplemented the "Thief Takers", and they sometimes numbered nearly 200. Fielding and Welch both instilled an *esprit de corps* that helped galvanise the group into an effective crime-fighting force. It was this spirit of comradery which contributed to the myth in what Critchley (1967) asserts:

"This roisterous body of men some of whom made substantial fortunes out of shady business in trafficking in crime, undoubtedly... creating in their own lifetime the myth of the Bow Street Runners."

Critchley was making this assertion based on a later evaluation of Bow Street's reputation towards the end of their tenure, around the 1830s.

To appreciate how the myth of Bow Street materialised and was re-enforced, sense needs to be made of the connection between all these forces at the Court. These early and professional officers had different titles as time went on. How were our early Constables selected, dressed, equipped and organised? What were their duties? What people, problems and issues did they encounter whilst out on the streets? In this book we seek to add clarity to what has already been written about Bow Street, and also perhaps to rediscover what information may have been lost. In essence, how did the reputation of Bow Street develop into this myth – was it manufactured or real?

Today, crime television programmes are very popular. We appear fascinated with crime investigation, especially of homicide. Our need to understand and find out how a serious crime was perpetrated is important and natural for our self-preservation, but how did police crime investigation and practice develop in Britain, and where were these methods developed, introduced and learnt? Perplexingly, why was it that the Metropolitan Police Commissioners removed some selected uniform police officers from the force and transferred them to the Bow Street patrole? Was it to gain practical street level experience? In other words, where did the art and science of policing originate? We look to Bow Street for likely answers.

The main role of a Justice of the Peace was to preserve the King's Peace and deal with disorder. They were given powers to call in the civil forces made up of Constables from the parishes or the military in serious disorder matters. Only when serious riots occurred in 1780, known as the Gordon Riots, was this problem brought into sharp relief and the Government realised that their police system was woefully inadequate, and a new system needed. Resolving this issue was a very slow and painful process, because it relied on a suitable balance being struck between the public fondness for their liberty and their need of increased security. The problem was succinctly put in 1822 when a Parliamentary Select Committee reported its findings into the State of the Police of the Metropolis:

> "It is difficult to reconcile an effective system of police with that perfect freedom of action and exemption from interference, which are the great privileges and blessings of the society of this country; ... the forfeiture or curtailment of such advantages would be too great a sacrifice for improvements in police or facilities in the detection of crime"

A centralised professional uniformed police was a good idea, but libertarian freedom was preferential and the development of a proper police of the metropolis would take nearly a further half century to achieve.

Research undertaken by the authors also reveals the detailed daily workings of Bow Street Public Office, its justices, the early peace officers, the later principal officers, runners and the patroles, including its minutiae. There has been a great deal of misunderstanding over what and who the Bow Street Patroles were, especially given the numbers of officers operating out of this office at various intervals. Over time these patroles, originally formed by Henry Fielding in 1749, were often given new individual names or titles as their roles, responsibilities and jurisdictions changed, which created further misunderstanding. Assumptions by newspaper reporters, authors and other commentators added to this confusion, since no matter where in London and the environs the police operated, they all mainly sought to link these Constables to Bow Street. All this added to the myth of Bow Street and contributed greatly to its success. We shall see that even police authors since those times have not really got to grips with the identity of these groups and how they operated. We explain how and why this may have happened.

Following the Gordon Riots in 1782, we see the transformation of the Foot Patrole from a reactive selection of Constables to a more proactive body numbering between 100 and 200 men. We help clarify, contextualise and differentiate those groups. Commencing with the Bow Street Thief Takers, then later Principal Officers, afterwards erroneously labelled "Runners" (perhaps an epithet better associated with the other members of Bow Street), the Bow Street Horse Patroles, Bow Street Foot Patroles, the Bow Street Dismounted Horse Patroles, the Bow Street Unmounted Horse Patroles and to finish with, the Bow Street Day Patroles.

Recognising Bow Street's success, Sir Robert Peel encouraged Bow Street patroles to join his New Police – something that many of them did. By this time, many experienced Principal Officers or Runners (and not only at Bow Street but the other Public Offices as well) had got too old or were long in service, and none wished to join the New London Police. This left a gap in detective ability and investigation for the Metropolitan Police. Bow Street was relieved of most but not all of its policing responsibility in 1829 on the formation of the Metropolitan Police but the so-named Bow Street Runners still existed, continuing for another ten years, investigating mainly property crimes until they were dissolved and pensioned off. The lack of detective skill amongst its officers would later become a significant problem.

Here we challenge the hypothetical notion of "Runner" by examining and scrutinising original documents and publications in detail to find the truth: "Principal Officer" or "Runner"? We see perhaps that the term "Runner" may be have been attached personally to John Townsend (1780–1832) as its most famous Principal Officer because of his background as a turnkey and his very long association with Bow Street.

Note should be made of the word "Patrole", which is used in its original form throughout this work where we have found it. The words Patrole and Patrol have been used interchangeably by newspaper reporters, historians and authors at the time and since. The meaning and context of these terms are problematic, since they are socially constructed by those very authors and others. We need to be able to understand and differentiate the context, since "to patrol" and "the patrole" are different. One refers to an action, whilst the latter refers to a body of men.

Writers have added to the confusion by making assumptions about what the role and function of those early police officers or patroles were. As the changing task and purpose of "the Patrole" developed in time and jurisdiction then so did the misunderstanding, leading to conflating all of the patroles into one body, "the Runners". Unsurprisingly, even Constables from other Public offices who co-operated with Fielding's Bow Street men in making arrests of known characters (see Grubb, pages 152-153) were reported as "Runners", and further examples are cited. Also, our modern day perception of the term "patrol" may be interpreted differently to the 18th and 19th Century understanding and so mean different things to different people, in different places and at different times. This in turn leads to a lack of consensus and agreement. For example, the original 1763 Horse Patrole were not "peace" officers, i.e. officers of the watch, and so could not intervene in domestic matters and breaches of the peace as their role was purely to detect and arrest highway robbers on the roads and highways leading into the metropolis. Hence the term "Patrole" does not include the "Principal Officers" who started life as "Fielding's People", but the uniformed and non–uniformed versions, although members of the patrole did supplement the runners from time to time.

Patrole is also difficult to determine as an action, since Government papers at the time use "Patrole" and on "Patrol" interchangeably when referring to the Bow Street patroles. It is this confusion mixed with assumption that has caused writers, historians and the public to create the myth in London that Bow Street was the crucible of policing with its ability to quickly detect, arrest and bring to justice perpetrators of serious crimes. Browne (1956) asserts that the finale "e" was dropped in 1822 in official documents, although he noted that the earlier spelling did occasionally find its way into Victorian texts (p73). In attempting to define patrole, it seems to be:

"A body of non or semi–uniformed men sworn as Constables with or without warrant appointed to patrol the streets, roads and highways of London, mounted or on foot, during the day or night to pursue, detect, arrest and bring into custody highway robbers, footpads, pickpockets and violent offenders".

Before the story commences it is worth reminding ourselves of the spatial context in which the Bow Street forces operated. Approximately three–quarters of a million people lived in London in 1760, rising to a little over 1.4 million inhabitants by 1815 making it the largest city in the western world.[1] By 1800 almost one in ten of the entire population of Great Britain lived in London. 18th Century London consisted of narrow streets, lanes and alleys which were often thronged with busy travellers. Street sellers mixed with knife grinders, chair menders and others to reveal a picture of noise and chaos. Traps, carriages and carts vied for position, dodging the unlucky foot passengers in their way. Sedan chair passengers, horse-drawn cabs and coaches slowly conveyed their paying guests along these busy thoroughfares. London Bridge was a particularly arduous bottleneck and traffic jams were a frequent nuisance all around the metropolis.

Situated within the parish of St. Paul's, Covent Garden was the site of London's first "Public Office", located at no. 4 Bow Street, two doors south of the Covent Garden Theatre, now the Royal Opera House. Across the road in Russell Street was the Drury Lane Theatre whilst to the north was Long Acre, where just a stone's throw away was the notorious area of St. Giles with its centre of prostitution, drinking dens, high unemployment, low-class housing[2] and the infamous rookery around Seven Dials. At the rear of the Public Office was Covent Garden Market, instituted in 1677 by a lease from the Duke of Bedford who granted a licence for two local residents to trade in fruit, flowers, roots and herbs.[3] The busy piazza with

1   www.bl.uk/georgian–britain/articles/the–rise–of–cities–in–the–18th–century accessed on 30th October 2017.
2   Inglis, L. (2014) *Georgian London – Into the Streets*. Penguin, London, p. 141.
3   Ibid, p. 128.

Fig. 1: St. Giles Rookery

its collection of old buildings thronged with noisy costermongers, farmers, tradesmen and grocers buying and selling their wares.

London was also changing economically, and its prosperity was linked to its trade. The metropolis had become a hub for business and exchange with its huge market trading goods from the Americas and Asia. Goods such as silk, tea, tobacco and sugar were arriving, making London a transit port handling 80 percent of Britain's trade. Lloyds of London helped the metropolis become a dominant financial market too. New business opportunities attracted people into the metropolis, with many migrating from the countryside and abroad, many into low-class slums in search of work. The arriving numbers also expanded the environs of London, for example Somers Town, only adding to the chaos. The New Road between Paddington and the City of London was built in the 1750s to bypass the congested London streets and ease the jams. Somers Town grew up north of this road and before the turnpikes, attracting middle-class families, often from abroad escaping the French Revolution.

London had become a magnet from people in other countries, with a third of London's population not born in Britain, the largest group originating from Ireland. These slum locations became a melting pot occupied by heterogeneous populations experiencing economic deprivation and poverty, an ideal setting for a criminal underclass to proliferate. The Fieldings understood the built environment and also the consequences of urban and social change. Familiar to them were the slums, also called rookeries, with their cramped, disorganised, unstable and unhygienic neighbourhoods. Places like St. Giles, Saffron Hill and the Seven Dials were dangerous places too for the unsuspecting visitor or outsider, who became easy prey.

In summary, London was a grimy, busy, overcrowded, noisy and generally unsanitary place which suffered badly from dirt and smoky pollution.[4]

---

4   www.bl.uk/georgian-britain/articles/the-rise-of-cities-in-the-18th-century accessed on 30th October 2017

Bow Street Public Office

In this chapter we start by looking at Thomas de Veil, a Trading Justice who originally chose a house at 4 Bow Street in the centre of Westminster as his headquarters through which to administer the law. The reputation of these Justices of Westminster at that time was not a good one. They were seen as corrupt self-serving men of low class who would line their own pockets by trading justice with complainants. Whilst Thomas de Veil came from humble beginnings, his tenacity, skill and ingenuity helped him rise up to become an important magisterial figure who certainly helped to start the myth of Bow Street – as a place to be feared by felons and law breakers. We plot how the system of Courts developed and how changes in the arrangement of public examination of prisoners before the court enabled and enhanced the powers of the justices of the peace.

Part of the success at Bow Street was Henry Fielding's policing plan – how to tackle the increased level of crime – a multi–faceted method rooted in victims reporting crimes at one central point, using a system of criminal records where information was recorded for the first time in registers. The ultimate success of Bow Street was how the plan was implemented.

Thomas de Veil

Sir Thomas de Veil, a Westminster and Middlesex Justice, established a Magistrates' Court at number 4 Bow Street in 1740. De Veil took on the role of investigating and detecting crime in the neighbourhood, something he did independently and most

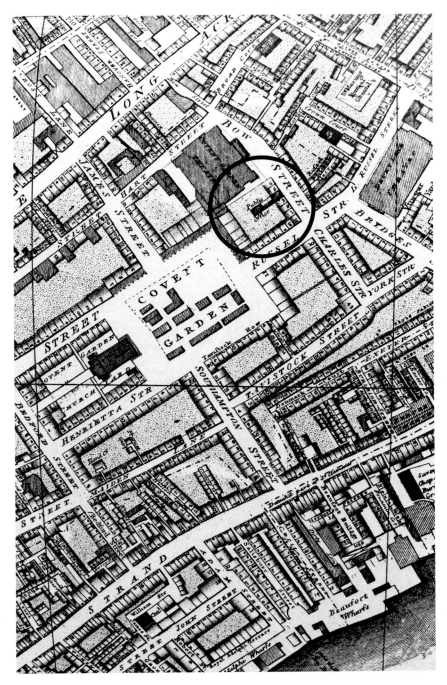

Fig. 2: Map showing the location of 4 Bow Street - the Public Office

vigorously. He was at the time described as a "Trading Justice" who would trade certain benefits for a fee, and whilst he was enthusiastic and efficient in his role against crime, he took advantage of his position both financially and socially. It was said that:

> "They [the Trading Justices] were also accused of engaging in corrupt activities, such as committing alleged prostitutes to prison in order to share the fees with the gaolers, and fomenting disputes among the poor in order to profit from the fees of complainants."[5]

De Veil was born in 1684 near St. Paul's, the son of Dr Hans de Veil, an impecunious Huguenot minister who had educated his son well. In so doing he taught Thomas about Hebrew and rabbinical literature; however, by age 16, because of his father's financial situation, he had to abandon his academic education and adopt a trade, becoming a mercer's apprentice in Cheapside. All went well for a year, when without notice the mercer became bankrupt and Thomas was cast out into the world on his own. It was now that de Veil enlisted as a private soldier and joined the ranks of the British Army. Commissions were purchased at huge sums, which de Veil did not have, although some were obtained in the field and at 17 years of age he set himself on his army career with enthusiasm in the knowledge that ahead were years of strict discipline, submission and hardship.

De Veil's skills in making the right friends, his courageousness, due diligence and also being forward and opinionated helped shape his career.[6] He excelled himself in the field, both as part of William III's Flanders campaign and later as part of Toby Caulfield's regiment in Portugal and Spain. Probably because of his linguistic skill and ability in interpreting foreign languages, he rose to become a sort of "secretary to Viscount Galway", the Commander of the Iberian

---

5   London Lives 1690–1800: Crime Poverty and Social Policy in the Metropolis. www.londonlives.org/static/Pretrial.jsp#toc3 accessed on 27th July 2015.
6   Anon, (1748) *Memoirs of the life and times of Sir Thomas de Veil*.

Forces.[7] By 1702, still only aged 20, he secured a commission as an ensign in the Dragoons and two years later at Lisbon was promoted to Captain. On his return to England after the Treaty of Utrecht in 1713, when his regiment was disbanded, he was placed on half pay. He was by now married and starting a family.[8]

His debts, the need for company and a taste for pleasure could not be sustained on the meagre income from the army. He set up an office in Scotland Yard and offered his services to disbanded officers and other persons in drafting petitions to the Treasury and the War Office seeking grants, privileges and favours, something he was extremely good at. This was also profitable work, and de Veil's ability to network and find favour, especially in Government circles, enabled him to seek a higher occupation through being granted his own sinecure. He suggested that he might become a Justice of the Peace for Westminster and Middlesex and was duly recommended. In 1729, when he was aged 45, he set up his first office in Leicester Fields (now Leicester Square), then a rough, sparsely-populated heath overrun with footpads and robber gangs. He set himself the task of apprehending and convicting these felons, which he soon did very well indeed.[9]

De Veil made no secret of his sexual weaknesses. He had four wives and twenty–five legitimate children, although all his wives and most of his children pre-deceased him. He was also no hypocrite, always open about his morals. He made it his business to find out what was going on in London. He often talked of the experiences of a magistrate friend, a euphemism about his own practices. The magistrate wanted to know where the "kept women" of London lived. "Kept women" at the time were those ladies who were supplied with comfortable or even lavish apartments by a wealthy gentleman in order that the lady was available for his sexual pleasure. De Veil ensured that he found out where these were, so

---

7   Babington, A. (1969) *A House in Bow Street*. MacDonald and Co., London, p. 43.
8   Ibid.
9   Ibid, pp. 44–45.

that he could discreetly visit their lodgings by cab without being seen, being dropped off right by the rear door.[10] He took advantage of his position and managed to glean useful information from them, not only without their male benefactors finding out but also availing himself of the facilities whilst he was there. De Veil's sexual appetite was also demonstrated when he would receive women at his home and take them to a private room to discuss their applications with him in secret, and he made no secret of the fact that they could pay in kind if they wished.

De Veil was untrained in law, as was often the case of Middlesex trading justices. According to Henry Fielding, who succeeded him, de Veil "boasted that he took £1,000 per year in his office and not all of that could have come from fees and fines".[11] He was ably assisted by Joshua Brogden, his clerk who was a Captain in the Westminster militia and who went on the serve both Henry and John Fielding in the same measure. De Veil was a trusted justice who acted with great courage, zeal and ability. He not only investigated matters but sought to arrest those responsible and ensure they were tried, acting as police officer, judge and jury, a seemingly unfair situation where justice was balanced in favour of the prosecutor, a factor which would not be tolerated today.

Such was the trust exercised by Government that de Veil was bestowed with another lucrative sinecure in 1738 – that of Inspector General of Imports and Exports. From here he was able to tackle the manufacturers of spirituous liquor, especially gin. De Veil also helped the Government when it came to matters of public unrest, and he often resorted to reading the Riot Act proclamation to a crowd in order to disperse them. It was perhaps his over-zealous single-handed enforcing of the Gin Act (1736) that was his biggest mistake and led to mass disturbances. His fellow magistrates did not react in the same way to "Queen Gin", as it became known,

10   Pringle, P. (1955) *Hue and Cry – The Story of Henry and John Fielding and their Bow Street Runners.* William Morrow and Sons, London p. 56.
11   Ibid p. 67.

perhaps knowing the consequences of over-reaction. Not only did his actions contribute to compromising both the personal safety of himself, his family and his servants, but also on one occasion led to a Government snub. In January 1737 a mob had gathered outside his house in Thrift Street, Soho with the object of causing harm to two informants who had given information on illicit gin production. De Veil found that the courthouse was surrounded and everyone in it in personal danger. He therefore read the riot proclamation to the crowd and had two men arrested and committed to Newgate Prison, one being John Allen. De Veil decided a prosecution was required but the Treasury Solicitor declined to support the action, advising against it; however, the magistrate's determination pushed the matter through and in May 1738 the case came before the court. Whilst Allen was found guilty he escaped punishment on the grounds of insanity. Outside the court, following the case, a huge crowd had gathered to hear a speech by the jubilant Allen, much to the obvious displeasure of de Veil.[12]

This matter did not sour his determination to proclaim a riot on a number of further occasions. He attended scenes of public disturbance and helped quell the public's anger by breaking up the gatherings by use of the military if necessary. These actions by de Veil were of considerable benefit to the Government, who in the eyes of the general public had distanced themselves with the responsibility for matters of public unrest, but also in many respects with enforcing the Gin laws.

In 1848, the unofficial memoirs of de Veil were published, entitled *Memoirs of the life and times of Sir Thomas Deveil* [sic] by Webb, where the author explained further his role of the magistrate as the "principle magistrate of Middlesex and Westminster". De Veil was also appointed "Court Justice", a role officially unrecognised but secretly given to the Justice of the Peace for Middlesex in which "the Government would give instructions and on whom they required

12   Armitage, G. (1932) *The History of the Bow Street Runners.* Wisehart and Co., London, p. 29.

prompt and immediate action in any emergency".[13]

In many respects, de Veil understood London society at all levels and particularly its many weaknesses, and this enabled him to be able to properly judge others fairly and impartially. He held himself above his fellow trading justices with a level of integrity which saw him take only what was right and fair. He kept scrupulous accounts, knew and understood the law, which meant that his application of justice was also unbiased, balanced and equitable. His main skill was that of detective-solving cases by visiting and observing the crime scene, active listening and inquisition of witnesses, his ability to tell the truth from lies, deduction from observed facts, a mind capable of understanding the evidence needed for prosecution and bringing offenders to justice.[14]

His reputation and his experience of people helped secure him a place in police history, and he anticipated what was later to become common practice of Bow Street and modern CID officers, as the first investigator to be invited to help solve a provincial murder case.[15] Against the backdrop of a corrupt society, he helped raise the status of the magistrate in his 18 years' service at the bench, and innovations he introduced during his tenure at Bow Street aided the next incumbent.

Henry Fielding (1707–1754)

Henry Fielding's life was a short one, yet in his six years at Bow Street he challenged previous conventions of crime control during a period of great change.

De Veil helped to lay the foundations on which both Henry and John Fielding were able to build, and it was in 1748, two years after de Veil's death, that his place was taken over by Henry Fielding, a justice for the City and Liberty of Westminster, and later by his blind

---

13 Anon, (1748) *Memoirs of the life and times of Sir Thomas de Veil Knight*, and Zirker, M. R. (1988) *Henry Fielding – An Inquiry into the causes of the late increase of Robbers and related writings*.

14 Browne, D., (1956) *The Rise of Scotland Yard*. George Harrap and Co., London, p. 24.

15 Ibid.

half–brother John, who had been his assistant.[16] He was the son of an army lieutenant and a judge's daughter; educated at Eton School and studied at the University of Leiden before returning to England where he wrote a series of farces, operas and light comedies. He was not a well man and increased ill health prevented Henry from continuing his legal practice which he had to give up; however, his appointment as magistrate was a sinecure and seen in some way as compensation for his assisting Tory supporters against Horace Walpole together with his support of Government.[17]

Fielding was a rare breed of gentleman for his time – a man not only of social vision, but also highly principled, honest, understanding and fair. He was also aware of critics who were watching his every move in the hope of catching him out and seeing him profiting from this political privilege and position. One of Fielding's concerns was the inadequacy of the traditional institutions, particularly the corrupt nature of the magistracy.

Not a rich man, and not very good with money, Fielding nonetheless had managed to secure a small private stipendiary out of secret service funds in order that the normal business of running a public office could be carried out without recourse to bribery.[18] This set him and Bow Street apart from the other justices, who relied on court income and were labelled "Trading Justices", since they allegedly treated the office primarily as a source of income, as indeed de Veil had done, with numbers increasing gradually to nearly 500 Justices of the peace in Westminster in 1761.[19] Fielding was aware of this reputation and ineptitude demonstrated by the magistracy, and as such he distanced himself from being seen as a trading justice.[20] How London Magistrates were viewed at the time

16 The 80 year old Justice Poulson succeeded de Veil who was hopelessly unfit for the job and it was only on his death two years later that Henry Fielding succeeded him.
17 Ascoli, D. (1979) *The Queen's Peace*. Hamish Hamilton, London, p. 36.
18 Pringle, P. (1955) *Hue and Cry – The Story of Henry and John Fielding and their Bow Street Runners*. William Morrow and Co., London, p. 37.
19 London Lives 1690–1800: Crime Poverty and Social Policy in the Metropolis. www.londonlives.org/static/Pretrial.jsp#toc3 accessed on 27th July 2015.
20 Landau, N. (1984), *The Justices of the Peace, 1679–1760*. Berkeley, Appendix A.

was best summed up in the House of Commons by Edmund Burke in 1780, when he said:

> "...they were generally the scum of the earth – carpenters, brick makers and shoemakers some of whom were notoriously men of such infamous characters that they were unworthy of any employ whatever, and others so ignorant that they could scarcely write their own names".[21]

Horace Walpole described the officers of justice "as the greatest criminals in town" in 1742. The trouble was it was not only the magistracy that was corrupt. Those appointed men who delegated their responsibilities as Constables to hired deputies as cheaply as possible were often people of the worst character who made their living on the meagre money. Also, the watchmen were mainly old, infirm and generally unfit for the task. The watch "was very irregular and various".[22]

The City of Westminster differed from other places in its annual selection of Constables, and once sworn they had jurisdiction over the whole city, not just the parishes. The Constables were usually drawn from local small tradesmen and they were expected to perform this duty by rota; however, this duty was often challenging, difficult and dangerous.[23] Leslie–Melville (1934) asserted that:

> "Some of the appointed Constables were corrupt, many were lazy but most were ignorant of their powers. They did their duty according to the spirit of the law; their routine business amounted to very little more than keeping a record of newcomers to the locality and going out with the watch periodically, one Constable in each parish performing this duty every night."[24]

21   Webb, S. and Webb, B. (1906) *English Local Government (Vol. 1) – The Parish and the County.* Longmans, London.
22   Moylan, J. F. (1929) *Scotland Yard and the Metropolitan Police.* G. P. Putnums and Sons, London, p. 11.
23   Leslie–Melville, R. (1934) *The Life and Work of Sir John Fielding.* Lincoln Williams, London, p. 36.
24   Ibid, p. 37.

This was an imperfect system and Henry Fielding was well aware of it.

Recruitment of Constables

The office of Constable in the City of Westminster was an evolving one. While Constables were originally appointed separately for each parish, they became in the 18th Century Constables for the whole of the city and liberty being appointed at the Westminster Court Leet, where the Deputy High Steward presided over the burgesses. There were some 80 Constables whose main responsibility was to attend the Houses of Parliament, often neglecting their role of supervising the night duty watch.[25] In the growing suburbs of Middlesex and Surrey, outside of the nine parishes of Westminster, there was a variable assortment of parish Constables, beadles and watchmen. In effect, this was an imperfect system since the parish Constables had two masters – the Justices whose instructions they carried out in executing warrants, assisting witnesses and providing information, and the burgesses who appointed them.

In 1750, Henry Fielding created his small group of six trusted "people", on the recommendations of Saunders Welch, from the latest batch of 80 newly-sworn Constables in the City and Liberty of Westminster.[26] He also used other paid officials on temporary or fixed-term employment on expenses to deal with problems as they occurred, such as the rise of highway robbery or burglary.[27] Later on, his brother John recruited seven men. Once engaged these men were initially called "thief takers" and their prominence soon earned them unpopularity and hostility in equal measure, even amongst those who they were seeking to help.[28] The reason for this was the public's inability to differentiate between the spy, the informer

25   Moylan, J. F. (1929) *Scotland Yard and the Metropolitan Police*. G. P. Putnums and Sons, London, p. 10.
26   Pringle, P. (1955) *Hue and Cry – The Story of Henry and John Fielding and their Bow Street Runners*. William Morrow and Co., London, p. 88.
27   Pringle, P. (1968) *Henry and John Fielding – the Thief catchers*. Dennis Dobson, London, p. 54.
28   Reith, C. (1938) *The Police Idea*. Oxford University Press, London.

and the public-spirited police volunteer. When the latter called for assistance to secure or overcome a difficult prisoner it was likely that he would be attacked instead. Even in court, "Fielding's people" were accused of being private "thief takers", a name they resisted. Suffice to say, Fielding at the time wished for his men to remain anonymous in case of public repercussions – on one occasion he had to give evidence himself at the Old Bailey when the character and integrity of one of his trusted Constables, William Pentlow, was called into question. Pentlow was accused by the witness as being a private thief taker and Henry realised that he had a problem, with the public unable to differentiate his own trusted people with those private thief takers who were abhorrent to them. He needed to attend and assert in evidence his total support, thereby ensuring the conviction of the felon. Occasionally, "Fielding's people" were referred to as "Myrmidons" by Fielding himself to deflect these accusations, since the term referred to the legendary brave, devoted and trained warriors taken from Greek history as being commanded by Achilles. Fielding needed to divert public attention towards his brave and trusted men, not the private "thief takers". In so doing, Henry used publicity and the newspapers to report their brave deeds and thereby raise the profile of his "Myrmidons" in a corporate marketing way.

There also appeared to be a general feeling of impending gloom; that the country was descending into moral decline and degeneracy by the early 1750s. John Brown, the essayist, wrote at the time about railing against corrupt juries and people in positions of power, but also suggested that the country was "...by a gradual and unperceivable decline ... gliding down to ruin".[29] Brown also commented on the leniency of the law and reluctance of juries in capital cases, especially of highwaymen and robbers, to convict, suggesting that compared to other counties the metropolis was most compassionate.[30] Yet this compassion may not deter the felons,

---

29   Brown, J. (1757) *Estimate of the manner and principles of the times.* Davis, L. and
      Reymers C. Holborn, London, p. 149.
30   Ibid, p. 21.

who were another problem for Fielding.

When Fielding arrived at Bow Street in 1748 a new wave of crime was underway. Few offences were ever reported, and as Pringle (1955) suggested, "until Fielding started publishing advertisements not one in a hundred thought of reporting a robbery to police".[31]

Doubtless troubled at the high incidence of highway robbery on the roads leading to London, Henry set himself to inquire and research the problem. Once he had devised his plan of eliminating the current crime problems and preventing fresh outbreaks, within a few months the newspapers were reporting encouraging results with a number of high-profile offenders being captured, prosecuted and incarcerated.[32] Fielding had started work by setting his aims. These were to include: i) active public co–operation, ii) a stronger police, iii) advertisement of reported offences through the newspapers, and iv) removal of the circumstances under which crime and its conditions flourished.[33] Furthermore, Fielding ensured that the newspapers reported the positive aspects of Bow Street as well – when robbers etc. were arrested and imprisoned he knew that not only would the incarceration of a criminal in prison help reduce further crime by removing one felon, but it would provide a warning to others and at the same time increase the public's feeling of security and safety. The winter of 1748/49 saw the newspapers reporting:

> "Not only pickpockets but street robbers and highwaymen are grown to a great pitch of insolence at this time, robbing in gangs, defying authority, and rescuing their companions and carrying them off in triumph".[34]

Not only did Fielding invite news reporters into his own court, he also set up his own newspaper called the *Covent Garden Journal*

---

31   Pringle, P. (1955) *Hue and Cry – The Story of Henry and John Fielding and their Bow Street Runners.* William Morrow and Co., London, p. 81.

32   *London Magazine* 18th February 1749.

33   Ibid.

34   *London Magazine*, December 1748.

in 1752, on which he was helped by a small group of assistants including his dependable clerk Joshua Brogden.[35]

Within six successful months Henry Fielding was nominated to the commission of the peace for Middlesex and by May 1749 was elected Chairman of the City and Liberty of Westminster Bench, making him the most junior and at the same time the principal London magistrate.[36] Henry also had a plan which would help bring order to what he saw as chaos, so he wasted no time in waiting for others to do something. By June of the same year Henry delivered his first "Charge to the Grand jury", which was a brief survey of the causes of crime and contained hints on how they could be removed. So well was the "Charge" received that it was published three weeks later by order of the Court and the Grand Jury. Henry had already commenced his plan with the introduction of a "mixed patrol of troops and his selected peace officers", who were quickly put to good use because no sooner had the Charge been delivered than trouble broke out just as Fielding was travelling to his country retreat for the weekend.[37] This trouble demonstrated how volatile matters had become, especially when, as Fielding knew well, the civil powers of the traditional policing system were far too weak, uncoordinated and parochial to deal with outbreaks of mass violence.

Three sailors from Wapping, whilst on shore leave, visited a brothel in the Strand kept by a man named Owen. Whilst there they were robbed of thirty guineas, and when they complained they were thrown out. Angry and upset, they went back to Wapping, collected some shipmates and returned to the brothel which they wrecked, setting fire to it and even ripping the clothes off the women's backs. A large crowd gathered shouting "Pull the house down", and at the same time the fire threatened to engulf the adjoining buildings. The Parish Fire engine was sent for but wisely never turned up, whilst at the same time an attempt by the Beadle Nathaniel Munns

---

35   Babington, A. (1969) *A House in Bow Street*. MacDonald and Co., London, p. 99.
36   Pringle, P. (1955) *Hue and Cry – The Story of Henry and John Fielding and their Bow Street Runners*. William Morrow and Co., London, p. 83.
37   Browne, D., (1956) *The Rise of Scotland Yard*. George Harrap and Co., London, p. 27.

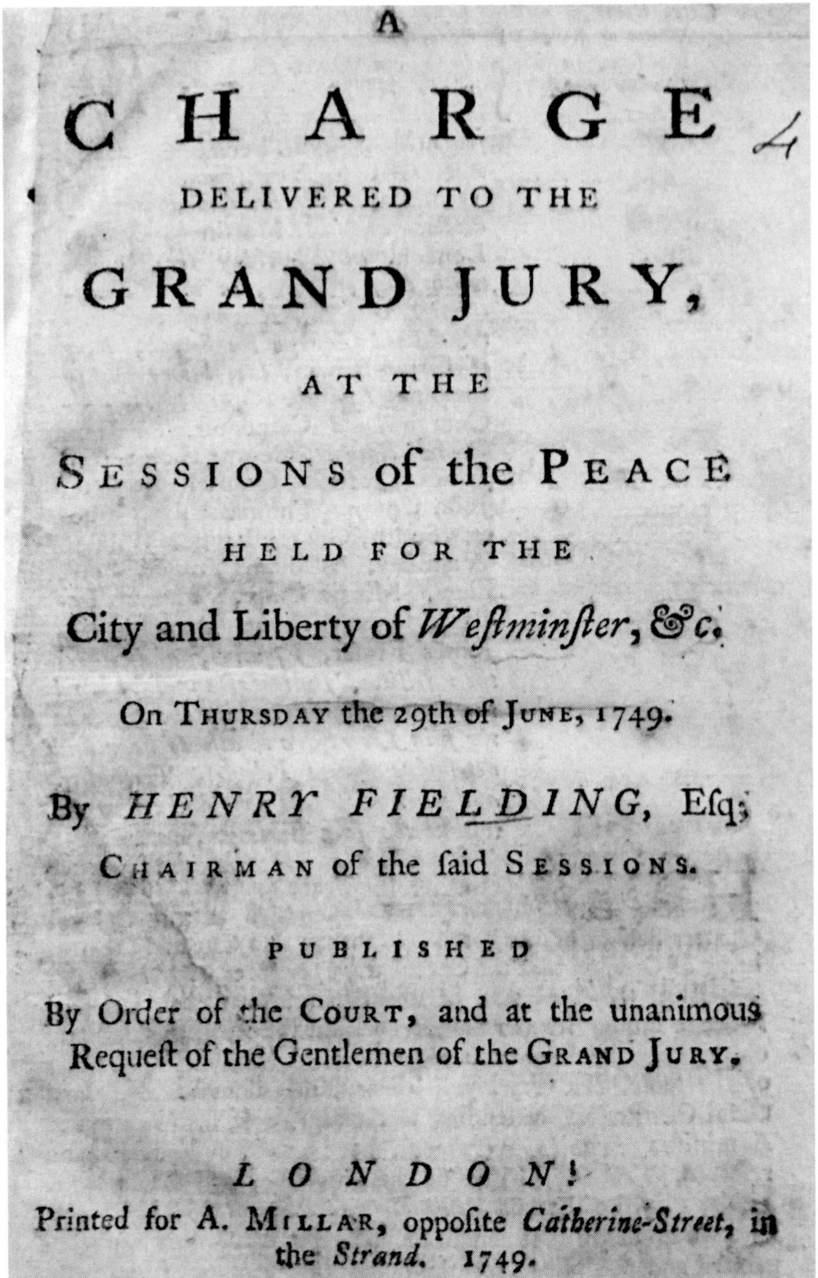

A

CHARGE

DELIVERED TO THE

GRAND JURY,

AT THE

SESSIONS of the PEACE

HELD FOR THE

City and Liberty of *Weſtminſter, &c.*

On THURSDAY the 29th of JUNE, 1749.

By *HENRY FIELDING*, Eſq;

CHAIRMAN of the ſaid SESSIONS.

PUBLISHED

By Order of the COURT, and at the unanimous Requeſt of the Gentlemen of the GRAND JURY.

L O N D O N!

Printed for A. MILLAR, oppoſite *Catherine-Street,* in the *Strand.* 1749.

Fig. 3: Fielding's Charge to the Grand Jury

to arrest one of the ringleaders resulted in him being threatened. Concerned over his personal safety and aware that Fielding was out of London, Munns went to Somerset House and obtained a party of twelve soldiers under a corporal from General Campbell. The troop returned to the scene and arrested two ringleaders, who were taken to the night prison – a cellar room under Nathaniel Munns' house. The gathering throng grew larger and a Constable asked for re-enforcement from Campbell, who sent another forty more soldiers. The angry mob, who were pelting the soldiers, also threatened to wreck another brothel owned by a man named Stanhope, however they broke up between two and three in the morning.

The following day at 10.00am they were back, and a concerned Stanhope went to see the High Constable of Holborn – Saunders Welch – to discuss the problem. Welch said he would only act under a magistrate's protection; however, the brothel keeper never came back as he probably couldn't find a magistrate. Later in the evening the sailors returned to Munns' house and by wrenching the bars of the cellar windows liberated the two prisoners. They then went back to Stanhope's house and wrecked that in the same way they had done to Owen's brothel the day before. A request for soldiers that evening was declined without the protection of the magistrate's authority. Saunders Welch, on returning from an evening out, saw the glare of fires in the Strand and immediately went to muster a troop of soldiers. After much argument an officer and twenty men were assigned to him; however, in the meantime another brothel, belonging to Peter Wood, had been wrecked although the troops prevented the furniture and building being burned. Several ringleaders including John Wilson and Bosavern Penlez were arrested and taken to the New Prison, and by 3.00am order was restored.

The next day Fielding returned to Bow Street by the afternoon, and under the protection of a detachment of Guards ordered the ringleaders to be brought from the New Prison in closed carriages in order to be examined at Bow Street. All the time the mob were still hanging around and causing trouble. Welch noticed how the crowd had grown outside the court and urged them to disperse, and even

Fig. 4: New Prison Clerkenwell, 1809

Fielding from his upstairs window addressed the crowd without any effect. Fielding sent a message to the Secretary of State for assistance in protecting the court and to prevent the prisoners being liberated. By the afternoon Fielding had examined the prisoners and committed nine of them to Newgate; however, whilst escorted by a troop of Guards, the mob tried unsuccessfully to smash into the sealed coaches to release the prisoners.

Rumours circulated that a huge mob had gathered at Tower Hill and was on its way to Temple Bar. Fielding ordered the troop and his Constables to patrol the Strand in sufficient force to make prospective rioters think again. The result was that the expected riot did not take place, even though Fielding, Saunders Welch and the Officer of the watch sat up all night.

A month later, two of the rioters appeared at the Old Bailey and were tried under the Riot Act, with the proceedings attracting public attention and critical comment. They were convicted and sentenced to death which caused an even greater stir because of its apparent unfairness. Such was the public upset that not only the jury who had convicted them, but at least 900 parishioners of the Strand area petitioned the Prime Minister for a reprieve. John Wilson, thanks to Fielding, was reprieved but the sentence against Bosavern Penlez, a wig maker, was carried out and he was hanged. Pringle (1955) asserts that the reason for this prejudice focussed on the fact that Penlez, in addition to being a rioter, was also a thief because he was arrested carrying a bundle of women's clothing stolen from Peter Wood's brothel. So he had been charged with burglary as well as riot whilst Wilson was just a rioter – facts the public were unaware of.[38] The public agitation was further compounded by the fact that the troops had been called out irregularly, since no magistrate had read the proclamation of the Riot Act as prescribed by the law. The Government came in for much criticism and even Fielding had to defend himself against the vociferous public and political criticism by issuing a pamphlet entitled *"A true state of the case of Bosavern Penlez",* which included the true facts of the burglary and seemed to quell the affair.

Rioting did not stop in 1749, and the troops were again called out because of a fraud perpetrated on a theatre audience who were charged over a hoax performance. The audience rioted because they had been duped into paying out money after seeing an advertisement allegedly by the Duke of Montague proposing the forthcoming performance. They knew they had been duped when no one turned up, and rioting followed.[39]

In the winter of 1748/49 a large number of highway robberies had occurred, spurring the Government into action. Horse Guards were strategically placed on all the roads and footpaths in the towns around London with instructions for them to patrol from town to town. Their patrol commenced from 5.00pm in the evening until

---

38   Pringle, P. (1955) *Hue and Cry – The Story of Henry and John Fielding and their Bow Street Runners.* William Morrow and Co., London, p. 85.

39   Pringle, P. (1955) *Hue and Cry – The Story of Henry and John Fielding and their Bow Street Runners.* William Morrow and Co., London, p. 87.

11.00pm at night, and these guards were to be made up of regular soldiers receiving extra pay.[40] The employment of Horse Guards in this way rankled the Government, who however had no other plan.

Henry had 80 parish Constables under him, mostly deputies, who were inefficient and corrupt – but this was not unusual. Strengthening his police was going to be a real challenge. Henry was very fortunate to have a trusted practitioner at his side – Saunders Welch, the experienced High Constable of Holborn and later magistrate, who is perhaps one of the real unsung heroes in the creation of Bow Street.

Some 80,000 men in total had been disbanded from both the army and the navy following the ending of the war of Austrian Succession in 1748.[41] Returning soldiers from abroad were marching back to be discharged and of course this included the lame, disabled and incapacitated. The onset of winter in 1749 did not deter criminal enterprise, and soon the robber gangs were back and reports of their activities were being reported in the newspapers. Such was the level of crime that Horace Walpole warned a friend that:

> "You will hear little new from England but of robberies; the number of disbanded soldiers and sailors have taken to the road; or rather to the street; people are all but afraid of stirring after it is dark".[42]

Walpole had not overstated the problem, as a significant number of crime reports or "informations" were being made at Bow Street. Henry's mission had started, and although early results were encouraging they were small compared with the level of crime generally. "Fielding's people" remained active throughout the spring as they had public unrest and allegations of attempted murder to cope with during this time in addition to their other duties. However,

---

40   *The Ipswich Journal*, 21st October 1749.
41   Black, J. (2015) *British Politics and Foreign Policy, 1744–57: Mid-Century Crisis.* Ashgate, Farnham, p. 150.
42   Walpole, H. (1859) *Journal of the reign of King George III and The Letters of Horace Walpole* (ed Mrs P. Toynbee (1903–5) 16 volumes. Oxford, Clarendon Press, and supplemented by 3 further volumes (1918–1925).

concern by the Government over rising crime levels caused them to revive the old scheme of rewarding £100 per convicted felon to anyone who was interested. This in Fielding's view would have consequences and produce the opposite effect. The high reward money would not only increase crime, but also involve innocent people being framed by perjured evidence given by people of dubious character; Fielding was not wrong.

Fielding's small body of men could be called on at short notice to track down some of the most notorious and violent highway robbers, but gradually as their role changed they became more involved in the detection and recovery of stolen property. This was unchartered territory, as these men knew their work was dangerous and that they were only semi-official in status. As we know, Fielding tried to keep not only their identities secret but their methods as well. Fear of reprisals and rejection by the public was Henry's prime motivation in what was a new method of crime control. Saunders Welch oversaw the training of this small band of officers but they needed a guide – directions and instructions. Ably assisted by Henry, Welch wrote down his experiences of policing the alleys, streets and thoroughfares of the metropolis as a guide to other Parish Peace Officers on the relative pitfalls of the office of Constable, so as not to fall foul of litigation that would certainly ruin them (see Appendix 1 for a précis of *"The Office of Constable"* by Welch).[43] This instruction book became the early perceptual blueprint of policing from which the wise advice was widely recognised and taken to heart by the Constables. This guide has been added to and enhanced by a range of other police authors ever since; it was built on lessons learnt through failure – failing your way to success in other words! It was perhaps at this point that policing as both an art and a science was born.

Due to Fielding's need for secrecy it has been notoriously difficult during our research to identify these first officers and differentiate

---

43   Armitage, G. (1932) *The History of the Bow Street Runners.* Wisehart and Co., London, p. 46.

Fig. 5: Newgate Prison

between the various members of "Fielding's people". A main problem is that these encompassed a variety of roles – Constables, informants, orderlies, turnkeys, clerks and messengers; many of the relevant documents now available to us often just reveal a last name, so the authors have been circumspect in their identification of certain members of Bow Street.

Henry's publicity machine was brought into play to win approval and support, since within a short time the effectiveness of his plan saw significant results. The newspapers heralded the success of Fielding's small group of officers when they said:

"...nearly 40 highwaymen and street robbers, burglars, rogues, vagabonds and cheats have been committed within the week last past by Justice Fielding".[44]

44   *The General Advertiser* (1750) 5th February.

Fielding knew he would have a problem sustaining his accomplishments of the previous winter since his six trusty men, real thief takers who had been trained up, were threatened by the group's retirement at year's end.[45] The appointed Parish Constables' year of office was coming to an end and he was now looking at losing their services so he asked them to stay on. Miraculously they all agreed.[46] It would appear from our research that Fielding's initial six officers included Thomas Hind, William Pentlow, Samuel Phillipson, Edward Gaul, Robert Street and William Marsden.[47]

Henry had the ability to inspire a sense of loyalty in those around him, more especially towards his common purpose of ridding society of crime. Not only within his officers, but his brother John, Saunders Welch and Joshua Brogden were dedicated to Henry. For this respect and loyalty he rewarded them well and not necessarily financially, but perhaps through a favour when they had problems of their own such as illness, injury or family issues. Such was the mutuality of this esteem that in 1749 Henry Fielding had applied to Lord Chancellor Hardwicke to make Brogden a justice for Westminster; but even though this was recommended, the Commissioners regarded Brogden no better than a 'Hackney Clerk', so this did not materialise.[48] We see this respect and dedication rewarded when Henry applied to the Duke of Newcastle for his most trusted Constable William Pentlow to be put forward as Keeper of the New Prison. Pentlow was rewarded with this sinecure over the Duke of Newcastle's own preferred candidate. We hear more about Pentlow in the next chapter.

In 1755 John Fielding, now in place of his deceased brother,

45 Armitage, G. (1932) *The History of the Bow Street Runners*. Wisehart and Co., London. p. 48.

46 Pringle, P. (1955) *Hue and Cry – The Story of Henry and John Fielding and their Bow Street Runners*. William Morrow and Co., London, p. 88.

47 These early Bow Street men served as Constables for longer than their statutory one year for their parish and the expenses they obtained are shown in Fielding's Accounts seem to indicate these were his anonymous officers.

48 Battestin, M. C. (2000) *A Henry Fielding Companion*. Greenwood Press, Westport, p. 216.

produced a pamphlet seeking to obtain recompense for another officer, Thomas Hind, who had been injured whilst arresting a notorious felon and subsequently died of his injuries in the line of duty. John did not have the funds or the authority to compensate the family for their loss – only the Government did. The arrests of Burk and Gill (who were involved in the injury to Hind) led to the capture of their gang of robbers and John wished to reward the now fatherless family who had paid the highest price in some way.[49] We do not know the result of his letter as no reply appears to have survived. Henry Fielding was forever the compassionate man, and it seems John carried on his brother's sense of kind–heartedness.[50]

Fielding was beginning to make an impact on metropolitan crime. It was later reported that by 1753 four of the robber gangs had been largely broken up[51] and the following year John Fielding's records show that the

> "...then reigning gang of desperate street robbers were attacked and within a space of three months no less than nine capital offenders were brought to justice though not without bloodshed as one of Mr Fielding's people was killed."[52]

Increased powers were bestowed on Justices during the mid- to late-18th Century, such as measures relating to the summary conviction of offenders. However, it was the pre-trial review that Henry Fielding introduced to inquire into allegations against suspects, in what has been described as "essentially a new stage in the pre-trial procedure", which was effective although not strictly legal.[53] Justices were not expected to take pre-trial matters into their

49   Armitage, G. (1932) *The History of the Bow Street Runners*. Wisehart and Co., London, p. 48.
50   Babington, A. (1969) *A House in Bow Street*. MacDonald and Co., London, p. 99.
51   Pringle, P. (1955) *Hue and Cry – The Story of Henry and John Fielding and their Bow Street Runners*. William Morrow and Co., London.
52   Armitage, G. (1932) *The History of the Bow Street Runners*. Wisehart and Co., London, p. 58.
53   Beattie, J. (2007) Sir John Fielding and Public Justice: The Bow Street Magistrates Court, 1754–1780, *Law and History Review*, 25, text after note 30.

own hands, but to commit all suspected felons to prison for trial by jury and not to dismiss them before trial.

In his manner Henry had, uniquely for the time, begun collecting evidence into the causes of crime, which he published under the title of *"An Enquiry into the causes of the late increase in robbers"* in 1751. In court, men of violence who killed or destroyed property were punished harshly by Henry Fielding. People who he felt were impoverished victims of very low social standing were treated with compassion, understanding and shown mercy. Fielding's unique research not only highlighted the causes of crime, but showed up an inept system of prosecution and a flawed legal profession.

By 1751 Henry was quite unwell and his health was failing despite having tried various medications, even resorting from time to time to a well–known quack, one Dr Thomson.[54] In the meantime John Fielding began to take over many of his brother's responsibilities and had settled in as his assistant.[55] This allowed Henry to concentrate on writing, and during this time he wrote a romantic novel – *Amelia* – for which he was paid £1,000, a sum soon swallowed up by the daily management of his household.[56]

The Universal Registry Office

Henry and John Fielding were also forward-thinking and innovative businessmen for their time. Their foray into this world was highly successful and included the building of the Universal Registry Office, which opened in Cecil Street, Strand, in October 1750. Principles developed here helped them later to transfer these skills into another area – crime. Their knowledge and experience here created a method for identifying and enabling the apprehension of offenders.

Prompted by the increase in commercialisation, this was a combination of employment bureau, investment agency, travel

54   Babington, A. (1969) *A House in Bow Street*. MacDonald and Co., London, p. 96.
55   John Fielding aged 19 years had been blinded in an accident whilst serving in the Royal Navy.
56   Babington, A. (1969) *A House in Bow Street*. MacDonald and Co., London, p. 98.

agency, information office, estate agents and insurance company.[57] John ran it single-handed while in his spare time brother Henry taught him law. The importance of the Universal Registry Office seems to have been understated, perhaps misunderstood and not really publicised by scholars, writers and biographers since that time. Both Henry and John Fielding recognised the importance of the collection, understanding, coordination and promulgation of information in their age, because their view was of a utopian and perfect world. The perfect society would be closer in the world of business and commerce, because the theory was the more transactions there were the better things would get as it would grease the wheels of business making people richer, providing more employment and improving the general state of society.[58]

This was a matter which was essential for society, especially when it came to the imperfect situation that led to crime. The Universal Registry Office compiled information in an innovative way through a series of registers, such as places and employments, property to buy or rent, investors and investments. For example, for a fee of one shilling an unemployed person could register for a job with the Registry Office while a person with a position to fill could inspect the register of the employable searching for a job, again for the same payment. These "wants" and "talents" were quickly brought together, leaving satisfied customers and saving time.[59] Ogborn (1998) suggests that the Fieldings' achievement was also due to their understanding of modernity, social progress and integration, together with overcoming the problems of time, space and communication. Successful commerce and business united the country, but this understanding was hampered by geography and communication. The Fieldings applied the same innovative ideas and methods to their plan of preventing and detecting crime. Their knowledge of the spatial and temporal transformations and social

---

57   Ogborn, M. (1998) *Spaces of Modernity – London Geographies 1680–1780*. Guilford
     Press, New York
58   Ibid, p. 213.
59   Ibid, p. 219.

changes of 18th Century London saw Henry Fielding organise a new and better system of crime prevention and detection, as we see later, in the development of "the plan".

Fielding stressed the importance of maintaining a good character because this would invoke trust between employers and employee. Without trust, this could not be guaranteed so when publicising vacancies in newspapers he would address the reader thus: "To the faithful, honest and industrious", paying careful attention to "hierarchy, property, morality and time discipline".[60] The Fieldings also felt that successful crime detection relied on gathering a group of reliable Constables at the Bow Street office, "collected together, known to each other and bound by the conditions of good fellowship, friendship and the bonds of society".[61] In essence this meant they chose those of high moral and trustworthy character and good reputation. Furthermore, the understanding of communication, both its problems and disadvantages, was also central to the "one uniform plan" as John Fielding called it later.

There had been a positive expansion of the road system in the 1740s, especially given the growth of trade not only from increased overseas business but improved home markets as well. With this in mind, the Fieldings not only focussed on advertising and circulating information, but developed an understanding of physical geographical communication specifically relating to the road network. This involved understanding the arteries of communication throughout the country, not only spatially but temporally as well. For example, knowing when and where the Leeds coach would start from, its route, where it would stop and when this would happen was a useful way of appreciating the spaces and times in which they might be attacked en–route. A list of the lonely open spaces, the heaths, forests, and places outside the urban areas was made

60   Fielding, J. (1755) *A Plan of the universal register office, opposite Cecil Street, and that in Bishopsgate Street, the corner of Cornhill*, 8th ed. London.
61   Fielding, J. (1758) *An Account of the origin and the effects of a police set on foot by his grace the Duke of Norfolk in the year 1753, upon a plan presented to his grace the Duke of Norfolk by the late Henry Fielding*. London, p. 38.

and identified as likely places for crime. The toll gates and turnpikes were very important and Henry realised he needed to include the toll gate keepers in his plan, since these acted as "pinch points" through which most travellers on the highways were channelled. The toll gate keepers were provided with horns to alert attention and the patroles were, with the exception of one gate, allowed free access and egress. Apart from this, the toll gates were identified through Fielding's research as useful places where information could be gathered on travellers, handbills posted up about felonies and news of robberies taken down. This was the plan which would become most useful to the "patrole", as will be seen.

The First Policing Plan

The men who were "Fielding's People", later to include the patrole, were originally just another part of "the plan". The idea of "the plan" was way ahead of its time and was perhaps the earliest theory of crime prevention and detection. We see later how John Fielding, as he takes over the reigns as Magistrate, develops "the plan" further very successfully, even expanding its practice beyond the metropolis into the counties. What seems to have made "the plan" so appealing was the credibility of both Henry and John Fielding in their understanding of the problem, and as a result they were able to persuade politicians and the Government to accept likely solutions. Such was their knowledge, especially understanding how London had expanded with its new streets, roads, alleys and passages. As the poverty-stricken descended on London they tended to gather in low-class areas with cheap and badly-maintained impoverished residences. These areas began to expand, and with this development came the proliferation of slums and rookeries which were ideal locations for felons and footpads.[62] Otherwise, no-one else had any idea of the context of criminality, nor did they really appreciate why the disparate nature of policing in London was not really working.

In the last months of his life Henry Fielding, despite being

---

62   Footpads were street robbers who preyed on pedestrian traffic.

desperately ill, was commissioned by the Duke of Newcastle at short notice to provide his plan to "put an immediate end to the murders and robberies which were everyday committed on these streets".[63] Henry understood the failings of the current police system: there was no proper system of reporting crimes, nor a place where they could be recorded. The plan, once delivered, included a remedy for victims reporting criminal matters and was immediately accepted by the Duke of Newcastle, because the Government had no other formula or scheme to tackle this growing problem. Copies of Henry Fielding's original plan have not survived because it was never published; however, an abstract of it survives in the British Museum. It was only later that John Fielding explained what it was and how it worked. Few scholars, writers and researchers have acknowledged its proper origin, its importance as a scheme or given due credence to understanding "the plan" and how it worked, but perhaps more importantly why it worked in practice. In other words, this was the very first detailed structured policing plan.

Today, policing plans are a normal everyday part of the police world, and understanding a strategy created over 260 years ago was perhaps central to the success of Bow Street. We see, perhaps unsurprisingly, how practical lessons learnt from mistakes and experiences as originally outlined by Saunders Welch devolved into a system of better management; practice and experiences later copied by Robert Peel in the formulation of his modern police force.

This scheme shows the perceptive ability of Henry Fielding in identifying crime using his knowledge of the criminal world and dealing with its causes. This sets Fielding out as one of the great reformers of 18th Century England. Such a grasp of the problem certainly helped to prove the adage that "knowledge was power" and this was especially true when it came to dealing with successive Governments who required evidence of worsening crime conditions and criminality in order to provide grants to combat these issues.

---

63   Fielding, J. (1758) *An Account of the origin and the effects of a police set on foot by his grace the Duke of Newcastle in the year 1753, upon a plan presented to his grace the Duke of Newcastle by the late Henry Fielding.* London, p. 37.

"The plan" was once described by John Fielding in a letter to the Duke of Newcastle as "simple and exceptional", because not only did the detail deal with the arrest of felons, but also the underlying causes of crime. Its implementation, which was now being properly funded by the Treasury, later caused a delighted Fielding to comment that "during the remaining part of November and the whole of December not only no such thing as murder but not one street robbery was committed."[64]

In 1753 Fielding had presented his plan to the Treasury stating a cost of £600; the latter was not keen to pay the full amount immediately and awarded just £200, but this was enough for Henry to act. He mobilised his six men, and within a short time the Mason Welsh gang were neutralised. Mason and Welsh were caught in their sleep and a further five were arrested the same night after furious fighting, whilst the rest fled the capital.[65] The informant was paid in cash up front, as he had asked. Further information was purchased for a small amount of money regarding the Dennis Neal gang, who were also apprehended and later convicted.

Still keen to advertise the successes and victory over crime in a way which sought to destroy the confidence of would-be felons, Henry suggested that there was now nowhere a felon could hide. Some examples of success have been recorded; however, it was often the promulgation of such information contained in the registers through issuing handbill or advertisements that provided the best leads. He placed an advertisement in the *Public Advertiser* on 7 December 1753, stating:

> "The two desperate gangs who added murder or extreme cruelty in every robbery they committed are now totally broke by the conviction of Welsh, Mason and Neal yesterday at the Old Bailey; except one who has escaped into the country, and is supposed to be the person who has committed several robberies near Bristol

64 Pringle, P. (1955) *Hue and Cry – The Story of Henry and John Fielding and their Bow Street Runners*. William Morrow and Co., London, p. 38.

65 Pringle, P. (1968) *Henry and John Fielding – The Thief Catchers*. Dennis Dobson, London, p. 70.

with his usual cruelty, and he has been pursued by a warrant from Justice Fielding and actually taken there upon the vigilance of the Mayor of Bristol and is now in custody there".

This was a dangerous gang who were most organised, and consisted of fourteen men under the leadership of Welsh and Mason. No-one was safe from the gangs, who were blatant and brazen, for the first time robbing people during the day. One such occasion occurred one summer's evening when the King was walking in the gardens of Kensington Palace when he was robbed in broad daylight by a gang of his watch, money and shoe buckles.[66] The crime was reported, descriptions taken down and recorded in the registers. Henry, desperate for evidence, resorted to advertising for informants to come forward. One witness did so, but he wanted paying in advance for the information. An irritated Henry Fielding did not have the means nor the authority to pay, as it was usually only on conviction that rewards were payable by the trial judge. The case was unresolved, and the Welsh gang escaped conviction on this occasion. In time, the paying of informants by the runners out of their own pockets became an everyday occurrence.

Henry died in 1754 in Lisbon, where he had gone on doctor's orders for the good of his health. He was aged just 48. Despite just six short years at Bow Street, Henry's legacy was to reform the administration of the poor given the huge growth of the city, highlight and reform the nature of imprisonment, reform the parish watches and create a proper centrally-controlled body of unified mobile police in the metropolis. To achieve the latter required constitutional change, and since the public preferred liberty above security it would involve removing traditional institutions, at that time impossible to achieve. It would take another 75 years before the London police were unified, paid, co-ordinated and professionalised.

Henry had managed to lay down a scheme designed to combat the increasing levels of criminality very successfully. It was his younger

---

66   Pringle, P. (1968) *Henry and John Fielding – The Thief Catchers*. Dennis Dobson, London, p. 66.

brother John who, from then onwards as a Westminster Justice himself, took over 4 Bow Street and devoted all his time and energy in carrying out his brother's vision.

John Fielding (1721–1780)

Following Henry's death, John shouldered the responsibilities of the Bow Street Public Office. Together with Saunders Welch he set about reconciling the problems with an extremely inefficient and ineffective parish constabulary system of policing. John Fielding's first action was to secure, like his brother had done before him, a stipend from the Government secret service fund for both himself (£400) and Saunders Welch (£200). This action was not copied by magistrates operating in other public offices, which for them meant that abating crime, catching offenders and prosecuting them was more to do with their own personal gain than it was about creating a more professional system of preventing crime and keeping the peace.[67] This is what set Bow Street above all the other public offices and helped to transform this office as the headquarters of London policing, the "Centre Office" as it became known.

In carrying out his brother's "plan" of policing the metropolis, John did not have an easy path in counteracting the ever-increasing danger of being robbed whilst travelling the highways into London. Using his great powers of persuasion, backed by criminal intelligence on robber gangs taken from the Registers, Fielding managed to secure a further grant from Government of less than £1,000. This gave him authority to implement part of his scheme as an immediate response to deal with highway robbery. It is to these Criminal Registers we now intend to focus, and look at how the foresights learnt from the Universal Registry Office were applied to crime control.

---

67   Ascoli, D. (1979) *The Queen's Peace*. Hamish Hamilton, London, p. 41.

Central Reporting and the Bow Street Criminal Registers

The Fieldings realised that understanding criminal minds in predicting, apprehending and preventing crime was an essential part of any plan. The collating and cataloguing of felons (and their physical descriptions) with their criminal and family networks was also crucial to this task, especially since there were no criminal statistics available at the time. The problem was that no one individual knew what the shape of crime was like, and until crimes were reported and recorded there would be little or no appreciation, understanding and knowledge of crime or criminals. Until then, the matter of reporting felonies locally involved victims visiting watch houses within the parish where the offence took place and making a report. These matters were never circulated, yet another example of parochialism of an imperfect police system. There was no central point where victims of crime could report. But this was to change under the Fieldings at Bow Street Public Office, when incentives were given for victims to report their losses immediately, and later reports of highway robbery, murder and violent offences began to come in. The plan also put forward the introduction of a Foot Patrole, improved street lighting (which came in properly in 1807), a regiment of light horses to be stationed at the turnpikes out of London, and a newspaper established by law to advertise all things relative to the discovery of offenders.

Henry Fielding encouraged the reporting of crime and victims, even paying their expenses if they would travel to Bow Street and make their reports. In essence, the world of crime was coming to one place. Here both Henry and John Fielding were ahead of their time, because they had copied the principles learnt by running the Universal Registry Office and applying the collection of information and its dissemination to apprehending those responsible for crime.

Henry Fielding and Saunders Welch targeted the growing problem of street robbery. During December 1753 and January 1754 a street robbery happened every night. Welch had an understanding of the criminal mind and suggested that the robberies were committed by the same men, or put another way, most robberies were committed by a small number of men who were generally known. So by quickly identifying and targeting those small numbers by collecting information against them from informers, Constables and prison staff would bring fast and sure results. The small numbers problem besets society even today, as research in 2013 suggested that 63 percent of crime was committed by 1 percent of the population.[68]

Fielding and Welch realised that quick reporting of crime to Bow Street was to be encouraged, which enabled an immediate pursuit to catch the offenders. Once supplied with descriptions of a suspect they urged routine checking of the records, and when descriptions and clothing were compared against the records it was possible to identify the offender and their methods of operation; also revealed were previous crimes or convictions, last known addresses and any other useful information. Armed with this knowledge, handbills were printed describing the suspects and distributed near the scene of the crime on notice boards etc. Articles were also placed in newspapers, reaching a wider audience, encouraging information to be taken to Bow Street. Once suspects were identified then Fielding's men would follow and apprehend them. Today this is not exceptional practice, but in mid-18th Century England this was a brilliant, simple yet radical plan and perhaps the reason why it was kept secret.

As already stated, "the plan" needed consistency for victims to report their crimes at one central collection point no matter where the crimes had occurred. This led to the development of the first police crime reports, which were recorded in registers. A register of crimes reported, list of property stolen and register of wanted felons formed the earliest Criminal Record Office. A report would be made at Bow Street to an orderly (one of the officers), who enquired into "the truth of Informations" and to a "Register-clerk to keep an exact Register of all robberies", and the victim or witnesses would

68   University of Gothenburg. "One percent of population responsible for 63% of violent crime, Swedish study reveals." *Science Daily*, 6th December 2013. www.sciencedaily. com/releases/2013/12/131206111644.htm.

then, most importantly, provide "exact descriptions of persons and things".[69] There was an orderly present at Bow Street 24 hours a day to take reports and information from the victims of crime.[70] The orderly was a privileged person, often an older, responsible Constable who received a separate salary for this function. It was here that the origin of the registers developed into what we understand of today's indices – the wanted missing, stolen property and methods index.

These registers not only recorded the crime as told by the victim, but also if there were any suspects. Each offender's name was taken down and recorded, along with their detailed descriptions, any addresses, associates, family members, method of operation, and who could identify them. It is now absolutely understandable that a second strand to the plan was a formation of a small group of thief takers who could apprehend the suspect and bring them before the justice of the peace. These men needed to know the criminal underworld, their haunts and crime associates. For this reason the Fieldings employed keepers of the prisons, turnkeys, informants and honest and hardworking Constables, since they knew the felons and their ways best. Sometimes offenders or felons switched sides by becoming witnesses themselves to events they had seen and later gave evidence against their co-conspirators with the result they occasionally were recruited into the Fielding's honest thief takers.[71]

This scheme was indeed a masterstroke. It meant that even if the victim, who had reported the crime, could offer very little or no evidence of identification to Bow Street, they still had a far better chance of catching the culprits later. By not only searching through the registers but also advertising the crime, offering rewards, and by circulating handbills to pawnbrokers, innkeepers, turnpike keepers and stable owners, they maximised their opportunities for success.

---

69 Fielding, J. (1758) *An Account of the origin and the effects of a police set on foot by his grace the Duke of Norfolk in the year 1753, upon a plan presented to his grace the Duke of Norfolk by the late Henry Fielding.* London, p. 38.

70 Pringle, P. (1955) *Hue and Cry –The Story of Henry and John Fielding and their Bow Street Runners.* William Morrow and Co., London, p. 88.

71 See Darvall and Yates pp. 53-55.

Obtaining evidence in this way was laborious and time-consuming, however informants were also a valuable source of information and evidence. When this information was added to searches of the method index it could eliminate certain suspects, but also bring others to prominence. It was the responsibility of the Bow Street back room staff to deal with the court's daily administration. This all helped propel Bow Street towards its success and revered status. However, matters would not go all John's way for long, and soon public unrest threatened the security of London.

Many victims of felony still remained ignorant of the fact that reports were to be made at Bow Street quickly, so John Fielding added another sentence to his now historic advertisement:

> "...and if they would send a special messenger on these occasions... Mr Fielding would not only pay the messenger for his trouble but would immediately despatch a set of brave fellows in pursuit who have been long engaged for such purposes and are always ready to set out to any part of this town or Kingdom on a quarter of an hour's notice."

At the end of December 1754 three gang members – Armstrong, Courtney and Welch – were arrested after a fierce fight. They were taken before Fielding and questioned. Fielding was happy to advertise success in order to increase the public's perception that "his people" were not common thief takers, but "peace officers" or "Myrmidons". Accordingly, he stated in an advertisement that any victims of the fourteen or so robberies that had been committed in the previous four months by this gang should attend Bow Street for examination on the following Monday in the hope of identifying and prosecuting any of the culprits.[72]

Crime was being reduced and was less frequent than it had been, but by 1765 the message for victims to come to Bow Street quickly was still not completely being heard. A man name Kirby was walking

72   Pringle, P. (1968) *Henry and John Fielding – The Thief Catchers*. Dennis Dobson, London, p. 76.

past Somerset House when he felt his pocket being picked. The assailant was a small boy, and when the theft was detected by the victim and the suspect detained, two men sprang on him, making him release the pickpocket. Once released, another accomplice drew a knife and cut Kirby to the bone on his nose, from which he bled profusely. After staggering to the nearest tavern a doctor dressed his wound and put him to bed. The doctor came to Bow Street as the victim was too unwell to take the trouble. Fielding despatched one of his officers, a turnkey named Henry Wright, to speak with Kirby, who could offer very little in the way of a description, saying he would not even have been able to properly identify his assailants.

Wright consulted the Register of Crimes and Criminals in their methods index for men who used boys as pickpockets and stood by to rescue them in case of need.[73] There were several men suspected of this, but not enough to reduce the list significantly. Marsden, the Chief Clerk, was told by John Fielding to advertise the crime through the *Covent Garden Journal* and as a result a witness came forward who was able to name the assailants as Barney Carrol and William King of an address in St. Giles. Wright, who knew Carrol well and could identify him, drew a cutlass from the armoury and went in search of his suspect. Often these were desperate men, and as their fate was likely to be the gallows they would stop at nothing to evade arrest, even mortally wounding an officer to ensure their escape, so surprise was important in any capture. On arrest Carrol had a clasp knife on him, which he was thankfully unable to use and this was removed from his possession by Wright and kept for safe keeping. He was then taken to the roundhouse and detained until the morning and identified as the assailant by the informer. Wright arrested King later. They were tried at the Old Bailey, convicted and hanged for their crime.[74]

The registers became a huge success and felons began hiding their features in order to avoid detection. On one occasion a masked gang

---

73   Pringle, P. (1968) *Henry and John Fielding – The Thief Catchers.* Dennis Dobson, London, p. 96–97.
74   Ibid, p. 97–98.

raided a house of a man name Clewen, and the occupants were sent to bed and told to cover their heads with the bedclothes, but there were some glimpses and distinct voices heard by the victims. A messenger was sent to Bow Street and one of the officers despatched to question the occupants of the household. The officer returned to Bow Street to consult the Registers, and identified the suspects who were all arrested before dawn.[75]

John Fielding extended his brother's idea and by 1773 had instituted a national scheme of sending information out into the counties and boroughs, encouraging dialogue between magistrates.[76] Whilst policing had its boundaries crime did not, so providing information in this way allowed officials, leaders and magistrates to make connections and contribute for the first time in a unified way to better criminal detection.

The power of superior knowledge was not lost on Fielding, which he knew certainly from a legal perspective tended to help prove his case. So when Sir John Fielding was interviewed by a House of Commons Committee in 1772, not only was he able to deliver statistics on burglaries and robberies, but he included details of property, their values, lists of premises broken into and their locations, all taken from his central Bow Street Registers in a way no one had done before.[77] Even fugitives from justice in the country could find few hiding places. They would often travel to urban areas and London was a key location to remain hidden; however, sharp-eyed Bow Street men often surprised these felons by arresting them with a warrant signed by a magistrate from the district they had recently left.[78]

Next on Fielding's agenda was the compilation of a *Quarterly*

75 Pringle, P. (1968) *Henry and John Fielding – The Thief Catchers*. Dennis Dobson, London, p. 99–100.
76 Fielding, J. (1758) *An Account of the origin and the effects of a police set on foot by his grace the Duke of Newcastle in the year 1753, upon a plan presented to his grace the Duke of Newcastle by the late Henry Fielding*. London.
77 Home Department (1772) *Report from the Committee of the House Of Commons into the Burglaries and Robberies committed in the Cities of London and Westminster*.
78 Pringle, P. (1955) *Hue and Cry – The Story of Henry and John Fielding and their Bow Street Runners*. William Morrow and Co., London, p. 194.

Fig. 6: Sir John Fielding

Review and later a *Weekly Review* or *Extraordinary Pursuit,* a scheme which would receive great publicity. Information from the Registers was published and issued free to all magistrates and sent throughout the country. This review contained an alphabetic list of all crimes and prosecutions, including a list of stolen property together with a directory of wanted felons who had escaped justice from the metropolis. John Fielding even placed advertisements in newspapers, requesting such information of offenders coming before the magistrates including their descriptions and offences committed in order for him in cases of doubt to send a member of the patrole to make enquiries. He encouraged the Government to make Bow Street the centre for recording information through his system of registers that would contain the details of criminal trials and convicted felons. This enabled the identification of felons returning early from transportation – a capital offence – or having escaped from detention whilst awaiting transportation. Even deserters from the army were recorded at Bow Street, and lists would appear in the *Quarterly Review*. The latter was particularly important, as often those deserters not only kept their uniforms which belonged to the army and sold them, but also because often their knowledge of horses and guns made them useful highway robbers.

Such was the publication's success that it soon became the *Weekly Review* and later under John Fielding's successor Sampson Wright, the *Public Hue and Cry*. On the formation of the Metropolitan Police this publication later morphed into the *Police Gazette,* a pamphlet we still have today. Given the complexities of life and the increased migration of people and their changing habits crime flourished, but once the Fieldings' plan was in full swing there was nowhere to hide for the felon.

At Bow Street, the art and science of policing had begun, replacing the old idea – the amateurish parish Constables and the complicated and multifarious system of delegated officers – with a system which was more organised, systematic and useful in bringing offenders to justice.

It is widely believed that the Bow Street Horse Patrole commenced in 1805. However, 42 years before, a Horse Patrole had been introduced and experimented with for a short time and although widely successful, it was incredulously abandoned. This is not to be confused with the two horses kept at Bow Street by John Fielding's police patrol. The purpose of the 1763 initiative was to patrol and protect the highways into London, a visible form of crime prevention to help the travelling public by apprehending highway robbers.

John Fielding, like his brother before him, became more open when advertising crime through newspapers, but again like his brother, he kept operational matters very much to himself. Once a report came into Bow Street of a highway robbery or other serious crime, time was of the essence. To do this the Fieldings' problems were many. Firstly, he had to get an officer to the scene of the crime as quickly as possible. John Fielding frequently repeated the office motto "Quick notice and sudden pursuit", and his officers were expected to provide an instant mounted response in the pursuit of offenders.[79] This meant that an officer of his court had to travel some distance at speed in all weathers and have the flexibility to cover rough ground as well as journeying on the rough roads and highways. The immediate response vehicle at the time was the horse, and Fielding only selected those of his officers for the job if they were highly skilled. There were two horses kept at Bow Street police office for use by these specially selected officers at a moment's notice day or night – in effect, a fast response horse patrol, except these did not really patrol but pursued.[80] To do this his men had to be fit, active and have a sense of bearing. His recruits also had to have a sense of purpose – they had to be public-spirited, honest and brave. Not only did the officers have the ability to be good horsemen, probably the reason he often chose ex-cavalry soldiers who had served the army with credit, but they also had to be able to care for their steeds as well. Familiarity with firearms was also essential, and the need to be

---

79   Pringle, P. (1955) *Hue and Cry – The Story of Henry and John Fielding and their Bow Street Runners.* William Morrow and Co., London, p. 132.
80   Ibid, p. 133.

a good marksman might well save the officer's life, perhaps another reason for using people with military experience.

Fielding realised he had no time to set up a training school to teach his officers their craft, although he issued orders and instructions almost daily for distribution to his men. These men had to "learn the practical arts on the job", but he used people he could trust who often had been in the Horse Guards, military, or had been efficient Constables in their parishes. He even employed some ex–felons and turnkeys for some years who knew, and more importantly, could recognise the people that passed through the prison gates. These people also knew the serious criminal fraternity and their associates, which enabled Fielding's men to recognise identify and locate suspects. "Mr Fielding's People", or as he put it his "Real Thief-takers", were not to be confused with those reprehensible and distasteful common thief takers such as Jonathan Wild, a notorious villain and master criminal who played both sides of the law. As a gang leader, private thief taker and master manipulator of the criminal system, he enticed young, defenceless and vulnerable people into committing crime and then arrested them, claiming the £40 reward on their conviction.

Henry Fielding had written a pamphlet in 1754 in which he sought to differentiate both groups and alleviate public suspicion. He wrote of his own officers that:

> "These persons who are entrusted with the execution of this plan are commonly styled thief takers are all of them house keepers, men of tried courage, picked from peace officers and moreover, the moment anyone of them commits an act either of cruelty or injustice, he is immediately discharged from the office of thief–taker, and never admitted again".[81]

By January 1755 both the newspapers and Old Bailey transcripts reveal that the terms "Mr Fielding's People" or "A Servant of Mr

---

81   Armitage, G. (1932) *The History of the Bow Street Runners.* Wisehart and Co., London, p. 58.

Fielding" were often used when referring to officers and Constables at Bow Street. From time to time John Fielding, or Justice Fielding as he was called, had to appear and give evidence himself at the Old Bailey on matters relating to the reporting of crimes at Bow Street and on occasion regarding the conduct of his officers, as we shall see later. The newspapers often reported very favourably when it came to "Mr Fielding's People", recording deeds of great heroism and bravery which resulted gradually in a rise of their status, greater respect for their situation as Bow Street thief–takers and perhaps more importantly, a public acceptance.[82]

As far back as 1755 there had been some successes, as by year's-end a number of notable highwaymen had been apprehended and locked away. This was despite the Government being slow to provide the necessary funds as requested in support of Fielding's crime control efforts. Fielding was happy to quote the costs of running his horse pursuit, which totalled £400 a year, but he never revealed his own stipend, which was the same amount.[83]

Next, Fielding decided to deal with the great numbers of pawnbrokers who were only too ready, he felt, to deal in stolen goods and turn them into money. There were procedural problems with the convicting of fences and receivers. Whilst receiving stolen goods was not an offence, at this time a receiver could be charged as an accessory but the principal thief had to be convicted first. Adverts were often placed in newspapers by victims for the return of their property, and pawnbrokers sometimes acted as middlemen to help them, providing no questions were asked. By 1752 it became an offence for any person to advertise a reward for the return of lost or stolen property, punishable by a fine of £50.[84]

John Fielding had become a magistrate in Westminster and his principal officers and patrole overlapped with the local parish

82   See *Derby Mercury* 7th January 1755 which records the bravery and heroism of Mr Pentlow keeper of the New Prison and Mr Gee a Constable.
83   Pringle, P. (1955) *Hue and Cry – The Story of Henry and John Fielding and their Bow Street Runners*. William Morrow and Co., London, p. 133.
84   Browne, D. (1956) *The Rise of Scotland Yard*. George Harrap and Co., London, p. 92.

watches in what was a complicated system of beadles, watchmen, Constables, headboroughs and street keepers. There seemed to be sufficient numbers of the watch in order to contain and deal with crime but there were big problems. In 1770, the Government inquired into the state of the watch system in Westminster. The High Constable reported that:

The Parish of St. Margaret's there were 41 watchmen

The Parish of St. George's there were 57 watchmen

The Parish of St. James' there were 50 watchmen

The Parish of St. Anne's there were 23 watchmen

The Parish of St. Martin's there were 43 watchmen

The Parish of St. Paul's (Covent Garden) there were 22 watchmen

The Parish of St. Clement Danes there were 22 watchmen

The Parish of St. Mary le Strand there were 3 watchmen[85]

This made a total of 261 men on duty in an area of 17,000 dwellings, however the level of public protection was woeful, with the watch being inefficient and parochial, with them declining to operate outside their designated or assigned areas. There was also jealousy between the parish authorities and the Bow Street Patroles. Their feelings manifested in often hostile, antagonistic and aggressive ways, where on occasion Bow Street officers were assaulted and apprehended by watch officers in somewhat dubious circumstances. Co-operation and the exchange of information between them was virtually non–existent, and given the complex policing arrangements and overlapping jurisdictions of many parish officials and watch officers, this made the situation even more unworkable.

Fielding encouraged the Government to provide better street lighting to illuminate stretches of road that were unsafe and had a bad reputation.[86] Government provided £10,000 in 1764, and 89 street lamps were erected between Hyde Park corner and

85   Howard, G. (1953) *Guardians of the Queen's Peace*. Odhams, London, p. 102.
86   Browne, D. (1956) *The Rise of Scotland Yard*. George Harrap and Co., London, p. 31.

Kensington, a notorious stretch of road.[87] This important measure provided not only better visibility for travellers, but also afforded better identification of criminal acts and the felons who committed them. Fielding's men began to overcome the prejudice towards them by a more accepting public, who had misunderstood the thief takers to be from the corrupt and dishonest school of Jonathan Wild.

By the early 1770s Bow Street and its officers had begun to develop a good, sound reputation through the ability to detect and arrest serious offenders, but a serious outrage soon began to threaten that status. This occurred in 1771 when Fielding investigated a gang robbery in the Kings Road, when a farmhouse owned by Elizabeth Hutchins was raided by nine men. In the course of the raid a labourer named Joseph Slew was fatally shot in the shoulder. It was suggested that the gang had been Jewish, and as a result three men of that faith were arrested and interviewed, but released without charge for lack of evidence. Weeks went by without any further arrests, and John Fielding asked the Government to issue a reward of £50 for information leading to the conviction of these felons. Soon a man named Isaacs came forward to give information, although he was not blameless in the robbery. This is what we know today as "King's or Queen's evidence", and in so doing Isaacs gave up the names and descriptions of most of the gang. These were predominantly central European Jews, one of which was a well-educated medical man called Levi Weil, who had a degree from Leyden University. The others were Arthur Weil, Markus Hartogh aka Asheburgh, Jacob Lazarus aka Hyam, Dresden aka Hyam Lazarus, Solomon Porter aka Moses, Lazarus Harry and Abraham Linevill, who had not been detained with the others. Handbills were printed revealing the detailed descriptions and names of the wanted suspects and sent out far and wide to every postmaster in the land including Edinburgh and Dublin – a novel and new idea, never before tried. Nicholas Bond, at the time one of the principal thief takers, acted on a tip off and went to Birmingham, bringing back Weil and three accomplices. Several

---

87   Browne, D. (1956) *The Rise of Scotland Yard*. George Harrap and Co., London, p. 31..

more were arrested days later. They were charged and convicted at the Old Bailey, with the exception of Lazarus Harry who was found not guilty and acquitted. They were executed at Tyburn.[88]

Fielding encouraged the newspapers to report cases appearing at court, even providing the printers with a desk, pen and ink.[89] He also persuaded the interested general public and witnesses of crimes to attend the court and observe events, providing benches for them to sit. In this way Fielding had an audience, but more crucially, other victims of crime could identify their perpetrator from those being examined on another matter.

In January 1777, probably as an adjunct to the Universal Registry Office, John Fielding, now in his waning years, embarked on another literary enterprise and published the *"Universal Mentor"*, or *"Entertaining Instructor"*. This paper was composed of extracts from observations, sentiments and objects of virtue by famous historians, biographers and moral writers, in order to make the world a better place; Fielding's view of a utopian world. Priced at 3s, it was sent out to booksellers in towns and around the country.[90] The idea was to set standards of decency and behaviour for the public to follow, so that they became model citizens.

John retired in the last years of his life, three months before his death becoming ill and confined to his home at Grove House, Old Brompton (near the current site of South Kensington Station). His work was being carried out at Bow Street by Sampson Wright and William Addington, both of whom would later become senior magistrates.[91] At the time of his death John was not only supporting his own family, but also that of his late half–brother. Additionally, he had played a prominent part in helping to set up, with Saunders Welch, three philanthropic charities: the Marine Society, the

---

88   Browne, D. (1956) *The Rise of Scotland Yard*. George Harrap and Co., London, p. 38.
89   Beattie, J. M. (2012) *The First English Detectives*. Oxford University Press, Oxford, p. 99.
90   *The Oxford Journal*, Saturday 18th January 1877.
91   Babington, A. (1969) *A House in Bow Street*. MacDonald and Co., London, p. 152.

Magdalen Hospital and the Royal Female Orphanage.[92] These charities, in fact, gave Fielding options when sentencing young boys and girls who he felt were deserving of support – in effect achieving two objectives, firstly taking them out of the criminal classes by giving them a sense of purpose, and secondly to reduce levels of crime on London's streets. For example, in 1756 the Marine Society commenced when Fielding advertised to raise money in order to send to sea with the British Navy what he described as the "ragged and iniquitous, pilfering boys that infest the streets of London." So having successfully raised £600 through his advertising campaign, Fielding was then able to immediately send some 400 boys for their nautical training.

Further social changes began to threaten the fabric of society. Between 1760 and 1815 British society was in a state of great flux and change, bringing with it a range of associated problems which challenged 18th Century social order. These changes not only saw Britain move from an agrarian economy to an industrial one, but also huge movements of population into the towns and cities, away from the country. In 1801, when the first reliable modern census was taken, Greater London recorded 1,096,784 inhabitants, with numbers rising to a little over 1.4 million by 1815.[93] The metropolis saw the largest growth, with Manchester, Glasgow and Birmingham reaching populations of 140,000, 125,000 and 100,000 respectively.[94]

There were also positives to the nature of societal change and regional migration. There was better hygiene, increased fertility, improved child mortality, increased childbirth and changing patterns of behaviour. Demographic changes, especially for young migrant inhabitants of London, saw patterns of courtship, marriage and illegitimacy also change for the better. Women continued to

92   Pringle, P. (1968) *Henry and John Fielding – The Thief Catchers*. Dennis Dobson, London, p. 109.
93   www.oldbaileyonline.org/static/Population–history–of–london.jsp#a1760–1815 accessed on 1st October 2015
94   Ascoli, D. (1979) *The Queen's Peace. The Origins and Development of the Metropolitan Police 1829–1979*. Hamish Hamilton, London, p. 59.

*Fig. 7: Grove House, Brompton,
home of Sir John Fielding from 1768 until his death in 1780.
Taken from a painting by the favourite Chelsea artist W. W. Burgess*

dominate the population during this time, with females in the metropolis making up 54 percent and both courtship and marriage were taking place earlier in life, now under the age of 25 rather than in their late twenties. Better hygiene saw infant mortality in the metropolis reduce, where children were three times less likely to die than in 1730.[95] Urban development, new roads, infrastructure and better transport links encouraged more housing to be built, initially along the main highways but later gradually in-filling of the fields, meadows and other available areas. London expanded dramatically both north and south. The cheapness of the new Royal Mail coaches saw a greater regularity and movement of commuters in and out of London. The roads also saw migrations of people, often the poor, including injured soldiers and vagrants, moving towards urban areas like London. All these changes resulted in rising levels of drunkenness, crime and violence.

95   www.oldbaileyonline.org/static/Population-history-of-london.jsp#a1760–1815 accessed on 1st October 2015.

John Fielding extended and enlarged the plan which he put into operation, and while the efforts of the Fieldings were modest, the suggestion of a unified police system by two moderate hardworking and honest magistrates had been placed into society's consciousness and it would only be a matter of time before sensible policy makers introduced it. John summed up the success of Bow Street by paying tribute in 1758 to all those magistrates who had assisted him, but not forgetting to acknowledge

> "The general good behaviour, diligence, and activity of the Constables of the County of Middlesex and the City and Liberty of Westminster who have never been backward in their duty, however hazardous on occasion."[96]

According to Browne (1956), "Mr Fielding's people" soon became recognised as a valuable nucleus of trained police and were soon to receive the stamp of public approval,[97] probably by the nickname "Runner". Fielding remained as magistrate until 1779, covering a 25-year period. He died on 4th September 1780 at his Brompton country home, and was buried at All Saints Churchyard, Chelsea.[98]

Sampson Wright – Chief Magistrate (1780–1797)

Sampson Wright become a magistrate at Bow Street in 1772 and registered his property qualifications in September 1774. He often covered for John Fielding in the latter years of his life, when ill health caused him to gradually relinquish his magisterial activities. About the same time Saunders Welch had ceased to operate as a magistrate, in 1776 retiring to Taunton Dean in Somerset where he died in 1784. He is buried in St. George's Church, Bloomsbury where there is a memorial plaque in the porch.[99]

---

96   Fielding, J. (1758) *An Account of the origin and the effects of a police set on foot by his grace the Duke of Newcastle in the year 1753, upon a plan presented to his grace the Duke of Newcastle by the late Henry Fielding.* London.
97   Browne, D. (1956) *The Rise of Scotland Yard.* George Harrap and Co., London, p. 38.
98   www.findagrave.com/cgi-bin/fg.cgi?page=gr&GRid=14108206 accessed on 26th June 2016.
99   Babington, A. (1969) *A House in Bow Street.* MacDonald and Co., London, p. 152.

Sampson Wright succeeded John Fielding as Chief Magistrate in 1780, at a challenging time when public disorder was threatening to destabilise the country and it was Wright's responsibility to do something about it. What he was able to do in the light of serious challenges also set him apart as a truly great magistrate. Public discontent had been bubbling below the surface of the country for a little while and this were blamed on high taxes, unjust and repressive laws, Government profiteering and the pressing of men into the army and navy. It was now the turn of religious zealotry, in the attack of the Catholic Church. In 1780 Lord George Gordon called for the repeal of the Catholic Relief Act of 1778 and a return to the repression of Catholics, which seemed to touch the public consciousness and stir them into demonstration and later rebellion. The 1778 Act had repealed seemingly harsh anti–Catholic legislation from the 17th Century and excused Roman Catholics from swearing the oath of allegiance (with its implicit recognition of the Church of England) on joining the army.[100] This had been designed to get more Roman Catholics to join the army and help fight in the highly unpopular war with America, the War of Independence. The idea of tolerating Catholics in Protestant Britain was highly distasteful at the time.

Gordon and his followers, numbering 60,000, had gathered in St. George's Fields on 2nd June 1780 and made their way to Parliament Square. Gordon inflamed the situation by encouraging revolt amongst his followers who, wearing blue cockades and carrying banners proclaiming "No Popery", besieged the Houses of Parliament. Their intent was to peacefully present a petition to discourage "Popery", but matters turned to violence with peers and members of parliament being accosted, breaking their coaches and causing a disturbance. Parliament refused to debate the petition and a new wave of destruction commenced. Lord Stormont, Secretary of State for the Home Department, sent a letter to the Secretary of War requesting troops remain in readiness in the event of further

---

100 www.nationalarchives.gov.uk/pathways/blackhistory/rights/gordon.htm accessed on 18th October 2015.

public disorder. He also advised Sir John Hawkins, Chairman of the Middlesex Magistrates, to take what action was necessary to protect Parliament, its peers and members. The same afternoon, William Addington arrived with troops and cavalry, although even with swords drawn he was unable to make any impression on breaking up the demonstration.[101] Lord Stormont required that Hawkins should arrange for the Bow Street and Litchfield Street courts to have sufficient number of justices, Constables and peace officers to secure the Lords and Parliament to allow access and egress during the next session. The focus of the mob's attention turned to ransacking Catholic chapels attached to the Sardinian and Bavarian Embassies. The ex–High Constable of Westminster, Sampson Rainforth, and some of his men managed to arrest one of the rioters in the Sardinian chapel but he was immediately rescued. Later Rainforth, with some 100 troops who had drawn bayonets together with Bow Street officers, managed to return and arrest a further thirteen of the ringleaders. The next day the prisoners appeared at Bow Street under a strong military presence before Justice Sampson Wright and Justice William Addington. Sunday, 4th June saw more riots, and this was to be the trend for a further week and became known as the Gordon Riots.

In that time, whilst John Fielding was in his final days at his home in Brompton, the mob ransacked Bow Street and burnt many of Sir John and Henry Fielding's manuscripts and papers. The houses of Sampson Rainforth, Lord Mansfield and Justice Hyde were also sacked and burnt, whilst Newgate, built like a fortress, was also broken into, sacked, burnt with the freed prisoners joining their rescuers.[102] Fires were started in numerous other places including the Fleet Prison, the King's Bench and a distillery in Holborn owned by a Catholic named Langdale. The newspapers at the time commented on the "infernal humanity and one of the most dreadful

---

101 Babington, A. (1969) *A House in Bow Street*. MacDonald and Co., London, p. 153.
102 Browne, D. (1956) *The Rise of Scotland Yard*. George Harrap and Co., London, p. 40–41.

Fig. 8: Firing of the New Gaol at Newgte by rioters in 1780

spectacle", as the now drunken rioters broke open the containers to let the spirit flow out into the streets and down the gutters.

An emerging black population were seen during the riots, with former slave John Glover taking a leading role in the sacking and burning of Newgate prison. Charlotte Gardiner, an African, and Mary Roberts stormed the house of an Italian Catholic innkeeper. Both were captured and charged with riot.[103] When the spirit caught fire it resulted in many stupefied rioters perishing in the flames. Martial law was proclaimed and the military congregated in the City of London, although many members of the Honourable Artillery Company (HAC) with some Guards acted as personal protection to the Lord Mayor (Brackley Kent), instead of repelling the rioters or protecting the citizens of the City of London.

Some 326 people were tried for their part in the Gordon Riots, of which less than twenty were condemned to death and at least half of these were reprieved. On 11th July, five rioters were hung in London; three of these were on Tower Hill – William McDonald and the only

103 www.executedtoday.com/2011/07/11/1780-five-for-the-gordon-riots accessed on 11th November 2016.

two women, Charlotte Gardiner and Mary Roberts.[104] None took place at Tyburn, the usual place of execution, as it was considered too risky and would probably have caused disorder along the three-mile route to the gallows from Newgate. William Brown and William Pateman were executed in Bishopsgate Street and Coleman Street respectively, near where their crimes were committed. In the meantime, the HAC acted to protect not only the Sherriff of the City of London, but also his offices from being wrecked and accompanied him to the executions at Tower Hill. Requests from the Sherriff for the assistance of the HAC continued for other executions during July 1780. These were those of Enoch Flemming, who was hung in Oxford Road on 13th July; James Jackson at the Old Bailey; George Staples in Coleman Street on 20th July; and Jonathan Stacy in White's Alley, Moorfields, on 21st July. There was no disorder at the local hangings and as such these were regarded as a success.

The military involved in establishing order included the Horse Guards, Foot Guards, Inns of Court Yeomanry, the HAC, line infantry including the various county militias and the Queen's Royal Regiment (West Surrey). The HAC had been fully occupied with the riots during June, taking part in shooting rioters in Broad Street, the Poultry and Blackfriars Bridge.[105] Without any proper consent from the Court of Assistants, the Justices of Westminster felt, given their authority and the state of emergency, that they could requisition premises when they wanted. They came to the HAC headquarters at Armoury House and established a Rotation Office (a court of hearing)[106] to hear and examine the prisoners taken. Also without consent, they housed the prisoners in the cells below ground. The Court of Assistants chaired by Lt. Col. Harriott voted to prevent Armoury House from being used again as a Rotation Office in future.

---

104 www.executedtoday.com/2011/07/11/1780-five-for-the-gordon-riots accessed on 11th November 2016

105 Gould-Walker, G. (1986) *Honourable Artillery Company (1537–1987)*. HAC, London, p. 172.

106 Rotation Offices were established in 1763 and lasted until 1792 as small courts with justices who issued warrants and heard cases.

The inadequacies of the magistrates and the total failure of the current system of policing had been highlighted. Something needed to be done and this required a show of force, and it was when the King stepped in suggesting that he would take the troops out personally and give the order himself to fire on the mob that matters came to a head. Rumours were circulating that evening suggesting the Bank of England was to be overrun and ransacked and an urgent response was necessary. The Guards marched down Threadneedle Street with their new instructions and so when the mob turned up with their sticks, stones and clubs the Guards stepped forward with loaded rifles and immediately fired on the advancing menace.[107] Many were killed, some due to inebriation or drinking unrefined spirit, whilst others were shot. Some 300 died, with a further 200 being wounded as a result and in the wake of this show of force the rioting ceased and the point had been made.[108] The Government had realised that they had come within a whisker of rebellion and that the current system of policing was inadequate.

Sampson Wright returned his focus to Bow Street, where he continued the good work laid down by John Fielding.

One of the most troublesome crimes was fraud in all its particular guises. Whilst the arrests were being undertaken of well–known swindlers and fraudsters, there was one character who was evading Bow Street. He was Charles Price, commonly known as "Old Patch", who had eluded Sampson Wright at Bow Street for many years. He came near to being captured when Wright made it his business to inquire into the antics of this forger and master conman and ensure he didn't get away.[109] Price, also known as Powell, was then a large, overweight man, aged about 50 years. He was well-dressed, often wearing a tie-wig, ruffle shirt and buckle shoes.[110] He defrauded people through forged documents and false lotteries of all kinds to

---

107 Browne, D. (1956) *The Rise of Scotland Yard*. George Harrap and Co., London, p. 41.
108 Howard. G. (1953) *Guardians of the Queen's Peace*. Odhams, London, p. 111.
109 Babington, A. (1969) *A House in Bow Street*. MacDonald and Co., London, p. 165.
110 Fitzgerald, P. (1888) *Chronicles of Bow Street Police–office*. Gilbert and Rivington, London, p. 90.

begin with, gradually moving on to other fraudulent enterprises. He advertised the launch of a brewery, and later a bakery to unknowing and gullible punters in his efforts to get them to invest their money in what was essentially a sham. He was a skilled and persuasive man, and a serial liar. He engraved his own plates, watermarked his own paper and made counterfeit bank notes. By 1780 Price was flooding London with forgeries to such an extent that an alarmed Bank of England issued a reward of £200 for the arrest of a man they described in detail:

> "He appears about 50 years of age five feet six inches, stout made very sallow complexion, dark eyes and eyebrows speaks in general very deliberately in a foreign accent; has worn a patch over his left eye, tied with a string round his head; sometimes wears a white wig, his hat flapped before and so nearly so at the sides a brown camlet greatcoat, buttons of the same and a large cape which he also wears to cover the lower part of his face, appears to have very thick legs, which hang over his shoes as if swelled, his shoes are very broad at the toes and little old fashioned narrow silver buckles, black stocking breeches and walks with a short crutch stick with an ivory head, stoops or effects to stoop very much and walks slow as if infirm, he has lately hired many hackney coaches in different parts of the town and been frequently set down in or near Portland Place in which neighbourhood it is supposed he lodges".[111]

Price was a master of disguise; a headache for the authorities, since no one really knew what he looked like. In 1784, working on the premise that no one could identify Price, Sampson Wright tried another approach – to identify his female partner in crime instead. He placed an advert of his own in a newspaper headed "Bow Street Public Office", describing a female accomplice of Price. He offered a substantial reward for her capture, but alas got no result. The trail had gone cold, but Bow Street refused to let the matter rest.

---

111 Armitage, G. (1932) *The History of the Bow Street Runners*. Wisehart and Co., London, pp. 111-112.

Despite the above precise description Price remained at large for a further six years. However, a member of the patrole remained on his tail for the duration and one day received a lucky break. Members of the patrole regularly enquired at pawnbrokers to see if stolen property had been pledged. Aldus, a pawnbroker who knew Price well and had done a great deal of business with him, had become suspicious so he had Price watched. From this he deduced that Price and Powell were the same person. Aldus alerted the patrole to his suspicions and they kept a discreet watchful eye on the premises until their suspect turned up.

Price was confronted by Thomas Ting, a conductor of the Bow Street Foot Patrole, after cornering him in Aldus's pawnbrokers' shop. Initially Price became truculent and claimed Ting was there to rob him, but when another Bow Street officer by the name of Clarke arrived and greeted him with his proper name – Price - his whole attitude changed.[112] Forever the conman, Price even offered Ting a bribe of £115 in notes to leave the shop to tell his wife what had happened, the money being security on his safe return. Price's luck had run out, as this was declined.

Price had been finally arrested and was brought before a very pleased Sir Sampson Wright, who remanded him to Tothill Fields, Bridewell. During the pre–trial procedure Price was identified by another member of the patrole, and on this evidence committed for trial at the Old Bailey. However, he dodged justice by taking his own life in the Bridewell before his trial.[113] Buried as a suicide at a crossroads near the Bridewell, he was afterwards dug up by his widow and removed.[114]

---

112 Armitage, G. (1932) *The History of the Bow Street Runners*. Wisehart and Co., London, pp. 120-121.

113 Suicide was regarded as shocking and blasphemous, and a coroner's verdict of "felo de se" – literally crime against oneself – usually resulted in the body being buried at a crossroads, with a stake driven through the heart, and with no religious ceremony. The suicide's property could also be confiscated. www.historyextra.com/qa/end–road accessed on 3rd November 2015.

114 Armitage, G. (1932) *The History of the Bow Street Runners*. Wisehart and Co., London, p. 121.

This was a fine capture, relying on the tenacious ability of the patrole over a long period together with a piece of luck – a classic example of proper police work, which only helped cement further the myth of Bow Street.

In 1782 Sampson Wright developed Fielding's idea of a plain clothes police to patrol the environs of London, up to a distance of four miles from the court. The commencement dates of these innovations are sometimes disputed, although according to Treasury accounts they commenced in August 1783. This Foot Patrole or Night Patrole was a temporary measure and probably trialled in order to measure its success. Needless to say, this initial measure was a great achievement and within a short time was placed on a permanent footing. By 1790 Sir Sampson Wright personally oversaw these patroles as Chief Magistrate.[115]

Wright also championed, with other magistrates, a campaign against betting and gaming. He particularly disliked the game "Even and Odd", which Parliament was encouraged to outlaw. Wright appreciated how gambling brought misery and hardship to addicted gamers and their families. This was a game that affected everyone who played it; not just the upper classes, but the poverty-stricken poor as well. Wright led raiding parties with his colleague Addington and the runners in order to capture roulette tables. In August 1782 alone they managed to break up 17 tables situated in houses of fashion about the town.[116]

In 1783 Wright said that runners were able to earn a "comfortable livelihood with reputation to themselves and benefit to the public", and that they developed in consequence a sense of group identity, camaraderie and cooperation – the sense, as Wright went on to say, of being "a sort of Society".[117] What he meant here was a sort of early police sub-culture, which had originally been recommended by Welch who subscribed to his officers about forming a 'union' in 1754. John Fielding had underscored the suggestion in a pamphlet

115   Ibid, p. 124.
116   TNA 42/1, ff 246/7.
117   chs.revues.org/212 accessed on 3rd November 2015.

four years later when he stated that it was the role of the magistrate to promote the best attributes of his Constables:

"He should keep the civil power alive; that is to say, the Constables, constantly instructing them in their duty, and paying for dangerous and extraordinary enterprises; and, above all, promote harmony amongst them; for when the civil power is divided it is nothing, but when the Constables are collected together, known to each other, and bound by the connections of good fellowship, friendship and the bonds of society, they became sensible of their office, stand by one another, and are a formidable body".[118]

Wright built on the words of his mentor John Fielding, further galvanising his officers into a solid and remarkable force for good. This did not just affect the principal officers, but the same team-building principals applied to the other patroles as well. The advantages of good cooperation, acting as a collective and promoting the harmony of these officers for a common purpose, was to him success in policing.

This method of communication and sharing information became of great value and was welcomed by the magistrates, vestries and parish Constables in the counties. Often those shown in these lists distributed from Bow Street could also be linked to crimes perpetrated locally. This useful medium, as Leslie-Melville suggests, created a National Detective Office at Bow Street.[119]

Sampson Wright saw many changes during his 19-year tenure at Bow Street. He had been seriously tested during the riots of 1780 that later led to the introduction of regular Foot Patroles. The types of crime being committed in the metropolis had also changed, with increased gaming, fraud and forgery cases that kept the courts busy as villains moved to less violent, but perhaps easier and more

118 Fielding, J. (1758) *An Account of the origin and the effects of a police set on foot by his grace the Duke of Norfolk in the year 1753, upon a plan presented to his grace the Duke of Norfolk by the late Henry Fielding.* London.
119 Leslie–Melville, R. (1934) *The Life and Work of Sir John Fielding.* Lincoln Williams, London.

lucrative modes of crime.

Sir Sampson Wright died in 1793, having been a magistrate from 1774 and Chief Magistrate since 1780. His place as Senior or Chief Magistrate, still an unofficial position, was taken by his friend and colleague William Addington.[120]

William Addington (1728–1811)

William Addington had been a supporting magistrate to John Fielding, his mentor, since 1774 alongside Sampson Wright. Addington was born in 1728 and was already 65 years of age when he succeeded Wright as principal magistrate. By 1793 there were three salaried or stipendiary magistrates at Bow Street; in addition to Addington, who had been quickly knighted, were Richard Ford and Nicholas Bond. Bond had been the clerk to Sampson Wright, and had been rewarded and elevated in this way for his loyal service.

One of John Fielding's suggestions that would come to fruition during the tenure of Addington was the introduction in 1792 of "seven public offices" based on the Bow Street model that was funded directly by Government.

On the establishment of the other Public Offices, Bow Street still continued to have a separate place, a wider role and jurisdiction than the others. There were no prescribed limits to their officers' jurisdiction and they could go anywhere they wanted, whilst the other offices had responsibility for limited areas. Bow Street maintained six officers while the rest had from six to ten.

Bow Street maintained a national function, retaining its "Centre Office" status. Addington also had the responsibility for the Foot Patrole or Night Patrole, which now consisted of 68 armed, plain clothed officers divided into 13 parties of four-to-five men under the supervision of a captain. Eight of these parties patrolled the different roads leading to London and their duty was to "prevent robberies and detect offenders". The other five performed the same

120   Babington, A. (1969) *A House in Bow Street*. MacDonald and Co., London, p. 170.

role, but were assigned closer to Bow Street on the streets of the capital.

Some of the Foot Patrole deputised for the runners in the event that Bow Street became busy and they were short of investigating Constables. For this additional service those deputies would be compensated financially by the victim. This galvanised group of experienced men were trusted enough by Addington to become in effect an investigating detective. Details taken from the 1797 Select Committee report show that the magistrates were all paid £400 per year, whilst Addington received an extra £300 "in lieu of fees and emoluments". They were ably assisted by four clerks, who received salaries ranging from £80 to £160 per year, and administration was carried out by an office keeper, a house keeper and messenger.[121]

From 1799 to 1815 Britain was at war with France. This meant the Government having to fund the war through increasing taxation leaving many British men and women in desperate misery, not only from high taxes but rising food and fuel prices, unemployment caused by wartime trade restrictions and the increased use of labour-saving machinery. These economic struggles forced many men to sign up for the army.[122] Once the war was over, large numbers of demobbed British soldiers and seamen thronged the roads and cities, many with wounds and deformities – the result of combat. This produced its own problems not only in the form of increased levels of crime, but also begging and vagrancy.

William Addington retired in 1800 and lived for a further eleven years, his place being taken by Richard Ford.

Richard Ford (1800–1806)

Richard Ford was born in 1758, the fourth son of Dr James Ford of Albermarle Street, the co-manager of the Drury Lane Theatre and physician to Queen Charlotte. Ford was perhaps best known for his

---

121 The Report of the Select Committee on the Police of the Metropolis 1797.
122 www.bl.uk/romantics–and–victorians/articles/the–impact–of–the–napoleonic–wars–in–britain#sthash.ooYzFm2z.dpuf accessed 22nd March 2016.

liaison with the actress Mrs Dorothea Jordan.[123] Mrs Jordan went on to become the mistress and companion of the Duke of Clarence, later King William IV, with whom she had ten children. Ford was in his 20s and had recently qualified at Lincoln's Inn as a lawyer, in the 1780s, when Jordan moved in with him, and the couple would have three illegitimate children. On realising Ford was never going to marry her, Jordan moved out, transferring all her money into his care and leaving her children behind.[124]

Ford's legal training helped him secure a position as Magistrate at the Shadwell Office in 1792, eventually moving to Bow Street in 1801. He also became a Member of Parliament in 1789 for East Grinstead; however, after about a year he was successfully elected to the Appleby seat in Cumberland instead. He was appointed as Superintendent of the Alien Office in 1800 and also employed by the Home Office to collect information on radical agitators and manage French agents.[125] He was asked to consider the recent prison reform proposed by Jeremy Bentham which he reported favourably on; however, by 1802 he had changed his mind, preferring transportation as a better solution. He was asked to draft the regulations controlling the entry of foreigners during the peace of Amiens, and as Bow Street magistrate was instrumental in unmasking the Despard conspiracy.[126]

Ford succeeded William Addington in 1800 as Chief Magistrate, having joined the Bow Street bench in 1793. He remained at Bow Street until his untimely death in 1806. Ford is fondly remembered for creating the Bow Street Horse Patrole on the model previously introduced by John Fielding in 1763, but with some exceptions. It is

123 Fitzgerald, P. (1888) *Chronicles of Bow Street Police-office*. Gilbert and Rivington, London.
124 Highfill, Philip H., Kalman A. Burnim, Langhans, Edward, A. (1984) 'A Biographical Dictionary of Actors, Actresses, Musicians, Dancers, Managers and others Stage Personnel in London, vol. 8: Hough to Keyse', *Southern Illinois Press*, p. 259.
125 www.historyofparliamentonline.org/volume/1790–1820/member/ford-richard–1758–1806 accessed on 5th May 2017.
126 Farington, I. 174; Geo. III Corresp. ii. 1369, 1512; Add. 33108, ff. 100–3; 33110, f. 318; 33542, ff. 75 seq.; R. R. Nelson, Home Office (1782–1801), 115, 120; J. A. Hone, *For the Cause of Truth*, p. 69.

Ford that can be thanked for creating the origins of the Metropolitan Police Mounted Branch, under whose control it passed in 1837.

The Bow Street Horse Patrole was a body of uniformed men who were able to protect the traveller on the main roads leading into the metropolis, becoming hugely successful after a short period of time riding the highways in search of robbers, footpads and thieves. These officers were more professional, had greater numbers, better equipment and different uniforms than its 1763 predecessor. One other very important feature was that this was also to be a preventive force.

Richard Ford was knighted, and the appointment and control of his mounted men was his direct responsibility. He had a particularly close relationship with Home Secretary the Duke of Portland, who had provided him with an office in the Home Department. Ford was perceived by Portland to be a trusted magistrate, able to do the Government's bidding by openly challenging and taking action against radical societies.

Shortly after his promotion to Chief Magistrate in 1800 Ford learned from reports from a number of owners that their dogs had mysteriously disappeared. He sent out Robert Townsend (no relation to John Townsend, the famous Bow Street Runner), a member of the patrole, to investigate. At the time dogs would be stolen for their skins and a sophisticated network operated to steal, kill and skin the animals, disposing of their carcasses without detection. Townsend discovered that a house in St. George's Fields was being used for this purpose, occupied by Jane Sellwood and Thomas Pallet. On entering and searching the house he found up to 30 skinned dog carcasses in the back room. The place stank, and under the floorboards more carcasses and skins were found. Townsend later learned that another house near Blackfriars Road was also being used in this gruesome trade and immediately went to a two-roomed house in Bennett's Row occupied by Ann Carter, where in the back room he discovered a recently-skinned dog carcass. As a result of his inquiry, James Merrifield, Jane Sellwood, Thomas Pallet and Ann Carter were arrested and detained for examination before Sir Richard Ford at

Bow Street.[127] The examination revealed a network where houses would be rented by the women and dogs stolen and taken back to these premises, where they would be killed and skinned, and their carcasses buried underneath the floorboards. When the stench became unbearable the inhabitants would abscond with the hides without paying any rent.[128] After examination all were committed for trial.

Ford also had to deal with offences against the Combination Laws, the 1799 and 1800 Acts which in effect were early matters relating to unionism. These were passed under the Government of William Pitt the Younger, making it illegal to combine forces with other workers and strike during a conflict that would force employers and the Government to accede to more pay or time off. In one such action the men, who were journeymen boot and shoe makers, were charged under the Combination Laws at Bow Street with a number of others. Their defence case hinged on the fact that with rising food prices and the cost of living they could no longer support themselves and their families on their existing wages. The employers, on the other hand, were able to prove that the men had combined together against their masters to extract better wages. Common-sense prevailed under Ford who, with the other magistrates, withdrew the charges but reconciled both sides to agree terms under which both sides could survive.[129]

In 1805 the murder of a Rotherhithe shipbroker caused great excitement at Bow Street when the accused and witnesses were examined. Certain members of high society and the nobility went to see the spectacle. It was said that a special box had been erected for royalty to attend.[130] The case focussed on a man named Richard Patch, who had gained employment in 1803 at Mr Blight's shipbroking firm, a business where two of his relatives

127 *Morning Herald* 28th January 1801.
128 Ibid.
129 Armitage, G. (1932) *The History of the Bow Street Runners.* Wisehart and Co., London, p. 140-141.
130 Ibid, p. 136.

had positions, even though Patch's father had been a smuggler. He worked hard, showed aptitude, saved money and was considered industrious. This led to Blight offering Patch a third-share in the firm for £12,000, which Patch immediately accepted. Patch issued a promissory note underwritten by a local respectable tradesman from Bermondsey for the payment of £1,000 to Blight. When the note was not honoured Blight went up to London to investigate and was shot dead in his house. Bow Street, who were called in, were not happy with what they found, especially that the conflicting explanations given by the two witnesses were very suspicious. Both were arrested immediately, taken into custody and later examined. It transpired that Patch had been lying whilst the other witness, a maid, told the truth. Patch had shot dead his master to avoid being exposed to offering a forged note for the money. He was committed for trial and found guilty, sentenced to death and executed, protesting his innocence to the last.[131]

Sir Richard Ford was an industrious and hardworking man. Not only was he a Bow Street Chief Magistrate drawing the necessary recompense for that position, but he also received £500 a year for supervision of the Horse Patrole together with another £500 per year as Acting Magistrate for the Secretary of State's Office. In the latter position he was able to take part in examinations conducted by the Secretary of State.[132] Ford died unexpectedly in May 1806 aged 48 years after a short illness, which came as a great shock to all those officers and staff at Bow Street. John Townsend and his men went into deep mourning for Ford as his position as Chief Magistrate was taken up by James Read. In 1813 the operational responsibility for supervision of the Horse Patrole passed from Bow Street to the Home Office.

131 Armitage, G. (1932) *The History of the Bow Street Runners*. Wisehart and Co., London, p. 136.
132 Babington, A. (1969) *A House in Bow Street*. MacDonald and Co., London, p. 200.

James Read (1806–1814)

In 1802 James Read was a sitting magistrate at Bow Street, hearing cases such as allegations of pickpocketing, armed robbery, rioting, breaches of the peace, duelling, public disputes and cases of libel.[133] Read often sat as examining magistrate together with his senior colleague Richard Ford. Read had become an industrious, experienced and trusted magistrate, and was recommended for elevation to Senior Magistrate following Richard Ford's unexpected death. On Read's appointment to Senior Magistrate in 1806 he declined the traditional award of a knighthood, which was a usual nomination for a man in his position at the Bow Street court.

His first job was reported in August of that year, a case of bigamy. The case involved "a young and very attractive" woman who went through a ceremony of marriage to a man named Whitford at Gretna Green, "by a tobacconist for a certificate" against her father's wishes. The father was a respectable businessman in Basingstoke who soon forgave his daughter and son-in-law, even setting them up in business in Southampton. However, the business soon failed and the couple moved to London into a small house in Kensington and seeking employment. Mr Whitford noticed that his wife's affections had soon cooled. Furthermore, one day when he returned home he found the spare room made up for a guest. His wife had rented out the spare room to Robert Jacques James, an elderly man aged about 60 years who outwardly was a gentleman. Whitford welcomed James into his house warmly, but from the day of his arrival his wife's attentions cooled further towards him, causing suspicions that there may be more to this situation. One day when he arrived home Whitford found his wife and lodger no longer there and a note written by his wife stating their relationship was at an end. Whitford found her and she not only admitted adultery to him, but also that she had married James in May in St. Mary's Lambeth. Whitford went to Bow Street to make a criminal allegation of bigamy and she was soon arrested and tried. On finding the accused not guilty, the judge

---

133 *Morning Post* 31st August 1804.

suggested that there was doubt that a legal marriage had taken place, giving the defendant the benefit of the doubt.[134]

Soon Read was dealing with cases of duelling. He received information from Carpmeal, one of the officers in waiting at Bow Street, that a duel was to take place at Chalk Farm. The two participants were Francis Jeffreys of Edinburgh and Thomas More of Bury. Both were arrested together with their seconds by Bow Street officers, who brought them before the court. Read bound them all over to keep the peace with substantial sureties. When disarming Jeffreys' pistol to make it safe it was found that there was not a ball in the gun, but a pellet of paper instead. Carpmeal had been assisted by two members of the Foot Patrole in the arrests, Crocker and Wilkinson.[135]

Also in 1806 Read heard the case of two housebreakers named Kelly and Edwards, who had stolen a quantity of Irish linen valued £800. To avoid discovery of the stolen property they had hidden it in hampers smuggled into Newgate Prison. Wilkinson of the Patrole had discovered it on a search with the Keeper of the Prison and the Under City Marshall, who were in luck as they also found £150 in bank notes and a well-used set of prison skeleton keys.[136]

Apart from his other duties Read updated the fabric and buildings at Bow Street during his tenure. The premises were too small for the current task, and so space was created to accommodate the increased numbers of victims, lawyers, Constables, patroles, felons and court officers using the space. Although the premises at 4 Bow Street had been significantly altered since 1781 with the introduction of a large "Publick Office" nearly 30 feet wide by 20 feet long which replaced the yard and the "back building", by 1806 the buildings were again becoming cramped and overcrowded, with no space available for the housing of prisoners. New buildings were sought nearby, and fortunately No. 3 Bow Street became available for rent.

---

134 *Morning Herald* 6th August 1806.
135 Armitage, G. (1932) *The History of the Bow Street Runners.* Wisehart and Co., London, p. 148.
136 Ibid, p. 149.

Read managed to secure the lease and by 1813 a refurbished room for "Felons" was quickly established.[137]

Read resigned his office in 1813 and was succeed by Nathaniel Conant.

Nathaniel Conant (1813–1822)

Nathaniel Conant was born in 1745 at Hastingleigh, Kent, where his father the Rev John Conant (of Pembroke Hall, Oxford, MA 1730) was rector from 1734 and vicar of Elmstead from 1736 until his death on 9th April 1779.[138] Conant came from a very distinguished religious background.[139] Nathaniel was brought up at Canterbury School and intended for business, a pursuit he gave up in 1781 when he became a justice of the peace in the Commission of the Peace for Middlesex.[140] He was the first to suggest the idea of the new establishment of the police in 1792 and was very instrumental in forwarding the design.

There were three magistrates at Bow Street in 1814 and they were each paid £150 per quarter, making their yearly salary not inconsequential. Conant, as principal magistrate, received a further £150 per quarter in payment for his attendance to the Home Secretary. The responsibility for the administration of funds received and the paying staff and expenses rested with the chief clerk. In 1814 this was John Stafford, who kept a very tight rein on the monies. There were two other clerks at the office, William Woods and Samuel Keene. Each year accounts had to be published and submitted to the Treasury for accounting purposes. Stafford and all other chief clerks before and after him needed to reconcile the costs of running the Bow Street Office, ever-conscious of external criticism. He not only dealt with salaries but also expenses to the

---

137 Babington, A. (1969) *A House in Bow Street.* MacDonald and Co. London, p. 201.
138 *Gentleman's Magazine,* April 1822.
139 He was the great grandson of the celebrated Dr John Conant, Regius Professor of Divinity, and head of Exeter College, Oxford, in 1609, afterwards Arch Deacon of Norwich, and Vicar of All Saints, Northampton, near which place he possessed considerable property part of which is still in the family.
140 *Gentleman's Magazine,* April 1822.

Runners, pensions and annuities to wives of deceased magistrates, members of the Patrole, sick pay to injured officers, expenses to publish the *Hue and Cry*, parish rates, King's taxes and rents.

Conant had been one of the magistrates at the Marlborough Street Office, where he dispensed justice until 1813 when he became Chief Magistrate of Bow Street, and was knighted by the King. Conant, who lived at 11 Portland Place, also had other responsibilities and had been appointed as one of the

Fig. 9: Sir Nathaniel Conant
Courtesy Mr Edward Conant

Commissioners for Sale of the Land Tax for the County of Middlesex.[141] His son John Conant of Berners Street had, in the meantime, been recommended and appointed as a magistrate at Great Marlborough Street Court.[142]

In 1816 Conant, as Chief Magistrate, was called before the Parliamentary Committee appointed to enquire into the state of the police of the metropolis. The Committee was concerned about a number of matters, especially about offering rewards for stolen property and principal officers frequenting public houses of low repute - called "Flash Houses" - which seemed to attract the criminal classes. He was asked a number of questions, but prevaricated with his answers in a way that left the Committee feeling he had been disingenuous. For example, when asked about Flash Houses and his officers frequented them in order to gather information on felons, he was reluctant to admit this fact. He claimed he did not understand

141 *The Royal Kalender, and Court and City Register for England Scotland Ireland and the Colonies 1820.*
142 Ibid, p. 301.

nor could explain this art, even though some of his own principal officers, namely Townsend, Vickery and Sayer, had already admitted to the Committee that going to Flash Houses had been in operation for as long as they could remember, and that their existence in fact aided their ability in detection.[143] Conant was questioned further by the Committee and at length about the issue of rewards and remuneration paid to his officers, and he defended their reputation stating that they were paid one guinea a week as a retainer plus expenses. He added that if they were required to travel great distances at short notice and devote all their time to an inquiry, in his eyes the retainer was not enough.

If the inquiry was outside London the principal officer was paid at a rate of one guinea a day plus expenses, and Conant seemed to suggest that this was not unreasonable given they were often placed in some great danger.[144] The ability to pay rewards and the expenses of his officers was another line of questioning on which the Committee chose to tackle Conant, suggesting that if, as a victim, you were poor and unable to pay, it was unlikely an officer would be allocated to the case given there was little chance of recovering the outlay. Conant suggested it was always the magistrate's discretion that dictated whether an impecunious person would be supported in a prosecution or inquiry by his office. The Committee appeared unhappy at Conant's response, because in their eyes the reality of the situation was that it was the propertied classes from outside London who were more likely to use the principal officers and earn rewards and fees, with the poor, poverty-stricken majority being left to fend for themselves.[145] This very point was brought into sharp relief when the Metropolitan Police were formed in 1829, and for ten years the Runners and New Police co-existed. The Runners dealt with all the jewel robberies whilst the New Police were left to deal with the murders. All the murderers were apprehended, whilst only

---

143 The Report of the Committee on the police of the metropolis 1816.
144 Ibid.
145 Cox, D. (2010) *A Certain Share of Low Cunning – A History of the Bow Street Runners 1792–1839*, p. 77.

one sixth of the jewel thieves were detained.[146]

Conant was one of the first stipendiary magistrates, and he and William Mainwaring, the Chairman of the Westminster and Middlesex Benches, had submitted a plan to the Government to overcome the paucity of good, strong candidates sitting as magistrates at the Rotation Offices. They suggested copying the Bow Street model was the answer, and that a magistrate should have a group of paid Constables available to aid him thereby not relying on fees taken at the Office. They also suggested that salaried magistrates needed to be present at the Rotation Offices, and also sit at regular hours.[147] The proposals had been included in the Bill of 1785, but buried by more prominent elements that rendered the suggestions as ineffective.

By 1792 the situation was becoming worse with "the deficiency of magistrates and the abuse of office itself", so backbencher Francis Burton raised a Bill in parliament for a stronger court administration.[148] This manifested itself in the formal establishment of seven separate magistrates' courts, administered from the Treasury in the same form as Bow Street. Each court was staffed by three stipendiary (paid) magistrates and up to six paid principal officers or Constables. In addition to Bow Street, the new offices were set up at Queen's Square (Westminster), Great Marlborough Street (Westminster), Worship Street (Shoreditch), Lambeth Street (Whitechapel), Shadwell, Union Hall (Southwark) and Hatton Garden. A river police (Thames Police Office) was created later at Wapping in 1798. By 1816 there were between seven and eight officers at each station. The Shadwell Office had closed, but a new one was opened in Marylebone High Street.

Conant resigned his position at Bow Street in 1820 on account of his declining health following a fall. He lived a further two years and

---

146   Moylan, J. F. (1929) *Scotland Yard and the Metropolitan Police*. Putnam's, London, p. 150.

147   Paley, R. (1983) The Middlesex Justices Act of 1792; its origins and effects. pp. 213–218 Ph.d. thesis University of Reading.

148   Parliamentary debates, 29 (1791–2) 1034.

died on 12th April 1822 in Portland Place, London, aged 77.[149]

Robert Baker (1820–1821)

Robert Baker had a short tenure at Bow Street and is principally remembered for his role in the riots and funeral arrangements of Queen Caroline in 1821. Popular public affection for the Queen had risen out of her bad treatment by the King and his ministers, including the great and powerful. This popular affection often spilled over into public expressions of noisy disorder. Caroline had died following an obstruction of the bowel at Brandenburg House, Hammersmith on 14th August 1821. Even some six months before her death, when the King visited Covent Garden Theatre angry crowds repeatedly shouted their support for the Queen at him and his retinue. Grave disturbances had been thwarted by the supervision of Sir Robert Baker, who had received extra funds of £3,103 from the Government to keep the peace during the acrimonious divorce proceedings brought against her by the King.

The Queen had expressed her wish to be buried in Brunswick, Germany in the event of her death. The Government were concerned that the progress of the Queen's funeral entourage would engender more public unrest, while the King had quietly removed himself and made his way to Ireland on a visit. Her body was kept at Brandenburg House under the supervision of a Bow Street Officer named Perry together with a party of the Foot Patrole. Their role was to ensure the body was secure and prevent everyone who was not named on an official list from entry to the house. Discussions overseen by Prime Minister Lord Liverpool on the royal progress were debated by Government who came up with a circuitous route, avoiding the City of London. Arrangements on the ground had been left in the hands of Mr Bailey, who had arrived after a squadron of the Blues from Regent's Park Barracks had formed up outside the house at 6.00am. Their object was to take the body to Harwich, where it

149 www.lyndon-estate.co.uk/04%20History/NConantKt/NConantKT.html accessed on 28th November 2015.

would proceed to Germany by ship.

Outside the house the Queen's executors complained to Mr Bailey that the arrangements on the Queen's movement had not been communicated to or consulted with them. By 7.00am in the front drive there was an empty hearse harnessed to eight plumed horses, and behind that were 13 mourning coaches and 13 other carriages. This was a large procession which drew a large number of onlookers, but progress to Harwich was going to be slow.

Next to arrive was Sir George Nayler, Garter King–at–Arms, accompanied by Mr Hood, who was the Herald. He had with him an official letter authorising the removal of the body. There was a standoff between Mr Bailey and Dr Lushington, the Queen's executor, over possession of the body, with Lushington accusing Bailey of contravening the wishes of the Queen. Lushington's accusations did not lead to violence or force and so the Queen's body was placed in the hearse and after a slight delay set off for Harwich. The official route had been announced, commencing at Hammersmith then passing through Kensington, Uxbridge Road, Bayswater, Edgware Road, Islington, City Road, Old Street and Mile End, via Bow, Stratford, Ilford, Romford, Chelmsford and Colchester, ending at the port town of Harwich.

The weather was atrocious and it was raining hard as the entourage left, but this did not stop thousands of people with their umbrellas lining the route, with many of the houses being draped in black. On the way through Kensington a party of Bow Street Constables were directing traffic away from Hyde Park Corner. They were oblivious to the route, and as the lead coaches passed there were repeated shouts of "Through the City".

Baker had brought 40 of the Bow Street Police establishment, assisted by 50 police from the Thames Police Office, 80 Westminster Constables and seven or eight Constables from each of the Public Offices to help him keep the peace, but it wasn't enough. A skirmish broke out between the police and protesters, resulting in fatalities on both sides. The mob quickly obstructed the procession by erecting barricades, which brought it to a standstill. After an hour and a half the entourage moved off again, this time towards Hyde Park Corner having been denied access to the Park by the mob at Kensington Gore. Sir Robert Baker and a squadron of Life Guards who had turned up could not force access to the Park. At Hyde Park and Hyde Park Corner, large numbers of the Queen's supporters had gathered and the entourage was stopped again; this time a very serious riot occurred. The Military had also been subject to a good deal of stone-throwing and, noticing the procession was moving through Hyde Park towards Cumberland Gate, the mob went ahead to prevent them from exiting into the end of Oxford Street.

At Cumberland Gate the procession was halted once more. The situation was becoming desperate for the troops against an equally determined mob. Some 40 to 50 shots were fired into the crowd killing at least two people, and many others were injured. The determined mounted soldiers fired recklessly in all directions as they forced their way through the crowds towards Tyburn Turnpike. It was now 1.30pm as the entourage proceeded up the Edgware Road towards Paddington then right into the New Road to Islington. As it was about to pass the end of Tottenham Court Road the procession was halted once more by an obstruction, forcing it to turn towards The Strand and the City of London, through which it passed without incident.

Only one further incident occurred later at Colchester, where the procession had stopped for the night. A sympathiser who had accompanied the procession had fixed a plate to the coffin bearing the inscription "Here Lies CAROLINE OF BRUNSWICK the injured Queen of England". An altercation arose as the person in charge quickly removed it. The Queen's remains arrived in Brunswick a week later. Having left England, the plate was re–attached and buried with her as was her wish.

Baker was castigated by the authorities for his lack of determination in dealing with the angry crowds. This was shown when faced with obstructions en–route, where he failed to declare and read the Riot Act to them causing Richard Birnie, who accompanied him, to take responsibility himself and declare a riot. Baker was removed from office over this and replaced by Birnie.

There were only two other events of note reported in the newspapers for which Baker would be remembered during his time at Bow Street. The first happened in February 1821, when Baker heard a case involving a dispute over a stolen trunk. Sir James Crawford appeared before him on a charge of threatening the servants of the French Ambassador with a pistol. Crawford had stayed at the French Hotel in Albermarle Street and had left without settling his bill. His trunk containing his personal papers had been removed pending reconciliation of the account. Crawford had also threatened the hotel owner's wife with a pistol. When the case was before Baker, the location of the trunk was established as being safe and not stolen. Crawford, however, was inconsolable and would not agree to sureties or being released, preferring instead to go to prison pending his trial at the Middlesex sessions later in the year.[150]

Another event four months later also came to notice when two opposing groups of (Low) Irish from St. Giles and Bloomsbury were involved in a massive street fight. Both groups, dressed in different colours, met at Buckridge Street armed with knives, sticks and other weapons and a serious disturbance commenced. This was only quelled on the arrival of a parish Constable from Holborn and 20 assistants who separated the troublesome groups. This only provided a brief respite, as the word had been sent to Bow Street for help. Baker despatched a strong detachment of armed Foot Patrole who charged the warring factions with drawn swords, apprehending 13 principal rioters. They were removed and appeared at Bow Street, where they were committed to prison for trial later.[151]

Richard Birnie (1821–1832)

Sir Richard Birnie presided over the final stages and breakup of the Bow Street Foot Patrole and Dismounted Horse Patrole. He watched

---

150 Armitage, G. (1932) *The History of the Bow Street Runners*. Wisheart and Co., London, p. 227–228.
151 Ibid.

the introduction of the New Police that replaced them, although his Horse Patrole would last until 1837 and the Runners until 1839.

He was born about 1760 at Banff in Aberdeenshire. After serving an apprenticeship to a saddler he came to London, and worked for the house of Macintosh & Co., in the Haymarket, saddlers and harness-makers to royalty. He struck up a favourable relationship with the Prince of Wales and, probably as a result, was made foreman and later a partner in the business. He married the daughter of a wealthy baker and moved into rented accommodation in St. Martin-in-the-Fields.[152] Here he took an active interest in parochial affairs, serving as a parish Constable, overseer, auditor and churchwarden.[153]

He was an active, compassionate and intelligent man, establishing almshouses for the poor in Pratt Street, Camden Town. He was also a social climber who thought it essential to show some military experience, so he enrolled in the Royal Westminster Volunteers, in which he became a captain. With his star still rising he was put forward as a justice of the peace at the request of the Duke of Northumberland and placed in the commission of the peace. After sitting at Bow Street in the absence of Sir Richard Ford and Mr Graham, he was later established at Union Hall court in Southwark in his own right as magistrate. After a few more years he was transferred back to Bow Street as a magistrate, during which time he gave devoted service. He was upset, however, when the post of Chief Magistrate became available and Sir Robert Baker from Marlborough Street was chosen instead.

On the resignation of Baker following the debacle of Queen Caroline's funeral Birnie became Chief Magistrate and was bestowed with a knighthood. At the ceremony, which took place at the Carlton Palace, Birnie was called over by the Duke of Wellington to Lord Sidmouth and the Earl of Liverpool, who all surrounded George IV. Birnie fell down on one knee and the King took the sword from the

152 Birnie, Richard, *Dictionary of National Biography*. London: Smith, Elder & Co. 1885–1900.
153 *The Gentleman's Magazine and Historical Chronicle*, Vol. 102 Part 1.

Duke of Wellington and placed on the shoulders of Birnie, saying "arise Sir Robert Birnie" causing some mirth. When Birnie said in a very contrite manner "If it please your Majesty", and since his name was Richard, the King corrected his error.

In addition to his magisterial duties, Birnie headed and supervised the Bow Street Foot Patrole and became a very experienced magistrate, but he was also a brave man as well. With no thought as to his

Fig. 10: Sir Richard Birnie

personal safety, in February 1820 he led a team of officers in the apprehension of the Cato Street conspirators - Thistlewood, Brunt, Tidd, Ings, Davidson and company. Although one of his officers was killed in the storming of the building, all of the conspirators were rounded up and taken before the court. For this he won immense Government approval and gratitude. Birnie was an influential man and his experience saw him appear from time to time before Government Select Committees on the Police of the Metropolis. There was also another side to him, and he could be an arrogant man who played to his audience in the court at Bow Street.

In 1829 Birnie watched as the Bow Street Foot and Dismounted Horse Patroles, which had already been brought under Government control, were disbanded. He saw how some of his men had been transferred voluntarily to the New Police, while others had been dismissed or superannuated. He was opposed to the New Police and was happy to criticise young Constables in open court during many of the cases he heard before him. Birnie was visited by ten of his men who expressed their concerns over being terminated from their occupation and with it removal of their badge of office. As such they were no longer Constables acting on behalf of Bow Street Court. He heard how many had stalwartly declined a transfer to the New Police and lamented sadly at the loss of their experience, loyalty and courageousness. John Upson, one of the Police establishment, expressed his personal thanks to Birnie and placed no blame on him or Bow Street for their situation.[154] Steggles, another of the Patrole, asserted that Upson and himself were attached to a section in Surrey to which no New Police were yet allocated, and expressed his upset at having been terminated at such very short notice.

For several months in 1832 Birnie had been ill, and he died from "pulmonary affection" on 29th April at Bow Street aged 73 years, leaving two sons and a daughter.[155] The funeral was a big affair and practically the whole of the Bow Street police establishment and old members of the Patrole attended, such was the esteem under which he was held. Amongst those present were officers Taunton, Salmon, J. J. Smith, Ellis, Ledbitter, Birchall, Dodd, Godison, and Fall.[156]

Frederick Adair Roe (1832–1839)

In 1832 Frederick Roe became Chief Magistrate at 3 Bow Street. In 1836, the year he was created a Baronet, he was assisted as magistrates by George Rowland Minshull and Thomas Halls. The support staff included three clerks - Mr Stafford (Chief Clerk), Mr Burnaby and Mr Vine, all paid 25s a week. There were ten Constables or Principal Officers, with one of these officers being office bound as Summoning Clerk in receipt of 4s less pay than he would have received.

A particular bone of contention was the fact that Roe's Constables were directly answerable to the magistrates and not to the Commissioners of the New Police, and this situation would remain

154 Fitzgerald, P. (1888) *Chronicles of Bow Street (Vol. 2)*. Chapman and Hall, London.
155 *Drogheda Journal, or Meath & Louth Advertiser* Saturday 5th May 1832.
156 *Morning Post* Monday 7th May 1832.

so until 1839. These Constables were George Ruthven, James Smith, James Ellis, James Ledbitter, Richard Gardener, Henry Fall, Abraham Fletcher, Henry Goddard, William Ballard and Francis Keys. Mr Day was conductor of the Horse Patrole and their control would pass to the Commissioners in 1837. The other Public Offices created in 1792 also retained their Constables in the same manner as Bow Street.

Roe became King's Counsel in 1836.[157] He was an influential man and was in daily attendance at the Home Office seeing the Secretary of State and his deputies on Government business. He would often also attend Windsor Castle at the King's wish.

He was called before a number of the Government Select Committees inquiring into the Police of the Metropolis to give evidence, even though he had only served as Chief Magistrate for 12 months by 1833. He was also no fan of the New Police or the Commissioners, and used his appearances before the Committee in May 1833 and 1834 to vent the full force of his feelings. He prized the old system and dearly felt under threat that more of his Patroles would be removed to the Commissioners. He had already witnessed the transfer of the Foot Patroles and could see that disbanding his Bow Street Constables and Horse Patroles would be the next step, as this was what the Commissioners had been suggesting earlier. Roe was responsible for the Horse Patrole and in his evidence he stated that he issued warrants as a result of informations put before him, and most often he only gave them to his own Constables to execute unless there was a reason not to do so. In other words, he didn't give them to the New Police to deal with which caused some great difficulties, especially if a Metropolitan Police officer had possession of any evidence or incriminating property. When asked from the country Roe would send his officers to deal with criminal matters (and not inform the New Police at all), for which they received 10s a day for their pay and 12s a day for their living and coach hire there and back.[158]

157 *The Royal Kalendar, and Court and City Register for England, Scotland for 1836.*
158 Home Office (1833) *Report by the Select Committee into the state of the Police of the Metropolis*, p. 88.

He gave full vent in his evidence about exactly what he thought. He said that neither he nor his brother magistrates had been given information about the regulation and organisation of the Metropolitan Police. As such, there was no communication on areas of difficulty by both parties. He continued by saying that the New Police were governed like an army, with the private reporting up the chain of command for directions. The new police were deferential and civil enough when appearing before him but they considered in his view that his authority was now just purely magisterial and not extending into matters of policing as they had done before. Roe felt the New Police were no longer subject to the authority of the magistrates, despite there being many matters on which a Constable needed a magistrate's direction. These included very delicate, complicated and sophisticated matters requiring tact and discretion, such as a duel between gentlemen or allegations of espionage. Roe felt that their authority as magistrates would not only be eroded but also sidelined. In other words, they would lose their importance.

He felt that appointing and instructing Constables who answered to him was the best way to maintain secrecy, whilst the new system was open to failure in that objective. He suggested that the new corps system was destructive, inefficient and compromised integrity. He cited the numbers of Constables who since the start of the Metropolitan Police had been dismissed, discharged or resigned as supporting his case. On the issue of corruption and the taking of money by his officers, Roe indicated no suspicion of their dishonesty in the present or past.[159] Taking another swipe, he suggested that Inspectors and Superintendents, without being particular, "do very extraordinary things". On the issue of maintaining the peace, Roe was questioned about the threat of public disorder. Roe had gone to White Conduit Fields in 1831 on the instructions of Lord Melbourne because of a threat of disorder, but felt superfluous given there were over 500 Metropolitan Police officers present and no communication was made to the magistrates there as to the arrangements. When

---

159 Home Office (1833) *Report by the Select Committee into the state of the Police of the Metropolis*, p. 91.

an Inspector was asked by Roe what the instructions were there seemed to be confusion, because he now appeared to answer to two masters. The arrangements on the ground as to who was in charge were not properly delineated.

The commissioners were frustrated when a warrant was issued to a Metropolitan Constable as Roe also expected one of his Constables to be present to execute it. His reasoning was that on other occasions he had granted a warrant, only to find that 12–14 men ransacked every room in the house without waiting for one of his officers to attend to see what was going on.[160] Roe also admitted it was unnecessary for any of his officers to seek the assistance of a Metropolitan officer in any cases that he knew and in the case of riot he felt there was an issue of jurisdiction, leaving him with no power over the Metropolitan Constables in ordering them to act in preserving the peace should he say so.

Roe was also aware that the Commissioners had called for new legislation to extend their boundaries and take over other police responsibilities when the vacancy of Chief Magistrate should become available.[161] The Commissioners suggested that because of the lack of cordial cooperation on the part of the magistrates, the Secretary of State should create a distinct line between the duties of the magistrates and the Commissioners.

Roe was a belligerent man and fought very hard to blame others instead of himself for obstructing the ends of justice, but his days were numbered. It had become clear to most people through the Select Committee evidence that a change was necessary. As already stated in the intervening period, the Bow Street Horse Patrole was absorbed into the Metropolitan Police by 1837. On 17th August 1839 legislation was passed for improving the Police of the Metropolis, and a week later another Act was introduced regulating Police Courts in the Metropolis. Cox (2010) suggests that there were no

---

160 Home Office (1833) *Report by the Select Committee into the state of the Police of the Metropolis*, p. 95.
161 Ibid, p. 449.

clauses in the legislation which specifically disbanded the principal officers, and so those remaining had their positions terminated.[162] Two principal officers, Ballard and Goddard, went on to use their detective skills and became private detectives elsewhere once dismissed.[163]

It was clear that Roe had lost, and since his position was untenable given the new situation he resigned. The work of Bow Street Court still carried on in its new guise. The magisterial changes were reported in the newspapers:

"At Bow–street Police Court, yesterday, a communication was received from Lord John Russell, acquainting the sitting magistrate that Mr Halls, of Hatton–garden Police Court, has been appointed Chief Magistrate, with a salary of £1,200 a–year, in the room of Sir F. Roe, resigned; and Mr Jardine, the barrister, second magistrate, with a similar salary, in the room of Mr Minshull, who retires on a superannuated allowance. Mr Twyford, who has been a police magistrate seventeen years, continues to officiate as third magistrate, with a salary of £1,000 a–year."[164]

162 Cox, D. (2010) *A Certain Share of Low Cunning – A history of the Bow Street Runners 1792–1839*, p. 225.
163 Ibid, p. 235.
164 *Morning Post* 4th September 1839.

– 2 –

Principal Officers *or* Runners

There was no police force as such located at Bow Street at the time of Thomas de Veil, and it was only when Henry Fielding took over that Constables became "Fielding's people" and operated from his house. Noted also is the secrecy around which these groups operated, being shielded from the public misconception that Mr Fielding's people were corrupt private thief-takers rather than "honest householders actuated by a truly public spirit against thieves".[165] In taking this action the Fieldings not only thought it essential to do so in order to maximise their success as investigators of crime, but also to keep "the plan" secret.

The Bow Street Patrole(s) have often been confused with the Bow Street Principal Officers, sometimes called Runners, and vice versa. These were Constables and officers of the court who carried out the executive function in the execution and enforcement of the law. As we have seen, the Principal Officers, as they were later called, were a small group of non-uniformed men founded in 1752 by Henry Fielding, originally known as thief-takers and later as "Fielding's people", Principal Officers and lastly Runners.[166]

They operated at the same time there was a pool of some 80 Constables under the direction of Saunders Welch, from which

165 Critchley, T. A. (1967), *The History of Police in England and Wales.* Constable and Co., London, p. 33.
166 Newman, G. (1997). *Bow Street Runners. Britain in the Hanoverian Age, 1714–1837: an Encyclopaedia.* London: Taylor & Francis, p. 69.

six of the best were drawn to form the core of officers.[167] The term "Runner" is said to have been first used in the press on 5th March 1785, written in the *Morning Herald*.[168] It was written by the Rev Henry Bate on the famous occasion when Nathaniel Hone, in a painting called *The Conjuror*, accused Sir Joshua Reynolds of plagiarism. One verse ran:

> What's Raphael, Guido and the rest?
> Poor dogs, Sir Joshua, at the best!
> If no idea bright
>
> They lose – without Hone's demi–devil
> Like Bow Street runner – most uncivil –
> Bringing the theft to light!

There is no indication in the poem to whom the term "runner" refers. It might mean any of the Bow Street Patroles, just as equally as it could to the Principal Officers. This was not a term they used themselves, in fact the Principal Officers disliked the name, considering it derogatory.[169] However, in 1754 the term "a runner" was referred to in proceedings at the Old Bailey in the case of Charles Flemming, who had committed highway robbery. A turnkey or prison officer at Newgate Prison saw the accused being picked out from a group of other prisoners by a witness in what was an early form of informal identity parade. Flemming said that the "runner" had winked at the witness in order to ensure selection of the right person, identifying him.[170]

This suggested that Runners had a particular role or occupation involving prisons, but more insight can be gained in the following example. Again in 1755, a reference to "a runner" was in relation to

---

167   Pringle, P. (1955) *Hue and Cry –The Story of Henry and John Fielding and their Bow Street Runners.* William Morrow and Co., London, p. 88.

168   Metropolitan police in private correspondence to Mr Pike dated 17th May 1971. Metropolitan Police Historical Collection, ESB, London.

169   Cox, David J. (2010) 'Ruthven, George Thomas Joseph (1792/3–1844), police officer', *Oxford Dictionary of National Biography*, Oxford University Press, September.

170   Old Bailey Proceedings Online (www.oldbaileyonline.org, version 7.2, 25 March 2016), October 1754, trial of Charles Flemming , otherwise Johnson (t17541023–39).

Edward Wright, a turnkey, who was also an officer at Bow Street and local publican. He was said to be a "runner at Mr Fielding's Office who was required to carry persons backwards and forwards", as Beattie points out, "to one of the Westminster or Middlesex gaols and if necessary bring them back for re-examination."[171] This role was as a court functionary, working as part of the court's administrative staff and earning additional expenses for such work. In fact, even in 1816, in a report inquiring into the state of the police, the committee never referred to the Constables as runners but as "officers at Bow Street".[172]

Often in those early days those working for the court would be reported as "Fielding's People", "Sir John Fielding's men" or "Fielding's men", and not until much later was the term "Runner" applied to describe the officers not only at Bow Street but at the other offices as well.[173]

For example, in 1811, following the Ratcliffe Highway murders "... two runners hurried up from the Shadwell Office which was nearby" and "a score or more of runners from four different offices... and a strong corps of Bow street patrole were at one time or other involved in the inquiry".[174]

Almost certainly the confusion of patroles at Bow Street caused the newspapers to describe all of the patroles as "runners", not just the Principal Officers, when in fact this could have been the title for members of the Dismounted Horse Patrole or Foot Patrole.

The original term "runner" was meant:

> "...as a derogatory nickname that denoted a person who worked as an assistant to bailiffs in the disreputable job of arresting debtors or involved in escorting offenders to jail who had been

171 Beattie, J. (2012) *The First English Detectives.* Oxford University Press, Oxford, p. 33.
172 Report from the Committee on the state of the Police of the Metropolis 1816.
173 Old Bailey Proceedings Online (www.oldbaileyonline.org, version 7.2, 10 August 2015), February 1765, trial of Joseph Sparrow, Richard Perry, John Taylor (t17650227-30).
174 Browne, D. (1956) *The Rise of Scotland Yard.* George Harrap and Co., London, p. 55–56.

committed for trial by the court". (Beattie 2012)[175]

The title attributed to them was Principal Officer for the six non-uniformed Constables, probably derived from the magistrates themselves as at Bow Street John Fielding and his successors were described as Principal Magistrates in Westminster.[176] It appears fitting and understandable that their official title of Principal Officer thus separated them from the rest of the Patroles. In fact Browne (1956), like other writers, seems confused on the issue of who the Runners were and how they operated, since he asserts "the Runners, whether at Bow Street or elsewhere," seemingly conflating the term to mean the Principal Officers at all the Rotation Offices. Reith (1948) asserts that the initial group of Fielding's men came popular and famous, especially in the following century, when they became to be called Bow Street Runners.[177]

Later on we see that the most famous so-called Bow Street Runner, John Townsend, commenced his career at Bow Street by starting first as a turnkey at Newgate, then later a member of the Bow Street Foot Patrole before being promoted to Principal Officer and engaged in royalty protection.

Immediate pursuit

From the very early days at Bow Street the business of inquiry, pursuit and arrest of criminals was at first conducted by those original six (later eight) officers. Each had taken his practice and training from the school of Jonathan Wild, the thief-taker.[178] Wild referred to himself as "Informer General", and such was his arrogance he even paid newspapers to refer to him as "Thief-Taker

175 The term Bow Street runner was used for the first time in the newspapers – the *Northampton Mercury* and the *Oxford Journal* simultaneously on 27th January 1787 when referring to the capture of an infamous pickpocket and his later mysterious escape from custody. The Old Bailey records show the same term used in proceedings in January 1800 and April 1802.
176 Browne, D. (1956) *The Rise of Scotland Yard*. George Harrap and Co., p. 39.
177 Ibid, p. 34.
178 The term thief taker was at the time practically synonymous with that of informer.

General", thereby creating a myth which was felt to be equivalent to a whole host of Constables.[179] Under John Fielding, however, the issue of thief-takers became a problem where the magistrate had to differentiate between his honest full-time officers attached to Bow Street and dishonest ones like Wild.[180]

Fielding's patroles were irregular as his budget could not always support them, and they were only sent out when the need arose. The newly-appointed Constables had little guidance in how to perform the onerous tasks attached to their office. Many just coasted along, not upsetting the status quo, while others embraced the role wholeheartedly. Many underestimated the difficulty of the position and some were themselves sanctioned for failure or neglect of duty.

Saunders Welch appreciated the need for guidance of Constables and as such wrote down and published his experiences in book form. This small booklet, published in 1754 by A. Millar in The Strand and priced at one shilling, provided a guide for his parish Constables on matters which are still relevant and useful today.[181] This was, perhaps, the very first Constable's instruction book, and was aimed at the inexperienced parish Constable probably for the County of Middlesex in which Welch was High-Constable of the Holborn Division. This was a system Welch had developed (most probably with Henry Fielding) following his eight years' "experience highlighting the problems and pitfalls that could befall a Constable during his one year" in office.[182]

This advice would benefit not only sworn officers of the watch and servants of Bow Street, but was applicable to all those engaged in law enforcement. Unless a nominated Constable held a "Tyburn Ticket" which exempted him from performing his duty for a year as

---

179 Moylan, J. F. (1929) *The Blue Army in Country Life*. May edition.
180 Moylan, J. F. (1929) *Scotland Yard and the Metropolitan Police*. G. P. Puttnams and Son. London.
181 Browne, D. (1956) *The Rise of Scotland Yard*. George Harrap and Co., London, p. 26. See Appendix 1 for a précis of Millar's book.
182 Householders had a responsibility to become a Constable for a year in each parish unless they were in receipt of a Tyburn Ticket exempting them from this duty.

Constable he was required to serve the parish, although he could nominate and pay for a deputy to serve in his place. The system of the watch was a complicated parochial issue where vestries appointed Constables, a factor not lost on Welch.

The appointed Constables were unpaid and annually appointed through the vestry from a list of householders or small tradesmen of the parish. In practice, the main burden of the work was carried out by paid deputies, whilst watchmen were paid by the parish authorities at a rate of between 8½d and 2s a night.[183] Their duty was for one year. In urban parishes there was more than one Constable appointed, and in the case of Westminster five Constables per parish were selected. They performed their duty at night time and worked with the beadle who had, in most urban parishes, become a minor paid official.[184] The Constable did not need to do duty each night but attended the watch house in rotation with the other Constables. In the early days the parish Constable system meant that each man had to carry on their ordinary jobs during the day as well. Such were the numerous laws being introduced that a Constable in a year could not possibly learn all the legislation needed to do the job.

The Constable or beadle, or both, supervised and inspected the night watch as they reported for duty and again later when they paraded in the morning before being booked off duty. The Constable and beadle would walk around the parish at least twice and check that the watchmen were properly at their posts and awake.[185] There were minor expenses or rewards for serving court summonses and executing warrants. Petty crime or misdemeanours were often overlooked, in the hope that the Constable would find the person committing more serious felonies – "weighed forty pounds" (£40), the amount of reward payable by the court to a witness or Constable who assisted in the arrest and successful conviction of the felon. If

---

183   Leslie–Melville, R. (1934) *The Life and Work of Sir John Fielding.* Lincoln Williams, London, p. 37.
184   Tobias, J. J. (1972) *Nineteenth – Century Crime: Prevention and Punishment.* David and Charles. Newton Abbot, p. 98.
185   Ibid.

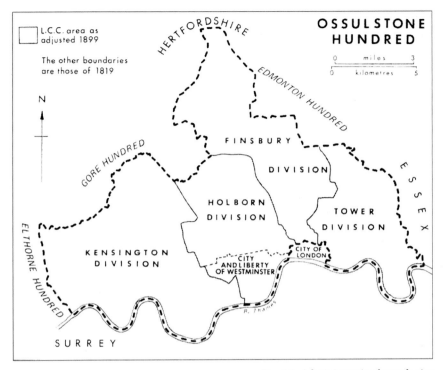

*Fig. 11: Administrative boundaries
of the Ossulstone Hundred*

a witness or member of the public was involved in such a case the judge might issue a "Tyburn Ticket" to them, thereby exempting them from duty as a sworn Constable of the parish. Yet in practice this body of Constables and watchmen were neither combined nor co-ordinated and it took the riots of 1780, as we have seen, to lay bare the problem of not having a civil power sufficiently strong enough to counter any threat not only against the King's Peace but also against crime in general, which had spiralled out of control.

There was the City and Liberty of Westminster, Holborn Division, Tower Division, Kensington Division and Finsbury Division. Separately there was also the City of London, and all these areas were bordered to the south by the River Thames. Welch was High Constable of Holborn Division, which also meant he supervised the City and Liberty of Westminster Constables. The City of London had their own separate system of policing, as they do today.

Applications were made to Bow Street to join those original thief-takers, and it was likely that they were interviewed by Saunders Welch. Welch felt that there was a general lack of knowledge and understanding amongst the Constables of their powers, and that this often resulted in failure to use them properly. At the beginning of his treatise Welch provided a warning that anarchy would prevail if the civil powers failed, because the honest citizen would then seek military intervention and redress instead.

From the very beginning, Welch's message was that the office of Constable should be exercised in an understated, impartial and subtle manner. Georgian England was gradually developing into a more civilised society, with a better balance between public freedom and consent, and the State's use of coercive force. Welch was conscious of the fact that excessive forceful intervention into the lives of citizens might lead to riot or revolution. He asserted that there should be no excessive use of those powers derived from their office unless the Constable was in danger of assault or death. Welch had seen for himself that the excessive use of force by Constables representing the will of the King did not earn respect, but hatred instead. The standard for him meant that the use of force had to be justified, proportionate, appropriate and necessary.

He also felt the fundamental starting point was that a "proper union" amongst colleagues was essential for co-operation and spreading information. This *esprit de corps* was vital, bearing in mind the difficulties of the job. Welch was, in essence, establishing a notion of camaraderie which was hinged on co-operation, solidarity and mutual respect. This bonding of a group as comrades in this way sought to create solidarity amongst them, where decisiveness, energy, toughness, courage and a willingness to take action were central features that would set them apart as people to be respected, not feared. Binding and bonding the Constables together in this way helped not only to re-enforce their social relationship each time they were on duty, but also assisted them in overcoming their nerves, anxieties and fears given the often tenuous duties they needed to perform. Today we might call this "a police occupational sub-culture".

Despite the fact that his constables came from all walks of life and given the fact that each had different perceptions and understandings it was essential to fashion them into a cohesive group. This meant that when performing their duties as constables it was crucial that they adhered to a common set of values, standards and behaviour. The art of policing is a social duty where decisions and responsibilities of the office of Constable are bound up in social proximity (perceived and actual) – a tendency for individuals to form interpersonal relationships.[186] Attached to it is the notion of a central frame of reference on how and to what extent these duties should be carried out. Successful "union" meant that the Constables could share information, experiences and knowledge, and behave with integrity and honesty when carrying out the duties of their office as part of this group.

The responsibilities of the parish Constable differed to those of the Bow Street Constable, although in the early days sometimes one was also a servant of the other. The parish Constable could only enforce the law within his own parish, whilst the jurisdiction of the Bow Street Constable extended beyond Westminster into Surrey, Kent, Middlesex and Essex. The parish Constable was unable to cross a parish boundary to enforce the law unless he was acting under the High Constable of his Division, whose authority he would share. An Act of Parliament in 1735 outlined the duties of the parish Constable for the Parish of St. Paul, Covent Garden within the City and Liberty of Westminster:

He..

> "Shall attend every night by turns and shall keep watch and ward from the hours of 9 in the evening until 7 in the morning...by endeavours to prevent as well all mischiefs happening by fire, as all murders, burglaries and robberies and other outrages

---

186 Newcomb, T. M. (1960). 'Varieties of interpersonal attraction'. in D. Cartwright & A. Zander (Eds.), *Group dynamics: Research and theory* (2nd ed., pp. 104–119).

and disorders and to that end to arrest and apprehend all night walkers, malefactors, and suspected persons who shall be found wandering or misbehaving themselves and shall carry the persons apprehended as soon as conveniently to one or more justice or justices of the peace..."[187]

Initially these Bow Street men were unpaid, but by John Townsend's time they were paid a modest retainer and their pay was supplemented in a number of other ways including rewards, presents and perquisites from those whose property they had recovered. They appeared to have no rules or system, as they responded almost daily to matters being reported to Bow Street from victims. Originally they were, with the exception of one, all former Constables of Westminster who had been chosen for their "public spirit against thieves".[188] By the early 1800s they had become more of a private detective agency than a public service.[189] As the 1837 Parliamentary Committee suggested, they "were private speculators in the detection of crime rather than efficient officers for the ends of justice." In other words, they only reacted really to property crime, coining or forgery offences which stood the chances of them being paid more. They appeared not the least interested in murders unless a substantial reward had been offered, or as Moylan puts it:

"Although only 8 in number they did not confine themselves to London being available to the highest bidder for their services in any part of the country".[190]

William Pentlow and William Bond, two of the earliest Runners, were referred to in court proceedings at the Old Bailey as "Fielding's people" and not as Runners. Thomas Hind had been a turnkey, but

---

187 An Act for the better regulating the night watch and beadles within the Parish of St. Paul, Covent within the Liberties of the City of Westminster pp. 249–250.
188 Welch, S. (1754) *Observations on the office of Constable*. Millar, A. Strand. London.
189 Moylan, J. F. (1929) *Scotland Yard and the Metropolitan Police*. G. P. Puttnams and Son. London.
190 Moylan, J. F. (1929) *Scotland Yard and the Metropolitan Police*. G. P. Puttnams and Son. London, p. 150.

later became the Deputy Governor of Tothill Fields, Bridewell (called The Bridewell) until his death in 1755, and later his colleague Henry Wright was the Under Keeper of Tothill Fields Bridewell from 1764, were both attached to Bow Street.[191]

Some of the principal officers had acquired specialist knowledge, such as George Ruthven who was attached to the Bank of England from time to time to detect forgery and coining offences. John Clarke (a Principal Officer from 1771-93) was an expert in coining offences, experienced in the metalwork trade and had been a silver cane head and button maker. Clarke, like Ruthven, was paid a retainer from the Bank of England to attend on certain days of the month. Ruthven also advised the Russian and Prussian Governments on forgery and false coinage.

In 1811 the Runners doubled their number from six to twelve officers.[192] A number of Runners became famous in their own right as they were often seen at the theatre, Windsor Castle, the Derby, at Royal Parties and events, protecting a notable person or being in the presence of the King, who paid and retained two of them to accompany him. In fact, Bow Street Runners became the early precursors of the Metropolitan Police Royalty Protection. One such principal officer was John Townsend, who built up a good relationship with King George III. Townsend would accompany the King on walks and it is said tell the monarch risqué jokes which George enjoyed immensely.

There were other unofficial Bow Street Principal Officers who militated from being one of the officers attached to Bow Street and moved to other duties. For example, John Rivett, who served as a Principal Officer from 1794 until 1811 then served in the Royal retinue from 1811 until 1837. Thomas Dowsett, was for a short while a Runner between 1798 until 1799, when he was also moved

191 Beattie, J. (2012) *The First English Detectives*. Oxford University Press, Oxford, and Cox, D. (2010) *A Certain Share of Low Cunning: A History of the Bow Street Runners, 1792–1839*. Willan, Cullumpton, p. 106.

192 Critchley, T. A. (1967) *A History of the Police of England and Wales*. Constable, London, p. 42.

to the Royal Retinue where he stayed until 1837.[193]

Pay, allowances and conditions of service

Principal officers were originally paid 1s 6d a day as a retainer, or 9s 6d a week. They were also hired out for detective work in any part of the country at a daily rate of 10s a day plus 12s expenses.[194] This increased to one guinea and 14s expenses, or by rewards for the return of stolen property, or from court funds following successful prosecutions of felons where up to a maximum of £40 could be distributed.[195] Bow Street officers were also allowed to undertake private enquiry work from anyone who could afford to pay them. By 1798 this retainer had increased to 11s 8d per week rising to a guinea per week in 1817, with rewards and expenses added if the enquiry was successful.[196]

Rewards

Parliamentary rewards, often called "blood money", were introduced towards the end of the 17th Century and were designed to improve the general state of lawlessness in the capital. The aim was to reward the more serious offences of felony, which ranged from £40 downwards to be split between prosecutor, witnesses, informers, watchman and police Constables. One unintended consequence of this ill-conceived idea was that the officers tended to neglect minor crimes which paid no reward.[197] Much later Principal Officer John Townsend, in evidence in 1816, suggested that each officer received, on average, between £20 and £30 in rewards per year, although it was felt by the committee that far more was received.[198]

---

193 Cox, D. (2010) *A Certain Share of Low Cunning: A History of the Bow Street Runners, 1792–1839*. Wilan, Cullumpton.
194 The Report from the Committee on the police of the Metropolis 1834, p. 88.
195 Howard. G. (1953) *Guardians of the Queen's Peace*. Odhams, London.
196 The Report from the Committee on the police of the Metropolis 1834, p. 88.
197 Browne, D. (1956) *The Rise of Scotland Yard*. George Harrap and Co., London, p. 21.
198 Fitzgerald, P. (1888) *Chronicles of Bow Street Police–office*. Gilbert and Rivington, London, p. 124.

The Parliamentary Committee enquiring into the Police of the Metropolis in 1817 asked Samuel Taunton, an experienced Bow Street officer since 1801, about the system of remuneration and rewards. He stated that his salary of a guinea a week was inadequate given they had to pay out for information and lose out when not rewarded by the public. He stated that a figure of £100 a year would sustain him, which would amount to double his pay. The Committee pointed out - and Taunton agreed - that the Bow Street magistrates had the power to reward work done outside the metropolis at a guinea a day plus expenses.[199] Taunton was in favour of removing the parliamentary reward in favour of rewards made at the discretion of the trial judge or magistrate, probably because the private thief-takers could frame unsuspecting innocent people.[200]

In 1820 there were eight Constables at Bow Street under the direction of Sir Nathaniel Conant. These were listed in that year's *The Royal Kalender* as John Townsend of Pimlico, John Sayers (sic) also of Pimlico, Stephen Lavender of 40 Long Acre, Harry Adkins of 33 Bow Street, John Vickery of 54 St. John Street, Samuel Taunton of 27 Duke Street, Daniel Bishop of 41 Great Queen Street and George Ruthven of 15 Holles Street. Also at Bow Street, the Conductor of the Horse Patrole was Mr Day and the Conductor of the Foot Patrole was Mr Stafford.[201]

Health and welfare

The Magistrates at Bow Street were well aware of the dangers and precarious nature of policing the streets of London and so made provisions for medical attention to those officers. Mr John Andrews, a surgeon, was retained at Bow Street from about 1803.[202] His duties included "...medical and surgical advice and attendance which

---

199 The Committee on the State of the Police of the Metropolis 1817, pp. 392–394.
200 Ibid.
201 *The Royal Kalender, and Court and City Register for England Scotland Ireland and the Colonies 1820*, p. 301.
202 Bow Street Accounts T38.762.

included giving medicines etc. to the officers and the patrole."[203] The Runners and members of the Dismounted and Mounted Patrole received free medical treatment, and the yearly retainer for the surgeon was £35 per quarter in 1814/15.

Andrews not only saw to the Patroles, but also was called in to deal with victims of crime like those of an indecent or sexual nature to prove the violation in court proceedings.[204] Andrews had been the surgeon at Bow Street since about 1794 and his appointment was by order of the Secretary of State. He was still practising there in 1818. By 1821 John Fisher had become surgeon to the Patroles and was appointed in the same capacity in 1829 to examine applicants for the Metropolitan Police.[205]

There was a genuine sympathy for those family members left behind with no means of support when the breadwinners had lost their lives in the line of duty, so care was taken to look after the widows financially in these cases. Bow Street, through the magistrates, often wrote to the Secretary for the Home Department calling his attention to such occurrences. Records show that By Order of the Secretary of State the widows Mary Barnett, Ann Mayner, Rebecca Jealous and Elizabeth Fugion were allowed £20 per annum each.[206] Mary Barnett was the wife of William Barnett, a Principal Officer murdered on duty in 1779 executing a warrant. Ann Mayner continued to receive her annuity until 1827, whilst Elizabeth Fugion accepted payments for her children and herself until 1827.[207]

203 *The Third Report from the Committee on the State of the Police of the Metropolis House of Commons* (1818), p. 190.

204 *Reports of Cases Argued and Determined in the Consistory Court of London* (1822) Volume 1 by Church of England. Diocese of London., John Haggard, William Scott (Baron Stowell) London.

205 Browne, D. (1956) *The Rise of Scotland Yard.* George Harrap and Co., London.

206 *An account of the Establishment of the Public Office, Bow Street for the years 1814 and 1815,* p. 270. The Committee on the State of the Police of the Metropolis 1816.

207 Bow Street Accounts T38.762.

Standards of police behaviour and discipline

It was necessary that the conduct of principal officers and members of the Patroles should be appropriate at all times, whatever the circumstances. Their role should be understated and they should not be overbearing, brutal or vicious. Amongst the qualities necessary to be a member of the Patrole was a sense of "service to the public", and this was seen as an essential objective for an officer who should have "good temper and sobriety" with "courtesy and good humour". They should not be easily provoked by the ill-manners of others and "avoid passion and resentment".[208] One should avoid overbearing conduct and any form of superiority or power-crazed nature. Creating a good impression and winning the sympathy of bystanders was essential, since any future contact would render the bystander more likely to aid a Constable in distress. Quiet but firm methods rather than acts of violence would always win the day, especially when dealing with mobs or crowds who should be cautioned against failing to keep the peace.

James Read, as Chief Magistrate, issued instructions regularly from his office at Bow Street giving advice and assistance to his officers. The law was becoming ever-more complex, with the increase in statutes being produced and Read advised his men, for example, on the protections offered by executing warrants on the one hand but cautioning against always using them since some offences were arrestable if seen by the officer. He also gave instructions to his officers over the use of force and violence. In so doing he used a direct quote taken from Saunders Welch in 1754: "Never strike a person except in absolute defence but striking should be avoided at all if possible and the sword of justice not the arm of the Constable should be the punishment."[209]

208 Pringle, P. (1955) *Hue and Cry –The Story of Henry and John Fielding and their Bow Street Runners.* William Morrow and Co., London, p. 165.

209 Welch, S. (1754) *Observations on the office of Constable.* Millar, A. Strand London, and Pringle, P. (1955) *Hue and Cry – The Story of Henry and John Fielding and their Bow Street Runners.* William Morrow and Co., London, p. 152.

3

Fielding's People
and Principal Officers

The following pen pictures appear in date order of when they appear in the Bow Street records and are of early and more prominent Bow Street Constables from 1749 until 1839. These show the daring, dangerous and often difficult work they needed to perform. Information and identification of early Constables has been very difficult to obtain, not only because there has been a lack of consistent record-keeping and some loss of records, but also because of variation in the spelling of many names in those records.

William Pentlow (sometimes Pentilow, Pentelow, Pantlow and Pentloe) (1749–1773)

William Pentlow, who in 1749 was a Constable and also a Headborough of St. George's Parish, Bloomsbury, was one of Henry Fielding's earliest and most trusted people. Fielding described him as "a good man of integrity and high morale standing". Fielding often chose family men for his trustworthy Constables, who had served their time skilfully in the parishes without recourse to deputies, and later invited them to join his small band of officers on special occasions.[210]

Fielding's men were also honourable, honest and brave. In 1750 Pentlow arrested two violent robbers named Thomas Lewis and Thomas May, and quickly distinguished himself for his courage. Later the same year a pistol was aimed at his head whilst he attempted to

---

210 Reith, C. (1938) *The Police Idea*. Oxford University Press.

arrest a boxer named Field on arrest warrants for robbery, burglary and other crimes. An armed soldier knocked the man down and Saunders Welch assisted in taking him into custody.[211]

Pentlow was a brave man and had narrowly escaped death on many occasions. By 1751 Fielding was so impressed with Pentlow's hard work and dedication that he recommended him for the position of Keeper of the New Prison at Clerkenwell, a largely honorary position which was often purchased by the incumbent. This allowed Pentlow to continue as an officer of the court whilst at the same time having a regular paid occupation that allowed him to support his family. As Keeper of the Prison Pentlow came into contact with known and convicted felons, and he was able to not only gather intelligence on suspects but also, and perhaps more importantly, to recognise and identify these individuals at a later date.

From time to time throughout the 1750s when exigencies of a situation demanded, Fielding kept Pentlow and others available to go out and investigate reports of serious crimes, usually highway robbery. They travelled on horseback or in a carriage called a post chaise.[212] Pentlow was not the only prison officer or turnkey, as they were called, employed by Fielding. Three of Pentlow's fellow turnkeys at the New Prison were attached to Bow Street – Robert Saunders, Edward Gaul and Thomas Street.[213] At Tothill Fields, Bridewell there was Thomas Hind and Henry Wright, while at Palace Court William Norden was also active as a Bow Street man.[214]

In April 1754 Fielding sent Pentlow to investigate a highway robbery and violent theft of a coach by a masked assailant on the Harrow Road. Based on the description of the clothing and information given by the coach driver, who had also seen the suspect unmasked a short while later, Pentlow quite by chance discovered

211 *Derby Mercury*, 14th December 1750.
212 A fast two or four-wheeled horse drawn carriage.
213 Beattie, J. (2012) *The First English Detectives*. Oxford University Press, Oxford, pp. 32-33.
214 Old Bailey Proceedings Online (www.oldbaileyonline.org, version 7.2, 27 June 2015), December 1755 (unnamed) (t17551204-31).

Charles Flemming (aka Johnson) in Paddington and took him into custody to Newgate. There he brought the coachman to an informal identity parade consisting of 14-15 people, where Flemming was picked out. Another Bow Street officer called Jackson also appears to have been involved but was too ill to attend court at the Old Bailey. The prisoner was found guilty and sentenced to death.[215]

In January 1755 Pentlow and a Constable named Gee were involved in the capture of two ruthless and desperate highway robbers who had wounded another of Fielding's Constables, Thomas Hind, the Deputy Governor of Tothill Fields, Bridewell. Hind was so badly hurt that he later died from his injuries, the first of Fielding's people to do so.[216] Pentlow, like Hind, would have known these notoriously dangerous men and likely to have wanted them quickly apprehended. More information had been received by John Fielding that the mother of one of the highway robbers lived at Hyde Park Corner and sold old clothes. He despatched Pentlow and Gee to make inquires. In their search for Joseph Gill and William Burk they entered an alehouse called The York Minster and there they saw both the robbers in a back room. Fielding's men resolved to arrest them immediately; however, the robbers had sensed a trap and both drew their pistols in an attempt to fight their way out of the situation, which they did. It was only later they were apprehended (see pages 31 and 116).

In April 1755 Pentlow foiled an escape plot from the prison which would have involved a mass breakout of prisoners, but at the Old Bailey all were acquitted due in insufficient evidence.

John Fielding's accounts show that Pentlow was also active in preventing crime, as he was paid expenses of 2s 6d a night for his periodic patrols with Bob (Robert) Street and Hyde of the squares during November and December 1756 and January and February

215 Old Bailey Proceedings Online (www.oldbaileyonline.org, version 7.2, 27 June 2015), October 1754, trial of Charles Flemming, otherwise Johnson (t17541023–39).
216 Cox, D. (2010) *A Certain Share of Low Cunning: A History of the Bow Street Runners, 1792–1839*. Willan, Cullumpton, p. 104.

Fig. 12: Islington Turnpike looking towards St. Mary's Church

1757.[217]

Between 1753 and 1759, as Keeper of the New Prison William Pentlow used the *Public Advertiser* as a means of finding and apprehending escaped prisoners for whom he was prepared to pay a reward. One such escapee was John Middlemas, described as 5ft 10 inches tall, about 30 years old with light eyebrows, a fair complexion and wearing a light cut wig. Pentlow offered the standard reward of five guineas.[218]

It was the determination, persistence and co–operation with other members of John Fielding's people that gave them results. In October 1756, after a pursuit of nearly 40 hours Mr Barnes (the High Constable of Westminster), Pentlow and others apprehended one Jonathan Hurst (aka Johnson) at Potters Bar with accomplice Thomas Browning. Both were former soldiers who had become street robbers and had attacked a Captain Robert Brudenell. They had committed robberies in Berkley Square for the past two years.[219]

In 1761, while investigating another case Pentlow gave evidence at the Old Bailey against two felons, Dupey and Whalley, for highway

---

217   John Fielding's Accounts T38.762.
218   *Public Advertiser*, 26th February 1759.
219   *Ipswich Journal*, 16th October 1756.

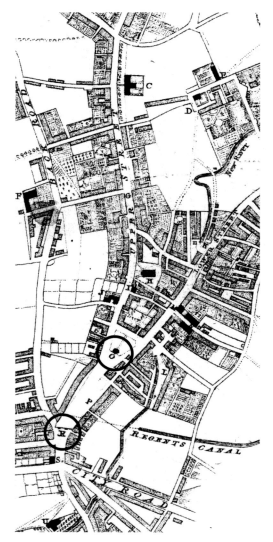

Fig. 13: Upper Street, Islington.
'R' indicates the turnpike, 'O' the Watch House

robbery. Both were found guilty and sentenced to death.[220]

Pentlow was paid expenses £14 5s 6d for pursuing a man called Hurst to Deptford and Potters Bar, and also chasing two others, Pallister and Ball, to Portsmouth and arresting them before conveying them back to London in carriages.[221]

There were further payments to him for arrests and conveying detainees to and from prison. John Fielding recorded these in his accounts as follows: Jones and others to Newgate on 16th February 1757; Walker and wife to Lambeth to search Shirley's address on 21st February 1757; with Barnes for taking after the Highwayman Page, 16th March 1757; and tracking Kenny the Street

220 20th April 1761 Ordinary's account for Newgate – Old Bailey.
221 John Fielding's Accounts T38.762.

Robber, 11th November 1758.[222]

It was, however, a serious error of judgement by another Bow Street officer in 1761 which nearly ended William Pentlow's career.

Pentlow was sent out by Fielding with William Darwell, a reformed highway robber, to protect the coaches heading out along the main highway north along the Holloway Road.[223] In the early morning of 1st April, on the stretch of road to Barnet, there had been at least three reported robberies.[224] They went to the Islington Turnpike situated on the Upper Street junction with Liverpool Road in a carriage, where they stopped and were speaking with the toll keeper about an individual who was robbing the stagecoaches when their attention was drawn to the Warrington coach, which was coming towards them from London. They followed behind it up to Holloway (along Upper Street to what is now the Holloway Road).

Whilst on their way up the hill they were themselves held up by a man on horseback who pushed his pistol into the carriage and threatened "to blow their brains out". Pentlow fired his blunderbuss and Darwell his pistol at the highwayman, who reeled back and rode off apparently uninjured.

Then the Leeds coach came up from London and was at the bottom of Highgate Hill with what appeared to be an armed man on horseback riding beside it. Thinking this was the same highwayman who had fired at them earlier, Darwell fired his pistol at him, injuring the horseman severely in the upper arm but also fatally wounding a passenger named John Lee, a servant who was sitting in a basket on the back of the coach. The horseman was in fact William Richardson, an ostler of The Swan With Two Necks in Lad Lane who was a guard hired by the coach company to protect it on its outward journey from London. Their carriage did not stop but headed back to London, not knowing the fate of John Lee, who died at Highgate later that day. On hearing of the death Darwell immediately gave

---

222 John Fielding's Accounts T38.672.
223 TNA: T 1/387, ff1–5.
224 Old Bailey Proceedings Online (www.oldbaileyonline.org, version 7.2, 28 June 2015), April 1761, trial of William Darwell, William Pentlow (t17610401–28).

himself into custody.[225]

Both Darwell and Pentlow appeared and gave evidence at the coroner's inquest, where a verdict of Murder was passed by the jury. Both Darwell and Pentlow later appeared at the Old Bailey. Although charged with murder, Darwell was convicted of manslaughter and given "benefit of clergy", meaning that he was branded on the hand in punishment. Pentlow was acquitted of aiding and abetting. John Fielding had also given evidence during the hearing, stating his reasons for sending Pentlow and Darwell on this mission in the first place. The register was produced in court and details of the allegation were read out in open court by Fielding's clerk, justifying the taking of action to capture the suspects.

After this case Pentlow resumed his Bow Street career until May 1764, when his position as Keeper at the Prison passed to Thomas Hopkins. Pentlow had shared in the undisclosed rewards given by trial judges at the Old Bailey and other Sessions cases following the successful conviction of his prisoners. He had needed to supplement his income, since his meagre salary from the prison alone could not sustain him and his family. Pentlow was getting older and had distinguished himself not only in his role as Keeper but also as one of John Fielding's trusted men. He died in July 1773.[226]

Bob (1756–1757)

Bob was an early Bow Street officer who first appears in John Fielding's accounts in November 1756, when he was paid for patrolling the squares. It is likely that because of his short duration as a Constable once he had served his yearly appointment he returned to his own occupation. In 1757 he was paid to fetch a prisoner called Craddock from Walthamstow who had been distributing handbills describing a highwayman in Kentish Town. In February of the same year he was required to go after a highwayman to Henley, whilst a month later he was paid to track down the highwayman Page (aka

225   The Leeds Intelligencer, 3rd March 1761.
226   The Craft Man and Says Weekly Journal, London 31st July 1773.

Williams) to Maidenhead and Moorfields.[227]

Leonard Yates (1757–1758) and Gibbon Smith (1758)

Smith and Yates are described together since they often worked as a pair and were intrepid thief catchers. Yates was very closely associated with pickpockets and had become one of Fielding's men given his knowledge of criminal enterprise. The art of pickpocketing is notoriously difficult to detect, since it involves a group of people who work very closely to the victim, using sleight of hand to remove the item. They immediately palm the property to another and then another so that by the time the victim has realised the theft, the stolen item is at least four people from the thief. Given the close proximity of the crime, the lack of a clear view, the confusion and distraction created by the thieves who can also crowd the victim, there is little chance of detection. In the meantime, the property is getting further away with the victim accusing a person who certainly no longer has the property.[228] It was useful for Fielding to have people who knew the pickpocketing underworld well, and reformed pickpockets were employed on occasions by Bow Street. Often informants play both sides of the law, and it was possible Yates was looking for the rewards from the prosecutions either on conviction or remuneration from the owners of the property once returned.

In 1757 Yates gave evidence at the Old Bailey in at least four cases. In two cases he acted as informant and knew the gang of pickpockets, but there seemed to be some problem with the continuity of his evidence since Gorman and Walker, who had stolen a watch, were acquitted.[229] This case would have made Yates a possible target for members of the pickpocketing underworld. However, in the other

227 John Fielding's Accounts T38.761.
228 See the Old Bailey case of Mary Jones who had picked the pocket of James Banti a man from Florence who spoke no English in the Bavarian Ambassadors Chapel in Golden Square. Old Bailey Proceedings Online (www.oldbaileyonline.org, version 7.2, 27 June 2015), October 1754, trial of Mary Jones (t17570223-28). Also although acquitted she was tried for returning early from transportation.
229 Beattie, J. (2012) *The First English Detectives.* Oxford University Press, Oxford, p. 33.

two cases his actions had enabled some members to be shielded from being apprehended and allowed to escape, or to set up the victim creating a suspicion that he was also involved in the gang.[230]

When new to Bow Street, one of Yates tasks was to post handbills (wanted posters) in certain areas to detect felons.[231]

In February 1758 Yates was assigned by John Fielding with Gibbon Smith, another officer from Bow Street, to go after a gang of thieves who were wise to the problems of the parochial boundaries in Westminster and sought refuge in the City of London. Fielding therefore issued a warrant for the arrest of Hugh Kirby, whom they knew was hiding in the City. Armed with the warrant they went to a public house in Threadneedle Street where they found Kirby. When challenged with the warrant the suspect drew a clasp knife and wounded both officers very severely. He stabbed Yates in the left leg and a number of times to his body before turning to Smith and stabbing him in the right leg and body as well.[232] Kirby made good his escape; however, a witness raised a hue and cry by shouting, "Stop thief; murderer", a number of bystanders chased him as he still wielded the clasp knife. In the account of Kirby's arrest the knife was described as being a foot long. He was apprehended by Captain William Wallford who drew his sword, causing Kirby to drop his knife immediately.[233]

He was taken before the Lord Mayor, who immediately committed him to Newgate. Both Yates and Smith were sent to St. Bartholomew's Hospital where it was felt their lives were in great danger and it was unlikely that they would both survive.[234] The indictments for wounding both officers were put to Hugh Kirby, who described himself as a labourer and pleaded not guilty. But the injuries to Yates and Smith were so grave that there needed to be several remand

230 Old Bailey Proceedings Feb–Mar 1757 Lawrence Gorman and Thomas Walker t17570223-11 accessed on 9th January 2016.
231 Beattie, J. (2012) *The First English Detectives*. Oxford University Press, Oxford, p. 38.
232 London Metropolitan Archives CLA/047/LJ/01/0912.
233 *Derby Mercury*, 10th February 1758.
234 *Sussex Advertiser*, 20th February 1758.

hearings before the case was satisfactorily dealt with.[235] Yates (on crutches) and Smith came to court and gave evidence on 9th September 1758. The jury found Kirby guilty and he was sentenced to five years' imprisonment in total at Newgate for both assaults. Both not only gave evidence that the wounds had lost them the use of a leg each, but Yates' leg had been removed as a result of the attack.[236]

The evidence suggested that both victims' injuries meant that they were "unable to labour and provide industry" in the future, indicating that their time at Bow Street was over.[237] This turned into fact, as neither Gibbon Smith nor Leonard Yates appear in the records at Bow Street and no longer worked or were associated with Bow Street again. At no time was evidence given at the trial that both of the wounded men were officers of the court at Bow Street. John Fielding was known as a compassionate man, and as such would have asked the Home Department for a stipend for both these men, but to date no records exist to verify this.

John Bowen (1758)

It is unclear from John Fielding's accounts dated 3rd November 1758 whether Bowen was an officer, a watchman or an informant; however, he was paid for services to the court. He appears in an account of an early patrol sent out from Bow Street in order to curtail crime. For this he was paid the sum of £3 3s 0d for three weeks' observation on Swift, Eckly and others in order to prevent robberies.[238] Given that Bowen fails to appear again we may assume he was a Westminster Constable performing his directed duty for the allotted one year.

---

235 The law at the time stipulated that if an injured person died within 6 months the assailant could be charged with murder. The Criminal Attempts Act 1981 allows for the crime of attempted murder to be put the assailant in a severe case of very serious injury where death does not occur.
236 London Metropolitan Archives CLA/047/LJ/01/0912.
237 Ibid.
238 John Fielding's Accounts T38.671.

William Darwell (also Darvill and Darvall) (1758–1761)

William Darwell had been a notorious highway robber in his time operating with another felon named Page. Henry Fielding had been trying to capture Page for some time without much success, but his fortunes turned when Darwell, who was in jail, turned King's evidence and supplied information sufficient for Page to be arrested, convicted and hanged. Darwell knew he could not return to his old ways once at liberty so he was allowed a second chance and joined the forces at Bow Street. His insider knowledge of the criminal fraternity, their haunts and his ability to identify them led to a number of significant captures. This also would earn him significant rewards and expenses.

Early records show that Darwell first appeared on 2nd December 1758, when he was paid 10s for "procuring the names of the persons committed to different gaols for fraud or felony, serving of summonses". Seven days later he apprehended an infamous felon known as Scampy the Jew, who was not only a known thief but a fence for stolen property.[239] For this he was paid £3 3s 0d.

Over the New Year period he was again paid for seven nights' patrolling in Islington, for going to Stratford after five persons who had returned from transportation, and also for watching a man named Brown, who was suspected of stealing a portmanteau. He was paid on 20th January 1759 for chasing a highwayman, and again on 24th March when he enquired into the robbery of Mr Creed of Faversham. On 10th March Darwell had rented a room in Kingsland Road (probably near the turnpike, now the Balls Pond Road junction with Kingsland Road) to watch for a prisoner who had escaped from Faversham Gaol.

Records show that on 24th April that year Darwell went to Chelsea to apprehend a housebreaker, and performed one night's patrol and four weeks' attendance as an orderly at Bow Street. In April he was paid to go to St. Pancras to prevent gaming and was paid as orderly

---

239 A fence is a receiver of stolen property who sells on the ill–gotten gains.

until September 1759.[240]

He was a trusted Bow Street officer by now, as shown by the fact that he was placed in charge of the Criminal Registers.

This officer was involved with Pentlow in the matter of the accidental shooting of John Lee on the Leeds coach on 1st April, as reported above. Darwell was found guilty and sentenced to be branded on the hand as punishment. This was referred to as "benefit of clergy".[241]

Little if anything is heard of him after that and it appears that this error of judgement and conviction meant that his tenure at Bow Street ceased at this point.

Thomas Hind (1749–1755)

Hind was another of the initial group of Fielding's trusted men. He was also the first Bow Street Constable to give his life in the line of duty. Hind was originally a turnkey who was later to be appointed Deputy Governor of Tothill Fields, Bridewell and also a publican. He was ideally placed to know the felons that graced the prison as well as his public house. Not only could he identify them but also knew their aliases, relatives and associates as well – in the days before photography, fingerprinting and DNA this was a valuable skill. He regularly attended court, ferrying prisoners to and fro from the prison to Bow Street and was therefore often present when other persons were examined. Whilst there, he would be on standby to witness other matters and events.

In 1749, in evidence at the Old Bailey Hind introduced himself as a turnkey at the Bridewell and spoke confidently about a

---

240 John Fielding's accounts T38.671.
241 Benefit of clergy meant that – the royal judges turned this clerical immunity into a discretionary device for mitigating the harsh criminal law by holding that a layman, convicted of a capital offence, might be deemed a clerk and obtain clerical immunity if he could show that he could read, usually the 51st Psalm. Later, a layman was allowed to claim benefit of clergy only once. www.britannica.com/topic/benefit–of–clergy accessed on 28th October 2015.

confession that was made to him by a prisoner under his charge.[242] Hind appeared many times at the court, with the transcriber often dropping the 'H' at the beginning of his name and recording it as Ind, an occurrence that even today in some parts of London is a fairly common colloquial occurrence. Hind gave evidence in the more serious matters such as highway robbery, violent theft, coinage matters and burglary cases.

It was early on in his Bow Street career (1750) that he became acquainted with Pentlow, who was the Headborough of the Parish, and the pair worked together on apprehending felons on behalf of Bow Street.

By 1752 Hind had become the keeper of the Crown and Sceptre public house in Drury Lane, which was managed by his wife when he was absent.[243] This was the sort of establishment which would attract trouble so Hind kept his brace of pistols close at hand just in case.

As a turnkey, Hind would transfer prisoners to the courts from prison or collect them from county gaols to bring them into the metropolis for trial. He also became adept at finding hidden locations where stolen property might be stored, and appreciated the laws of evidence that were necessary against a suspect to prove a conviction. The Old Bailey records show Hind was often present in cases and would have shared in the rewards of £40 offered against the conviction of a person for a felony. Hind seems to have had knowledge relating to base metal workings and false coin making, something which required special expertise.

The Old Bailey proceedings describe in detail the circumstances relating to the case of Burk and Gill, two notorious highwaymen who Hind went in search of. At the time of his arrest, William Burk was

242 Old Bailey Proceedings Online (www.oldbaileyonline.org, version 7.2. 13 January 2017) 22nd February 1749. Nicholas Mooney, Violent Theft – highway robbery, (t17490222–7).
243 Old Bailey Proceedings Online (www.oldbaileyonline.org, version 7.2, 13 January 2017) 19th February 1752. The Trial of James Hayes, Richard Broughton, Violent Theft – highway robbery. (t17520219–2).

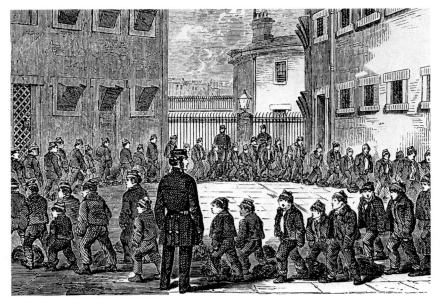

Fig. 14: Boys exercising at Tothill Fields Prison

aged 30. He was born in Monmouth Street, the son of William Burk, coachman to a nobleman of Ireland, from whose service he was discharged. His father became coachman to a gentleman in Jamaica, where he died. Burk Jr was left alone aged about six-years-old and, being destitute, a person at Epping took care of him. From this time on Burk stole whenever he had the opportunity and he was arrested and convicted on a number of occasions. In 1750 he was convicted and transported for seven years to Maryland in America, where he escaped by stealing a canoe and travelled to Philadelphia, where he met Gill.

They were of a like temperament and character and on their return to England agreed to "go on the highway". Their common haunts were about Drury Lane at one part of the town, and in Rosemary Lane at the other. When they had had enough of the town they left for the country, robbing on the Essex Road, which they continued to do for some time. They had not been in England more than two months when they were arrested. On Saturday, 21st of December

1755, Gill and Burk robbed several people on the Epping Forest Road, near the four-mile stone. On the 26th they were advertised and described, having robbed a farmer of several items including a bay mare. The mare had been kept upstairs in a friend's house. This friend had previously been tried with Gill for receiving stolen goods, but had been acquitted. The horse was sold and put into a hackney-coach; the original owner happened by chance to see the mare, challenged the driver and after some trouble recovered her again. Burk and Gill started robbing again, until December 28th when they robbed John Manby Esq on Tower Hill in a coach at about 1:00am in the morning. The robbery, including descriptions of the assailants, was quickly reported to Bow Street and men were sent out to their haunts to apprehend them. They were taken soon after.

Burk had been badly wounded, having fought desperately, and given Hind the wound from which he later died.[244] Fielding assigned Pentlow and another Constable called Gee to tackle these dangerous men and they were discovered in a tavern near Hyde Park. When challenged the felons put up a determined fight and escaped from Pentlow and Gee, although the officers found Burk's mother who gave them an address in Shadwell where they might be found. A prostitute soon alerted the fugitives to the approaching officers and again they escaped, this time to The Strand.

Here they were discovered by a group of Fielding's people – a patrol who were likely to have been other Constables returning to Bow Street from another inquiry. The Constables challenged Burk and Gill who put up a fierce fight, with the former nearly losing his arm whilst both sustained other injuries as well. They were detained and taken into custody at Covent Garden Roundhouse. In the meantime another of Mr Fielding's people had had his knee put out, collecting several bruises and one desperate wound in his hand.[245]

During the course of the inquiry other officers from Bow Street

---

244 Pringle, P. (1955) *Hue and Cry –The Story of Henry and John Fielding and their Bow Street Runners*. William Morrow and Co., London.
245 Old Bailey Proceedings Online (www.oldbaileyonline.org, version 7.2, 12 October 2015), Ordinary of Newgate's Account, March 1755 (OA17550317).

were able to identify and detain associates of Burk and Gill, namely Welch, Armstrong and Courtney, and bring them also to justice. In the fight to detain Burk and Gill, Hind's arm was very badly injured and needed to be amputated. He sustained life-threatening injuries following his determined sword fight whilst trying to arrest suspects Burk and Gill,[246] and it was from this that he died.

Hind was described at the time in the newspapers as "the greatest terror to thieves", and "in his death the public have lost one of the most useful members of the public and having always been afflicted in such a manner that there can be no reproach against his character."[247] No mention had been made that Hind was one of Henry Fielding's Bow Street officers. He was buried on 16th June 1755 at St. Bride's, Fleet Street, City of London, leaving a wife and two dependent children.[248]

John Hyde (1756–1757)

Hyde was a headborough, a publican who took over the Crown and Sceptre in Drury Lane following Hind's death. His was married to Mary Hyde.[249]

Hyde gave evidence of character at the Old Bailey in the case of Anne Palmer and Jane East on 14th July 1756 after they had stolen a quantity of fabrics, the property of Thomas Martin. This was a serious matter, as the offence was grand larceny. The value of the goods stolen was over 6s. Hyde stated that he had seen the prisoners at Bow Street as he had some business at the office for Justice Fielding.[250] His business, as a trusted headborough and publican, was the identification of suspects which would have been very useful to Fielding.

246 Armitage, G. (1932) *The History of the Bow Street Runners*. Wisehart and Co., London, p. 59.
247 *Derby Mercury*, 17th March 1755.
248 National Archives.
249 Old Bailey Proceedings Online (www.oldbaileyonline.org, version 7.2, 03 January 2016), April 1758, trial of John Briggs (t17580405-7).
250 Old Bailey Proceedings Online (www.oldbaileyonline.org, version 7.2, 03 January 2016), July 1756, trial of Anne Palmer Jane East (t17560714-28).

In November 1756 he was paid expenses of 2s 6d for helping other Constables to suppress an illegal meeting of servants and apprentices at a dance in the Golden Lion near Grosvenor Square. On another occasion he, Pentlow, Doctor and Street collected and brought to Bow Street two prisoners named Armstrong and Noland who had been detained in Portsmouth. For this he received his share of £5 10s 0d.[251]

Although not directly employed by John Fielding, Hyde remained in contact with the Constables of Bow Street as an informant and was useful in assisting them should they ask for help. In September 1765 he gave evidence at the Old Bailey in the case of William Healey and Eleanor Boyd, who had stolen a quantity of pewter plate valued £12–£14, the property of Michael Mayo. Hyde had been walking through St. Giles when he saw Edward Wright, one of Justice Fielding's men, who asked for help in obtaining evidence against Boyd and Healey and he went after them. Hyde managed to secure some of the stolen property from Boyd, who had hidden it in a ditch in Long Fields on the pretext he wanted to buy some of it.[252]

John Bryan (1757)

In February 1757 John Fielding paid expenses to Bryan and Scott to proceed to Colney Hatch in pursuit of two highwaymen who had robbed Lord Ferrers.[253]

Edward Gaul (or Gall) (1756–1763)

Gaul was an early Bow Street officer who was described as one of "Sir John Fielding's people" and was also a trusted turnkey at the New Prison under Pentlow.[254] Involved in very few cases at the Old Bailey but working under the direction of John Fielding, he was

---

251 National Archives: John Fielding's Accounts T38.671.
252 Old Bailey Proceedings Online (www.oldbaileyonline.org, version 7.2, 03 January 2016), September 1765, trial of William Healey , otherwise Keeley Eleanor Boyd , otherwise Nangle (t17650918-2).
253 The National Archives: John Fielding's Accounts T38/673.
254 Beattie, J. (2012) *The First English Detectives*. Oxford University Press, Oxford, p. 33.

sent out to find and apprehend people probably as he could identify them and bring them for examination at Bow Street.

In December 1756 he was paid for work completed when he was sent on an inquiry to Trinity Lane, Duke's Place and Hill Street, for which he was paid 2s. Fielding sent Gaul to see Sir Samuel Gowers, another Middlesex Magistrate and a known corrupt justice, and was paid one shilling. He was sent to see a Mr Stevens and was paid 1s, and then paid 3s for going twice to Hammersmith. He was also paid 6s for escorting robbers from the new gaol at Southwark.

He teamed up with officers from Bow Street including Pentlow, Bob, Ryley and Davies to arrest a man called Walker and his wife at Cripplegate in February 1757. Afterwards he went to Lambeth on a house search regarding the prisoner Shirley, for which he was paid 12s. The cost of coach hire and other disbursements for a prisoner escort of 8s was also paid for when Gaul and Curd had collected a man from prison and had him taken to court.

In January 1758 Lucretia Philips, a spinster, was indicted at the Old Bailey for stealing one silver watch valued at £3 ls 0d, the property of William Patrick, at the dwelling–house of Frances Dun, a widow. Gaul could not find the stolen watch when he searched Philips at Bow Street in front of Mr Fielding, and it was only later that she brought it to him. Philips appears to have been a prostitute and went to bed with the owner of the watch, William Patrick. Apparently she asserted that having no money to pay her and being 'in liquor' Patrick had asked her to pawn it, which she did. She was subsequently acquitted because doubt was raised that she had stolen the watch in the first place.[255]

In another case as a servant to the keeper of the New Prison, Gaul searched George Albeat and found a silver buckle on him which was thought to be the property of one John Barrett, but again the prisoner was acquitted because the prosecutor could not establish

---

255 Old Bailey Proceedings Online (www.oldbaileyonline.org, version 7.2, 02 June 2016), February 1758, trial of Lucretia Philips (t17580222-8).

beyond doubt that the buckle was his.[256] In another case Gaul was instructed by Fielding to apprehend a woman named Catherine May in an alehouse, which he did. When she was searched she had 10 guineas in her pocket, but again it could not be established if this was part of the proceeds of a crime and she too was acquitted.[257]

William Marsden (1757–circa 1768)

William Marsden was another of Sir John Fielding's active and trusted men who appears in the early Bow Street accounts. Marsden was to establish himself favourably at Bow Street, which later saw him elevated to the position of Chief Clerk.

Fielding sent him to Windsor in February 1757 in pursuit of Woods and Hardridge and was paid £2 2s 0d. Marsden was also tasked to pursue Page, the notorious highway robber and one of Bow Streets most wanted felons. For this he was paid 10s 6d for three days' horse hire in March 1757, and a further 13s for expenses relating to the same inquiry. He was sent on another inquiry to Newington Lambeth with another officer, in pursuit of a forger named Adams. He was sent to Eagle Court to prevent an illegal gathering of servants and apprentices at a dance, and was paid 2s 6d. Marsden was paid 6s to go to Ranelagh Gardens, a famous Chelsea amusement park, with other officers to apprehend six sailors who had broken into the Waterman's Arms in June 1757. In the same month Marsden was paid £1 2s 0d in order to travel to Colnbrook in pursuit of Evans, who was wanted for murder.

Page had still not been caught, and intelligence gleaned suggested that he had gone to Scotland. Later it was discovered that he had returned and once again Marsden went in pursuit. This time Page had linked up with Keys, another dangerous highwayman and felon. For this Marsden was paid the sum of £4 1s 5d. It was in August 1757 that Scott and Phillipson successfully arrested William Page

256 Old Bailey Proceedings Online (www.oldbaileyonline.org, version 7.2, 02 June 2016), May 1758, trial of George Albeat (t17580510-9).
257 Old Bailey Proceedings Online (www.oldbaileyonline.org, version 7.2, 02 June 2016), December 1759, trial of Catherine May , otherwise Castost (t17591205-12).

after a pursuit through Kent, Buckinghamshire, Hertfordshire, and Berkshire.[258]

Curiously, there is no record in the Bow Street accounts for Marsden in 1758, and Beattie (2012) suggests this was because the Patroles were being paid for by the Government for these duties.[259]

In 1759 Marsden was paid £1 2s 7d, this time for pursuing the highwayman who had robbed the Clapham coach. By April 1759 he had taken up a position as Register Clerk at Bow Street and was paid half a year's wages of £15 14s 0d, and a similar payment was made in June 1759.[260]

As a Register Clerk, Marsden's responsibilities were to maintain the records and take down the details of all crimes reported to him in the Particular Registers at Bow Street. This meant that he would take down in the register a criminal's name and description, including marks, scars and other identifying features, their criminal method, a list of property stolen and any other information that would be useful. The information would then be circulated to the trusted officers of Bow Street and later disseminated throughout the country.

Following his time as an administrator of the registers Marsden's worth was recognised, and he was promoted to Chief Clerk at Bow Street – a most responsible position. By 1767 he was paying the expenses of Bow Street including the court staff, principal officers and Foot Patrole Constables, and was responsible for the immediate distribution of those fees, for which he needed to account as quarterly expenses to Sir John Fielding.

In March 1767 reports started coming in to Bow Street of violent robberies taking place up the Holloway Road to Hornsey. This involved a gang of sailors who had been paid off from their ship, some of whom were Irish and had frequented an Irish public house in Hornsey, The Angel and Crown. They had been drinking all day and were clearly drunk, arguing both amongst themselves and

258   Beattie, J. (2012) *The First English Detectives*. Oxford University Press, Oxford, p. 39.
259   Ibid, p. 41.
260   The National Archives John Fielding's Accounts T38/671.

with other customers. Then one of the gang, Thomas Brown, pulled a pistol out and threatened a man that he would blow his brains out. They left and moved onto another alehouse and later, possibly because they needed more money, stopped a post-chaise, robbing it of just 2s and taking the shirt off the post-boy. Disappointed and angry they tried again, this time stopping a coach travelling from Holloway to the city with four men inside. Francis Gorman, one of the sailors, produced his pistol and went to the other side of the coach, threatening the occupants. When John Griffiths, one of those inside the coach refused to give up any money Gorman put the pistol to Griffiths' head and discharged his weapon, killing him instantly. They robbed the others of £15 before moving off to attack another target. The killing of Griffiths did not deter them, prompting immediate action at Bow Street.

Buoyed by their success the previous evening, two more of their shipmates joined the gang and Brown encouraged the band of sailors to rob another coach. The unfortunate coach was the Newington Stagecoach, where the gang abused the occupants and stripped them of valuables, clothes and a watch before cutting one of the passengers and making off. Such was the violence of this particular gang that it drew the full force of Bow Street office into the detection and apprehension of the gang. Heading and coordinating the operation was Marsden himself, who was put in charge by Fielding. It was Marsden's determination in seeking out the felons that in addition to his expenses of £4 3s 0d he was eventually rewarded with the sum of 10 guineas for his devotion to duty.[261]

Marsden directed the full force of his Bow Street officers to this outrage, including John Noakes, William Haliburton, John Heley, Joseph Stephenson, Nicholas Bond and Henry Wright. Noakes went to Whitechapel in pursuit of the Gorman gang and was led by Thomas Fitzpatrick, the son of the landlord of The Angel and Crown at Hornsey, who knew the men. Fitzpatrick identified to Noakes two of the suspects in the street, Thomas Brown and Jeremiah Ryan; however, when they went to arrest them Brown escaped. Ryan was

261 Beattie, J. (2012) *The First English Detectives*. Oxford University Press, Oxford, p. 82.

Fig. 15: The mail robbed near Colnbrook

provided with indemnity to prosecution by Fielding who made him a witness to the Crown rather than as an accused, in what is called today King's or Queen's Evidence. Ryan provided very useful information as to the whereabouts of Francis Gorman and three others, knowing where they lived or were to be found.

The Bow Street men made a round of the public houses in search for the men. First inquiries were made at The Angel in St. Agnes le Claire, where one of the gang, a man named Sweetman, had lodged then to The Three Goats at Whitechapel, and then onto The White Lyon at nearby Shadwell Docks. Ryan had provided information that the gang were likely to be at the boxing match being held at the Lyon, where they were all successfully detained although not without a vicious fight. One of the men sustained a head injury during the arrests and needed treatment.[262] Two of the suspects, Francis Gorman and Henry Johnson, were tried, convicted and sentenced to the death penalty, which was carried out within a week.[263]

Marsden remained an active officer in addition to being Clerk of the Court up until 1768, but no further details of him appear after this time.

Samuel Phillipson (1751–1758)

The very first case Samuel Phillipson was involved in at the Old Bailey related to Thomas Clements for burglary in early 1751. Not that Phillipson was involved in the arrest or visited the scene of the crime - he simply heard the confession of the accused Clements and gave this account in evidence.

Another of Phillipson's early cases at the Old Bailey concerned George Gibbons, who was charged that in the early hours of 26th February 1752 he broke into the dwelling house of John Allen and stole four silver watches, one silver hilted hanger, one silver salt salver and two silver teaspoons. The case was tried on 25th June, and Phillipson said that he was called to Newgate Prison to George

262 Beattie, J. (2012) *The First English Detectives*. Oxford University Press, Oxford, p. 82.
263 Old Bailey Proceedings Online (www.oldbaileyonline.org, version 7.2, 02 July 2016), April 1767, trial of Francis Gorman Henry Johnson (t17670429–51).

Gibbons who wished to confess to a crime. Gibbons had broken open a shop's front window and stolen the property, which he had pawned in Grub Street. Phillipson went and acquainted Justice Chamberlaine with the facts, who stated that the prisoner should be taken from Newgate and the watches found. On this order Phillipson and the keeper went with Gibbons to the house of a pawnbroker named Mr Belomey, who was asked for the shagreen watch which he had pawned in his own name for 7s 6d and redeemed it. He was then asked for a silver watch in another name, which was also produced. The prisoner then took the officers to the house of Mr Allen, who was asked to confirm that his house had been broken into.[264] Gibbons pleaded guilty at trial and was transported.

Phillipson's next case at the Old Bailey, in September 1752, involved Daniel Lovyer, Sarah Holmes, John Cornhill, Ruth Morris, Peter Pearvoy and Mary Lovyer, who were indicted for theft and grand larceny. Phillipson was working on a case where some pack horses were robbed on Highgate Common and property stolen. Information had been received that resulted in Phillipson, together with Booth and Hall, two other officers, searching the house where Ruth Morris was staying, and recovering some of the stolen goods.

Phillipson said:

> "I took Cornhill, and had him in my house; a little time after which he desired to go backwards to the necessary house. I went with him; but he shut himself in. After we had taken him before the justice, my little girl found a tobacco box in the necessary house, with two silk handkerchiefs cram'd into it, and when I came back she told me. I went there and found a powder horn and a little brass plate, and another silk handkerchief. He was searched before the justice, and three more handkerchiefs were found in his pocket".[265]

264 Old Bailey Proceedings Online (www.oldbaileyonline.org, version 7.2, 03 January 2016), June 1752, trial of George Gibbons (t17520625-3).

265 Old Bailey Proceedings Online (www.oldbaileyonline.org, version 8.0, 19 July 2018), September 1752, trial of Daniel Lovyer, otherwise Glovey Sarah Holmes John Cornhill Ruth Morris Peter Pearvoy Mary Lovyer, otherwise Glovey (t17520914-25).

All were found guilty and transported.

On 18th July 1753 Phillipson again gave evidence at the Old Bailey, in the case of John Stockdale and Christopher Johnson. Both were indicted that on the King's highway they murdered Zachariah Gardiner, a penny postman, also stealing one silver watch valued at 30s and one silver seal valued at 1s 9d. Phillipson had obtained information into the murder and went to arrest Stockdale, who when confronted with his crime wished to disclose the whereabouts of the real culprit, a man by the name of Johnson. Stockdale took the officers to a halfway house and they saw Johnson coming along the road; Stockdale identified him as the murderer.

Phillipson jumped out of the chaise and got over a ditch, and took Johnson by the arm. Phillipson quickly searched him and under his coat found a cutlass. Another officer named Jones searched Johnson's pockets and in his left-hand side found a pistol.

Phillipson then said of the arrest:

> "I was tying his hands with his handkerchief, he turned round and saw Stockdale in the chaise; he said that little scoundrel I suppose sent you after me; I said he did; said he, did he say I shot the man; I said he did, he said he is a scoundrel, it was he that shot him; we put him into the chaise and drove to the Red–lion at Brentford, there the two prisoners argued about shooting the postman; Stockdale said, you villain you asked the man what is it o'clock, he pulled out his watch, and you demanded it, he put it in your hat, and you shot him directly, and the man gave a jump, and you laughed; Johnson said to him, you little scoundrel you shot him, and I had a good mind when we were on Hounslow–heath to have shot you, and had my hand on my pistols".[266]

They were both convicted and sentenced to death.

In February 1757 John Fielding had a problem with trying to apprehend William Page, the notorious highway robber, as seen on page 130, and he committed the full force of the Bow Street

266 Old Bailey Proceedings Online (www.oldbaileyonline.org, version 7.2, 03 January 2016), July 1753, trial of John Stockdale Christopher Johnson (t17530718–33).

resources to capture him. All the officers were committed to achieve his apprehension, as he was a most elusive felon.

Fielding decided to send Jones and Phillipson to Hicks End after Page, for which Phillipson received the sum of £1 2s 6d for his trouble. Three weeks later they were both committed to watch The Red Lion near Westminster Bridge and they received the sum of £3 10s 6d. In March 1757 they were again paid for horse hire and given expenses, where both Phillipson and Scott were paid £1 2s 10d to follow a man who had robbed the Norwich Mail Coach and apprehend him.

Still on the trail of Page, Phillipson and Scott were sent to Tunbridge then to Windsor on the same inquiry, receiving £2 2s 0d for each excursion. By mid-September 1757 Page had still not been caught, but excursions into Kent, Bucks, Middlesex and Berkshire earned Phillipson £10 10s 0d.[267] In late September Phillipson was still on the trail of Page, and it was only when Darwell was detained that real progress was made in capturing him, as we have seen.

Steven Scott (1756–1758)

Shown as one of "Fielding's People" and a likely Constable of the City and Liberty of Westminster. There are no records to show that Scott ever appeared at the Old Bailey.

John Spensley (Spencley) (1756–1759)

John Spensley described himself as "a Constable of the night" at a trial at the Old Bailey in 1756 at which Margaret Chambers was accused of pickpocketing. His evidence was given professionally and showed how he had found a stolen watch in the accused's hand together with a stock and buckle, the property of John Hall. Chambers was convicted and sentenced to seven years' transportation.[268]

In a case of forgery and deception by Richard Vaughan in 1758

267 National Archives T38/671
268 Old Bailey Proceedings Online, September 1756, trial of Margaret Chambers (t17560915-1).

Fig. 16: Highway robber William Page

Spensley was still a Constable, and his evidence included the fact that the prisoner was hiding something in his mouth which turned out to be a forged £20 bank note. Some 48 of these notes had been forged by the prisoner, who was convicted and sentenced to death.[269]

Later the same year Spensley was again at the Old Bailey, giving evidence in a case of burglary and theft where John MacKelvey had

269 Old Bailey Proceedings Online (www.oldbaileyonline.org, version 7.2, 06 June 2016), April 1758, trial of Richard William Vaughan (t17580405–30).

gone to a public house and taken a silver beer tankard worth £7 home with him. Spensley had come by information which had been overheard by a witness that the tankard had been stolen, cut up and sold as scrap silver. In this case, because the property was no longer in existence and therefore could not be directly linked to the prisoner, he was acquitted. Interestingly, Spensley had stated that he expected no reward for evidence in this matter.[270]

In February 1769, in a case against William Wilson who had been indicted for stealing carpenters' tools which Spensley had found at the prisoner's address. Still described as a Constable, he was able to show continuity of evidence that the items found were those stolen and identified as the property of the owner. Wilson was convicted and sentenced to seven years' transportation.[271]

No further cases involving Spensley have been discovered after this date and it appears he retired.

John Barnes (1756–1758)

John Barnes was another of John Fielding's men, and he was also a High Constable of Westminster and an experienced official in the parish. Barnes was involved in the case of William Cannecott, who had killed his first wife with a pair of sharp scissors and covered up the matter. Barnes was able to extract a confession from the murderer, who was later executed for his crime.[272]

Barnes was hired to inquire into allegations of crime which had been reported at Bow Street. He received £4 12s 0d in January 1757 for travelling to Kick's End to track down the notorious William Page, who on this occasion had cut open the portmanteau from behind a chaise and stolen property belonging to Captain Barratt. Fielding employed a number of his men including Pentlow, Saunders, Street,

270 Old Bailey Proceedings Online (www.oldbaileyonline.org, version 7.2, 06 June 2016), June 1758, trial of John MacKelvey (t17580628–12).
271 Old Bailey Proceedings Online (www.oldbaileyonline.org, version 7.2, 06 June 2016), February 1759, trial of William Wilson Mary Harris (t17590228–13).
272 Old Bailey Proceedings Online (www.oldbaileyonline.org, version 7.2, 07 June 2016), Ordinary of Newgate's Account, September 1756 (OA17560920).

Phillipson and Marsden at various places around London and the surrounding environs in the attempt to capture this serious felon.[273] In March 1757 Barnes was paid again for undertaking further inquiries with regard to Page.

He investigated a murder the following month where he was attempting to track down a suspect by the name of Evans. At the end of May he was paid for coach hire involving inquiries relating to the highwayman Douglas, and in June he was sent to Guildford to make inquiries in tracing a highway robber by the name of Small.[274]

In addition to the apprehension of offenders, Barnes' other responsibilities were numerous as he answered to a number of masters and was required to carry out the instructions of the justices of the peace, coroners and vestry.

In March 1758 he was responsible for the apprehension of Page at The Golden Lion by Grosvenor Square Gate. On the prisoner he found three loaded pistols, two horse pistols and a pocket one, a powder horn full of powder, and about half a dozen balls. Also found was Page's disguise – a wig and a cockade.[275]

No further matters were reported relating to Barnes after 1758 and it is assumed he retired from his post.

William Gee (1756–1757)

William Gee appears to have been a parish Constable who had served his one year term. In September 1756 James Baythorne stole seven cloth coats valued at £7, two fustian frocks valued £2, seven cloth waistcoats valued £3, one pair of cloth breeches valued 5s, four pairs of worsted breeches and two duffel surtout (frock) coats, the property of William Leader. Baythorne had worked for Leader as a servant but had been stealing whilst there. The clothing was found by William Gee at several pawnbrokers in the Bow area, and

273 Beattie, J. (2012) *The First English Detectives*. Oxford University Press, Oxford, p. 39.
274 National Archives John Fielding's Accounts T38.671.
275 Old Bailey Proceedings Online (www.oldbaileyonline.org, version 7.2, 07 June 2016), February 1758, trial of William Page, otherwise Williams, otherwise Gage (t17580222–28).

was proved to be Leader's property. Baythorne was convicted and sentenced to death.[276]

Gee also worked at Bow Street, appearing in John Fielding's accounts when later in the year he was paid £4 4s 0d with Flanagan for a fortnight's patrolling in the fields regarding information about two soldiers. In January 1757 Gee and Flanagan were together again, searching for a highway robber and paid 15s. Later that month both were again paid 15s to enquire after a robbery in Kentish Town.[277]

Gee does not appear in the Old Bailey records after January 1757, so it appears that as a parish Constable he did not remain on the Bow Street staff.

Robert Street (1756–1758)

Robert Street was one of the early Bow Street officers and also a turnkey at the New Prison under Pentlow. There were at least three other officers by the name of Street, so identifying and separating the particular duties assigned to any of them has been difficult, especially since in his record of accounts John Fielding often did not use first names.

Of those we can individually document, Robert Street commenced in November 1756 and with others were sent to patrol the squares. In December that year Street and Hyde were paid £5 10s 0d to bring Armstrong and Noland from Portsmouth.

In March the following year Street was sent with Bob to Moorfields as part of the extended attempt to apprehend William Page, but without success. They were each paid £1 1s 0d. By early June 1757 Street paid a Mr Bevans £1 8s 0d for the hire of a pair of horses in order to pursue Page to Maidenhead, again without any success. Saunders and Street went to Henley-on-Thames in pursuit of Page in the winter of 1756/57. [278]

---

276 Old Bailey Proceedings Online (www.oldbaileyonline.org, version 7.2, 08 June 2016), October 1756, trial of James Baythorne (t17561020–25).

277 John Fielding's Accounts T38/671.

278 Beattie, J. (2012) *The First English Detectives*. Oxford University Press, Oxford, p. 37–39.

In early November 1758 Street was paid £1 1s 0d to watch Noland in prison.[279]

Thomas Street (1756–1766)

One of the officers at Bow Street who became a member of the very first Horse Patrole in 1763, but was also a turnkey at the New Prison under Pentlow where, in addition to his duties, he also "kept the tap", providing beer and ale for any of the inmates who could pay for it.

William Parsons (1757–1758)

William Parsons was described in the Old Bailey records as a "servant of Mr Fielding" when William Green and his accomplice robbed Thomas Manners, a clerk, on the highway near the turnpike about seven miles from London. Armed and on horseback, the robbers stole £2 2s 0d, a watch and a ring. Parsons went in pursuit and found Green at Hockley near Dunstable, where he was arrested. On searching the prisoner a watch and a ring were found, which Manners later identified as his. Green was sentenced to death for his crimes and later executed.

In September 1758 Parsons described himself as "a Constable" when he appeared at the Old Bailey to give evidence regarding the theft of goods from a cow keeper in Bethnal Green.[280]

Parsons was an active officer, as he appears in the same court where he gave evidence in a case of highway robbery by Richard Pousam (aka Spencer) and Mary Bulger in which he recovered property from the crime. Both prisoners were found guilty and sentenced to death.[281]

---

279 National Archives T38/671.
280 Old Bailey Proceedings Online (www.oldbaileyonline.org, version 7.2, 21 March 2016), September 1758, trial of Anne Wheatley (t17580913-36).
281 Old Bailey Proceedings Online (www.oldbaileyonline.org, version 7.2, 21 March 2016), September 1758, trial of Richard Pousam, otherwise Spencer and Mary Bulger (t17580913-37).

George Baxter (1759)

Only one entry in John Fielding's accounts existed for Baxter, a payment of £1 1s 0d for apprehending a suspect called Field who then turned King's evidence against a gang of 20 sky farmers – so called because as fraudsters they promised much and cheated others.[282]

Given his short duration at Bow Street, Baxter was likely to have been an appointed parish Constable serving his statutory one year in office.

Thomas Adams (1763)

One of Fielding's men who became a member of the Horse Patrole.[283]

Nicholas Bond (1768–1779) (Clerk/Chief Clerk 1779–1785, Magistrate 1785–1807)

Nicholas Bond (sometimes erroneously referred to as John Bond) was another famous Bow Street officer used by John Fielding who was elevated to Principal Officer, leader of the Principal Officers, Register Clerk, Clerk of the Court, Chief Clerk and then Magistrate.

As Paley (1983) contends, Bond had been a strong and valued character at Bow Street over a long time and was especially appreciated by Sampson Wright, John Fielding and the Home Department. Described as a disreputable individual, he had been a journeyman carpenter before he joined Bow Street. Bond had a strong character and was regarded as ruthless, ambitious and a mercenary.[284] He was also industrious, knowledgeable and single-minded.

282 Sky Farmers are cheats who impose on their benevolence and compassion of the charitable who pretend they were farmers in the isle of sky, or some other remote place, from their farms being in the clouds. findwords.info/term/sky–farmer accessed 28th December 2015.
283 Fielding's Accounts GA65 and Notes on Bow Street and other Middlesex Justices Officers and related staff.
284 Babington, A., (1969) *A House in Bow Street*. MacDonald and Co., London, p. 169.

These attributes made him ideal to become an officer at Bow Street, and he became a particular favourite of John Fielding. He certainly got results, and because of his good organising capabilities and motivational skills became head of the small group of Principal Officers at Bow Street.

One of his first cases involved him in a case of burglary at the house of a jeweller where a vast quantity of valuable jewels had been taken. Bond had obtained information where the stolen jewels could be found, and armed with a search warrant went to the house of one Andrew Martin, finding incriminating evidence. Martin was convicted and sentenced to death.[285]

In 1771 Bond was sent on a special errand as an officer of Bow Street by John Fielding to Birmingham to arrest three members of a gang who had taken part in a robbery at a house in Chelsea where the servant was murdered. The case involved a gang of Jewish men who were eventually caught, tried and convicted. Four of the six gang members were executed for their crimes, attended "by a crowd greater than one ever seen" and their bodies later displayed for dissection at the Surgeons' Hall. Such was the wave of anti–Semitism at the time that the trial judge complimented the Jewish community for their laudable conduct during the investigation.[286]

Up until 1789 Bond was involved in 40 cases at the Old Bailey, marking himself out as a very prolific and enthusiastic thief-catcher. He was also allocated to special duties, and with Donaldson was hired regularly by the Covent Garden and Drury Lane theatres to prevent disorders during the performances.[287]

In 1785 he became a magistrate at Bow Street, a reward for his loyal service, having been recommended by Sir Sampson Wright. It is said that on becoming a magistrate Bond started charging newspaper journalists for reporting proceedings in court, causing

---

285 Old Bailey Proceedings Online (www.oldbaileyonline.org, version 7.2, 01 June 2016), December 1768, trial of John Andrew Martin (t17681207–9).
286 Pringle, P. (1955) *Hue and Cry –The Story of Henry and John Fielding and their Bow Street Runners*. William Morrow and Co., London, p. 191.
287 Babington, A., (1969) *A House in Bow Street*. MacDonald and Co., London, p. 188.

The Times to cease publishing accounts altogether.[288] In this way he lost the respect of sections of the press, but perhaps realised the newsworthiness of cases appearing before the courts.

Bond's elevation to the highest level was seen as an attempt to fill the void of appointing strong candidates as magistrates,[289] as many were seen as weak.

Sir Richard Ford, who became Chief Magistrate in 1800, was selected by the Government to tackle revolutionary ideas, but this upset Bond who had been passed over several times. Ford was a trusted magistrate and specifically chosen over the head of the more senior Bond, with 32 years' loyal service. Bond had not been told formally that he was not to be made Chief Magistrate, but heard it from another source. The reason for his lack of promotion was that he was considered someone from humble social origins, and he therefore had no support to succeed either Sampson Wright in 1793 or William Addington in 1800.

He was upset by the Government's decision to appoint Ford over his head but remained a magistrate, working tirelessly until his death in May 1807 at his house in Queen Street, Brompton Road.[290] He was buried in the Parish of St. Anne, Soho on 1st June 1807.[291] His wife later received an annual pension, as was the practice at the time.

Robert Saunders (1755–1758)

Robert Saunders was one of John Fielding's men and turnkey under Pentlow at the New Prison, often working with another turnkey, Thomas Street. In 1755 he was involved in the discovery of a prisoner of Irish extraction named Winifred Farrell in a bid to escape from the New Prison. This involved three visitors to Farrell, who used a disguise in an attempt to trick the turnkeys into allowing

288 Ibid, p. 170.
289 Paley, R. (1983) The Middlesex Justices Act of 1792; its origins and effects, pp. 213–218, Ph.d. thesis University of Reading.
290 *Morning Advertiser,* 27th May 1807.
291 National Archives.

the prisoner's escape dressed as one of the visitors. However, since the escape attempt was discovered and the prisoner did not escape, the four suspects were acquitted.[292]

In 1758 Saunders was involved in a case of shoplifting and at trial described himself as "a servant to the Keeper of the New Prison". His evidence involved sending a message to the accused, Ann Mathews, from the prosecutor, which on the face of it looked as if the latter was looking for monies from the prisoner to drop the case against her. The accused was found guilty and fined.[293]

There were no further cases reported at the Old Bailey involving Saunders after 1758.

Morgan Whalan (1758–1759)

At the end of November 1758 Whalan appears in the accounts of Bow Street for delivering handbills to pawnbrokers, summonses to publicans and other messages, and was paid £1 1s 0d. A few days later he was delivering cautions to inns and stable keepers, and other messages for which he was paid £9. In January 1759 he was ordered to wait at turnpikes at Chelsea for a highway robber who had robbed a gentleman on the other side of the River Thames.

He was next required to find witnesses and arrange transport for the solicitor of the Royal Mint in the case of Fuller, a coiner, including coach hire which came to £5.

In February 1759 he was paid £5 to prevent a lottery taking place, and by the end of that April was paid 10s 6d for the delivery of summonses to publicans and bakers.[294]

Whalen was likely to have been an appointed parish Constable, serving his statutory one year in the office.

---

292 Old Bailey Proceedings Online (www.oldbaileyonline.org, version 7.2, 05 June 2016), April 1755, trial of Bridget Golden John Jordan Matthias Duffey, and Anne, his wife and Matthias Duffey (t17550409-40).

293 Old Bailey Proceedings Online (www.oldbaileyonline.org, version 7.2, 05 June 2016), February 1758, trial of Ann Mathews, otherwise Cole, otherwise wife of Thomas Tobin, and Mary Dean, otherwise Mary wife of Richard Rusty (t17580222-27).

294 John Fielding's Accounts T38.671.

Cupon (1756)

Cupon was paid 10s 6d by John Fielding for searching after the suspect who robbed a mail coach.[295]

Woodcock (1756–1757)

Woodcock appears in Sir John Fielding's accounts on 12th December 1756 when he was paid 4s to go to Tower Hill with Ruff (a prisoner), and in mid–January 1757, together with William Pentlow, Bob and Street he was paid £10 to patrol the squares. In January 1757 he was paid £5 6s 0d for patrolling nine nights to find a suspected house of gamblers.[296]

From the short duration that Woodcock served it is highly likely he was an appointed parish Constable for his statutory one year.

John (Jonathan or Jonah) Fordsam (1758–1763)

Fordsam was John Fielding's coachman and was appointed by him as one of the first members of the Horse Patrole.[297] In December 1758 he was sent to all the turnpikes in London to post handbills in relation to the current spate of robberies and was paid £4 4s 0d, which included his costs in hiring a post-chaise.[298]

John Noakes (Noaks) (1757–1775)

Noakes was a trusted, prominent and long-serving officer of Bow Street who was involved in a great number of criminal cases. In 1757 he was a Constable who, with John Cartwright, was sent by John Fielding to apprehend some soldiers who had robbed Luke Rashbrook. All three soldiers were indicted and later appeared at the Old Bailey. One ringleader was sentenced to death for his crime.[299] Noakes described himself as a Constable in the City and

295 Ibid.
296 Ibid.
297 John Fielding's Accounts GA 65.
298 Ibid.
299 Old Bailey Proceedings Online (www.oldbaileyonline.org, version 7.2, 05 June 2016), January 1758, trial of Samuel Ong, John Davis, John Allen (t17580113–26).

Liberty of Westminster, and when he gave evidence at the Old Bailey against Joseph Guyant and Joseph Allpress he stated that he went with "John Fielding's People".[300] He worked closely with Haliburton, Heley, William Bond and Henry Wright when in pursuit of the Gorman gang and shared in the substantial reward for their capture in Whitechapel.[301] Noakes was involved in a number of other cases.

Richard Fuller (1763)

Fuller was an original member of the Horse Patrole and discovered the Coventry gang.[302]

Joseph Stephenson (Stevenson) (1765–74)[303]

Stephenson worked with other Bow Street officers, notably Noakes, Haliburton, Heley, William Bond and Henry Wright, and together they detected the Gorman gang who were arrested, mainly in Whitechapel.[304] Stephenson described himself when giving evidence at the Old Bailey as "an officer" during his time at Bow Street.

In April 1767 John Lacuse, an apprentice smith sleeping at The Kings Head in Covent Garden, was robbed in his bed of his master's £41 10s 6d, some silver buckles and buttons. On discovering the theft and armed with some information that a chairman called John the Saylor was seen acting suspiciously at the time of the theft, Lacuse went to Bow Street and saw John Fielding, who gave him a search warrant. Joseph Stephenson and the victim returned to the scene, but on their way they saw the suspect enter another public house in Prince's Street so went in pursuit. Stephenson, who knew John the Saylor well, took him to The Brown Bear to be searched,

300 Old Bailey Proceedings Online (www.oldbaileyonline.org, version 7.2, 30 May 2016), June 1772, trial of Joseph Guyant, Joseph Allpress, otherwise Allprice (t17720603-44).
301 Beattie, J. (2012) *The First English Detectives*. Oxford University Press, Oxford, p. 82.
302 John Fielding's Accounts GA 65.
303 Beattie, J. (2012) *The First English Detectives*. Oxford University Press, Oxford, , p. 82.
304 Ibid.

and this revealed a large amount of money and some identifiable shoes buckle belonging to the victim. The prisoner was convicted and sentenced to seven years' transportation.[305]

In July the same year Stephenson (who described himself now as a Constable) was with William Bond and others at the The Brown Bear and on information received went in search of some highway robbers named Boswell, Spires and Harford. All three were arrested and tried but later acquitted.[306]

There were five further cases up to 1772, after which Stephenson's attendances at the Old Bailey ceased.

John Heley (1766–1778)

John Heley was first shown as a Constable at Bow Street as one of "John Fielding's people" in 1766, where he appears in the accounts for executing search warrants relating to theft and a coining offence. The accused in these cases appeared at the Old Bailey but were later acquitted through lack of direct evidence to convict them. In fact the first four cases at the Old Bailey in 1766 involving Heley resulted in acquittals, but the Constable was still learning his trade and this would change. Heley would become one of the most productive and industrious Principal Officers at Bow Street, appearing in over 80 cases at the Old Bailey alone.

Later in 1766, also at the Old Bailey, he described himself as a headborough when he was involved in a sexual offences case.[307] In a pickpocketing case in December 1766 he described himself as a Constable who with Noakes, also a Constable, submitted evidence connecting two thieves to the property although, again, the accused were acquitted. In a case of burglary in June 1767 Heley and Haliburton gave evidence relating to finding of stolen property on

---

305   Old Bailey Proceedings Online (www.oldbaileyonline.org, version 7.2, 07 June 2016), April 1767, trial of Thomas Donnelly (t17670429-10).

306   Old Bailey Proceedings Online (www.oldbaileyonline.org, version 7.2, 07 June 2016), July 1767, trial of Francis Boswell John Spires John Harford (t17670715-46).

307   Old Bailey Proceedings Online (www.oldbaileyonline.org, version 7.2, 31 May 2016), September 1766, trial of Christopher Pearson (t17660903-70).

the prisoner Joseph Morehane, who was found guilty and sentenced to death.[308] The next case was a highway robbery investigated in July 1767, involving Bond, Heley, George Sale and Stephenson, who were in The Brown Bear when they got word of a robbery from Bow Street. The group went immediately in a Hackney coach to Pancras Wash, where the robbery had taken place. There they found four men who fitted the description of the accused given to them. One was caught with a pistol whilst the others had nothing incriminating on them. One of the gang immediately wanted to turn his evidence to help convict his three accomplices. When the men were indicted the three faced two counts, one of highway robbery and the other of burglary. Heley did not have much luck convicting the prisoners, since again all three men were acquitted on both counts.[309]

In October the same year Heley, together with Richard Bond, Stephenson and John Noakes, was investigating a theft of linens, stockings and other haberdashery goods. They were able to locate the goods through useful information indicating that the property was at an address in Almonry where the four accused would also be found. Between 6.00 and 7.00am the Constables waited and immediately entered the house, arresting the suspects and taking possession of all the stolen goods. The prisoners were all tried, convicted and sentenced to be transported.[310]

In the next case Heley, Hartley and Noakes were involved in investigating a grand larceny – the stealing of a quantity of valuable silk and linen handkerchiefs. John Noakes had information that a prisoner, James Murphy, had bought stolen goods. Sir John Fielding granted a warrant to search his house, although the information given asserted that if they watched the house they would see the gang of pickpockets go in with things. Constables Noakes, Heley

308 Old Bailey Proceedings Online (www.oldbaileyonline.org, version 7.2, 31 May 2016), June 1767, trial of Joseph Morehane (t17670603-19).
309 Old Bailey Proceedings Online (www.oldbaileyonline.org, version 7.2, 31 May 2016), July 1767, trial of Francis Boswell John Spires John Harford (t17670715-46).
310 Old Bailey Proceedings Online (www.oldbaileyonline.org, version 7.2, 31 May 2016), October 1767, trial of James Chilcot John Beale Margaret Anne Worral Anne Harvey (t17671021-37).

Fig. 17: The Brown Bear, Bow Street

and Hartley went at seven in the morning and waited and watched. After some time Heley spotted the suspects entering the house, but Hartley ran across and took Lloyd before Heley managed to enter the house. Once inside they found more of the suspects, and a search of the house revealed property suspected of being stolen. These included a bundle of eighteen handkerchiefs, sixteen cotton ones and two silk, which were found between the grate and a board that stood before it in the front room. Sir John Fielding had advertised for the owners to come forward in the *Hue and Cry* without success. Out of the three accused, only Lloyd was convicted and sentenced to transportation.[311]

The next case involved Thomas Stapleton, John Curtis and Susanna Stapleton on charges of grand larceny in May 1768 at a house in Haverstock Hill. A large quantity of property of great value had been stolen including linens, a clock, horse pistols and women's nightwear. An informant had overheard two women who were drinking in The Nags Head by Monmouth Street to have knowledge of a robbery. She passed the information the next day to Sir John Fielding's office and he despatched Heley, Marsden and Noakes to investigate. They found some of the property at a house in St. Giles, and further information led to more of the property being recovered from a nearby pawnbroker's. On this occasion only Thomas Stapleton was convicted and sentenced to transportation.[312]

On 9th July 1768 Noakes, Heley, Haliburton and Bond were sent by John Fielding in a hired coach to investigate a highway robbery on the New Road at Highgate, where a woman named Sarah Rogers was robbed at gunpoint. On their way, when passing Tottenham Court turnpike Noakes identified to his colleagues two of the assailants who he had recognised from the description he had been given.[313]

---

311 Old Bailey Proceedings Online (www.oldbaileyonline.org, version 7.2, 31 May 2016), October 1767, trial of Thomas Lloyd, James Murphy and Sarah, the wife of James Murphy (t17671021–41).

312 Old Bailey Proceedings Online (www.oldbaileyonline.org, version 7.2, 31 May 2016), May 1768, trial of Thomas Stapleton John Curtis Susanna Stapleton (t17680518–19).

313 Frontispiece: Tottenham Court Road Turnpike with a view of St. James's Chapel (1798), in *Survey of London: Volume 21, the Parish of St Pancras Part 3: Tottenham*

No sooner had he said this when two of the robbers attempted to attack the Bow Street Constables, but their plan was thwarted and a man named Leicester was apprehended. He at once offered to turn King's evidence as his three accomplices had by now escaped. As a result Hanlon, Jones and Miller were later arrested at their lodgings, with property found connecting them to the robbery. Both Hanlon and Miller on being convicted were sentenced to death. Hanlon was further indicted with Jones for attempting to rob the Constables in their coach and Richard Bond gave evidence against them, supporting Leicester. Hanlon was again convicted and Jones acquitted.[314]

John Carey, otherwise known as John Clark, had returned from Maryland in America after being sentenced to transportation for stealing a quantity of goods the previous year. He returned to London on another ship and was soon apprehended, indicted again and faced trial in January 1769. Returning from transportation was a capital offence if convicted. Carey was sentenced to death after Heley gave evidence of his identity, having been present in court at the previous conviction.[315]

In January 1769 Heley was involved in the recovery of stolen clothing, the property of Thomas Booth. Acting on information received he went to Turnmill Street, where he saw two felons known to him named Hedges and Hussey, together with two women. One of the women appeared to be in possession of some of the stolen coats, which Heley quickly took possession of. The coats were indeed found to have been stolen and both Hedges and Hussey were indicted, found guilty and sentenced to be transported.[316]

Court Road and Neighbourhood, ed. J R Howard Roberts and Walter H Godfrey (London, 1949), British History Online www.british-history.ac.uk/survey-london/vol21/pt3/frontispiece accessed 17th April 2017.

314 Old Bailey Proceedings Online (www.oldbaileyonline.org, version 7.2, 31 May 2016), October 1768, trial of Patrick Hanlon William Miller Benjamin Jones (t17681019–29).

315 Old Bailey Proceedings Online (www.oldbaileyonline.org, version 7.2, 31 May 2016), January 1769, trial of John Carey, otherwise John Clark (t17690112–31).

316 Old Bailey Proceedings Online (www.oldbaileyonline.org, version 7.2, 31 May 2016), February 1769, trial of William Hedges, Catharine Hussey, Bridget Dalton (t17690222–55).

Peter Medley was indicted in April 1769 for having stolen a silver pint mug valued at £1 10s 0d, the property of Archibald Maughlin, and a woman named Winifred Carryl for receiving it, knowing the same to be stolen. Information had been received from Mrs Maughlin that Medley had come into their alehouse and insisted on drinking beer from a silver mug inscribed with her husband's name. She saw him put the mug under his jacket, never thinking he would steal it. Medley sold the inscribed mug to Carryl for 22s, which she placed under her mattress in her room and was later discovered later by Heley. Both were found guilty. Medley was sentenced to transportation for seven years, whilst the receiver of the property was punished more severely, with Carryl receiving 14 years' transportation.[317]

The next case involving Heley were crimes against a member of the gentry, when John Lister and Isaac Pemberton were indicted for breaking and entering the dwelling house of Sir Thomas Willson on 10th of January 1770. About 2:00am, the accused stole two damask napkins value 3s, 16 silver tablespoons value 16s and two silver candlesticks, valued at £2 1s 0d each. Sarah Hill, described as a spinster, was indicted for receiving the two damask napkins, knowing them to have been stolen. Constables William Taylor and John Heley had received information that Lister and Pemberton were active burglars, residing in Black Boy Alley. Both Constables went to the address and shortly afterwards both suspects turned up. On their persons were found chisels, and each had a loaded pistol. They were taken to Bow Street and later a search of the address revealed a napkin with the Willson coat of arms engraved upon it, which was identified as the property of Sir Thomas Willson. Stealing from a knight of the realm cost Lister and Pemberton dearly as they were both found guilty and sentenced to death.[318]

317 Old Bailey Proceedings Online (www.oldbaileyonline.org, version 7.2, 31 May 2016), May 1769, trial of Peter Medley, Winifred Carryl (t17690510-4).
318 Old Bailey Proceedings Online (www.oldbaileyonline.org, version 7.2, 31 May 2016), January 1770, trial of John Lister, Isaac Pemberton Sarah Hill (t17700117-37).

Fig. 18: Tottenham Court turnpike

May 1770 saw the conviction of James Lee and Thomas Cook for burglary which was investigated by Heley, and both were sentenced to be transported.[319]

In that same month a more serious matter occurred – a murder, which involved Bow Street officers albeit only by chance. John Shaw and Mary Leighbourn were walking together along the New Road, Islington (now Pentonville Road) towards The Angel public house. When they were about 200 yards away they were approached by three men, who attempted to rob them. Shaw defended himself well against the three robbers, until one of them produced a blunderbuss and fired directly at Shaw's stomach, injuring him fatally. The three men then made off. Mr Read, a Bow Street constable, and his colleague Roberts were nearby when the incident happened. They were immediately alerted by a witness to the three suspects making good their escape and quickly apprehended them. They searched the suspects, taking from them a blunderbuss, a pistol and a scabbard,

---

319 Old Bailey Proceedings Online (www.oldbaileyonline.org, version 7.2, 31 May 2016), May 1770, trial of James Lee Thomas Cook (t17700530–24).

the accompanying blade being found nearby. All three men were convicted at the Old Bailey and sentenced to death.[320]

Both Nicholas Bond and John Heley gave evidence in May 1770 of identity and conviction against John Read, aka David Miller aka John Miller, who was indicted for returning from transportation, and was convicted and sentenced to death.[321]

Another case involved Edward Millson and Charles Macdonald, who were indicted for highway robbery against John Tomlin. They had stolen a large amount of property including one silver watch value 40s, a steel watch chain value 6d, a silver seal value 1s, ten leather sheepskins value 15s, one blue and white linen handkerchief value 2d, a dozen knives and forks value 9s, a pair of spurs plated with silver value 6d, and 5s in change. Heley and Haliburton gave evidence of finding property connected to the prisoners, resulting in Macdonald being found guilty and sentenced to death.[322]

Heley continued to give valuable service to Bow Street. He was involved in many more cases at court until 1880, when it appears he had retired from Bow Street and, as was usual for Bow Street officers, took over an alehouse, the famous Swan and Two Necks in Lad lane.

Henry Wright (1766–1774)

Wright was the under keeper of Tothill Fields, Bridewell from 1764 whilst attached to Bow Street, although in evidence described himself as a turnkey.[323] He worked with Stephenson, Haliburton, and Bond in pursuit of the Gorman gang, and shared in the substantial

320 Old Bailey Proceedings Online (www.oldbaileyonline.org, version 7.2, 31 May 2016), May 1770, trial of Charles Stevens Henry Holyoak Henry Hughes (t17700530-47).
321 Old Bailey Proceedings Online (www.oldbaileyonline.org, version 7.2, 31 May 2016), May 1770, trial of John Read, otherwise David Miller, otherwise John Miller (t17700530-50).
322 Old Bailey Proceedings Online (www.oldbaileyonline.org, version 7.2, 31 May 2016), September 1770, trial of Edward Millson Cha. Macdonald (t17700912-39).
323 Old Bailey Proceedings Online (www.oldbaileyonline.org, version 7.2, 31 May 2016), January 1770, trial of William Moody Charles Burkitt John Jones, otherwise Posnett (t17700117-31).

reward for their capture in Whitechapel.[324]

In 1770 Wright was involved in a case of highway robbery, burglary or theft relating to the property of John Wood at Petty France. It was solved using informants who, rather than give details out of any public duty, were likely to have been rewarded for their trouble by Wright. In his evidence he said:

> "I am turn-key at Tothill-fields bridewell. There were informations brought to Sir John Fielding, of several robberies; upon which, six of us were ordered to patrole at Chelsea. We were out three nights: the third night I came from the road about half an hour after ten o'clock, which was the 15th of December, to bridewell. There was a person had been waiting for me two hours; he said, he could tell me where the people were that had committed robberies on Chelsea-road. I went as directed, with three or four people, to the Hole-in-the-wall, Bow-street, Westminster. There I apprehended Moody, Burkitt, and Settle: I searched them all, but found nothing particular on them, but a large knife".[325]

This was another example of information being brought to Bow Street and being used to identify, locate and apprehend felons. John Settle acted as look-out whilst Moody, Burkitt and Jones had broken into the house and stolen some money and other valuables. On being caught Settle wished to turn his evidence, and appeared in court for the prosecutor. On this evidence both Moody and Jones were convicted and sentenced to death.[326]

Henry Wright was still at Tothill Fields, Bridewell in 1784, having been promoted to keeper.[327] In 1771 he was involved with the Constables at Bow Street when he had received information from the wife of Michael Welch where stolen property may be found. Along with the Constables, Wright found the property resulting in

324 Beattie, J. (2012) *The First English Detectives*. Oxford University Press, Oxford, p. 82.
325 Old Bailey Proceedings Online (www.oldbaileyonline.org, version 7.2, 05 June 2016), January 1770, trial of William Moody Charles Burkitt John Jones, otherwise Posnett (t17700117-31).
326 Ibid.
327 Hartley, J. (1785) *History of the Westminster Election*. Debrett, J. London.

Welch's conviction and he was sentenced to be transported.[328]

The following year Wright gave evidence in another notorious case, but very little was reported of him after this with the exception of the following matter some years later. This was a case in 1784 where a Henry Morgan was indicted to the Old Bailey having killed Mr Charles Linton. Morgan had confessed to the murder, but later stated he had been entrapped into making it. Both Henry Wright and his wife were key witnesses to this fact and gave evidence during the trial which resulted in Morgan being found guilty and sentenced to death.[329]

Richard Bond (1767–1772)

Richard Bond was the brother of Nicholas Bond, whose pen picture appears earlier.

In February 1767 a Mr Kemp went to Bow Street to make a report about a theft and robbery by a black highway robber near the Marylebone turnpike. A purse containing coins was snatched from Mrs Kemp's hand whilst her husband was being held up by the robber. Richard Bond was sent from Bow Street to investigate the robbery after handbills giving a description of the robber had been printed and placed in the vicinity. Bond was in the area of Ryders Court, Cranbourne Alley when he noticed a man later identified as Mr Joseph Guy from New York, who had served as a sailor on a British Man of War and also been in the British army. Bond asked Guy to accompany him to The Brown Bear in Bow Street to ask a pardon of a man he is alleged to have assaulted. Guy appeared confused, although he went. Once opposite the Bow Street Office he was taken before Mr Fielding instead and remanded. In his pocket was the purse belonging to Mrs Kemp. Guy was found guilty and sentenced to death, although there was no record of his execution

---

328 Old Bailey Proceedings Online (www.oldbaileyonline.org, version 7.2, 05 June 2016), January 1771, trial of Michael Welch, Lettia Johnson (t17710116-20).

329 Old Bailey Proceedings Online (www.oldbaileyonline.org, version 7.2, 31 May 2016), September 1784, trial of Henry Morgan (t17840915-1).

ever being carried out.[330]

In 1771 Richard Bond and John Noakes were sent by John Fielding to investigate an armed robbery of the mail coach at Enfield. Some witnesses described the two suspects as Joseph Guyant and Joseph Allpress. Guyant lived in Edmonton, so armed with a warrant Noakes and Bond visited his house and left a message that he was wanted down at the local public house, where he was later apprehended. He was taken before John Fielding at Bow Street and later committed for trial, where he and Allpress confessed to their crime and were sentenced to death a month later.[331]

Thomas Carpmeal (1769–1808)

Carpmeal became a long-standing member of the Bow Street Establishment, serving nearly 40 years. In 1769 he was a victualler residing in Bow Street and attending the office at Bow Street as one of Sir John Fielding's men. Carpmeal became very good at detecting offences of coining, where false metal replaced silver in what was called a Royal offence which attracted the death penalty on conviction. In 1780 Mary Spencer Williams appeared at the Old Bailey for coinage offences and experts in this field, Bow Street Officers John Clarke and Prothero, gave evidence.

Carpmeal appeared very regularly at the Old Bailey during 1780 and 1781 for other cases of making false coinage. In 1781, together with Jealous, he arrested four men named Abrahams, Parker, Robus and Levy at The Falcon public house in Clerkenwell. The men had stopped and robbed a heavily laden cart coming from Towcester three days before, on the Barnet Road between the 12th and 13th mile stone. It was likely that Carpmeal had been tipped off by an informant, as they knew where to go and who to find for this offence. The offenders were questioned about the offences and appeared

330 Old Bailey Proceedings Online (www.oldbaileyonline.org, version 7.2, 27 June 2015), February 1767, trial of Joseph Guy (t17670218-38).
331 Old Bailey Proceedings Online (www.oldbaileyonline.org, version 7.2, 30 May 2016), June 1772, trial of Joseph Guyant Joseph Allpress, otherwise Allprice (t17720603-44).

at the Old Bailey, but only Parker was convicted and the others acquitted. Parker was sentenced to death.[332]

During his long service Carpmeal was also a well-known and trusted Bow Street officer who attended on the Royal family between 1800–1806, and he is shown being well remunerated for this duty.[333]

Thomas Carpmeal died in his apartments in Bow Street in January 1808, aged 66 years, after serving as police officer attached to Bow Street for some 38 years.[334]

Charles Grubb (1775–1783)

It is often difficult to determine Bow Street police officers from other industrious and committed parochial Constables and Charles Grubb certainly falls into this category. It appears he was a long-serving and committed Constable, and possibly originally a member of the Foot Patrole under Saunders Welch. In January 1775 at the Old Bailey Grubb was involved in the case of Henry Martin, who had been indicted for receiving stolen linen. A year later, in 1776, Old Bailey records give details of the burglary of watches by Sarah Crabtree and Robert Campbell.

Grubb seems to have been an officer at the Litchfield Street Office, possibly under Justice Saunders Welch, and good at detecting cases involving false coining. In September 1779, along with officers John Dixon, James Hyde and Dennis McDonald, Grubb was involved in the case of John Field for coining offences which was proved and he was sentenced to death.[335]

Later Grubb was shown as a Litchfield Street Constable, often involved in co-operation with Patrick MacManus, one of Fielding's

---

332 Old Bailey Proceedings Online (www.oldbaileyonline.org, version 7.2, 29 December 2015), July 1781, trial of Abraham Abrahams, James Parker, Moses Robus, Arthur Levy (t17810711-3).

333 John Fielding's Accounts T38/672.

334 *Morning Post*, 1st January 1808.

335 Old Bailey Proceedings Online (www.oldbaileyonline.org, version 7.2, 28 December 2015), 15th September 1779, trial of John Field (t17790915-47).

men at Bow Street. In September 1783 they were involved somewhat contentiously with the trial for burglary of Burton and Duxton.[336] The prisoners were found guilty and sentenced to death. A man named Doherty had perjured himself during the proceedings in an attempt to get the prisoners acquitted, and the trial judge had him committed to Newgate for his crime. He was later convicted.

No further instances relating to Charles Grubb can be found and it appears he may have retired at this point.

William Haliburton (1765–1783)

Haliburton first came to notice in 1765 in a case of theft and burglary against the accused, John Robinson, John Rouson and Anne Clark. Haliburton and Henry Wright had found stolen property which was identified as such. Rouson was found guilty whilst Robinson and Clark were acquitted. Rouson was sentenced to death.[337]

On 27th May 1777, while giving evidence at Bow Street Court he described himself as "a peace officer" who had brought in a 13-year-old girl for soliciting clients for prostitution. The Bow Street Magistrates asked John Heley, another of John Fielding's people, if the girl could be put under the custody of his wife.[338]

In April 1779 Haliburton was involved in a much-publicised case of murder, and his part related to the continuity of evidence involving an exhibit.

The Reverend James Hackman was accused of murdering the singer Martha Reay (sometimes Ray) on 7th April 1779. Reay was the mistress of the 4th Earl of Sandwich, who was separated from his wife as she was thought to be of unsound mind. Reay had lived under the protection of Sandwich for 19 years and with whom she

336 Old Bailey Proceedings Online (www.oldbaileyonline.org, version 7.2, 02 July 2016), September 1783, trial of John Burton, Thomas Duxton otherwise Duckston (t17830910–1).
337 Old Bailey Proceedings Online (www.oldbaileyonline.org, version 7.2, 02 July 2016), January 1765, trial of John Robinson John Rouson Anne Clark (t17650116–37).
338 *St. Martin's Scrapbook*, Victoria Library.

had nine children.[339] Hackman was for a short time a Reverend in Norfolk, had got to know Sandwich and was often invited to dinner at Hinchingbrooke. Hackman had become besotted with Reay over a period of time and suspected she had taken another lover, and as a result became jealous. He took two pistols and as she came out of the theatre in Covent Garden Hackman produced his firearms and immediately fired one, shooting dead Miss Reay, and then attempting to take his own life with the other gun which misfired. Haliburton gave evidence at the trial in respect of a letter which he had been given by Nicholas Bond, the Clerk at Bow Street, and testified that this had been found in the prisoner's pocket. It was addressed to Hackman's brother-in-law, Frederick Booth, and stated that by the time the letter was read the writer "shall be no more". A witness named Mahon identified it as a letter taken from the prisoner, saying that Booth had opened it and read in his presence.[340]

During his 18-year career at Bow Street Haliburton appeared 16 times in the Old Bailey list, giving evidence in a variety of cases of burglary, highway robbery and pickpocketing until 1782.

John Atkins (1783–1791)

Atkins worked at the New Prison before joining the Patrole in 1783, later becoming one of the Principal Officers at Bow Street. Atkins often worked with Moses Morrant and frequented the notorious Brown Bear opposite Sir John Fielding's house. There they would be sought out by victims and informants alike, and when following the information they received they would move to apprehend suspects.[341]

Moses Morrant (also Murrant, Morant) (1776–1793)

Moses Morrant was an extremely active Constable at Bow Street,

---

339 Sandwich was noted for ordering a slice of beef between two slices of bread – hence sandwich.
340 murderpedia.org/male.H/h/hackman-james.htm accessed on 28th December 2015.
341 Beattie, J. (2012) *The First English Detectives*. Oxford University Press, Oxford. p104 and Old Bailey Proceedings February 1784 Thomas Turner t17840225-29.

working with Clarke, MacManus, Jealous, Carpmeal and others. He became well known at doing a good job consistently, both in his own right or supporting others' evidence in coining offences, theft, burglary and highway robbery. Morrant was a long-standing Constable and one of the Principal Officers at Bow Street as one of six officers in 1793. He served Bow Street from 1776, where he stayed for 17 years.[342]

On 12th October 1778, William Jones and Richard Baker were indicted for highway robbery after they attacked John Tovey and stole a silver watch valued at 40s, a steel watchchain value 6d; a base metal watch key value 1d, a base metal seal value 6d, and one guinea and a half-guinea in change. In this case Moses and James Morrant both appear as Constables, and it is likely they were related. Moses had found stolen property in the lodging of one of the accused and was able to prove the case. Jones and Baker were convicted and sentenced to death.[343]

One very interesting case involving a number of Bow Street officers were the Gordon Riots of June 1780, where at least 500 people tried to burn down their station – the house and court building of John Fielding, who was desperately ill at the time and near death. Those recognised and charged were William Laurence and Richard Roberts, seen removing, damaging and burning property taken from the house. It would appear that Mr Bond, the Chief Clerk, was coordinating the defence of Bow Street and required MacManus to remain at the house. Prothero, who was with MacManus, helped secure the front door as a very large crowd gathered outside armed with clubs, iron bars and choppers, chanting "Newgate, Newgate, Newgate".

MacManus identified one of the ring leaders as William Laurence, who he knew previously. Other witnesses identified Roberts. The two officers secured the house with a chain and left through the

---

342 John Fielding's Accounts T38/673.
343 Old Bailey Proceedings Online (www.oldbaileyonline.org, version 7.2, 28 June 2016), December 1778, trial of William Jones, Richard Baker (t17781209–2).

back, at which point MacManus went home and put on his greatcoat and armed himself with his pistols and cutlass then returned to Bow Street. By then the crowd had broken into the house.

Morrant gave evidence regarding the condition of the house prior to the riot, which was being repaired at the time, and how it looked after the riot was over. He described it as "Pulled to pieces. The doors were broke to pieces, the window shutters were broke, the glass and frames of the windows were broke, and the household goods had been thrown out and burnt." There were fires out in the street where furniture, papers and books were being burnt. Laurence and Roberts were found guilty and sentenced to death.[344]

In another case Morrant was on duty at Sir John Fielding's house when a victim came and gave information about the theft of a trunk, and was able give the location of the prisoner. A cab driver named Thomas Grinley was indicted for stealing a hair trunk containing a great quantity of clothing on 30th December 1779, the property of John Plucknett. The mistress' servant William Gough seemed to be able to identify the coachman, who had left the dropping-off point without unloading a trunk and had made off without even collecting the fare. Morrant went to the address given and found the prisoner in bed and the stolen trunk, which had been broken open, in the room. The trunk and the remainder of its contents were removed to Bow Street where it was identified as the property stolen. Grinley was arrested and charged to appear at the Old Bailey, where he was convicted and sentenced to be whipped.[345]

In February 1782 Morrant gave evidence in a case of coining. The accused were John Jones, Jacob Levi and John Wheeler, who were charged with making false halfpenny coins. Benjamin Colborne, Joseph Atkins and James Pullen were also charged with counterfeiting, aiding, abetting and procuring Jones, Levi and Wheeler to commit that felony. Morrant had gone with John Clarke,

344 Old Bailey Proceedings Online (www.oldbaileyonline.org, version 7.2, 28 June 2016), June 1780, trial of William Laurence, Richard Roberts (t17800628-1).
345 Old Bailey Proceedings Online (www.oldbaileyonline.org, version 7.2, 27 June 2016), January 1780, trial of Thomas Grinley (t17800112-29).

Charles Jealous and Thomas Carpmeal. Colborne was acquitted of the main charge, whilst Jones and Wheeler were found guilty and transported to the West Indies. Colborne was later sentenced to six months' confinement and Levi to twelve months, both at Newgate.[346]

MacManus, Clarke, Morrant and Carpmeal had joined together to raid a house in Bowling–pin Alley on 17th March 1782 which was suspected of housing individuals who were making counterfeit halfpenny coins. There they found Thomas and Mary Morris together with Joseph Norton, who had blackened hands from working with grease used to make the counterfeit coins. All were found guilty and sentenced to various terms of imprisonment.[347]

Mary Davis and John Rosewell were charged with the theft of some geese from Col. Egerton at Ealing on 18th April 1787. Morrant, described in court as an officer of Bow Street, was involved in arresting Rosewell. Col. Egerton stated that he could identify the geese stolen from him and was sure the ones shown were his. However, both were found not guilty since there was a flaw in identifying the property.[348]

John Lott and Isabella Williams were charged with theft on 24th April 1790, when they took one gilt medal value 20s, four other medals valued at 42s, five laced velvet collars value 25s, three silk ribbons, value 50s, and two pictures. In court Morrant described himself as "an officer of Bow–street" before explaining "On the 28th of March last, I had these medals and pictures from Mrs Brown's, Castle–street, Oxford–market."[349] Both prisoners were found not guilty as there was doubt as to connection between the prisoners

346 Old Bailey Proceedings Online (www.oldbaileyonline.org, version 7.2, 27 June 2016), February 1782, trial of John Jones, Jacob Levi, John Wheeler, Benjamin Colborne, Joseph Atkins, James Pullen (t17820220–64).

347 Old Bailey Proceedings Online (www.oldbaileyonline.org, version 7.2, 27 June 2016), April 1782, trial of Thomas Morris, Joseph Norton, Mary Morris, otherwise Russel (t17820410–14).

348 Old Bailey Proceedings Online (www.oldbaileyonline.org, version 7.2, 27 June 2016), April 1787, trial of Mary Davis, John Rosewell (t17870418–97).

349 Old Bailey Proceedings Online (www.oldbaileyonline.org, version 7.2, 27 June 2016), April 1790, trial of John Lott, Isabella Williams (t17900424–36).

and the property.

Morrant's cases were numerous, including four of burglary, 19 of theft, 18 of grand larceny, one of pickpocketing, 16 of highway robbery, ten of coining, two of housebreaking, one of riot, two of receiving, one of shoplifting and lastly one of forgery and deception.

John Clarke (1768–1793)

John Clarke became one of the leading principal officers of his time, considered a man of dignity and honour. He was an expert, given his background in the metalwork trade as a silver cane-head and button maker. His knowledge of metal casting, including stamps and dies, was invaluable in the investigation and prosecution of coining offences. Coining offences were capital crimes and attracted large rewards for the likes of Clarke. According to Beattie (2012), he appears to have started as early as 1768, and was previously a parish Constable who left his post after a year or two to become one of "Sir John Fielding's people".[350] Given also his considerable experience of the criminal underworld, he was a formidable opponent to those he apprehended. Together with his experience as an investigator who knew the law, he was also used to giving evidence in court. Combining all these attributes meant that Clarke knew where to go, who to find and where to look in recovering evidence.

At the Old Bailey in 1780, in the case of Henry Barnett, Clarke said that when property was stolen and information had been received they would "go to the noted houses", indicating that they knew where the receivers of stolen property lived. This also meant that they knew their associates and co–conspirators. Clarke's experience, not only of coining offences, was considerably more useful than those of the parish Constables.[351] The Principal Officers became experienced in where to find the active receivers (also known as "fences"), probably through their early indices or registers kept at Bow Street. MacManus, when giving evidence, alluded to this when he said in

350 Beattie, J. (2012) *The First English Detectives*. Oxford University Press, Oxford, p. 268.
351 Ibid, p. 76.

1783 "...there was an information back at the office that such sort of people lived there, that stole trunks."[352]

Clarke's experience as an investigator and crime scene analyst came to the fore after a major burglary in 1776 where £200 worth of silver plate, clothes and jewellery were taken. Clarke went to the crime scene and spoke with a servant, who was the only witness. The servant said that three men had broken into the property and tied him up before ransacking the house of his master, stealing all the property. Clarke's detective skills established, from his close observations, that glass of the broken window was still intact, with the shards jutting outwards from the room and that a spider's web was unbroken on another damaged glass pane in front of it. This led Clarke to deduce that the window was broken from the inside, and suspicion thus fell on the servant. Once Clarke had learnt that the servant had a wife in lodgings he immediately dispatched officers to the address, and there they found the stolen property.[353]

Clarke was a respected witness and made 18 depositions during his time at Bow Street. These were in effect the officer's investigations given in oral evidence taken from his inquiries into a matter, and these would be sworn before the court.[354] Clarke organised raids on premises for coining offences, and even when locked premises were found where such practices were suspected, the Bow Street men sent for him because he knew what to look for.

Such was his standing as an expert witness that on one occasion, in the 1789 case of Thomas Denton and John Jones, whilst giving evidence at the Old Bailey under cross examination by the notorious Mr Garrow, Clarke asked to be excused from court, no doubt to be relieved. He promised not to speak with anyone, and when he turned to the prisoners and repeated himself, prisoner John Jones

352 Old Bailey Proceedings Online (www.oldbaileyonline.org, version 7.2 Feb 1783 the trial of Thomas Dudfield and Hart Levy (t17830226-3).

353 *London Evening Post*, 17–19 March 1778 and Old Bailey Proceedings Online (www. oldbaileyonline.org, version 7.2, 21st January 2017) March 1778, the trial of Francis Lewis otherwise Grimson (t17780429-7).

354 Beattie, J. (2012) *The First English Detectives*. Oxford University Press, Oxford, p. 111.

said, "You have too much honour to do anything of the kind Mr Clark [sic]."[355]

His conviction rate, probably because of his in-depth knowledge of criminal procedure and giving evidence over 20 years (1774–1793), was 82 percent, whilst for other coining matters investigated by his colleagues during the same period it was 40 percent.

Charles Jealous (1773–1794)

Charles Jealous resided at Brownloe Street, Drury Lane. He was a saddler by trade, and a Constable of the Bow Street office in 1794.[356] Like many of his contemporaries he was often involved in coining prosecutions.[357] His first case was in 1774, when he dealt with a case of theft or grand larceny when he recovered stolen property from a pawnbroker after discovering a pawn ticket on a prisoner named Patrick Shields.[358] During his time at Bow Street he was very industrious and conscientious, with 133 cases at the Old Bailey alone. It was the precedent at the time to pay the wives of officers an annuity in the event of their husband's demise, and after Charles Jealous's death his wife received £5 per quarter (£20 per year), which was still being paid in 1818.[359]

Patrick MacManus (1780–1817)

Patrick MacManus was a Constable of Bow Street residing at 10 Drury Lane. He became a Constable during the Gordon Riots, and was a colleague and trusted friend to John Townsend. In time he became part of the King's Retinue, when in 1795 he was ordered to accompany the monarch from Windsor to Weymouth.[360] One of

355 Beattie, J. (2012) *The First English Detectives*. Oxford University Press, Oxford, p. 132.
356 Howell, T. and Cobett, W. (1818) *A Complete Collection of State Trials and Proceedings for High Treason and Misdemeanours*. Hansard, London.
357 Sibley, M. (1794) *The Genuine Trial of Thomas Hardy for Treason. Vol. 2*. J. S. Jordon London.
358 Old Bailey Proceedings Online (www.oldbaileyonline.org, version 7.2, 02 July 2016), May 1774, trial of Patrick Shields (t17740518-34).
359 The Report of the Committee on the police of the metropolis 1818.
360 HO 65.1.

his first cases at the Old Bailey, in 1780, saw him give evidence with Charles Jealous and Moses Morrant in a case of burglary. He was not yet one of "Sir John Fielding's People", but started as a member of the Foot Patrole and was taken along initially to arrests in order to support Fielding's men, in this way gaining practical experience in accounting for stolen property in an evidential way.[361] Further cases followed this same pattern, where he worked with a number of other officers from Fielding's office including Clarke, Morrant, Carpmeal, Prothero, Jennings and Phillips. Many of these cases were serious crimes such as coining, robbery and burglary, and on conviction MacManus would receive a portion of the £40 reward at the judge's discretion.

At the Old Bailey in July 1784 MacManus described himself as one of the Foot Patrole when he was involved in a case of violent highway robbery, but within a year or so had been promoted to an "officer of Bow Street". By 1800 he had been involved in over 90 cases heard at the Old Bailey, making him one of the most prodigious Bow Street officers.

MacManus also appears very often in the financial accounts at Bow Street, especially between 1800 and 1807. In 1800 expenses were paid to MacManus and Miller to prosecute the driver of a coach who was riding furiously and deliberately tried to wreck their vehicle – a post-chaise – and causing them serious injury. The prosecution was successful, resulting in the coachman receiving three months' imprisonment. The following year further expenses were paid to the officers, allowing them to prosecute the coach owner. This time, however, the action was set aside and the prosecutors were ordered to pay costs of £94 6s 2d.[362]

By 1814 MacManus was receiving a retainer of £1 1s 0d per day, whilst also in receipt of £200 per annum for attending to the King and the Prince Regent on public occasions in town along with

361 Old Bailey Proceedings Online (www.oldbaileyonline.org, version 7.2, 21st January 2017 trial of Robert Anders otherwise Andrews and Richard Palmer (t17800223–34).
362 T38/672.

Townsend and Sayer.

MacManus became one of the more trusted of Bow Street officers, serving for 37 years. He died in 1817, and his widow received £35 per year annuity from the Bow Street accounts as was the custom.[363]

Edward Fugion (1784–1798)

In 1784 Edward Fugion resided at the Pleasant Retreat, Palmer's Village in Tothill Fields, not far from Bow Street. He was a shoemaker by trade, and one of the officers at the Bow Street Public Office.[364] In 1793, after nine years' service, he became a Captain of the Bow Street Foot Patrole after gaining invaluable experience in policing the streets of the metropolis.

In July 1796 he went with another Bow Street officer named Rivett to Bromley on a murder investigation, after the body of Elvi Manns was discovered. There they apprehended John Clarke as the main suspect,[365] but it appears that he never appeared at the Old Bailey charged with the murder.

Fugion became a Principal Officer on promotion in 1796, and was very energetic in the fight against gambling. He led a raid on a number of establishments in Leicester Square where two Englishmen and 17 Frenchmen were arrested.

In January 1798 he gave evidence against John Seymour, James Wright and William Wright, who had all been arrested for violent theft or highway robbery on the Edgware Road between the third and fourth mile stone.[366]

In June that year Fugion and other Bow Street Principal Officers were tasked to deal with cases of sedition and treason, often requiring them to travel out of from London. They are known to have

---

363 Committee on Police of the Metropolis (1818) *The State of the Police of the Metropolis* – Appendix 1, pp. 199–204.
364 Howell, T. and Cobett, W. (1818) *A Complete Collection of State Trials and Proceedings for High Treason and Misdemeanours*. Hansard, London.
365 John Fielding's Accounts T38/673.
366 Old Bailey Proceedings Online (www.oldbaileyonline.org, version 7.2, 28 December 2015), January 1798, trial of James Wright, William Wright and John Seymour (t17980110-24).

been involved in investigating at least 30 cases.[367] The Government was suspicious that treasonable correspondence was being passed between certain individuals and the French Government. Together with Rivett, Fugion was despatched to Gravesend in Kent to apprehend certain suspects against whom good intelligence had been obtained, and the prisoners were taken back to London for examination.[368]

Edward Fugion died suddenly of natural causes in 1798, a month after giving evidence in the above mentioned cases of treason at Maidstone. His death was reported with regret and sadness in the newspapers,[369] such was the interest and respect paid to Bow Street Principal Officers at the time.

Bow Street also supported the wives and children or deceased officers of the court, and application was made to the Government in this case. By 1800 Fugion's widow was in receipt of an annuity of £15 a quarter as ordered by the Secretary of State, which amounted to one-quarter of Fugion's pay, representing an allowance for his three children.[370] In 1803 the Secretary of State ordered £5 a quarter to Mrs Fugion and she was still being remunerated in 1827, probably continuing until her death.[371]

Christopher Kennedy (1793–1795)

Kennedy resided at Cross Court, Broad Court in Long Acre. He was a carpenter and one of the Constables of the Bow Street Public office.[372] In August 1795 the Secretary of State directed Kennedy to accompany the King on a journey from Windsor to Weymouth.[373]

---

367 Cox, D. (2010) *A Certain Share of Low Cunning: A History of the Bow Street Runners, 1792–1839.* Willan, Cullumpton, p. 88.
368 *Staffordshire Advertiser,* 10th March 1798.
369 *The Cumberland Pacquet and Wares Whitehaven Advertiser,* 24th July 1798.
370 John Fielding's Account T38.672.
371 John Fielding's Account T38.673.
372 Howell, T. (1818) *A Complete Collection of State Trials and Proceedings for High Treason and Misdemeanours.* Hansard, London.
373 HO 65/1.

John Miller (1793–1806)

Miller lived in Duke's Court, Bow Street and was one of the Constables of the Bow Street Public Office. In 1800 he was involved with MacManus when an assailant deliberately and recklessly crashed his carriage into the officers in an attempt to injure them.[374] This became a drawn-out affair in the courts, and Bow Street funds were used to support both men.

Thomas Jones (1794)

Jones lived in Milford Lane, The Strand, employed as a labourer and one of the Constables of the Bow Street Office.[375]

Roger Gatrell (1794)

Gatrell lived in Hemlock Court, Cary Street, and was a tailor or greengrocer as well as being one of the Constables of the Bow Street Public Office in Covent Garden.[376]

William Bond Sr[377] (Foot Patrole 1812–1822, Conductor 1823 –1827, Principal Officer 1828–1830)

Like most others who joined Bow Street, Bond first became a member of the Bow Street Foot Patrole, joining around 1812 following the end of the War with France. From the start he was a very industrious officer, often arresting people for serious matters and appearing in evidence against them at the Old Bailey. He was self–confident and skilled as a speaker, gradually becoming expert in giving evidence to ensure convictions at court. Clearly, he was a leader of men, and this attribute came to the notice of the magistrates

374 John Fielding's Accounts T38/672.
375 Howell, T. (1818) *A Complete Collection of State Trials and Proceedings for High Treason and Misdemeanours.* Hansard, London.
376 Howell, T. (1818) *A Complete Collection of State Trials and Proceedings for High Treason and Misdemeanours.* Hansard, London.
377 There have been a number of officers at Bow Street with the name Bond and given that often it was the surname which had been reported it makes the task of trying to identify particular individuals notoriously difficult. We know also that from the 1760s–1829 there were three individuals with the name William Bond so again providing difficulties of identification.

so after a while he was promoted to Conductor of Party No. 16 – a group of four men who patrolled a given area of the London environs up to four miles from Bow Street. He had also encouraged his son to join the Foot Patrole, making his application in 1825 and finally joining Party No. 13 in early 1826.

Bond Sr would perform other functions which earned him additional remuneration to his pay, and attended the Theatre in Drury Lane to keep the peace and prevent pickpocketing. He distinguished himself in his proceedings and was soon being considered for further advancement. In 1828 he was promoted from the Foot Patrole to become a Principal Officer at Bow Street. As part of his work he would be hired or sent out of the Metropolis to execute warrants or arrest felons who had decamped away into the country.

In December 1830 he was sent with others to help quell rioting in Kent, where he helped detain two rioters and take them before the court. He immediately returned to London on the Sevenoaks coach, but whilst alighting in Southwark he slipped awkwardly and fell, breaking his leg. People immediately went to his assistance and found that he was delirious, so Bond was taken to Guy's Hospital. The complicated fracture of the leg led doctors to recommend amputation, which he declined. He died of his injuries a short while later and was buried at St. Mary's Lambeth on 20th December 1830.

Henry Croker (1794)

Croker lived in Tottenham Court Road in the county of Middlesex and was a broker in addition to being a Constable attached to the Public Office at Bow Street.[378]

Christopher Cridland (also Creedland) (1791–1814)

Christopher Cridland lived in Kemp's Court off Soho's Berwick Street, employed as a shoemaker and as one of the Constables

---

378 Howell, T. (1818) *A Complete Collection of State Trials and Proceedings for High Treason and Misdemeanours*. Hansard, London.

attending Bow Street.[379]

He was very active and later became a captain of the Foot Patrole in February 1791, together with other Foot Patrole members John Shallard, Charles Brothwick and James Anderson,

Cridland's son Joseph was involved in the trial at the Old Bailey of John Rees and Thomas Goodman. The Patrole had stopped and detained the suspects for theft. They were found guilty and sentenced to seven years' transportation.[380]

On 8th June 1798 Cridland was involved in the case of William Green, whom he suspected of having stolen property in his possession. Green was later charged with the theft of copper valued at 10s, taken from the property of John Shepherd. In his evidence Cridland said:

> "I am an officer belonging to Bow-street: On the 8th of last month, between nine and ten at night, I was going upon duty down the Uxbridge–road, and under the wall, going to Bayswater, I saw the prisoner with a sack on his head, which contained this copper, (producing it); I asked him how he came by it, and he said he found it. I took him to the watch–house, and finding that Mr Shepherd had lost a copper, I desired him to come down to the office".[381]

Green was found guilty and sent to the House of Correction for twelve months.[382]

A further case of highway robbery in February 1802 at Notting Hill Green, near the Kensington Gravel Pits was quickly dealt with when Cridland, having received information about the robbery, went with other members of the Patrole in quick pursuit. Three men were stopped: Walter Duggan, James Condon and William Ogle, and when searched stolen property was recovered. John Wood, who reported

379 Ibid.
380 Old Bailey Proceedings Online (www.oldbaileyonline.org, version 7.2, 31 August 2015), February 1791, trial of Joseph Rees, Thomas Goodman (t17910216–12).
381 Old Bailey Proceedings Online (www.oldbaileyonline.org, version 7.2, 03 July 2016), July 1798, trial of William Green (t17980704–15).
382 Ibid.

the robbery, was later invited to Bow Street to attend what would today be described as an informal identity parade, and he was able to pick out the assailants. The reward in this case on conviction was a total of £120, so there was a handsome amount to be made by the Bow Street Patrole. The three were found guilty and sentenced to death, with the jury recommending for clemency.[383]

Cridland was involved in at least eight cases at the Old Bailey, mainly of theft. Intelligence received in 1801 relating to the attempted robbery of a shop by Benjamin Beale, who had struck the owner with a hammer three times, resulted in him being arrested by Cridland who had kept observation on the public house where Beale's brother was the licensee.[384]

In 1814 Cridland's career came to an end due to ill health. He had been unwell for 91 days, throughout which he was still being paid the sum of 3s 4d per day.

George Allan (1794)

Allen lived in Turner's Court, Bedfordbury in the county of Middlesex, and was one of the Constables attending the Public Office at Bow Street.[385]

Robert Beresford (1794)

Beresford lived at Bennett's Court, Drury Lane, where he worked as a tailor and greengrocer. He was also one of the Constables located at the Public Office at Bow Street.[386]

Nathaniel Birch (1794)

Birch lived in Vine Street in the Parish of St. John's, Westminster.

---

383 Old Bailey Proceedings Online (www.oldbaileyonline.org, version 7.2, 03 July 2016), February 1802, trial of Walter Duggan, James Condon and William Ogle (t18020217–21).
384 *Morning Post*, 30th April 1801.
385 Howell, T. (1818) *A Complete Collection of State Trials and Proceedings for High Treason and Misdemeanours. Hansard*, London.
386 Ibid.

He was a labourer by trade and a member of one of the Patroles located at Bow Street.[387]

William Pope (1794–1796)

Pope resided at Little Marylebone Street and his trade was as a blacking ball maker. He was an officer of the Patrole at Bow Street, according to accounts attached to William Black's party.[388]

John Shallard (1772–1794)

Shallard resided in Charlton Street, Somers Town in the county of Middlesex and was recorded as an officer, formerly a pastry cook. In 1772 he was an early captain of one of the Bow Street Foot Patroles.[389]

William Black

Black was a greengrocer of York Street, Westminster and one of the Constables attending the Public Office at Bow Street who later became a captain of the Foot Patrole.[390]

Duncan Grant (1793–1799)

Grant was a captain of the Foot Patrole who resided at a house in Strutton Ground, Westminster (very close to New Scotland Yard, situated in Broadway until 2017). Sadly Grant was one of the first Constables to be killed in the line of duty whilst executing a warrant of arrest (see page 273-4 for further information).

John Townsend (1786–1832)

Townsend was a long-serving, industrious man who became perhaps the most famous (some would suggest infamous) Constable

---

387   Ibid.
388   Bow Street Accounts T38.673.
389   John Fielding's Accounts T38/674.
390   John Fielding's Accounts T38/674.

of Bow Street, serving 46 years in total at the court. He was certainly a larger-than-life gregarious character, who had a nice respectable manner about him. There are a number of seemingly outlandish stories, apocryphal anecdotes and contradictions associated with him, which have all contributed to his reputation as a great curiosity.[391] Where possible, the authors have tried to verify them. He was disliked by those who had something to fear, but he also had an "effrontery, was clever, cunning and of low wit", qualities which helped to put him to the top of his profession.[392]

He was born in 1760 at the Middlesex Hospital and educated at St. Clement Danes, and he later subscribed to both institutions until the end of his life.[393] He began his working life as a costermonger selling fruit and vegetables, probably in Covent Garden Market. Costermongers at the time had an unsavoury reputation, with their "low habits, general improvidence, love of gambling, total want of education, disregard for lawful marriage ceremonies, and their use of a peculiar slang language".[394] It was his experience of life as a costermonger and London life in general which helped him learn the basics of his craft.

Townsend became associated with criminal London when he was appointed as a shoeblack at Newgate Prison. He described his role there more flamboyantly as "Valet" to the inmates, which meant that he would help dress those who were condemned to be executed.[395] He used to attend trials at the Old Bailey and watch proceedings, getting to know people and learning about them, making copious notes as to their descriptions, what they were accused of, and

---

391 Adam, Hargrave, L. (1920) *The Police Encyclopedia Vol. 1.* Blackfriars publishing Co., London, p. 110.
392 Ibid.
393 oxfordindex.oup.com/view/10.1093/ref:odnb/54374 accessed on 19th July 2016.
394 Hotten, J. C. (1859) *The Slang Dictionary.*
395 Ainsworth, W. H. Cruikshank, G. and Browne, H. K (1849) *Ainsworth's Magazine: A Miscellany of Romance, General Literature*, Volume 7. Published by John Mortimer, London and Southampton, p. 232.

whether they were found guilty or not.[396] He also noted down how offenders committed their crimes and who they were related to or associated with. This meant that when attending a crime involving the theft of valuable property, for example, he would often get a sense of who the culprit was and at which "Flash House" he could be found.[397] Certainly, he built up his personal informants who would be able to say where a particular suspect was located and Townsend would give the informant some financial inducement to reveal what was known. Because of this knowledge of the underworld network his reputation went before him, and he was quickly nicknamed "Counsellor double head".[398] He could strike fear into the hearts of anyone when entering any alehouse, gin shop or flash house.

Before Townsend became a member of the Bow Street Patrole, in 1780 he came to the notice as "a servant to Mr Richard Akerman", meaning he had risen from shoeblack and become valet to the principal turnkey or prison officer at the newly constructed Prison at Newgate. Akerman was in fact Keeper of the New Prison, which was a focus that year for riotous attacks during the Gordon Riots. The Keeper's house formed part of the overall structure and it was connected to the prison. It was also the weakest point, through which the rioters forced their way in and vandalised the rest of the prison. In fact Townsend appeared at court to provide evidence that he was present when the house was broken into, and identified several rioters who had previously been convicted and sentenced to transportation. Some of those convicted had returned from

---

396 Protheroe, M. (1931) *The History of the Criminal Investigation Department at Scotland Yard*. Herbert Jenkins, London.

397 A Flash House was generally a public house frequented by criminals. A combination of brothels, drinking places and centres for criminal intelligence, some were kept exclusively for young boys and girls. They were described as "hot beds of profligacy and vice" and usually situated in the rookeries described above. Some, like The Finish in Covent Garden, were under the nose of Bow Street. forromancereaders. wordpress.com/2009/10/03/rookeries–flash–houses–and–academies–of–vice accessed on 26th July 2015.

398 Fitzgerald, P. (1888) *Chronicles of Bow Street Police-Office. Vol.1*. Chapman and Hall, London, p. 100. Also Adam, Hargrave, L. (1920) *The Police Encyclopedia Vol. 1*. Blackfriars Publishing Co., London, p. 111.

Fig. 19: John Townsend
Courtesy Metropolitan Police Historical collection

transportation early, and once their identity was proved they were sentenced to death.

Later, of a convict named William Smith, Townsend said:

> "I belong to the office at Bow–street, I know the prisoner perfectly well, I was a servant to Mr Akerman at the time he was tried and convicted for coining a halfpenny in October session, 1782. I put him and Mary Jones to the bar, they were tried in the evening on the London side; and your Lordship, as you usually do, passed sentence on him on the last day of session".[399]

Smith was convicted and sentenced to death. The witnesses to his conviction would share in the £40 reward money payable from the court.

Townsend remained a turnkey until late 1783, when he was appointed at Bow Street as a Constable.[400] His early Bow Street career was as a member of the Patrole, where he was quite active and frequently found himself at the Old Bailey giving evidence which he did in a confident manner.

One of his first cases, in February 1784, involved other members of the Patrole John Cridland, Joseph Cridland and William Bowyer, the Captain of the Patrole. They were entering Hyde Park when three men who were acting suspiciously came towards them. Bowyer spoke to one, Samuel Selshire, who he immediately detained. This was the signal to the rest of the Patrole to apprehend the other two men, which they tried to do, but one produced a pistol as he ran off. The two men, Richard McDonald and John Jacobs, were pursued by the Patrole. McDonald fired his pistol at his pursuers narrowly missed John Cridland, who apprehended McDonald and recovered the pistol. When the three men were searched property belonging to Charles Chapman, who had earlier been robbed at gunpoint on the

399 Old Bailey Proceedings Online (www.oldbaileyonline.org, version 7.2, 06 July 2016), April 1786, trial of William Smith, otherwise Storer, Jospeh Robinson, otherwise Gosling (t17860426–13).
400 Old Bailey Proceedings Online (www.oldbaileyonline.org, version 7.2, 06 July 2016), September 1783, trial of Charles Thomas (t17830910–4).

road between Kensington and Kensington Gravel Pits, was found. The prisoners were convicted and sentenced to death, with leniency being recommended for Selshire and Jacobs who had displayed no violence.[401] Following the convictions the four members of the Patrole along with the victim shared the reward of £40 per prisoner, totalling £120 – a not inconsequential sum of money at the time.

In his next case at the Old Bailey, in 1784, Townsend appears to have been known to James Coyle, a robber. Townsend described himself as "attending the public office at Bow Street".[402]

By 1786 Townsend was a Bow Street Patrole Constable. He met Mr James Grey at The Brown Bear, who had gone to Bow Street to report that he had been attacked by highway robber John Kitsall at Highgate, his money and a seal stolen.

The cellar of The Brown Bear, which was opposite Bow Street Public Office, had a secure room in the basement where prisoners could be detained. Other members of Bow Street, namely Atkins, Sayer and Shallard, received a tip-off and went to Catherine Wheel Yard in Windmill Street, and Townsend went down and waited with them. A grey horse came into the yard and Townsend approached, distracting the rider as he got off, allowing him to take from him the pistol he had concealed in his greatcoat pocket. On a search of the rider once he was secured, Townsend found the seal which bore initials matching that stolen from James Grey. The prisoner was convicted and sentenced to death, the reward to the Constables amounting to £40 between them all.[403]

Another case saw Mary Benfield apprehended by Townsend and Thomas Ting, another member of the Patrole, for being in possession of counterfeit coins, *viz.* 7s 19d, which she had concealed in a bag

401 Old Bailey Proceedings Online (www.oldbaileyonline.org, version 7.2, 04 July 2016), February 1784, trial of John Jacobs, Samuel Selshire, Richard McDonald (t17840225–11).
402 Old Bailey Proceedings Online (www.oldbaileyonline.org, version 7.2, 04 July 2016), February 1785, trial of James Coyle (t17850223–13).
403 Old Bailey Proceedings Online (www.oldbaileyonline.org, version 7.2, 04 July 2016), February 1786, trial of John Kitsall, alias Wilmot, alias Smith (t17860222–55).

and a pocket. Richard King was an informant who had initially declined an offer from Benfield to buy false coinage, but a week later was approached again. This time he bought the bad money for 10s 6d, and took it to the expert Mr Clarke at Bow Street. Here, Clarke examined the coins and confirmed they were false. King then gave him information where Benfield could be found. She was found guilty and fined one shilling and sentenced to 12 months in Newgate prison.[404]

In November 1787 John Townsend married Ann Shepard at St. Clement Danes Church, Westminster. Ann had already given birth to at least one child, maybe more; however, as Robert John Townsend was born in 1782, it was likely that as she was pregnant again the couple decided to wed.[405]

A constantly active man, especially seen around the Central Criminal Court, John Townsend's expertise often gave reassurance to trial judges. For example, in court proceedings at the Old Bailey Townsend could influence the pardoning decisions of Judges after giving evidence "by quietly informing the judge regarding convicted persons' previous convictions (or a lack of them) after the defendant had been sentenced".[406]

Townsend was well-dressed, described by Gronow in 1889 as being "a fat man with a flaxen wig, kerseymere breeches, a blue straight-cut coat and abroad brimmed white hat".[407]

Following an attempt on the life of the King and the rise of republicanism in 1791, the Government thought it wise to protect the royal family, especially given, "the frequent appearance of mysterious looking strangers in and about Windsor Castle and its

404 Old Bailey Proceedings Online (www.oldbaileyonline.org, version 7.2, 04 July 2016), April 1786, trial of Mary Benfield (t17860426-105).

405 TNA.

406 King, P. (2000) *Crime, Justice and Discretion in England 1740–1820*. OUP, Oxford, p. 315.

407 Gronow. (1889) *The Reminiscences and Recollections of Capt. Gronow* 2 vols. and Dilnot, G. (1926) *The Story of Scotland Yard – its History and Associations*. G. Bles, London.

environs".[408] It was at this point that Townsend received his quite unexpected promotion. He would often put himself forward and was quite unperturbed when speaking with the King or any other member of the upper classes. When first introduced to the King he was instantly a success. He was accepted and elevated further since he was bestowed with the rank of "Private Privy Counsellor and personal protector of their gracious majesties George III and Queen Charlotte".[409] Described by some chroniclers at the time as a "blaggart", he "often boasted that the King copied him in his style of dress, and it certainly was true that that he wore the same trousers as Townsend."[410] An explanation given later by Townsend himself suggested that the King's tailor would be entertained by Townsend to a bottle of wine, and during the conversation would ask what had been ordered. The style and colour the King had recently ordered having been discovered, Townsend would then order exactly the same, ensuring he received his clothes before the Sovereign. Hence, he boasted that the King copied him when in fact the reverse was probably true.

Townsend allegedly accumulated a vast fortune and Protheroe suggested that he, "derived a large part of his income by receiving Christmas boxes from the nobility and of other parties of whose routs he was employed to detect or keep away improper characters, who he persuaded his patrons would be present, if he were not in attendance".[411]

Later he became the head of his profession and one of the most celebrated Principal Officers at Bow Street. There were three others who were just as industrious but perhaps not as infamous, and these were Sayer, Vickery and Ruthven.

408 Ainsworth, W. H. Cruikshank, G. and Browne, H. K (1849) *Ainsworth's Magazine: A Miscellany of Romance, General Literature, Volume 7.* Published by John Mortimer London Southampton, p. 233.
409 Ibid.
410 Protheroe, M. (1931) *The History of the Criminal Investigation Department at Scotland Yard.* Herbert Jenkins, London, p. 21.
411 Protheroe, M. (1931) *The History of the Criminal Investigation Department at Scotland Yard.* Herbert Jenkins, London.

Townsend was invariably found in the evenings at the theatre or behind the scenes at the Opera House, often in familiar conversation with King George III, whose good-humoured face was convulsed with laughter at his ribald stories. On one memorable occasion the King, in a fit of anger, swore over the tip he had given a Hackney carriage driver when going to the House. The cab driver expressed great disappointment at what he saw as insufficient. Thereupon Townsend, to the amazement of everyone, cried out from behind a screen: "Well said, Sir, I think your Majesty is d---d right!" The King, much surprised and amused called out: "Is that you, Townsend?" He replied "Yes, Sir, I am here to see that your Majesty gets fair play!" In fact Townsend suggested he should deal with the cab drivers on behalf of the King from that point on.

He also charmed and flattered the ladies. At an Installation of the Knights' of the Garter, the then Duchess of Northumberland accepted his arm and he conducted her through "a mob of Nobles and others" to her place in the chapel.[412]

Townsend was the senior Principal Officer at Bow Street, where he was in charge of ten others whilst Sayer was responsible for two. Although a little conceited and vain, he appeared on the face of it to be honest, since an attempt to bribe him was rebuffed. One such example concerned Mrs Usher, a well-known old pickpocket said to be worth £3,000, who was arrested by Townsend. He was offered £200 by a relative to withdraw from the prosecution.[413]

Opposite is a receipt from the Kings Theatre in 1810 paying John Townsend the sum of £4 4s 0d for the attendance of four officers attending four extra nights at the Opera.

Townsend's effrontery and ready wit, especially in the presence of the Prince of Wales (later King George IV), meant that he became a privileged person and could say and do very much what he liked. As such on a professional level Townsend's influence enabled him to make recommendations to the Magistrates at Bow Street for

412 Moylan, I. F. (1929) 'The Blue Army' in *Country Life*. May edition.
413 Griffiths, A. G. (1898) *Mysteries of Police and Crime*. Cassell and Comp, London.

the Patrole. He put forward his own nephew, Joseph Townsend, to become a Principal Officer in the early 1800s and he was duly selected; however, all did not go well for him and his career at Bow Street was short-lived.[414]

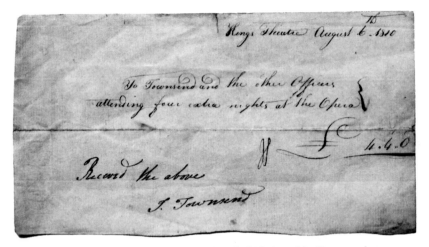

Fig. 20: Receipt for expenses dated 1810 signed by Townsend

There was an affray at the Palace on the King's birthday in 1804 involving Joseph Townsend, who was on duty preserving the peace. An altercation occurred which resulted in Joseph Townsend being accused of assaulting James Reilly, a private in the guards in Palace Yard. Instructions had been published by the Lord Chamberlain, who had issued tickets for entry into the Royal gathering in order to keep out uninvited guests. Townsend did not have a ticket and so was denied entry by the officer on duty. He had also brought a friend with him (likely to have been another Bow Street officer), and that person also had no ticket. The military version disagreed with the police evidence. When challenged Townsend apparently did not reply, but instead took out his truncheon and attempted to beat the

414 Joseph Townsend appears to have been John Townsend's son, not his nephew born in 1782 to Ann Shepard who later married Townsend in November 1787. Elizabeth Townsend was born in 1787.

corporal of the guard with it until the former was overpowered by the rest of the guard and placed in the "black hole". He was later charged with assault and appeared at Clerkenwell Quarter Sessions. Superintendent of the Patrole Christopher Jones and Michael Doyle (occasional Patrole) also gave evidence at the hearing, stating that "the guards were drunk and that they had hit the officer first with the butts of their rifles". Joseph Townsend was nonetheless found guilty, thereby ending his career at Bow Street.[415] This demonstrates the relative powerlessness of the police at the time, especially against the military.

On one occasion John Townsend was asked by the Duke of Clarence to publish his memoirs. He erroneously thought he wanted him to write about his "amours". When the Duke of Clarence asked him later whether he had fulfilled his promise, Townsend said:

> "Oh sir you've got me in a devil of a scrape! I had begun to write my amours as you desired, when Mrs Townsend caught me in the act of writing them, and swore she would be revenged; for you know your Royal Highness I was obliged to divulge many secrets about women for which she will never forgive me"[416]

This type of playful banter with Royals made him a privileged person, which Gronow suggested meant that "he could say what he liked".[417]

Townsend's basic salary as a Runner was set at £1 1s 0d per week, but he could supplement his income as the receipt voucher above shows by performing a range of duties. When he died he is said to have left investments totalling £25,000, getting on for £1,237,250 in today's money using the National Archives currency convertor, making wife Ann a very rich woman. Had he obtained this vast sum by corrupt means? There is some evidence to suggest that amongst some of the other Principal Officers this might have been so.

415 *Morning Post*, 11th September 1804.
416 Fitzgerald, P. (1888) *Chronicles of Bow Street Police-Office. Vol.1.* Chapman and Hall, London, p. 99.
417 Ibid.

Fig. 21: Gillray cartoon with Townsend in the left section of the image brandishing his tipstaff

Townsend himself probably got rich from the large fees he could demand, especially for taking up investigations on behalf of his new aristocratic acquaintances or receiving Christmas boxes from nobility and royalty alike.

In the early decades of the 19th Century all the Principal Officers seem to have been doing very well indeed.[418] Royal occasions would require ladies to wear their best jewellery, and the level of crime was such that they were not safe in and around Royal Court, so two officers were paid £200 a year for additional work as Royal detectives. Townsend gradually spent more of his time at the Palace, and, as the years progressed, became less adept at the cases his younger colleagues were undertaking. He seems to have been able to pick his own jobs and perhaps these tended to be the more lucrative ones. He also prevented innumerable duels, such as when the Earl of St. Vincent broke through the rules of etiquette and

---

418 www.lrb.co.uk/v34/n11/john–barrell/something–for–theresa–may–to–think–about accessed on 26th July 2015.

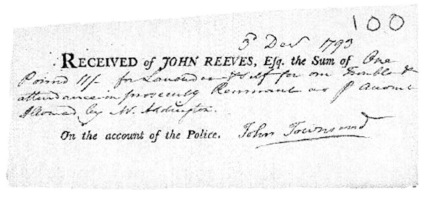

Fig. 22: Receipt dated 1793 signed by Townsend
Courtesy The National Archives

instead of sending second-in-command Sir J. Orde on the expedition to the Nile despatched Nelson. After the victory Sir John Orde sent a challenge to Earl of St. Vincent, and Townsend apprehended both the parties thus preventing them meeting.

It was not uncommon as a crime prevention measure to announce at some crowded 'Rout' where large numbers of people would gather an 'advertisement' that "Mr Townsend will attend."[419] He was entertainment to both royalty and nobility because of his popularity, and his background rendered him somewhat of a curiosity. This is demonstrated when on one occasion at the theatre the people of fashion would gather round him and ask, "How are you Townsend? What's the go?" Townsend's good-humoured manner and use of slang, much was virtually unintelligible, was amusing to them. However, on one occasion his confidence in this regard exceeded his ability when at the Haymarket he met his match. On duty that night was an officer of the guard who knew the whole slang repertoire inside out, as a group of listeners gathered round. Townsend was up for the match but was left quickly behind as the officer took the lead. Townsend could hardly keep up with the dialogue much to the

419 Fenn Clark, E. (1935) *Truncheons.* Herbert Jenkins London.

amusement of the gathered throng.[420] It wasn't often that Townsend was undone, but he was on this occasion. On the same subject, in October 1827 he happened to be at Bow Street when the Chief Magistrate Sir Richard Birnie had just granted a warrant against a Mr Summerfield, who had challenged a clerk named McDiarmid to a duel. Sir Richard pulled Townsend's leg by instructing him to execute the warrant, only to be met by an anguished plea by Townsend

> "that he should not be degraded after forty-six year's service by having to arrest a mere baker when he had been used to the honour of taking Earls, Marquises and Dukes".

Townsend died a very wealthy man on 10th July 1832 in Pimlico and was buried at the local St. Peter's Church a week later. He was survived by his wife Ann, who lived a further 14 years before passing away in 1846. She was buried at St. George's Church, Hanover Square.

John and Ann Townsend had two children, Robert (b. 1782) and Elizabeth (b. 1787). Robert died in 1832, the same year as his father. Ann did not need to work as she had sufficient assets from the estate to support herself. As all Ann's children had predeceased her, much of the property from the estate passed to her sister, Elizabeth Halstead of Chichester.[421]

There were few officers from Bow Street left who could show the same level of experience, ability and credibility as John Townsend. He could boast his connection and service at Bow Street court of over 50 years, back to the time of Sir John Fielding, and it was this sustained period of experience that gave him the senior position he held. He also made enemies, but because of his connection with royalty, the nobility and the gentry he remained protected, being regarded as something of a national treasure.

---

420 Fitzgerald, P. (1888) *Chronicles of Bow Street Police–Office. Vol.1.* Chapman and Hall, London.
421 Elizabeth Halstead was the great great great great grandmother of Louise Hurlow, who has kindly lent pictures of property owned by John Townsend.

George Ruthven (1793–1849)

George Thomas Joseph Ruthven became a member of the Patrole around 1810 and went on to become one of the most famous of the "Bow Street Runners". His appointment to Bow Street as a police officer had almost certainly being recommended by his father Archibald Ruthven, who had served at Bow Street himself, first as a Peace Officer in the 1780s and then being promoted to Conductor in 1793, the same year he married and son George born.[422] Not only did George follow his father into the profession, but his elder brother, also called Archibald, who had joined in about 1800. To supplement his Patrole wages Archibald continued his work as a baker.[423] While George made a distinguished career for himself, brother Archibald was implicated in corruption and his occupation terminated.

In 1816, aged 23, George Ruthven married Mary Ann Tamplin. He resided in Holles Street, a short walk from the Covent Garden Magistrates' Court. Some five months after his marriage his son George John William was born. His colleagues nicknamed him the "The Quaker" because of his rather relaxed attitude to his policing duties.[424]

In 1820 George became famous as he infiltrated the notorious revolutionary Cato Street gang, a small prominent radical group in London led by Arthur Thistlewood, and he helped bring them to justice.

The gang had protested against the impact of the industrialised world that produced rising inflation, food shortages and new patterns of factory employment. It was during this time of great social change that discontent and radicalism developed. Named after the street near Edgware Road where the gang met up, they aimed to overthrow the Government by assassinating the entire cabinet as they dined at Lord Harrowby's home in Grosvenor Square. During the assault on the building to arrest the conspirators Ruthven acted

---

422 Bevan, F. (2006) *Criminals and Conspirators in Ancestors*, November, p. 33.
423 Ibid.
424 goodgentlewoman.wordpress.com/tag/bow–street–runners accessed on 4th June 2015.

Fig. 23: George Ruthven
Courtesy Greg Ruthven

with great bravery, but in the hand-to-hand combat a Bow Street officer, 33-year-old Richard Smithers, was fatally wounded by Thistlewood, who stabbed him with a sword.

Proclaimed a hero because of his bravery, George continued to make his name with his detective work, some of which was very close to home. His wife Mary had run off with a horse dealer named James Haseldine, who was known as "Shock Jem". Haseldine had implicated some notorious felons, including some innocents in a fraudulent bankruptcy. He boasted about Mrs Ruthven playing a major part and even suggested when later examined by the magistrates at court that "she had money in her stays". Investigating this whole matter was George, who had been rather upset when his wife left him. On conviction Haseldine went to Newgate Prison to serve two years, so George got even on a personal front. Ruthven never saw his wife again and instead moved in and settled down with his common-law wife Mary Ann Harrison, with whom he had 12 children.

George continued his work despite the formation of the Metropolitan Police in 1829 and eventually retired in 1839, when the Bow Street Runners were disbanded. In retirement he became a publican and purchased the One Tun Inn in Chandos Street, close to his former beat. He received a pension of £220 from the English Government and similar amounts from both the Russian and Prussian Governments for his work on detecting forged currencies.[425]

He died in 1849 and was buried in the churchyard of St. Paul's, Covent Garden. His obituary published in *The Times* stated that he was "considered as the most efficient police officer that existed during his long career." Ruthven was a determined and charismatic figure but certainly a hero as well.

John Vickery (1799–1822)

Vickery was born in 1771 to parents of James and Phoebe Vickery

---

425 goodgentlewoman.wordpress.com/tag/bow–street–runners accessed on 4th June 2015.

and baptised at Odiham in Hampshire. He married Sarah Marriner on 9th January 1794 at St. Andrew's Church, Farnham in Surrey. The couple had two children over the next two years, and resided in Cheshunt in Hertfordshire.[426] In 1801 Vickery seems to have taken up with Ann Brown, with whom he had three children, all boys who he described in his Will as "my three sons".[427]

By September 1799 residing in Tyson Street, Bethnal Green, Vickery seems to have come to prominence when property was stolen from his premises where he was a saddler. He not only found the property which had been pawned, but investigated further and found witnesses who identified the culprit. He took the matter to Worship Street Police Court and later appeared at the Old Bailey, where the prisoner, John Hankins, was sentenced to six months' imprisonment and received a fine of 1s.[428]

By 1800 Vickery was an officer at Worship Street, working under the guide of John Armstrong who was an experienced officer. One of his first cases was the theft of some worsted yarn valued at £3, which was located at a house in Carters Rents, Bethnal Green, and stolen by George Martin and Judith Daly.[429] In this case Vickery is supporting Armstrong's evidence and learning about being able to identify stolen property and who stole it to the satisfaction of the court.

In 1800 he appeared at the Old Bailey to give evidence in seven cases alone, three of which involved false coining. By 1810 he had become a regular there, giving evidence in no less than 65 cases. In the same year, while still a Worship Street officer, he came to notice when he saw Ikey Solomons and Joel Joseph picking pockets in

426 www.rootschat.com/forum/index.php?topic=750229.0 accessed on 18th August 2016.
427 Ibid.
428 Old Bailey Proceedings Online (www.oldbaileyonline.org, version 7.2, 21st August 2016) September 1799 trial of John Hankins (t17990911–28).
429 Old Bailey Proceedings Online (www.oldbaileyonline.org, version 7.2, 21st August 2016) April 1800 trial of George Martin and Judith Daly (t18000402–55).

Westminster Hall.[430]

Vickery first appears in the Bow Street financial accounts in 1803, seemingly as a member of the Patrole, although he was and remained an officer at Worship Street until 1810. By 1811 he had transferred and become one of the principal Bow Street officers. Vickery later moved closer to his office and resided at 54 St John's Street, Clerkenwell, where he became a very active and respected officer in a short time.

In the Bow Street accounts there are some incidental charges made by John Stafford (the former Bow Street Principal Officer, now a magistrate), for the prosecution of James King, William Mansfield Evans and Edward Sadler for maliciously cutting Vickery in the execution of his duty, with intent to murder him. The sum allotted for this purpose was £36 18s 8d, and related to a matter which occurred on 30th December 1813 where Vickery had been seriously wounded. He was considered to be near death and it took three months for him to recover. Two of the assailants, King and Evans, were quickly arrested and appeared at the Old Bailey in February 1814. However, no evidence was offered by the prosecution, inferring that Vickery was too ill to be able to attend court and give evidence. Under the legal principle of double jeopardy neither men could face the same charges, again but Edward Sadler could. Sadler appeared at the Old Bailey in 1814, apparently on related charges, and was acquitted like the other two suspects.[431] It would appear that some, if not all of the suspects (Sadler), were prosecuted for other matters and convicted, sentenced to transportation, were capitally convicted or moved out of London, as no further was heard from them after the years 1814.

Vickery was employed separately by the Post Office to investigate mail coach thefts, thefts from banks, robberies and counterfeit money. In 1815 he went after a criminal named Cooke, who had robbed the Hertford Mail coach. The officer was involved in the

430 Tobias, J. J. (1974) *Prince of Fences: Life and Crimes of Ikey Solomons.* Valentine Mitchel. London, p. 5.

431 Old Bailey Proceedings Online (www.oldbailey online.org, version 7.2, 03 July 2016), February 1814, trial of Edward Sadler (t18140216–85).

Paisley Bank robbery investigation.[432]

At one time, law officers at Bow Street would have been treated badly had they entered flash houses, but by the time of the 1816 Select Committee report on the Police of the Metropolis they mixed freely with the criminals. John Vickery, giving evidence about Flash Houses before one such committee, reported: "I am always treated with great civility." This civility concealed more sinister happenings. Many officers were lazy, many were also corrupt. The Select Committee heard from several witnesses about "hush money" and underworld bribes, while other officers warned that they did not want their names known in case of reprisals. An anonymous witness, known only as A. L., supplied the Committee with a list of flash houses known to the police, and gave detailed notes on receivers of stolen goods.[433]

In 1820 John Vickery suffered an apoplectic fit and it appears this was serious enough for him to consider his future and seemingly caused him to write his Will.[434] His last case at the Old Bailey as an officer was in September 1822, when he gave evidence in the case of Edward Barber and William Goddard for conspiracy. They were found guilty and sentenced to confinement.[435]

In 1822 Vickery had had enough, probably due to his ill-health, and submitted an application to resign his position at Bow Street with his place being quickly taken by James Ellis.[436] The same year Vickery successfully applied to become Prison Governor or Keeper of the infamous Clerkenwell House of Correction, which had by then been renamed Coldbath Fields. In 1827 and 1828 Vickery published returns of prisoners held for felonies and misdemeanours, amounting to 4,900 men and women.[437] He remained in the role

432 Tobias, J. J. (1974) *Prince of Fences: Life and Crimes of Ikey Solomons.* Valentine Mitchel. London, p. 112 and 121.
433 forromancereaders.wordpress.com/tag/bow–street accessed on 7th June 2015.
434 www.rootschat.com/forum/index.php?topic=719112.9 accessed on 18th Aug 2016.
435 Old Bailey Proceedings Online (www.oldbailey online.org, version 7.2, 03 July 2016), September 1822, trial of Edward Barber and William Goddard (t18220911–153).
436 TNA T38/673.
437 House of Commons (1830) *Accounts and papers 13 Vols. Relating to Convicts, Criminals, forgery, debtors, penitentiary, police.* Bodleian Library Oxford.

until 1829, and after seven years' service when he was entitled to a pension.

He died suddenly on 18th June 1840, a rich man. In his Will he left two dwelling houses in his home village of Odiham, together with some land. The estate was left in trust to his son John Vickery Jr, although provision was made to Phoebe Vickery for his three other children.[438]

John Sayer (also Sayers, Sawyer) (1786–1832)

John Sayer was born around 1763, and in his adult life lived in Bridge Row, Pimlico, very close to Chelsea Hospital south east of Sloane Square.[439]

Between 1786 and 1832 he served as Principal Officer at Bow Street, a career spanning 46 years. He died in post.

Sayer is first mentioned in the financial accounts at Bow Street when he claimed expenses in October 1795; however, by July 1796 he is shown as one of the six Bow Street Principal Officers. By 1797 he was required to perform the duty of taking reports from victims of crime, and so he added Office Keeper to his title.[440] For this additional function he received an extra £8 15s 0d a quarter.[441] The positions of Office Keeper and, later for Sayer, Office Messenger attracted the same extra pay as he would need to run errands, serve warrants and post letters etc.

Sayer was involved in arresting a number of people for seditious and treasonable activities in over 1798 and 1799, a job he performed with the other officers from Bow Street most vigorously.

In 1796 Sayer had been posted to the Royal Retinue in attendance

---

438 PROB 11/1931 Prerogative Court of Canterbury and related probate jurisdictions: Will Registers 1354–1858 image 358/317.

439 Cox, D. (2010) *A Certain Share of Low Cunning: A History of the Bow Street Runners, 1792–1839.* Willan, Cullumpton, p. 49.

440 28th Report GA123.

441 The report from the Committee on the state of the police for the metropolis (1818), p. 189.

of the King, where he saw service at St. James's Palace and Kew.[442] George III had been attacked by a mad woman called Margaret Nicholson in 1786 and a number of people had been able to obtain entry to royal palaces without authority while the royal family were in residence. From this time, the King's security was attended to by the Bow Street officers and Sayer was included in protection duties when foreign royals and crowned heads came to the United Kingdom on official visits. The Emperor of Russia and the King of Prussia visited in 1814 and the Treasury paid £800 for the services of the Bow Street officers who accompanied them on events in London, Oxford and Portsmouth.[443] Sayer also performed bodyguard duty to George IV when he became King in 1820, and was still completing this duty in 1828.

In 1799 Sayer was sent to Gloucester Gaol to identify men who were held there on suspicion of committing offences in London, no doubt brought about by information from the registers and published in the Bow Street publication *Hue and Cry*.[444] On knowing two of them he brought back a man he knew as "Galloping Dick" and Thomas Clark, an accomplice of a man named Haines who had been hung a week before for shooting at two Bow Street officers. In fact, later in 1799 Clark was also convicted of this crime and sentenced to death (see full account on pages 308-310).[445]

Officers at Bow Street were able to make a comfortable living out of the fees they charged for their services, the rewards they received from victims for identifying suspects and the remuneration from the state for successful convictions of up to £40. On the face of it Sayer was an honest Principal Officer at Bow Street, but in later life he appears to have been tempted into corruption.

Combating forgers on behalf of the Bank of England was another lucrative duty that Sayer performed vigorously. He received remuneration for performing these duties of up to £200 per year

442 Beattie, J. (2012) *The First English Detectives.* Oxford University Press, Oxford, p. 193.
443 TNA. HO36/17, 419.
444 *The Times*, 4th March 1799.
445 *The Times*, 14th January 1799.

for his attendance at the Bank for ten days a quarter when the dividends were being paid. In 1811, with the permission of the Bank Sayer negotiated between a daring burglar, James MacKoull, and the Paisley Bank in Glasgow for the restitution of about £20,000 stolen from the Bank, on condition that proceedings should be dropped. Little more than half that sum was recovered, but shortly after Sayer's death in 1832 some notes, recognised as part of the Paisley Bank plunder, were found in the possession of his relatives.[446] Sayer lived in his house with the wife of the Paisley Bank burglar who died in 1820, and the presence of some of the proceeds has not been satisfactorily explained. Fitzgerald suggested that whilst Sayer may have known of the money's existence, he chose not to do anything about it in order to protect his lover's integrity.[447] This was a stain on the character of Sayer, especially since on the surface he appeared to be an honest and truthful police officer.

In 1814/15 he was recorded as in receipt of a guinea a week expenses (total of £54 12s 0d a year), £200 per year for his duties at the Bank of England and a further £200 for his attendance on Their Majesties the King and Queen, including the Prince Regent when attending events out of town in Brighton and Windsor.[448] As part of these duties Sayer was expected to be present during investitures, which would be reported in the newspapers. *The Morning Post* wrote of one such event in 1803:

"Townsend, Macmanus and Sawyer (sic) assisted by the whole of the Bow Street Patrole attended the investiture at Westminster Abbey of the installation of the Knights of the Bath."[449]

The Principal Officers were directed by the Bow Street magistrates to guarantee the safety of the King and his family during such events. Between 1803 and 1817 Sayer had submitted receipts for expenses

446 Griffith, Op. cit. supra note 143, at 242.
447 Cox, D. (2010) A *Certain Share of Low Cunning: A History of the Bow Street Runners, 1792–1839*. Willan, Cullumpton, p. 53.
448 Select Committee report into the Police of the Metropolis (1816) p510 Vol. V.
449 *Morning Post* 20th May 1803.

Fig. 24: Margaret Nicholson attacks the King in 1786

to Bow Street for work done for the magistrates or the Home Department. In 16 yearly quarters he received monies totalling £707, averaging £44 per quarter (or £176 per year just for expenses at Bow Street), the second highest total, only being excelled by John Townsend himself, who received nearly double Sayer's expenses.[450]

Sayer was earning over £500 a year for his duties, excluding his rewards from the State and private arrangements, a not

450   Beattie, J. (2012) *The First English Detectives*. Oxford University Press, Oxford, p. 204.

inconsequential sum of money at the time. Together with other members of the Royal Retinue he was also able to earn even more remuneration by accompanying lesser royals and nobles. Like the other Bow Street officers, Sayer was also called away to deal with private inquiries, for which he received additional financial recompense on an agreed scale.

By this time Sayer was well known in policing circles and had 30 years' continued service. He was a trusted and experienced officer, who was at times required to testify before Government Select Committees inquiring into the state of the police of the metropolis. He was confident and self–assured. Sayer gave evidence before the 1816 Select Committee in an over-confident and arrogant manner, and the Committee later commented that "they were not best pleased with his cocksure attitude and vanity". He was asked about the £40 parliamentary rewards and stated he felt the system often meant the officers could be out of pocket when expenses had been taken into consideration. He explained that there was a need to pay informants or people to obtain information, which they did up front out of their own pockets. His view was that these monies, once paid out to informants, were worthwhile since the information often led to an arrest where a reward, compensation or other expense was paid. Sayer ensured that his informants were not left out of pocket.

By 1827 Sayer was in his mid 60s and was not as active as he had been. His role by this time was shown as a Messenger at Bow Street, meaning that even though he was still a Principal Officer of the court, earning £1 1s 0d a week, he was no longer really involving himself in active investigations but earning a remuneration for office work, bank and royal duty.

He was a Bow Street officer for 28 to 30 years, having spent also some time at Litchfield Street Public Office then as a turnkey to Tothill Fields, Bridewell.

John Sayer died at his home on 10th September 1832 aged 69 years, still listed as an officer at Bow Street. His Will, written the day before he died, revealed that he was indeed a very rich man. He left many thousands of pounds to individual friends and beneficiaries, including several properties in Bridge Row.[451] He was buried in St. George's Hanover Square a few days later.[452]

George Donaldson (1795–1820)

Donaldson was a very active police Constable and his industry came to the attention of Bow Street. He first appears in December 1795 as a parish Constable of St. Martin-in-the-Fields, when he was involved in a case of grand larceny concerning Susannah King, Elizabeth Crompton and Henry Jones. A quantity of clothing and other items were stolen and later found at King's address in Monmouth Street. Later more stolen property was found by Donaldson at a pawnbroker's shop in Drury Lane. King and Compton were found guilty and sentenced to seven years' transportation each.[453]

Donaldson became particularly knowledgeable about pickpockets who operated in the vicinity of the Drury Lane and Covent Garden theatres. He was able to help identify them and prevent crimes taking place. When leaving the theatre he would mingle with the crowds calling out "mind your pockets".[454]

George Donaldson appears in the accounts for Bow Street in April 1803 and 1804.[455] He died at the The Brown Bear in Bow Street, next to the court. He was involved in no less than 67 cases at the Old Bailey, serving 25 years as a Constable and with it gaining an honourable and honest reputation.[456]

Henry Goddard (1800–1883)

The only officer of Bow Street to have written a biography of his

451 Cox, D. (2010) *A Certain Share of Low Cunning: A History of the Bow Street Runners, 1792–1839*. Willan, Cullumpton, p. 49.
452 National Archives.
453 Old Bailey Proceedings Online (www.oldbaileyonline.org, version 7.2, 07 June 2016), January 1796, trial of Susannah King, Elizabeth Crompton and Henry Jones (t17960113-71).
454 Babington, A., (1969) *A House in Bow Street*. MacDonald and Co. London, p. 189.
455 Fielding's Accounts T38.672.
456 Old Bailey Proceedings Online (www.oldbaileyonline.org, version 7.2, 07 June 2016), 1795–1820.

later life and to have had these diaries published. Goddard was born in 1800 and christened the following year in the parish of Christchurch in Surrey, the son of Joseph and Catharine Goddard. He died in 1883 having spent a lifetime investigating and detecting crime. Goddard earned a reputation as being a conscientious and efficient officer. In April 1824 he was appointed to the Bow Street Foot Patrole after being recommended by the Earl of Stradbroke and Lord Eastnor. Goddard had previously been a fishmonger by trade. He was described as five feet nine inches tall and well made. He was posted to party no. 12, where Luke Nixon was the Conductor. Goddard lived at 180 Drury Lane in the next street from Bow Street, and his foot patrol stretched from the end of Downing Street along to Vauxhall and Pimlico.[457]

Within a year, and probably due to his intuitive nature, Goddard had obtained a position as an officer covering aspects of security at the Drury Lane Theatre, replacing another Bow Street officer who had died.[458] This was a very fortunate appointment for Goddard, because such positions were reserved for Principal Officers and were paid a guinea a night, the equivalent of a week's patrol work. The other door keeper was a senior officer, a member of the Day Patrole called William Nettleton, who did not take kindly to Goddard at first. A group of pickpockets stole a watch from a gentleman and ran off to cries of "Stop! Thief!" Goddard, on vacating his position in the theatre and coming late to the cries, had instinctively taken a linkman and lantern with him and followed the trail taken by the fleeing pickpockets as they left the theatre in the dark.[459] One lesson that Goddard had learnt was that pickpockets discard incriminating evidence very quickly, fearing arrest if any is found in their possession. Goddard found the watch on some cabbage leaves a short distance away and later returned it to its grateful

457 Goddard, H. (1956) *Memoirs of a Bow Street Runner.* Museum Press Ltd., London, p. xxii (Introduction by Patrick Pringle).
458 Goddard, H. (1956) *Memoirs of a Bow Street Runner.* Museum Press Ltd., London, p. xxii (Introduction by Patrick Pringle).
459 A linkman possessed a lantern and escorted people for a fee through ill lit streets to prevent robbery.

owner. Once Goddard had gone back to the theatre to resume his position Nettleton ridiculed him for leaving his post at a time when the theatre production was ending; however, he soon looked on dumbstruck as Goddard produced the stolen property to him.[460] This sort of intuitive and instinctive style (part of the blueprint of policing) helped Goddard develop a most honourable and worthy reputation.

Within a short time he was transferred from the Night Foot Patrole to the first division of the Day Patrole, considered to be a promotion. There were three divisions of the Day Patrole, who still wore the same uniform of the Foot Patrole and also possessed the same weapons. For this he received 3s 6d per day and worked from 9.00am until darkness, which were longer hours.

By the end of 1826 Goddard resigned from the Day Patrole after successfully becoming one of the Principal Officers at Great Marlborough Street Magistrates' Court under the Chief Magistrate there Frederick Roe, a man he admired and respected. He stayed there until January 1834 when he transferred back to Bow Street where Frederick Roe had also moved, to become Chief Magistrate. At Marlborough Street in 1827 were Benjamin Schofield, George Avis, Clements and Goddard.[461] Sam Plank was the Chief Officer. Goddard remained there until the Bow Street Principal Officers were disbanded in 1839.

Almost immediately he was selected to become the Chief Constable of Northampton on a salary of £250 per year, a position he occupied until he resigned in January 1849.[462] He had been granted a gratuity of £150 in compensation for an injury he received whilst on duty. He returned to London and took up detective work, often being employed by the Forrester brothers who ran a detective agency located in the Mansion House building in the City of London.

460 Goddard, H. (1956) *Memoirs of a Bow Street Runner.* Museum Press Ltd., London, p. 34.
461 Goddard, H. (1956) *Memoirs of a Bow Street Runner.* Museum Press Ltd., London, p. 40.
462 Ibid, p. 33.

The famous Forrester brothers received much work from the City of London Corporation. John Forrester commenced from 1817, and Daniel from 1821. They operated outside the City of London police, the latter being formed in 1839. Goddard received work from the Forresters from as early as 1839, and was still accepting investigations into the mid-1860s.[463]

In 1825 he had married for the first time, to Hannah Davies at St-Martin-in-the-Fields. In 1835 Goddard solved a London murder by observing ballistics relating to the characteristics of bullets. He examined the moulds used and noticed marks on the bullets which he was able to prove connected them to the murderer.

In 1841, when he was Chief Constable of Northampton, he was aged 41 years and described as a bachelor living in Marchmeal Street, Marylebone. At the time of the 1851 census ten years later Goddard was residing as a visitor in a hostel outside of London in Sherwood, Nottingham most probably on an inquiry. In July 1858, by now a mature man aged 58 years, Goddard became betrothed to Rose Prior in St. Dunstan's and All Saints, Stepney. She came from Billericay in Essex and was 20 years his junior.[464]

In the 1861 and 1871 censuses he is shown living with Rose at 42 Maitland Park Road, Haverstock Hill, Kentish Town, and was listed as one of three door keepers at the House of Lords.[465] When he retired through failing health the House of Lords recognised Goddard's contribution as door keeper and not only reinstated his Bow Street pension of £100 per year which he was awarded in 1839 when Bow Street Principal Officers were retired, but also added a further £165 per annum.[466]

Although Henry Goddard did not live long enough to attain much benefit from these awards, when he died he had an estate of £1,067

463 Kesselman, B. (2015) *Paddington Pollakey, Private Detective. The Mysterious Life and Times of the Real Sherlock Holmes.* The History Press, London.
464 TNA.
465 Ibid.
466 Goddard, H. (1956) *Memoirs of a Bow Street Runner.* Museum Press Ltd., London, p. xxviii.

19s 8d.[467]

Peter Thomas Schonfield (also Schofield, Shanfield, Shanfeld, Schonfeld) (1809–1894)

Peter Schonfield was born on 12th September 1809, the second of three sons to Thomas and Hannah Schonfield of Dover in Kent. Not much is known about his early life, but he married Ann Beach in Southwark on 1st July 1830 when he was 21-years-old. Peter and Ann had eight children in 22 years. At about the same time Schonfield became a Bow Street Principal Officer to fill the vacancies left by the passing of Townsend and Sayer, and the retirement of Vickery. Ruthven was still at Bow Street and was disbanded with the rest in 1839.

In 1841 Schonfield lived in High Street South in Croydon, his employment was shown as "private police", although the Bow Street Runners had ceased to exist in 1839 so like Goddard he probably took on his own detective work. Within the next few years he set himself up as a tailor, employing three persons operating from 44 High Street, Croydon.[468]

Wife Ann died in 1861, and he married Mary Ann Howie in 1874. In 1878 he was still operating as a tailor from 6 Denman Road, Croydon.[469]

He was reputedly the last surviving Bow Street officer, dying in 1894 in Croydon. His last known address was the Croydon Almshouses, where he lived with his 77-year-old wife. Very little more is known about Schonfield or his police career, as his records at Bow Street appear to have not survived.

Schonfield probably joined Bow Street at the same time the Metropolitan Police were being introduced in 1829, when the reputation of the Bow Street Principal Officers was being denigrated.

467 mv.ancestry.co.uk/viewer/37f7ba2e–aae4–4617–9f03–8f3b097e84af/50500753/ 26655814856 accessed on 25th December 2016.
468 *Post Office Directory 1851.*
469 *Post Office Directory 1878.*

Indications were surfacing that the Runners were more corrupted - and corruptible - than was first thought. The magistrates at Bow Street still needed court officers to carry out their enquiries, and Schonfield was about 20-years-old by then. There is no record that he ever was involved in matters or gave evidence on criminal cases at the Old Bailey. It cannot be proved one way or the other whether Peter Schonfield was the actual last officer or not. The Police Act 1839 rendered the Bow Street Runners obsolete, and they were disbanded in receipt of a pension.[470]

470 Beattie, J. M. (2012) *The First English Detectives. The Bow Street Runners and the Policing of London, 1750–1840*. Oxford University Press, p. 257–58.

4

Bow Street Horse Patrole

This chapter reflects on the nature of serious crimes particularly highway robbery, which proliferated on the thoroughfares of London in mid to late-Georgian Britain, and what the police mounted response was to it. These were revolutionising times, with innovations in road design, faster modes of transport and improved business opportunities that also meant increased numbers of robbers and footpads who preyed on an unsuspecting travelling public.

The Fieldings at Bow Street had been watching these important changes and developments. John Fielding particularly wanted to ensure the safety of the travelling public on London's chaotic roads not only from a crime perspective, but also from a traffic point of view. Robbery with violence committed by highwaymen and footpads particularly alarmed him, but traffic fatalities and injuries from the wanton and furious driving of carriages was also of great concern. These concerns became an integral part of his plan in 1763 which led to the establishment of a Police Mounted Horse Patrole. His idea had originally fallen on deaf ears, but the disturbing increase in violence to "people of fashion" caused the Government to rethink its position, quickly authorising Fielding's request. What followed helped lay the foundations of the Metropolitan Police Mounted Branch.

The ability to respond immediately to a reported crime and to quickly apprehend the suspect has been a lesson not lost on our law enforcers down the ages. Speed was (and still is) essential in crime detection, and a horse with a trained rider was the answer for the Fieldings. The Bow Street officers were not restricted to London and its environs, unlike the parish Constables and watchmen. They could travel virtually anywhere when application was made to Bow Street. John Fielding's oft-quoted call "Quick notice – sudden pursuit" to anywhere in the country was no idle threat. Between 1755 and 1759 Fielding's People were called to various parts of the country including Windsor, Maidstone, Bristol, Barnet, Faversham, Newark, Maidenhead, Henley, Guildford, Tunbridge Wells and Oswestry.[471]

From the start of Henry Fielding's tenure horses were available for immediate pursuit at a moment's notice, and were either hired locally or kept at Bow Street itself. These horses and pursuers were not used for preventive measures, but retained as a reactive method to respond immediately before any felon was able to completely disappear and follow the trail to apprehend him before it got cold.

Early signs of horsemen being used at Bow Street can be found in the records, but these were drawn from Fielding's People or his honest Thief takers. From Christmas 1756 four pursuers, all Peace Officers, were retained for 12 months at Bow Street at a cost of £40, whilst the hiring and maintenance of appropriate horses also came to £40.[472]

During 1757 the roads around London were being plagued again by highway robbers, footpads and mail robberies and panic stirred in the ever-fearful middle and upper classes at the time. However, John Fielding was short of money to finance a roving patrole, but forever the entrepreneur he realised he needed to become more flexible and allow his trusty officers to be hired out privately. He had previously come to an arrangement for protecting theatres in and around Covent Garden, and so he encouraged businesses to hire his Bow Street mounted officers further afield, helping to defray some the costs out of court proceeds.

One of these first Horse Patroles was established in 1756, when two mounted men patrolled the roads to Ranelagh Pleasure Gardens in Chelsea during the season. The organisers paid 17 guineas for

471 John Fielding's accounts – PRO Treasury Papers T38/671.
472 Ibid.

the privilege, whilst the balance of £9 16s 10d was paid by John Fielding.[473] Fielding also sent the horsemen to protect theatre goers in May 1756 by patrolling the New Road in the evenings between Sadlers Wells, Clerkenwell and Grosvenor Square, Westminster. To ensure the success of the Patrole he encouraged the organisers to prepare reassuring protection advice in their theatre programmes, stating that "security was assured and that ladies were asked to arrive early and for their safety as an armed Horse Patrole would cover the roads" [474]

Immediate response was paying dividends, when for example in November 1757 on the instructions of the Justice Fielding, William Parsons and another officer from Bow Street were despatched on horseback in immediate pursuit of a highway robber to Dunstable. Thomas Manners, a clerk, and his lady friend had been robbed at gunpoint by William Green and his brother. The description of the suspects given, the speed of their pursuit led to the swift capture of one of the Green brothers in a small village beyond Dunstable, resulting in the perpetrator facing justice back at Bow Street. The prisoner was later tried at the Old Bailey, found guilty and sentenced to be executed.[475]

Bow Street were also beginning to take on a national policing role, given that crime and criminality fails to respect social, spatial, geographical or parish boundaries. They travelled into the environs of London and surrounding counties in order to capture felons who thought themselves beyond the reach of the law enforcers. They soon had a shock, but the few Bow Street officers who were available could only ever be a reactive force, catching up with felons once a crime had been committed. John Fielding realised there was a crying need for a regular preventive establishment. A dedicated

473 Pringle, P., (1955) *Hue and Cry – The Story of Henry and John Fielding and their Bow Street Runners.* Morrow and Co., London, p. 116.

474 Leslie–Melville, R. (1934) *The Life and Work of Sir John Fielding.* Lincoln Williams Ltd., London, p. 80.

475 Old Bailey Proceedings Online (www.oldbaileyonline.org, version 7.2, 21st January 2017) 7th December 1757, trial of William Green, Violent Theft – highway robbery. (t17571207–8).

routine uniformed mounted police was still some way off, however. Until then, only a fraction of crimes committed on the highways could be resolved in this way.

The 1763 Horse Patrole Experiment

John Fielding alerted the Government to the rise of highway robberies in 1763, when he wrote to a sympathetic Grenville. Fielding suggested that "It can only be stopped by a mounted patrol on the roads into the metropolis."[476] Grenville called John Fielding and Saunders Welch to a meeting, with their clerk Joshua Brogden taking notes. They discussed a plan which could deal with the problem, and by October 1763 John Fielding had secured a promise from the Government of £600 which would allow him to introduce a Horse Patrole for a six-month experimental period.[477] This is not to be confused with the £400 granted to Bow Street per annum to run the Public Office or for the £400 stipend to John Fielding himself; this was additional monies.[478]

Not until this time was there an organised, routine roving Horse Patrole on the roads of the Metropolis. The expenses were charged back to the Treasury, but the Government were often extremely lax in ensuring reimbursement to John Fielding, as he had found out all too often. This was probably because of mounting Government debts due to prosecuting wars in Europe and America. Fielding wrote to Grenville repeatedly, requesting immediate payment as the Bow Street accounts could not sustain subsidising the Government plan for long. A horse and rider were an expensive commodity, and seemingly beyond the limited financial resources available to Fielding, with each man and his horse costing £75 for the season 1st October to 31st May 1764.[479]

476 Pringle, P., (1955) *Hue and Cry – The Story of Henry and John Fielding and their Bow Street Runners.* Morrow and Co., London, p. 117.
477 The Bow Street Horse patrol was originally spelt differently with an additional (E) inserted at the end of Patrol and we had maintained the original spelling throughout.
478 Leslie–Melville, R. (1934) *The Life and Work of Sir John Fielding.* Lincoln Williams Ltd., London, p. 153.
479 Leslie–Melville, R. (1934) *The Life and Work of Sir John Fielding.* Lincoln Williams Ltd., London, p. 151.

The Bow Street Horse Patrole originally consisted of eight men (later augmented to ten) covering the principal roads; however, there was no flexibility nor backup or reserve in case of sickness and injury, hence the increase in numbers. Contrary to some suggestions, these were non-uniformed men and it was only the later 1805 Patrole who on occasions wore a distinctive red waistcoated dress. Otherwise they were to patrol during the hours of darkness for 4s a night each, notwithstanding incurred expenses.[480] Fielding was said to have recruited "Peace Officers... and which happened to just come in" as the press recorded them; however, their role was initially limited to the policing of highway robbery and later traffic matters.[481] The regular Horse Patrole would soon cause considerable disruption to the highway robbery on London's roads.

This initial Horse Patroles, known as Fielding's People, were unofficial; however, they were well armed, for all the weapons they carried between them cost Bow Street £23.[482] The horses were supplied by Mr Barber at The George in Long Acre, and he was paid 4s a night for each horse. A supervisor was also occasionally employed to ride around to ensure the Patroles were on duty.[483] The men selected, those whom Fielding knew well and trusted, included three parish Constables, two former Constables, a publican, an ex–soldier and a coachman. Some of these were William Pentlow, son of the keeper of the New Prison (a former soldier, late of Hales Light Horse), a Mr Partridge, Thomas Adams, William Smith, Richard Higgins, William Wright, John Fordsam, William Langrid and Richard Fuller.[484]

This preventative response soon curtailed the outbreak of highway robberies, but the mounted officers became involved in traffic

480 Ascoli, D. (1979) *The Queen's Peace*. Hamish Hamilton, London, p. 42–43.
481 *Derby Mercury*, 24th February 1764.
482 Leslie–Melville, R. (1934) *The Life and Work of Sir John Fielding*. Lincoln Williams Ltd., London, p. 153.
483 Ibid.
484 Leslie–Melville, R. (1934) *The Life and Work of Sir John Fielding*. Lincoln Williams Ltd., London, p. 153, and Pringle, P. (1955) *Hue and Cry – The Story of Henry and John Fielding and their Bow Street Runners*. William Morrow and Co., London, p. 165.

matters when John Fielding later expanded their role to regulate the furious driving of carriages and the particularly dangerous way carmen rode their carts. They patrolled the main arterial roads leading into and around London, which was their primary role, but they did not have enough officers to cover them all so one road was left unpatrolled each day. The Patrole were under strict instructions not to reveal to anyone which road remained uncovered, although additional men were later recruited to fill this gap. This was an onerous duty, and Fielding soon realised this. Experience was telling him that the daily grind of patrolling was arduous, not only for the rider but also the horse too. Their duty took place late in the day until midnight seven days a week, with no day off. Fielding wrote to Grenville expressing these concerns:

> "The labour of the Horse Patrole is so severe and hazardous that I am rather surprised than otherwise that I have such proper persons to undertake it for constancy."[485]

John Fielding realised the benefit of newspapers in helping to reduce the fear of crime. He frequently sent out reassuring messages to the public, using advertising space in the local newspapers informing the travelling public of his new Horse Patrole initiative. He also used the tollgate keepers as an important lynchpin, encouraging the public to report anything suspicious or important to them as they passed. He instructed his men to speak with the tollgate keepers, travellers and local residents and exchange useful information. Fielding gave the turnpike toll clerks a horn on which to quickly alert or summon the Patrole, and he even successfully negotiated with the turnpike trusts (with the exception of the Hyde Park Turnpike) for free access through the toll gates for his officers.[486] Toll gate keepers who came to Bow Street to alert the

---

485 Copy of a letter taken by Mr J. Paul de Castro in 1913 from the original in the possession of the late A. M. Broadley and reprinted in Leslie–Melville, R. (1934) *The Life and Work of Sir John Fielding*. Lincoln Williams Ltd., London, p. 154.

486 Rubenstein, J. (1977) *Henry and John Fielding – Police Philosophy and Police Technique in Pioneers in Policing*. Philip Stead (Ed) McGraw-Hill, London, p. 42.

Central Office of a felony or provide information and intelligence were also rewarded with expenses for their trouble, usually 1s.

The Road Network, Turnpike Trusts and Toll Keepers

Understanding the spatial and geographic dimension relating to the access and egress to London's road network was a key skill for the Horse Patrole. Of importance were the types of road, the varying travelling methods and the mechanisms for organising, repairing and managing the road network on which the travelling public journeyed. Here, both the Fieldings recognised the significant commercial importance of the turnpike system and road networks well, following their collation of information on travel at the Universal Registry Office; however, an ever-expanding road network brought its own problems.

The turnpike system created pinch points where people paid monies for access and where people came together, and for the Fieldings this meant that suspect behaviour could be observed or reported. Turnpike Trusts were responsible for the commercial privatisation of the road network, which allowed them to make huge profits but they were reluctant to involve themselves officially with the Fielding brothers. John Fielding had provided an incentive for individual tollgate keepers to help as informers, but also wished the co-operation of the Turnpike Trusts in the metropolis; however the local gentlemen, clergy and merchants who acted as Trustees felt such measures would incur unnecessary costs and as such defray their profits. The Trusts were not interested in defraying crime, just making money.

The proposal to turnpike a particular section of road was normally a local initiative but required an Act of Parliament, and once in place gave the Trustees responsibility for maintaining a specified part of the existing highway. These Trusts were allowed to take charges from travellers, whether on foot, horse or in a carriage, on main roads in Britain which were maintained by them. Initially Trusts were established for limited periods, often twenty one years,[487] although the time limits varied and were relaxed, resulting in some Trusts being responsible for roads up until the 1870s.[488]

By 1770 there were over 1,100 Trusts, administering 23,000 miles of road, with 7,800 toll gates.[489] At their peak, in the 1830s, over 1,000 Trusts administered around 30,000 miles of turnpike road in England and Wales.[490] This involved taking tolls at almost 8,000 tollgates and side-bars.[491] In effect the traveller did not need to journey far before they would encounter a tollgate, although a ticket covering all a Trust's gates could be purchased. Unsurprisingly, these improved roads increased the number of travellers but the tollgates reduced the speed at which they could travel.

The Trustees derived indirect benefits from the better transport, which improved access to markets and led to increases in rental income and trade.[492] The Trusts could demand statute labour or a cash equivalent, and appointed surveyors and collectors. In return they repaired the road and put up mileposts. They placed a barrier across a road and took a toll payment 24 hours a day, seven days a week, from each road user, except some pedestrians; the monies were then used in theory to support the maintenance and improvement of the road. The Trusts erected tollhouses that accommodated the pikeman or toll-collector beside the turnpike gate, and over and above running costs it left substantial profits on their operations over a year.[493]

---

487 *Tollgates London* (1801) by J. Cary – Old London Maps at www.oldlondonmaps. com/viewspages/0462.html. Licensed under Public Domain via Commons – commons.wikimedia.org/wiki/File:Tollgates_London_1801.jpg#/media/File: Tollgates_London_1801.jpg accessed on 30th January 2016.
488 www.turnpikes.org.uk/The%20Turnpike%20Roads.htm accessed on 30th January 2016.
489 www.aim25.ac.uk/cgi-bin/vcdf/detail?coll_id=12951&inst_id=118 accessed 27th January 2016.
490 Parliamentary Papers, 1840, Vol 280 xxvii.
491 Searle, M. (1930), *Turnpikes and Toll Bars*, Limited Edition, Hutchinson & Co., p. 798.
492 Webb, S. and Webb, B. (1922). *English local Government: Statutory Authorities for Special Purpose.* London: Longmans, Green and Co., London.
493 Webb, S. and Webb, B. (1922). *English local Government: Statutory Authorities for Special Purpose.* London: Longmans, Green and Co., p. 159.

The Roads out of London

The turnpike system dated from 1663, when Parliament authorised the erection of toll bars or barriers along the Great North Road following a line through Islington up the Holloway Road, tracing the former Roman road named as Watling Street. There was also the Great Essex Road, for example, which stretched from London to Harwich and broadly followed a line from Mile End, Stratford, Ilford, Romford, Brentwood, Shenfield, Ingatestone and Margaretting joining what is now the A12 as far as Colchester. The road then followed the same route as the A137 and B1352 to Harwich. This road was originally run by several Trusts, but became the Middlesex and Essex Trust in 1722. It consisted of 32 miles of roads, with six main gates and four side gates that made £14,205 per year in toll fees. In 1836 each gate was making over £2,368 annually.

The original starting point in London was from The Standard in Cornhill, but later measurements were taken from Whitechapel Church on the eastern boundary of the City of London. As Middlesex encircled the north of the City, the first milestone in Essex along the route was placed at Stratford.[494] In 1806 John Charrington became responsible for the Whitechapel Turnpike Trust, whose job it was to maintain the Great Essex Road from Stones End, literally where the paving stones finishes at Whitechapel Church, to Shenfield.[495] The Essex Second District Turnpike Trust, formed in 1695, consisted of 16 miles between Shenfield and Harwich. It had two gates and made much less than its Shenfield to London equivalent – some £296 per year.[496]

The Fieldings recognised how the road network was improving as the Trusts developed new sections of road to avoid obstructions and ease steep inclines and slopes. Existing roadbeds were replaced with carefully graded stones to create a dry, fast-running surface

---

494 www.aim25.ac.uk/cgi–bin/vcdf/detail?coll_id=12951&inst_id=118 accessed 27th January 2016.

495 Ibid.

496 www.turnpikes.org.uk/The%20Turnpike%20Roads.htm accessed on 30th January 2016.

(known today as Macadamising). Coach and carriage design also improved, which not only made the journey more comfortable but also shortened travelling times along these arterial roads. In 1843 the London to Exeter mail coach could complete the 170 mile journey in just 17 hours.[497] These improvements meant also that business would benefit, since animal produce and products could be transported greater distances much faster, opening up markets in London and elsewhere previously unrealisable. Further business opportunities to the benefit of rural merchants, towns and trades folk were also created. However, as the Fieldings had predicted, with the rise in commercial and passenger transport came the highway robbers, footpads and thieves. Even when Richard Mayne was giving evidence before the Select Committee on Turnpike and Tolls in 1836 he agreed, as the Fieldings had discovered over 60 years before, that:

"Constant and speedy communications is the foundation of police operation both for the prevention of crime but the apprehension of the offender."[498]

Leaving London, on the Great Bath Road a turnpike was created at Hyde Park Corner and in 1717 this road went all the way to Cranford Bridge through Kensington, Hammersmith, Turnham Green, Brentford, Hounslow and Harlington Corner. Hounslow was a busy staging post and the inns were capable of housing up to 2,000 horses,[499] so there was a great deal of activity. During the 1750s, when the 150 Trusts were formed, it also became their responsibility to erect milestones.

One of the busiest routes in and out of London was through the Tyburn Turnpike. Lewis Levi, a rich stockbroker, purchased the lease on the turnpike for £12,000 - a very large sum in those times, but a particularly wise investment.

At that time, tolls at Tyburn Gate were as follows: a carriage

497 en.wikipedia.org/wiki/Turnpike_trusts accessed 27th January 2016.
498 (16/5/1836 para 753).
499 Buchanan, B (1992) *The Great Bath Road 1700–1830*. Bath History Vol. 4. Millsteam.

drawn by one or two horses paid 10d, horsemen 4d and drovers 5d for 20 oxen and 2d for 20 pigs.[500] This gate alone made very high profits indeed, as it was one of the most important gateways into the metropolis. The Tyburn to Uxbridge Turnpike was formed in 1715, following the route of the current A40 to Oxford. This Turnpike Trust was responsible for mending the road from Brent Bridge over Hanwell Heath, through Hanwell, New Brentford, and Ealing to the Great Western Road, and for lighting, watching and watering the highway between Tyburn, Bayswater, and Kensington Gravel Pits to Kensington, Shepherds Bush, Acton, Ealing Common and Hanwell.[501] Coach travel along these roads was uncomfortable and awkward. This particular road attracted the heaviest wagons, sometimes drawing twelve horses, wrote John Middleton in 1798 which drew disapproval for its depth of mud, sometimes up to eight inches deep and the width of passable track being only six feet wide in winter.[502]

The mail coaches travelled the toll roads free of charge, so the post horn call was sounded to alert tollgate keepers to immediately open the gate under the pain of a 40 shilling fine should they fail to do so. Members of the royal family, soldiers in uniform, parsons on parish duties, funeral processions and prison carts were also exempt from tolls, as were pedestrians.[503]

There were a number of other very busy tollgates out of the metropolis. For example, the Elephant and Castle Tollgate was situated in the south bank area between Southwark and Lambeth and stood just 542 yards southwest of the Southwark Tollgate, and across from the tavern and coaching terminus of the same name. The Elephant and Castle tavern, the famous coaching terminus of routes from southern England which was founded in 1760, stood

---

500 www.georgianindex.net/ldn_tollgates/Toll_gate.html accessed on 27th January 2016.

501 www.aim25.ac.uk/cats/118/16628.htm accessed on 30th January 2016.

502 Robson, W. and Robson, W. (1993) *Britain – Access to History. 1750–1900.* OUP Oxford.

503 www.georgianindex.net/ldn_tollgates/Toll_gate.html accessed 27th January 2016.

Fig. 25: Entrance to Oxford Street looking east through the Tyburn turnpike, 1798

at the crossroads of the Kennington, Walworth, and Lambeth roads. The traffic at the crossroads was greatly increased in the mid-eighteenth century by the building of Blackfriars Bridge in 1769, the New Kent Road and the London Road. The area was notorious as a very confused traffic junction,[504] possibly because it needed proper regulation and control. Many bridges crossing the Thames were also turnpikes, including those at Vauxhall, Westminster, Southwark, Kew, Hampton Court. Located on the Great North Road was the busy Islington Tollgate, situated in Upper Street near the junction with what is now Liverpool Road. This was the last stopover for the farmers and drovers conveying livestock and goods to Smithfield market, hence the famous High Pavement situated on the northwest side which was constructed to allow pedestrians to proceed without being splashed by the passing carts and animals.[505]

504 www.georgianindex.net/ldn_tollgates/Toll_gate.html accessed 27th January 2016.
505 Ibid.

The Hyde Park Tollgate in the West End was also another busy point and was situated on the road to Bath leading from Westminster. Hyde Park was at the time essentially part of the open countryside pressing upon the western areas of the city. Other busy tollgates were located in the Mile End Road at Spitalfields on the road north–eastward out of London, and to the south of the Thames at Southwark, located on the London Road at the obelisk at St. George's. The Tottenham Court Road Turnpike on the Great Northwest of England Road was another very busy route in and out of London and it was at its busiest along Oxford Street, since this was yet another market route into town. This increasingly-complex road system was day-by-day getting busier and more dangerous, and the security of the travelling public became of paramount importance to Sir John Fielding. The opportunity for crime on the road was not the only concern, but also other actions of the travelling public with their often total disregard of other road users due to the wanton furious driving of carts, wagons and drays that injured and killed many other travellers. Fielding's concerns were expressed again in the *Public Advertiser* in November 1763:

> "Whereas persons of fashion and others are put in daily fear, and as many valuable lives of his majesty's subjects have been frequently lost, and our hospitals are daily crowded with miserable wretches under grievous afflictions of fractured sculls, broken limbs and fatal bruises; and these respective nuisances and misfortunes arise in a great measure from the wilful neglect or misbehaviour of the drivers of carts, cars and drays..." [506]

Fielding planned, organised and regulated his horsemen in an efficient manner, but as this was a new idea it was not without its problems. He tried to cover as wide an area as possible, stretching from inside the metropolis out into the suburbs and even some surrounding remote villages. The jurisdictions for the 1763 Horse Patroles were:

---

506 *The Public Advertiser*, 2nd November 1763.

"Pimlico to Chelsea and along the Kings Road to Fulham and through the turnpikes at Hyde Park to Hammersmith to Brentford, round Acton, Ealing, Tyburn, Paddington, Tottenham Court Road, Hendon, Highgate and through Holloway to Islington, Stamford Hill, Shoreditch, the new City Road, Whitechapel and on the Surrey side over Westminster Bridge to Greenwich, Clapham, Newington, Kennington lane and towards Wandsworth".[507]

In 1763 metropolitan London reached out to Park Lane in the west, the Angel Islington in the north, Whitechapel in the east and Kennington in the south.[508] The jurisdiction for the Horse Patrole covered the villages to Fulham from Pimlico, a distance of about four miles, while Hyde Park Turnpike to Ealing was about six miles. Hendon, Highgate, Holloway, Stamford Hill in the north, Acton and Ealing in the northwest and Clapham and Wandsworth to the south were distant places. The patrols were also few in number, given the task in hand and the distance to be covered each night, meaning that resources had been spread thinly. John Fielding soon realised that he needed to augment the eight officers to ten, and so he wrote again to Grenville securing an additional two Peace Officers for his Patrole. Fielding also soon appreciated the strain on these patrols, since this was a seven-days-a-week responsibility and there was no room for flexibility through absence caused by sickness, injury or fatigue. The Patrole's success would also soon reveal another abstraction from duty – obtaining and giving evidence in court.

The scheme became very successful and many highway robbers were apprehended, detained and tried for their crimes. Those robbers who had not been caught spirited themselves away, as the risks of detection outweighed any potential rewards. This meant that Patroles that had apprehended robbers would need to detain them in lockups or sometimes their own cellars or other secure locations before bringing them to Bow Street the next morning for inquisition before Sir John Fielding. Witnesses would also be

---

507 *The Public Advertiser*, 24th October 1763.
508 Leslie–Melville, R. (1934) *The Life and Work of Sir John Fielding*. Lincoln Williams Ltd., London, pp. 151–152.

Fig. 26: Barnes Common Toll House

instructed to attend Bow Street in order to give evidence. Such was the success of the scheme that soon the travelling public could use the main metropolitan roads in relative safety and without fear of attack.

Charles Jenkinson, the first Secretary to the Treasury, was constantly having to be reminded by Fielding to forward monies either for the Horse Patrole or the running of Bow Street itself, and so the 1763 experiment with the Horse Patrole for the moment came to an end, although Fielding still retained several horses and pursuers at Bow Street. Afterwards Fielding managed to supplement Patroles out of court funds, and where he could a foot and horse response was dispatched to where crimes had taking place. He wrote an angry letter to Jenkinson, stating that in that particular week there had been robberies in Finchley, Paddington, Ealing, Isleworth, Turnham Green, Kentish Town, Hounslow Heath and Islington, all within the eight-mile limit of the by then discontinued Horse Patrole.[509] Jenkinson had suggested that if the Horse Patrole was to be permanent there should be a "country charge", but this

509   Grenville papers, ii, pp.366–69, 385.

Fig. 27: Highgate Toll and Tavern, dated 1825

Fig. 28: Hounslow Toll Gate, dated 1864

was rejected by Fielding.[510] His angry letter was forwarded to Prime Minister George Grenville, and a further Patrole was authorised. The experiment was continued for a further six months before the grant was withdrawn, with no reason being given. The Horse Patrole had cost the Government a total of £1,014 18s 0d, amounting to £100 per horse and rider for twelve months.

Sir John Fielding lobbied Government vigorously for a continuation of the Horse Patrole to no avail. He became frustrated, considering that terminating this great success was very short-sighted on the part of the Government. Very quickly the metropolitan highways became dangerous places again, but not for another 41 years would a routine Horse Patrole be considered seriously again.

But for the moment this did not deter Fielding, as he reverted to his two mounted pursuers back at Bow Street to deal with reports of felonies being committed on the highways. One such incident happened in July 1767. Fielding had received speedy information from a coachman about robberies happening in the St. Pancras Way so, he despatched his private Patrole to apprehend the four footpads responsible. Within a short time Offer (aka Bradley), Boswell, Harford and Spires were arrested and brought to Bow Street.[511] The following year, in July 1768, Fielding sent his men out to Blackheath and Shooters Hill for a week in order to catch two footpads who were robbing travellers on the Dover Road. The Patrole engaged the footpads, who tried to rob the officers and an exchange of gunfire resulted in both being arrested and a robber having his ear partly shot away. They were taken before Sir John Fielding and committed to Newgate Prison.[512]

The 1805 Horse Patrole

By the early 1800s public concerns regarding the increase in highway robberies caused the Government to extend the scheme

---

510 Grenville papers, ii, pp.366–69, 385
511 *Derby Mercury*, Friday 3rd July 1767.
512 *Derby Mercury* Friday 15th July 1768.

that had been originally introduced by John Fielding in 1763, and in 1805 the Bow Street Horse Patrole was re-established by the Chief Magistrate, Sir Richard Ford.[513] The aim was to provide protection on all the main roads and thoroughfares within 20 miles of Charing Cross.[514] These areas included Hounslow, Blackheath and other unguarded commons. The plan was to establish the Horse Patroles, i.e. a few well-armed men patrolling lonely roads, meeting each other at fixed points. Originally it consisted of "thirteen parties…eight of 'country' and five of 'town', each with a Conductor."[515] The initial cost when the Patrole was revived was about £1,000, when eight men were employed at 4s a night and given a further 4s each for their horse. Some £23 was spent on arms, and an Inspector was appointed to ride around to ensure they were doing their duty.[516] Ford was seen in Government circles as a trusted ally in the suppression of radical societies, and was much favoured by Home Secretary the Duke of Portland, who was also a close personal friend. Portland had even provided Ford with his own office at the Home Department.[517]

Following the encouraging successes of the London Bow Street Horse Patrole, other towns in the United Kingdom considered implementing their own mounted patroles. These included Bath, Liverpool, Sudbury, Norwich (in 1813), Edinburgh, and Newcastle.[518] There was also a Horse Patrole in Dublin which appears to predate the London Patroles. As far back as 1802, the City of London had proposed a Blackfriars Bridge Horse Patrole and placed regular adverts for men to undertake the duty of patrolling the bridge from ten in the evening until four in the morning. The applicant was to

---

513 The 1822 Royal Commission was given incorrect evidence by Mr Day that the patrole had not commenced until 1809.

514 Fitzgerald, P. (1888) *Chronicles of Bow Street Police–office*. Gilbert and Rivington, London, p. 90.

515 Fenn Clark, E. (1935) *Truncheons*. Herbert Jenkins London.

516 Pringle, P. (1955) *Hue and Cry – The Story of Henry and John Fielding and their Bow Street Runners*. William Morrow and Co., London, p. 165.

517 www.lucienneboyce.com/assets/files/Bow–Street–Runners–Final.pdf accessed on 31st August 2015.

518 *Lancaster Gazette*, 3rd January 1807.

Fig. 29: Putney Bridge Toll House

supply his own horse.[519] Despite this, in 1817 the City of London rejected the idea of reforming the police via a Horse Patrole, sticking to what they believed was their own successful system of policing.[520] In policing terms, across London there were many different systems and some overlapped or worked against each other. Some worked better, such as the City of London, and others which were corrupt and inefficient. The point being that until Bow Street there was no really efficient and effective uniform system of crime reporting, detection or prevention in the parishes, and the Fielding brothers

519 *The Morning Chronicle*, 19th October 1802.
520 *Morning Post*, 3rd November 1817.

Fig. 30: The Toll Gate at Kennington

attempted with limited success to rectify the situation.

There has been a dispute as to what distances the Patrole operated along the thoroughfares and roads leading into the metropolis.[521] In 1805 the radius appeared to be 25 miles; however, in 1807 the radius the Patrole operated was 10 miles from the centre.[522] It should be noted that some other newspapers record distances of up to 19 miles.[523] The point here was that there was no uniform radius but rather some "roads and highways were patrolled up to 20/25 miles whilst others no more than 12 miles".[524]

On its re–introduction the Horse Patrole was significantly strengthened to more than 54 officers, two Conductors and 52 Patroles and they patrolled to a distance of 20 miles from Charing Cross, and later to 50 miles.[525]

Ford died rather prematurely in 1806; however, this resurrection

521 Howard. G. (1953) *Guardians of the Queen's Peace*. Odhams, London, p. 101.
522 *The Morning Post,* 8th October 1807.
523 *Staffordshire Advertiser*, 17th October 1807.
524 *Hampshire Chronicle*, 8th January 1805.
525 Howard. G. (1953) *Guardians of the Queen's Peace*. Odhams, London, p. 101.

Fig. 31: Kilburn Toll Gate

of an old idea proved its worth and went from strength to strength. Both the Bow Street Horse Patrole and later the Bow Street Dismounted Horse Patrole were set up and paid for by the Home Secretary and not from Bow Street Police Office funds, and this time there was no dispute about payment to keep it going. In 1806 Mr Read, the Principal Magistrate, was responsible for their day-to-day operation and organisation. The monies paid to him from the Government for this year was in the order of £3,596.[526] This was to be sustained, and by the following year had been reduced to £3,272.[527]

Unlike the experiment in 1763, the Horse Patrole officers were granted constabulary powers with the approval of the Government. This meant that as a sworn Constable their powers could be transferred into other jurisdictions including Essex, Kent, Middlesex and Surrey. Furthermore, even the grounds of Royal Palaces were included, since these were regular hideouts for criminals.[528]

526 *Bury and Norwich Post,* 14th October 1806.
527 *The Morning Chronicle,* 21st March 1807.
528 Howard. G. (1953) *Guardians of the Queen's Peace.* Odhams, London, p. 101.

When crimes in the metropolis increased, the outer Patroles were summoned into London to help combat the threat.

There were two Inspectors, four Deputy Inspectors and 54 Patrole Constables in 1805.[529] By the year 1822 this had increased to 72, whilst there were 100 Dismounted Horse Patrole.[530] The Patroles needed to cover the main roads into and out of London, of which the most important totalled eight in number. These were the Dover Road from London Bridge to Deptford and Dartford into Kent, the Portsmouth Road from Southwark Bridge through Wandsworth to Kingston and Esher into Surrey, the Bath Road from Hyde Park Corner to Kensington, Brentford, Hounslow to Staines and Windsor into Buckinghamshire, the St. Albans Road to Kilburn, Hendon, Edgware, Elstree, Radlett and St. Albans into Hertfordshire, the Great North Road from the City of London, Islington, Holloway, Highgate, Finchley Common, Whetstone, Chipping Barnet and Hatfield into Hertfordshire, from London Bridge to Hoxton, Haggerstone, Kingsland, Stoke Newington, Tottenham, Edmonton, Enfield onto Hoddesdon and Cambridge into Middlesex and Hertfordshire, and finally the routes into Essex were from Stratford, Woodford and Epping, the Great Essex Road from Stratford, Ilford, Romford and onto Brentwood. The routes can be viewed on the map at the front of the book.

Combatting highway robbery was not their only duty, since as a body of uniformed men they were put to other uses and their function was later adapted and modified to cope with social pressures at the time. The usefulness of horses became widely acknowledged, especially in public order situations and the Horse Patrole was at times sent into London to help quell disturbances or riots.[531] In this manner, the Government were acknowledging the value of the

---

529 Melville–Lee, W. L. (1901) *The History of Police in England*. Methuen and Co.
530 Report of the Committee of the State of the Police of the Metropolis (1822) House of Commons, p. 33.
531 The Horse Patrole was sent to deal with riots against the Corn Laws in March 1815. *Morning Post,* 15th March 1815.

Fig. 32: The Esher Toll House, dated 1870

Mounted Patroles.[532] The cost of the Horse Patrole kept on rising as numbers increased, and by the year 1815 it had risen to £6,695.[533] By 1816 it had jumped to £7,556, and the following year it had reached £7,740.[534] In 1822 notice was given for the improvement of the Bow Street Horse and Dismounted Horse Patroles, which now numbered 288 men.[535] One of the main problems for the Horse Patrole was finding suitable accommodation for a man and his family with an attached stable for the horse. Such houses were rare and advertisements were placed by the Conductor of the Patrole for suitable premises on the general roads into London.

Administration: Applications, Pay, Allowances and Superannuation

John Fielding applied pressure on the Government to give Constables better powers, a factor which he wanted to extend

---

532 *The Morning Post*, Saturday 7th December 1822.

533 *The Morning Post*, 29th April 1815.

534 *Report of the Committee of the State of the Police of the Metropolis* (1822) House of Commons, p. 284.

535 www.open.ac.uk/Arts/history–from–police–archives/Met6Kt/MetHistory/mhPolOffices.html accessed 25th May 2015.

also to watchmen. The Westminster Constables Act of 1756 introduced measures to allow his 80 Constables to operate beyond their parochial parish limits including the whole of the City of Westminster.[536] Saunders Welch, in collusion with Henry Fielding, produced a working guide for officers appointed as Constables an early police instruction manual (see Appendix 1). John Fielding, building on *The Office of Constable* by Welch also produced a set of simple practical instructions on the behaviour of his officers, and whilst some of these instructions originated from Henry Fielding as a result of his own experiences, one can see that many of these instructions would be familiar to police officers today. Clearly many of these practical experiences and general orders were adopted later by Robert Peel on the introduction of the Metropolitan Police in 1829.

Certainly in the case of the Foot Patrole, their records of 1824-1829 show that reputation was everything and that a recommendation by a notable member of society was a good start. Some conductors of the Horse and Foot Patrole even made recommendations as well, often putting forward their own sons for the job. Physique and stature were also important qualities, as it was necessary to have bearing in order to enforce the authority of the law. Mainly younger married men were chosen who also had a trade to fall back on in the event that no duties were available to them. In fact, as their duty was from the evening until midnight, outside those hours they could carry on their trade from home. In 1813 a member of a Patrole received 4s a night or 28s a week. They received expenses for shoeing of the horse and any turnpike fees that were incurred. Rewards were also paid to officers of the Horse Patrole who managed to get successful convictions at court, as it was for any other police officer.[537] The yearly expenditure for the Patrole was rising year on year, and

536 Pringle, P. (1955) *Hue and Cry –The Story of Henry and John Fielding and their Bow Street Runners.* William Morrow and Co., London, p. 165.
537 *Report of the Committee of the State of the Police of the Metropolis* (1816) House of Commons.

by 1814 had increased to £5,028.[538] From 1821 Home Secretary Lord Sidmouth ordered that there should be one Conductor, two Inspectors, four Orderly Inspectors and 72 Mounted Patroles.[539]

The Horse

There were strict instructions issued by Bow Street, through the Conductor, on the officers' responsibilities in how and where to keep the Horse Patrole Mount. The horse, which was supplied by the Chief Clerk together with forage, resided in a small stable usually at the back of the station. The Constable was not allowed, whilst on duty, to give his horse to another person or allow the horse to be out of his sight, to be stabled or for any other reason. If the Constable or the horse became ill or injured, Mr William Day, the Conductor, was to be immediately informed. If the horse became incapacitated the Constable was to proceed on foot in a dismounted capacity taking his pistols with him, but only covering half the distance usually covered whilst on horseback. Any failure on the part of the Patrole to rendezvous at the allotted time and place was to be communicated with Mr Day the following morning, and there was no excuse for not reporting this. The horse was not to be used for any other purpose other than his duty, nor was it to be kept feeding in any field without permission. Only in the case of illness was the horse to be entrusted with any other person.

The horse was to be looked after and not neglected. It was fed three times a day: at eight o'clock in the morning, one o'clock in the afternoon, and on his return to the stable after midnight. The horse was allowed a bushel and a half of oats, three bushels of chaff, a truss and half of hay and a truss of straw per week. At eight in the morning the Patrole was to remain with his horse for at least one hour to dress it and clean his appointments. From one o'clock in the afternoon the Patrole, now back at the station, was to remain with

538 In the accounts it fails to discriminate between the two arms of the patrole – the horse and the dismounted men but does not include the runners' salary etc.
539 Wilkinson, F. (2002) *Those Entrusted with Arms*. Greenhill, Pennsylvania, p. 145.

the horse for at least half an hour and on his return at night he was to ensure that the horse was clean and dry before leaving it in the stable for the night.

No Patrole was to be absent at any time for more than two miles from the place that he was stationed without permission, except when on duty, and he was also not to change his lodgings without giving notice of it to Mr Day. Together with the Inspectors, Mr Day was to inspect the Patroles in their respective districts at least once each month. They were to appear in the uniform of the establishment together with their arms and appointments with their horses, where it was expected that they would be in perfect order and fit for service.

The Inspectors in their respective districts were required to visit the Patrole on night duty and in the morning make any report to Mr Day of any particular occurrence or neglect of duty. The Inspectors were also required to report their own duty to Mr Day in writing every week and specify the conduct of the men and behaviour of the Patrole during that period. The Inspectors were also required to visit the stables of the Patrole at the hours set for maintaining the horses, and report any neglect or disobedience of the order to Mr Day immediately. When Richard Ford died in 1806 he was replaced by James Read, who would have assumed responsibility for superintending the Patrole.

The equipment supplied with each horse included a headstall with chain rein, bridle complete, saddle with holsters and flounces, girths, stirrup leathers with irons, surcincle, crupper, cloak, pad and straps, breastplate, horse cloth, cloak, sabre and belt, a pair of pistols, a turn-screw, a picker and worm, a pair of handcuffs and matching key, book and orders and warrant.[540] The accoutrements for the horse were supplied by Gibson and Peat in Coventry Street. Equipment for the stable was also provided and included a corn bin,

---

540 *Report of the Committee of the State of the Police of the Metropolis* (1816) House of Commons.

sieve, pail, measure, lantern, fork, shovel and carry brush.[541]

Early in 1810 the establishment was increased, and 52 officers appointed to eradicate the increasing highway robbery problem.[542] By the following year the arrangements for the Patrole were reduced and the Foot Patrole, who had hitherto operated up to a distance of four miles from London, were withdrawn into the metropolis from the environs and consequently an increase in street robbery was seen. From about 1810 there was therefore a Foot Patrole, a Horse Patrole and a Dismounted Horse Patrole in operation.[543]

Mr William Day was made Conductor of the Bow Street Police Horse Patrole establishment, which included the Dismounted Horse Patrole. Due to his position he had given evidence before two Government Committees during his service. These were the 1816 and 1822 Select Committees. He stated that in addition to these responsibilities he was also a "denominated Keeper of the Criminal Registers" in the Secretary of State's office since 1800. He was questioned by his own boss Sir Robert Peel who, as Home Secretary, had assumed the chair of the 1822 Select Committee. William Day was paid £100 per year as Conductor with £1 1s 0d a week for his horse, in addition to any monies he received as Keeper of the Criminal Records. He was questioned in detail by the Committees about the arrangements made regarding the various Patroles.

The duty of the Foot Patrole was to be confined entirely in the metropolis, whilst at the same time Lord Sidmouth, the previous Home Secretary between 1812 and 1822, had sought to extend the Horse Patrole. This was done in two ways, the first being to increase the overall establishment to 102 dismounted officers and 72 mounted Horse Patrole. The second method was by giving them different responsibilities,[544] with Day giving the following examples:

541 Bow Street (1827) *Orders and Directions to be observed by the Police Horse Patrole.* Downes, London.
542 *Report of the Committee of the State of the Police of the Metropolis* (1822) House of Commons.
543 Ibid.
544 Ibid..

"From Charing Cross to Blackfriars Bridge there was a foot patrol, then from Blackfriars Bridge to New Cross dismounted Horse Patrol and from New Cross out into the country to Dartford a mounted Horse patrol. And this was for all the roads into London. So the foot patrol come into London from Blackfriars Bridge and the Horse patrol stationed at New Cross travels to meet his opposite number stationed at Dartford". [545]

The evidence tends to suggest that these Patroles were effective and efficient in their roles and responsibilities, as seemingly suspicious travellers and other individuals could be observed by officers from three distinct Patroles. Bow Street did not pay more than £25 per horse and on average purchased 20 animals each year. Whilst cheaper horses were available they would not be of a sufficiently high standard, given they were expected to travel between 15 and 16 miles a day. Young horses aged between five and seven years were usually purchased. In Mr Day's experience, old horses were unable to take on the rigours of patrolling and even the horses of gentlemen were easily "knocked up", i.e. becoming lame.

The Horse Patrole had to find their own lodgings which needed to have stabling facilities, for which an allowance of between £3 and £10 per year was allowed for stable rent. Later on the Patrole had to pay toll charges when necessary, for horse shoeing and repairs to their appointments when the need arose. The Horse Patrole officers were reimbursed for these out-of-pocket expenses which would be added to their pay. In fact it was of great difficulty for the Horse Patrole to find suitable stabling, given the regulations and constraints on looking after the mount. It was desirable but not always achievable to have the stable adjoining the Constables' residence.

The Organisation

The organisation and management of the earlier Horse Patroles differed greatly from what superseded arrangements in 1805. The

---

545 *Report of the Committee of the State of the Police of the Metropolis* (1822) House of Commons.

earlier experiment had provided Bow Street with useful experience and knowledge, particularly on specific equine arrangements relating to the selection, management and feeding of horses. Whilst this was some 42 years earlier, these experiences informed a system of Horse Patroles which was more structured, professional and disciplined.

There were originally four divisions of the Bow Street Horse Patrole, but in 1837 this was increased to six prior to merging with the New Metropolitan Police. Each division was split into numbered patrols. New stations were added to each division along or near other popular main routes into London when they were needed. Once the main routes had been dealt with, other patrol areas were introduced on connecting routes, for example Wimbledon, Ewell and Kingston.

The Horse Patrole favoured married family men, and Mr Day was constantly looking for suitable houses situated in the right areas. An appropriate building was found on the Ridgeway in Wimbledon village, consisting of a brick-and-slate building with three bedrooms, scullery, living room and a yard with stable.

To ensure the divisions ran efficiently and effectively, a re-modelling of the divisions was necessary from time to time. The Horse Patrole stations and the routes on which they operated in 1816 were as follows:

Patrol Routes	Location of Horse Patrole stations
Dartford to Walworth	New Cross
Maidstone to Blackheath	Welling
Bromley to Bexleyheath	Dartford
Croydon to Sidcup	Bromley Common
Sutton to Kennington	Croydon
Epsom to Clapham	Tooting
Wimbledon and Kingston to Sutton	Ewell
Richmond to Westminster	Pimlico

Patrol Routes	Location of Horse Patrole stations
Hounslow to Putney Heath	Kingston
Staines to Wimbledon	East Sheen
Colnbrook and Windsor to Turnham Green	Hounslow
Staines to Bedfont and Colnbrook	Staines
Uxbridge to Bayswater	Hanwell
Edgware to Uxbridge	Paddington
Hampstead to Kilburn	Edgware
Highgate to Somers Town	Highgate
Barnet to Hampstead	Whetstone
Enfield to Barnet	Stoke Newington
Edmonton to Newington Green	Enfield
Epping to Enfield Highway	Stratford
Chigwell to Woodford	Woodford Bridge
Romford to Loughton	Romford

Horse Patrole – First Division

The first division covered south east London, primarily on the main routes into and out of London on the Dartford, Maidstone and Sevenoaks Roads. The Horse Patrole stations were located at Shooters Hill on the Dartford Road, where there were a pair of cottages (called a double station) for Patroles Number One and Two, situated near the eighth milestone.[546] In 1837 these were James Lingham and Edward Palmer, who not only got to know each other very well, but were also well known to the people living in the area. Palmer, the senior of the two, had a slightly different patrol to his neighbour and whilst they travelled the same road at the same time, this was to different locations. Lingham's Number One Patrole travelled from the eighth milestone at Shooters Hill to

546 Milestone measurements were calculated from London Bridge not Charing Cross or Trafalgar Square as they are today.

the sixth milestone at Blackheath and back, then progressing onto the seventh milestone before returning home, having covered 12 miles in total. Palmer's Number Two Patrole required him to travel 13 miles in total each day from the top of Shooters Hill, situated half a mile from his station, to Blackheath, then back to the seventh milestone between The Sun in Sands public house and Lower Kidbrook. The extra mile each day was needed to enable Palmer to return to his station. Lingham and Palmer would cross paths where they would stop and exchange dialogue, giving information and discussing suspicious activities about notable suspects seen on their routes. They would also stop and pass on or receive information in the same way with members of the Bow Street Foot Patrole situated in the Blackheath area.

At Welling, near the tenth milestone there was another double station for Patroles Number Three (James Mew) and Four (Thomas Whitbread), whilst a single cottage was situated at Bexley Heath to house Patrole Number Five which was positioned between the eleventh and twelfth milestones, then a further two cottages were situated at Lee Green for Patroles Number Six and Seven. At Eltham there was a station for Patrole Number Eight, whose beat was from Eltham village to Shooters Hill then on to Welling just beyond the tenth milestone, where he would meet up with both Mew and Whitbread. The single station at Sidcup was occupied by Patrole Number Nine, Lewisham station by Patrole Number Ten, Bromley by Patrole Number Eleven and lastly Patrole Number Twelve at Croydon.

In all there were 12 Horse Patrole officers in this division; however, by 1837 this had expanded to 16.[547] Nine of the Patroles covered the main road from London (Blackheath) from the sixth milestone to Dartford Turnpike and on to the sixteenth milestone. Four other Patroles covered the Maidstone Road from Lee Green, Eltham, South End, Sidcup, Foots Cray and Ruxley Wood to the fifteenth milestone

---

547   For a full list of 1st Division Horse Patrol stations and occupants in 1837 see Appendix 8.

at Garolls Wood. At Sidcup there was a turnpike and a lockup for lodging prisoners. Primrose Douglas was the Sidcup Horse Patrole, Number Eleven, and his neighbour was Thomas Thompson, the pair covering ten miles of the Maidstone Road between them. In 1836, the 48-year-old Primrose Douglas, a Scotsman, successfully joined the Metropolitan Police as one of their mounted officers.

Horse Patrole – Second Division

The second division of the Bow Street Horse Patrole covered south west London from Cheam to Kingston in 1827, and travelled through the principal towns and local villages in between.[548] These were North Cheam, Croydon, Sutton, Merton, Wimbledon, Robin Hood Hill, Kingston and Ditton Marsh. The Horse Patrole stations consisted of two cottages at Merton; Sutton, one cottage; Wimbledon, one cottage; Ewell, one cottage; Kingston Bottom, one cottage; Kingston (Hill), one cottage; Ditton Marsh, one cottage; Priest Bridge, two cottages; Hounslow Heath, one cottage; Bedfont, two cottages; Hounslow, a further two cottages and lastly two cottages at Harlington Corner. There were 17 Horse Patrole officers in this division.

The policing of the Kingston area before the 1820s was carried out and supervised by the various vestries and parish authorities. There was a fairly efficient police within the Surrey parishes, and these consisted of sworn Constables (including those of the Bow Street Horse Patrole), beadles and head-boroughs who would patrol during the day and night by rotation. In 1836 the Patroles were W. Wright covering Merton to Mitcham and Sutton, G. Drake covering Merton to the Ewell turnpike, and W. Richardson covering Cheam to Merton Gate. They were paid 3s a day. Sometimes the men were employed on what was termed "Special Service" to police fairs, races etc, and for such duty they received an extra day's pay.[549]

548 MEPO2/25.
549 www.epsomandewellhistoryexplorer.org.uk/PoliceEpsom.html accessed 25th May 2015.

Fig. 33: Horse Patrole Stations 18 and 19 located at 1 Brickfield Crescent, now 1 Oldfield Road and 3a The Ridgeway, Wimbledon Village

Records held by the Metropolitan Police show that in 1845 they had taken control of a double cottage belonging to the Horse Patrole at 1 Brickfield Crescent on the Ridgeway, now 1 Oldfield Road and 3a The Ridgeway, Wimbledon village. This is directly opposite what is now known as Lingfield Road. Today Wimbledon Lane continues into Wimbledon Hill Road, but in the early 1800s Wimbledon village was situated from Prospect Place along the Ridgeway down the hill, through to what is now the Broadway and back up Wimbledon Hill Road. Charles Churchill and his family had lived here prior to being transferred to the Metropolitan Police; however, on the introduction of the New Police, there was a re-organisation of the Patroles.

Lancastrian-born William Wright became Patrole Number 18 and his 37-year-old neighbour Drake from Bristol was Patrole Number 19. They occupied the two cottages mentioned above. Wright's daily patrol took him along the Ridgeway to Pettywad Wood to the left and Wimbledon Common to the right, where he would turn right into Combe Lane, over the Wandle at Combe Bridge towards Combe, then turning right up towards Kingston Hill between the eleventh and twelfth milestones on the Portsmouth Road (now the A3), where two other Horse Patroles were stationed – Thomas Barnes and Thomas Jones. Here Wright would exchange information and probably chit-chat, or pass on orders from the Patrole Inspector. Like all of the Patroles who would travel this road daily he would have been known to the local people, who would in some cases pass on anything suspicious they would see to the officer. Like many other villages it was the coming of the railways in the 1840s that saw expansion to the north towards Wimbledon Park and south towards Merton, creating New Wimbledon in the middle.

The Second Division of the Horse Patrole at the time of the transfer to the Metropolitan Police was reorganised and dovetailed into the new divisional system employed by the Metropolitan Police Commissioners at the time. Some of the Patroles were placed under the supervision of Inspector William Richardson, who had been the Mounted Patrole stationed at North Cheam. Richardson was a senior figure in the Horse Patrole and he was responsible for the stations at Croydon, Sutton, Merton (Millers Mead), North Cheam, Wimbledon (village), Kingston, Robin Hood Hill and Ditton Marsh.[550] His job was to visit each of his Patroles daily to ensure they were doing their job.

There were two patrol stations at Harlington village in 1837; firstly the more experienced Thomas Bray, Patrole Number 32, who was responsible for patrolling the Harlington to Hounslow Road then onto the Bath Road to Bedfont; and secondly William Thompson, who went in the opposite direction, passing Colnbrook onto the 20-mile stone at Upton and Slough village, a distance of seven miles. Thompson needed to return to Harlington then go back to Slough before returning to Harlington, covering 28 miles each day for which he was paid 28s a week.

Patrole Number 30 was Robert Stewart and Number 31 William Bassett, who both lived in a double cottage at Hounslow. Stewart travelled from Hounslow to Colnbrook turnpike, some six and a half miles, where he would pass William Thompson at least twice and

---

550   Brown, B. (date unknown) *The Metropolitan Police in the County of Surrey.*

Fig. 34: The twin Horse Patrole Stations at Bedfont
Courtesy Metropolitan Police Historical collection

where they would wait and exchange information before moving on.

In 1837 a section that was part of the Second Division of the Bow Street Horse Patrole was amalgamated with the Metropolitan Police as part of the mounted branch attached to V Division, under the command of Inspector Dowsett.[551] This was so even though the area was not included within the Metropolitan Police until 1839, when Kingston, Hook and Chessington formed part of the inner district of V or Wandsworth Division.[552] In January 1840 these areas were extended still further to their present limits, when another 13 Sergeants and 101 Constables were added to the V Division, with new stations being opened at Kingston, Epsom, Hampton, Sunbury and Richmond (the Surrey Constabulary not coming into existence for another decade).[553]

Richard Dowsett had been appointed as Inspector/Conductor

551 Kennison, P. Swinden, D. and Moss, A. (2013) *Discovering More Behind the Blue Lamp*. Coppermill Press, Essex.
552 MEPO 2/76.
553 Lambert, T. (2011) *A Brief History of Kingston upon Thames*. www.localhistories. org/kingston.html accessed on 25th January 2011.

in 1814 for the Horse Patrole, and was the Inspector in charge of Kingston by 1844. He was an experienced officer and remained in charge until he retired aged 60 in 1850, after 35 years in the saddle.[554] Dowsett would have known all the local offenders and most of the people living in the area. He was best-placed to guide his officers in the event of problems with crime in the locality. His pension records show that Dowsett was classified as being "worn out", and his annual pension amounted to £95 per year (when a Constable's typical pension was £27 per year).[555]

The Horse Patrole station situated in the Staines Road, Bedfont was rented from Mr Francis Newborn of Bedfont for the annual sum of £28. These provided three sets of married quarters where Constables and their families would live.[556] The Horse Patrole station acted as the principal police station in the area until the new one was built in 1866. It was still in use in 1881, and was described as "two semi-detached cottages on the roadside" which were occupied by two Constables and their families. Regular complaints were made from the occupants that the cesspool leaked, providing unhygienic odours in the yard at the rear.[557] The horses were housed to the side of each building and each had a hay loft for the storage of equipment and fodder.

Horse Patrole – Third Division

The Third Division of the Horse Patrole covered the area of north west London and comprised Hanwell, Hayes, Harrow, Hillingdon, Harrow Road, Hendon, Highgate, Edgware and Whetstone.[558] There were two Horse Patrole cottages at Hanwell, two more on Harrow Road, two more at Edgware, one at Hillingdon, one at Hendon and two cottages at both Highgate and Whetstone. In total, there were 13

554 *Kelly's Directory 1851.*
555 Metropolitan Police Pension Records 1840–1858.
556 Metropolitan Police Surveyors Records ESB, London.
557 Condition of Police Stations 1881.
558 Martin, S. (1970) *The Policing of Finchley Through the Ages.* MPS Historic Collection ESB.

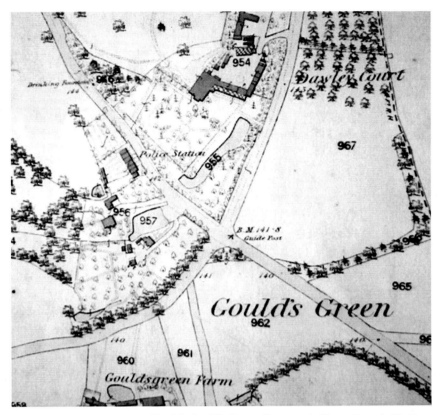

Fig. 35: Gould's Green, Hayes twin Horse Patrole Stations
Courtesy David Swinden

Patrole officers on this Division, which by 1837 had extended to 16. Their supervisor was Inspector Samuel Bonton, who was stationed at Kilburn in Middlesex.[559]

Leaving London from the Tyburn turnpike (today's Marble Arch) at the start of the Edgware Road was the highway to Uxbridge and into Buckinghamshire. This road was covered by six Bow Street Patroles in 1836. Patroles 35-40 were Joseph Spillman, John Denton, Moses Lander, William Fair (senior), Thomas Duggan and John Parnel. Spillman and Denton resided in a double cottage at Hanwell and patrolled west out of London from the seventh milestone at

---

559 Distribution of Horse patrols 1836. Records held at ESB. West Brompton, London.

The Old Hats inn at Ealing to Hillingdon Gate along the Uxbridge Road, a distance of seven miles. On their journey they would pass through Hanwell at the eighth milestone, Southall Park at the ninth milestone, then Southall, over Yeading Bridge towards the eleventh milestone, where there was a turnpike past The Adam and Eve, to the twelfth milestone near Hayes Park and onto Hillingdon Heath at the thirteenth milestone towards the Hillingdon turnpike, just shy of Uxbridge.

Fair and Lander did the same route but did not patrol together. As both lived at Gould's Green, Hayes, their patrol took them southeast along the Harrow Road to The Old Hats at Ealing.

Lander became one of the Bow Street Horse Patrole Constables to join the Metropolitan Police in 1836, when he was 27 years of age. Born in Kent in 1809, Moses Lander had joined the Bow Street Horse Patrole in January 1834 and by 1836 was paid 3s 6d per day. When he transferred over to the Metropolitan Police, he joined their ranks as Police Constable 15528 patrolling the roads to Uxbridge from Hillingdon Gate into London to The Old Hats.

It was a requirement that the men stayed in any given locality only for relatively short periods of time, to avoid the likelihood of familiarity arising between Patrole and populace.[560] Lander's next door neighbour was William Fair and his family. Fair was the more senior of the two, having more service and being paid a higher daily rate; however, he did not join the Metropolitan Police and therefore needed to vacate the house in 1836. The lifestyle obviously suited Lander, who stayed a further 18 years before finally resigning on pension on 1st April 1857 after 23 years' service in the saddle.

Thomas Duggan and John Parnel patrolled the Harrow Road from the fourth to the ninth milestone. On the Kensal Green Road they commenced west, leading away from London from the fourth milestone onto the Holsdon Green fifth milestone, passing the sixth milestone near Stonebridge. They continued towards Harrow on the

---

560 Elliott, B. (2001) *Peelers Progress* www.brynelliott.co.uk/peelers%20progress.pdf accessed 1st November 2017.

Hill, passing the seventh milestone, then onto the The Swan at the eighth milestone, and the ninth milestone at Sudbury. They needed to do this twice, a distance of 18 miles per day, seven days a week, 364 days a year. Duggan never joined the Metropolitan Police, but his 35-year-old colleague Parnel did, lasting until November 1840 when he resigned having completed four years' service with his new employer.

Chipping Barnet

There were ten Patroles that covered the Great North Road (now the Holloway Road and A1) out from the third milestone at Highbury to the twelfth milestone at Monken Hadley (Watford). Bow Street had rented two cottages for the Horse Patrole, at 47 and 48 Barnet Road (later Barnet Lane), which in 1837 were occupied by Thomas Norton and Samuel Collard. These were both taken over by the Metropolitan Police in the same year. When a review of housing stock was undertaken in 1845, the surveyors described the houses as consisting of standard brick and tile cottages, with a small garden and stable in each. Each had four rooms and a coal cellar. The cottages were rented from Mr Anderson of Anderson Cottages, Finchley for £10 per year with the cost of the stable being an additional £5. Norton travelled each day from Wellington Bar at Highgate near the fourth milestone to Whetstone Gate at the ninth milestone, a distance of five miles. Travelling to and fro twice, and then required to cover a return journey between the sixth and the eighth milestone four times totaled 18 miles each day. Collard travelled in the same direction from Finchley North, but on to Chipping Barnet at the eleventh milestone. He was required to ride, walk or patrol the Barnet Road from Wellington Bar to Barnet Gate, a distance of five-and-a-half miles, and between the eighth and ninth milestone four times per day.[561] When taken over by the Metropolitan Police they were in a sad state of repair and needed

---

561 Martin, S. (1970) *The Policing of Finchley through the ages*. MPS Historic Collection ESB.

renovation, which was immediately carried out, but the premises were given back to the landlord in 1849 and vacated by police.[562]

Two cottages with stabling from the original Horse Patrole were transferred to the Metropolitan Police in 1845, and were located at 49 and 50 Whetstone Road, Finchley Common. Patrole Number 49 was John Smith, and his neighbour was William Davis. They were the property of Mr Joseph Bourton of Willesden, who rented them out for £15 each per year. The buildings consisted of brick and slate and were in a good state of repair, having been renovated by the Metropolitan Police in 1844. There was a large garden to the rear with good stabling, a four-room wash house and a large water closet. There was also good clean water supply, which was important in those days in order to maintain health and keep infection away.[563] Davis's patrol route was along the New Finchley Road, from the station to Grand Junction Gate, a return journey of 12 miles; however, he had to cover between the third and fourth milestone four times each day, adding eight miles to his journey and totaling 20 miles per day.

Bow Street Horse Patrole Number 45, Joseph Higgs, lived in a station located on the Finchley New Road, and travelled his beat north up the Barnet Road to Grand Junction Gate, which was not a tollgate but near a junction where The Gate public house stands just beyond Arkley, a distance of five-and-a-half miles. Patrole Number 46, Robert Buffham, travelled the same route as Higgs except each officer had a dedicated instruction to patrol between two milestones at Monken Hadley and Chipping Barnet. Buffham's beat overlapped that of Higgs in that he patrolled, walked or rode Finchley New Road and Barnet Road to Grand Junction Gate for a distance of five-and-a-half miles twice per day, whilst patrolling from the second to the fourth milestone four times per day. Patrole Number 47, Norton, also walked, rode or patrolled the Barnet Road from Wellington Bar to Whetstone Gate for four miles twice a day, and from the sixth to

562 Metropolitan Police Surveyors Records. MPS Historic Collection ESB.
563 Ibid.

the eighth milestone four times a shift. In the rare event their horse was unfit for patrol on a given day, the Constable was required to proceed on foot but only needed to cover half the distance.

Number 4 Cowley Cottages, Hendon was a Horse Patrole station in New Brent Street (opposite the Congregational Schools and the junction with Bell Lane) and was rented by Bow Street.[564] The cottages stood until 1959, when they were pulled down to make way for the Foster Estate.[565] Aldenham near Watford was not a police station for the purposes of taking and holding prisoners, as there were no cells or a charge room for these purposes. This was a station that was a Bow Street Horse Patrole station. The Horse Patrole was first recorded in a cottage located near Finchley in 1818.[566] By 1828 its third division operated as far as Whetstone, and in 1836 four Constables worked from Finchley (Highgate), and two from Whetstone.

The two Patroles at Whetstone were Numbers 49 and 50. The first was allocated to a man called Smith, whose beat included patrolling, walking or riding from Barnet to Archway, Highgate, a distance of six miles twice a day, and from the eighth milestone to the ninth milestone four times a day. Horse Patrole Number 50 was a man called Davis, who patrolled in the opposite direction, either riding, walking or patrolling the Finchley New Road, from the police station to Grand Junction Gate, also a distance of six miles, and from the third and fourth milestone four times a day.[567] The distance travelled each day by each Patrole was 20 miles on average, and when the two Patroles met up, either patrolling or back at the station, they would exchange information which would also be passed onto other Patroles at Finchley (Highgate).[568] There was also still a Bow Street

564 French, I. (1984) *Hendon Police.* Local police charity publication in aid of 2 Area Widows and Orphans, p. 7.
565 Ibid, p. 91.
566 Babington, A. (1969) *A House in Bow Street.* MacDonald and Co., London, p. 194.
567 Martin, S. (1970) *The Policing of Finchley Through the Ages.* MPS Historic Collection ESB.
568 Kennison, P. Swinden, D. and Moss, A. (2013) *Discovering More Behind the Blue Lamp.* Coppermill Press, Essex.

Horse Patrole Station at Edgware on the Great North Road in 1851, which was occupied by four men.[569]

Horse Patrole – Fourth Division

The Fourth Division of the Horse Patrole covered primarily a section of north east London into Essex and included the main roads to and from Westminster, all of which had been turnpiked. These included the Great Essex Road, which ran from the Mile End Road through Bow, Stratford, Ilford, Romford, Brentwood, Ingatestone and Chelmsford, onto Colchester. The Great Essex Road maintained links with the Continent, since from Colchester the road ran to Harwich and the regular boat sailings to and from Holland.

The Bow Street Horse Patrole only operated from the fourth milestone at Stratford as far as Romford at the twelfth milestone, unless there were reasons to pursue felons further along these roads. There were two other roads in Essex worthy of attention by the Patrole; firstly one which forked left at Stratford (Maryland) through Harrow Green, Leytonstone, Chigwell to Abridge. Secondly, but much later, another route which was increasing in importance was the road which forked left just beyond Leytonstone, diverting to Buckhurst Hill, Woodford, Loughton and on to Epping, which ran to Cambridge via Newmarket and Norwich. There was another old road which was also gaining in popularity to travellers, the Woodford Bridge to Chigwell and Ongar Road.[570]

The Bow Street Night, Foot and later the Day Patroles were responsible for patrolling the road between Aldgate, along to Mile End and Stratford, whilst the Horse Patroles were posted along the road from Stratford, Woodford and Epping, as well as Stratford, Ilford and Romford along the Great Essex Road. Single Horse Patrole stations were located at Westminster, Enfield, Lea Bridge

---

569　www.british–history.ac.uk/report.aspx?compid=22507&strquery=police　accessed 9th November 2011.
570　Lockwood, H. H. (1996) 'The Bow Street Mounted Patrol on Essex Highways' in Kenneth Neale (ed) Essex – 'full of profitable things' Essex Archaeological Historical Congress, p. 313.

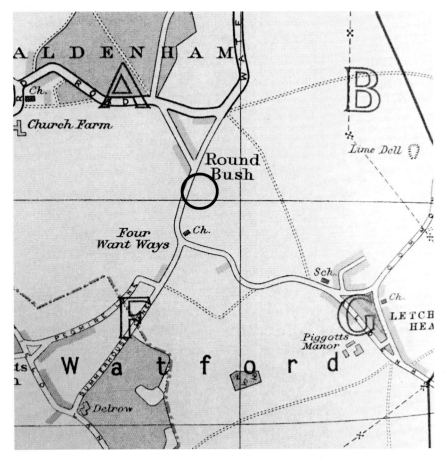

Fig. 36: Aldenham Horse Patrole Station

Road, Loughton, Epping, Ilford and Romford, with a pair of stations situated at Stratford and Woodford.

Originally the Division had 11 Patroles; however, by 1836 this had risen to 14, with the stations numbering 51–65. Supervision from 1813 had been undertaken by Mr Day, Principal Conductor, located at the Westminster Station; by 1836 James Carter had taken his place and he resided at 54 Holywell Street, Millbank.

Mr Barber owned Station Number 63 at Lea Bridge, this being manned by Constable Richard Glendenning in 1837. Glendenning patrolled from the tollgate at Lea Bridge to Leytonstone for six-and-a-half miles twice a day.

In 1836, Thomas Jacques was stationed at a cottage owned by Mr Wilks in Loughton as Patrole Number 57. Other stations nearby, both manned, were at Epping and Abridge. The Epping station, Number 58, was let from Mr Conyers of Copt Hall. There had always been a perennial problem with finding suitable accommodation to rent for the Horse Patroles, because the building had not only to be able to house a Patrole, his family and horse, but also be located in a specific place ideally along a main road. The Loughton Station, for example, was rented for some considerable time and was even passed into the responsibility of the Metropolitan Police from 1836. This house was constructed of brick with a slate roof, and the building was not finally ceded by the police until 1853 when it was handed back to the owners. Manned by Samuel Simmons that year, Station 60 was tasked with the patrol of the roads between Abridge, Chigwell and Woodford Bridge. From his base at Chigwell at the tenth milestone he would patrol twice each day the seven miles to Abridge and then return to Leytonstone. In the early 1800s this was a very rural and, in places, a heavily forested area.

There were Patroles at Romford Road (Maryland Point) and two in Ilford.[571] The Bow Street Horse Patrole operating from a rented house at Maryland Point, Leytonstone Road was owned by Mr Curtis of the Broadway, Stratford.[572] Romford formed part of the Fourth Division (later the Fifth Division), with further Patroles situated at Enfield, Lea Bridge Road, Woodford, Loughton, Epping, Stratford and Ilford.[573] The Stratford Bow Street Patrole Number 62 was Samuel Gutteridge, who was responsible for patrolling the High Road to Ilford from the fourth to the seventh milestone, which he did three times a day, travelling just over 16 miles a day. Gutteridge encountered many travellers on his journeys up and down the Great Essex Road, and one day stopped to speak with a suspect who he

571 Brown, B. (1990) *Romford Police: 'The Anniversary of a Change' in the Romford Record*, Romford and District Historical Society.
572 Metropolitan Police Surveyors Records, ESB West Brompton.
573 MEPO 14/40.

knew. The encounter quickly turned nasty and he was assaulted by Irishman Paddy Regan, who he arrested and detained to be brought before the court.[574]

The two Patroles in Ilford were stationed at what was deemed a double police station, situated about halfway between the seventh and eighth milestone located on the High Road (Romford Road) to Chadwell Street on the north side of the present junction at Green Lane.[575] These comprised of a double set of cottages for Patroles numbered 63 and 64, with facilities to house and care for their horses, usually a single stable with a small hay loft. This double station not only afforded a good view, but also allowed the two Constables to watch who and what was coming in and out of Ilford or Goodmayes when they were not on patrol. The officers knew their road very well indeed. At the tenth milestone, High Road Junction with Whalebone Lane, there was a turnpike, whilst halfway between the eleventh and twelfth milestone there were military barracks on the south side of the highway.

Very often these members of the Patrole had been living at these locations a long time and were also well known to the local inhabitants. They were used to being seen on horseback, and locals would stop and talk to them, passing the time of day. Anything suspicious they saw would also be passed on to them. Further to the east, a single Horse Patrole was stationed in Romford Town near the turnpike at the eleventh milestone.

Problem areas for the Patrole were located at Stratford Common just east of Maryland Point, Wanstead Flats east of Leytonstone, Chadwell Heath on the north side of the highway before Whalebone Lane, and large areas of Epping Forest. The two roads which were deemed most profitable by robbers were the Leytonstone to Woodford route continuing onto the Epping Road, whilst the Stratford to Romford Road was the other.

574 *Essex Standard*, 15th May 1835.
575 Lockwood, H. H. (1996) The Bow Street Mounted Patrol on Essex Highways in Kenneth Neale (ed) Essex – 'full of profitable things' Essex Archaeological Historical Congress, pp. 319–321.

William Hogg, based at the Stratford Horse Patrole Station dealt with a theft of potatoes on 20th April 1837, when he arrested two men named Skiggs and Sales with the help of William Davis, another Constable.[576] Skiggs had stolen a quantity of potatoes and had recently passed a bag on to Sales. When the Horse Patrole went to Sales's house they found a bag fitting the description in the larder which was later proved to be stolen from a farmer named Thompson. Both were found guilty, and Skiggs, aged 23, was confined for a year, whilst Sales, aged 39, received seven years transportation.[577] This was another fine result for the two Horse Patroles, who may have received a reward from the court for their trouble.

The Horse Patrole were called on in 1811 to deal with an outcry of panic amongst the people of Wapping and Shadwell. The Ratcliff Highway murders were vicious attacks within twelve days of each other on two separate families who lived along one of the main roads into London (now called The Highway) in December 1811. This was a run down, dark and dangerous area of dilapidated tenements, and the attacks resulted in seven deaths. The first attack took place on 7th December 1811 in the living quarters behind a linen draper's shop at 29 Ratcliffe Highway, on the south side of the street between Cannon Street Road and Artichoke Hill. The attacks caused panic amongst the local population.

The victims of this first attack were Timothy Marr, in his twenties, his young wife Celia, their 14-week-old son Timothy Jr, apprentice James Gowan and a servant girl, Margaret Jewell. All had been living there since April of that year. The location of the second attack was The King's Arms, a tavern at 81 New Gravel Lane (now Garnet Street). This time the victims were John Williamson, the 56-year-old publican who had run the tavern for 15 years; Elizabeth, his 60-year-old wife and their servant, Bridget Anna Harrington, who

---

576 Hogg had joined the Metropolitan Police from the Bow Street Horse Patrole but only remained for eight months having joined on 2nd January and resigned 3rd September 1837.

577 Old Bailey Proceedings Online (www.oldbaileyonline.org, version 7.2, 21st August 2016) April 1838 trial of James Skiggs and William Sales (t18380514–1369).

was in her late 50s. Concerns had been raised by Williamson on the same night to the parish Constables that a suspect in a brown coat had been lurking about their house and listening at the door.

Quite soon after a suspect was identified: John Williams (also known as John Murphy), a 27-year-old Irish or Scottish seaman, and a lodger at The Pear Tree, a public house on Cinnamon Street off the Highway in Old Wapping. Evidence was gathered from a number of people that Williams harboured a grievance against Marr from their days at sea. The Shadwell Police Office examined Williams as well as several other suspects. He had two pawn tickets on his person, some silver coins and a pound note. His last voyage had been on the *Roxburgh Castle*, an East India Company trading ship, and he had narrowly escaped being part of a failed mutiny attempt. He was educated and had a reputation for being honest, as he always paid for his rooms, and was popular with women. Williams had been seen drinking with at least one other man at The King's Arms shortly before the murders, so he was subjected to an intense interrogation. What aroused suspicion was his earlier mention that he had no money, although he was seen to have some after the murders. Williams proclaimed his innocence, claiming he had pawned articles of clothing afterwards and that the pawn tickets were proof of this, thus providing an alibi. No one investigated this alibi or checked the dates on the pawn tickets.

Pleading his innocence, Williams was remanded to Coldbath Fields Prison, also known as the Clerkenwell Gaol, where another suspect was also detained. The police were still not sure how many men were involved, and confined three suspects in all. Williams was detained for further examination at Shadwell Magistrates' Court, but he never went to trial as he hung himself by a scarf from an iron bar in his cell. No one discovered this until just before he was to be taken for another hearing before the Shadwell magistrates. An officer announced to the court that the accused was dead and that his body was cold. Williams's suicide surprised, everyone since a number of prisoners and a warden said that he had appeared to be in good spirits only the day before, believing that he would soon be exonerated and released.

The public outcry over Williams' death and his supposed guilt, was such that the Shadwell magistrates contacted Mr Ryder, the Home Secretary, of their concerns of public disorder if the situation was not managed properly. Ryder was more than happy to agree with the opinion of the Shadwell Bench, and ordered a parade of Williams' body through Wapping and Shadwell, declaring themselves happy that Williams was the murderer and that he was dead and no longer a threat. To ensure order during the procession a number of Thames Police and the Bow Street Horse Patrole, as well as the local Constables and watchmen, were instructed to oversee the occasion. Since the Bow Street Horse Patrole was required to attend as a body of men, they wore their distinctive red waistcoats as a mark of their uniform. In the event there was only one incident, when a Hackney carriage driver struck the body three times with his riding crop.

The cart carrying Williams's body stopped at Cable Street and Cannon Street, close to St George's Church where previously the Marr family had been buried, in order for the body to be placed in a pre-dug grave. After removing the body from the cart, a stake was driven through the heart and then dumped into its grave, the accepted burial away from consecrated ground for a suicide. The presence of the Horse Patrole helped maintain order at the event.

Functions

The Horse Patrole would travel up and down the main highways looking out for crime, criminals or victims of robbery and violence. Their duty was to prevent and deter highway robberies. The Patrole would seek information from the tollgate keepers, who would provide intelligence on the movements of individuals which was passed on to the Dismounted Patrole and later to the Foot Patrole. This was an efficient system, since information on suspicious people and their movements, including detailed descriptions, were recorded in each officer's occurrence book (an early version of a police pocket book), which they carried and passed between Constables at their rendezvous points.

Conditions of Service

In 1813 Sir Nathaniel Conant superintended the Horse Patrole from the Public Office at Bow Street with Mr William Day, the Principal Conductor, as his deputy, who ensured that all orders were properly promulgated. The Patrole were to live with their family in houses provided, keeping them clean and decent and not to have pigs or other animals which fed on corn. As corn was supplied for the horse, it was felt that allowing animals would cause difficulties. The Patrole were not to be absent from their homes for more than two miles without permission. Every Patrole needed to be correctly dressed when he left home and was to be in uniform. Any omission from this instruction was viewed dimly, suggesting that the officer was ashamed of his position and consequently unfit to be retained.[578]

The Patrole men had to be punctual when coming on duty, and to ensure they were familiar with all orders passed to them by their Conductor, Mr Day. They were required to travel along the designated road assigned to them at a pace that ensured they came to the extreme end of their journey at the allotted time, where they were to remain for ten minutes before returning homeward.

Any Patrole, whether a Horse Patrole or a Dismounted Foot Patrole, who lived or was stationed along the same road was required to meet and communicate at a given spot on the outward and return journey, and discuss any information they had been given about any robbery, successful or attempted, or about any suspicious persons who have been seen on the road. If any robbery or attempt has been committed, the Patroles should join up and proceed to the place and use every means to apprehend those responsible and ensure they were lodged securely at Bow Street. The Patrole was instructed that prisoners should be brought before the next sitting of the court at 11.00am, when any witnesses or victims were also required to attend. When they passed persons in carriages, the Patrole were required to call out in a clear and distinct voice, "Bow Street Patrole". This

---

578 Elliott, B. (2001) *Peelers Progress* www.eppingforestdc.gov.uk/library/leisure/ museum/collections/peelersprogress.pdf accessed on 9th February 2012.

was a clever requirement for a number of reasons. Firstly, people travelling on the same highways and byways could communicate any concerns or information on suspicious persons, and secondly they would be reassured as to their safety by his presence.

Role

The primary role of the Foot (Dismounted Horse) and Horse Patroles was to patrol their areas and roads of the metropolis and beyond as designated to deter crime, reassure the travelling public, gather information on felons and apprehend persons committing or on suspicion of having committed a felony or serious crime. Also, having a Justice's signed warrant in his possession to arrest the felon named thereon as soon as practicably possible. They should also converse with other people using the roads, highways and alleys in order to see what suspects were up, to or gather useful information on suspicious persons.

Discipline

The officers of the Horse Patrole were not to take matters into their own hands other than murder, robbery of severe violence on the roads and thoroughfares leading into the metropolis. In other words they were not peace officers, in the sense that they were parish Constables, but had a specific role beyond any parish in Westminster and Middlesex. Originally the role of the Horse Patrole was to be present on the main roads in and out of London and deal with serious criminal matters, but preservation of the peace or settling disputes between members of the public was not in their remit.

A case was heard at Middlesex Sessions in 1810 which involved a Horse Patrole by the name of Thomas Ashley who was on duty at midnight at the Kingsland Toll Bar when an altercation occurred between Mr Cambridge, the Toll Keeper, and Mr Severn, a trunk maker who was with two women in a post chaise, over the rate of toll charged. During the altercation Ashley had interjected on the side of the toll-keeper, which rather upset the trunk maker. However,

Mr Severn paid the disputed charge but alighted from his carriage in order to obtain the name of the toll-keeper, against whom he wished to make a complaint. The Patrole, who was present during the altercation, had words with Mr Severn and promptly drew his cutlass, swinging it three times at Mr Servern's head, the last swipe severely damaging his hat. This was corroborated by several witnesses, who agreed it was lucky Mr Severn was not injured by the Patrole. By the time of the trial the Horse Patrole had already been dismissed from his employment. Using a cutlass supplied for the protection of the public against an unarmed man also went beyond the officer's duty, and he was found guilty and sentenced to one month's imprisonment.[579]

An industrious Bow Street Horse Patrole named George Vaughan seemingly had a good reputation in arresting suspects; however, was not above faking evidence against innocent people. He conspired with others to set up young innocent, gullible or even mentally-impaired people to commit crimes in exchange for a part of the reward money. In 1816 he had been very active in gaining £40 rewards through the courts, using intermediaries to commit felonies. A one-legged man named Drake met with Vaughan at Sadler's Wells to hatch a plot to procure five men (three brothers, another man and a boy) to commit a burglary at Hoxton. Drake gave them the instruments to break into the house, along with an inducement of 10s "to lush them well". When it came to it they found the door unlocked, hesitated and ran off. The Patrole took a jemmy and made a mark in the lintel of the door with it. He then placed a lamp and jemmy inside the house. Drake led them to the place where the three brothers were staying, and the Patrole dropped a ring belonging to the woman of the house into one of their pockets. When they were arrested and later examined before the magistrates, it appeared that they had been put up to do this.

Ugly rumours circulated at the time pointed to the Horse Patrole, and Vaughan particularly, as being involved. Another house of

579 *Kentish Gazette*, 7th December 1810.

a friend was chosen in Grays Inn Lane by Drake as another likely target, but an argument with a watchman whose box was nearby caused the venture to be postponed. On another occasion two bad dollars and four bad shillings were passed from Vaughan to a man named O'Shea in order to procure an innocent man to enter a chandler's shop in Grays Inn Lane run by Vaughan's mother-in-law. A man named Mackay was found to do this, and once he had purchased the goods with false coinage he was arrested by Vaughan outside. At Bow Street the magistrates sought Vaughan to appear before them; however, he had decamped to the Whitechapel Road to the house of his uncle. Officers Limbrick (Hatton Garden) and Read were despatched from Bow Street and together with Freeman, the officer from Whitechapel Road Public Office, went in search of Vaughan, whom they found at the address together with two loaded pistols. Upon searching him the Bow Street officers found a pocket book which confirmed rumours that Vaughan was trying to entrap innocent victims in order to procure the £40 rewards plus gifts. Dickons, another Patrole, gave evidence against Vaughan, who was later charged to appear at the Old Bailey for his crimes.[580] He was convicted and sentenced to five years' imprisonment with hard labour.

Transfer to the Metropolitan Police

By Act of Parliament on 9th September 1837 the Bow Street Horse Patrole was transferred from Government control to that of the Commissioners of the Metropolis. This was not a transfer or change that was welcomed by the Horse Patrole and some resigned, others retired on pension for long service or resigned for health or injury reasons before the change took place.

On transfer, the pay remained the same at 25s a week plus the cost of their accommodation, stabling and forage for the horse. The Patrole also retained their weapons and accoutrements, which

---

580 Fitzgerald, P. (1888) *Chronicles of Bow Street Police–office.* Gilbert and Rivington, London, pp. 166–172.

became the responsibility of the Commissioners. Originally there had been just four Divisions of the Horse Patrole; however, through the transfer the Divisions had increased to six. Each Horse Patrole Division was transferred to the respective Metropolitan Police Division, where responsibility for supervision etc. passed to the Divisional Superintendent.[581]

The First Division consisting of Inspector Jason Beswick and 15 men who patrolled the Kent Roads up to a distance of 15 miles was transferred to the Met's R Division under Superintendent Mallalieu. The Second Division, consisting of Inspector Dowsett and ten men patrolling the roads through Surrey, were transferred to V or Wandsworth Division under Superintendent Becknell. The Third Division, who patrolled the western roads consisting of Inspector Samuel Bonton and 15 men, were transferred to T or Paddington head station at Turnham Green under Superintendent David Williamson. The Fourth Division of Inspector James Carter and ten men were transferred to S or Hampstead Division under Superintendent Jerimiah Carter. There were 15 Horse Patrole stations, numbered from 51 to 65, within the Fourth Division in 1836, including three at Woodford, two each at Ilford and Stratford, and single stations at Chigwell, Epping, Loughton, Leytonstone, Walthamstow and Romford.[582] The Fifth Division of Inspector Benjamin Pritchard and nine men patrolling the roads north of Hackney joined N or Islington Division under Superintendent Johnson. The Sixth Division of Inspector William Richardson and six men patrolling the Essex Roads and Epping Forest joined K or Stepney Division under the Superintendent of that Division, whose headquarters was in the Mile End Road.[583]

The Inspectors were experienced men, and the majority were long-serving Bow Street Patrole officers. The men, however, were unhappy at the transfer and the change of supervision. Their pay

---

581 *London Gazette*, 9th September 1837.
582 Elliott, B. (2001) *Peelers Progress* www.eppingforestdc.gov.uk/library/leisure/ museum/collections/peelersprogress.pdf accessed on 9th February 2012.
583 *Morning Post*, 9th September 1837.

of 25s a week with a supplement for long service was paid to them by the Commissioners from a special consolidated fund set up by Government, and the investigation of criminal matters and misconduct were now dealt with by magistrates in their respective areas rather than at Bow Street.

Some 66 members of the Horse Patrole transferred across to the Metropolitan Police when Bow Street was relieved of its responsibility,[584] with between them some 308 horses.[585]

584 Documents held by the Metropolitan Police at the Heritage Centre Empress State Building (ESB), West Brompton, West London.
585 *Morning Post*, 9th September 1837.

5

Bow Street Foot Patrole

In the previous chapters the role of the Bow Street Runners has been shown to consist of a small group of able-bodied omni–competent men who were used for a variety of purposes, from foot patrols, as pursuers on horseback chasing felons, arresting suspects, conducting investigations and carrying out the administrative function of the court. Gradually, as time progressed, the role of the Runners evolved into one of detective, leaving the other functions to newly-formed Bow Street forces. On the formation of the Metropolitan Police in 1829 there were no less than five different forces which constituted the Bow Street Police Establishment.

From the time of Sir John Fielding in the 1750s foot patrols in the metropolis developed at Bow Street in rather a piecemeal way, and these were not routine nor were they uniformed. Routine patrols were expensive and Henry Fielding had seen no immediate need for them. Touring the streets looking for or preventing crime was a matter that would come later, becoming well established by the 1780s. The title "Bow Street Foot Patrole" does not accurately reflect its function, since they operated during the darker hours and not during the day at all until the early 19th Century. In fact, no patrols operated anywhere during the daylight hours in England until 1821. Failure to appreciate their role and function in this way has caused writers from the 1780s onwards to conflate the different Bow Street Patroles into one organisation: The Bow Street Runners. From this developed their mythical status as being "the all–seeing and knowing," surely an impossibility for only eight "runners", but when other Patroles were included the total number of patrolling

Constables in London reached into the hundreds.

Whilst some foot patrols existed beforehand, it was not until 1782 that the Government agreed to Sir Sampson Wright's request for a night-time Bow Street Foot Patrole to routinely patrol the highways of the metropolis.[586] This created a band of 68 armed men who patrolled the roads on the outskirts of the metropolis to a distance of four miles.[587] As we will see, the Foot Patrole was improved, re-organised, extended and transformed at various intervals to increase their effectiveness and efficiency.

Evidence of foot patrols did exist before that, albeit in very basic terms and not only at Bow Street. The advent of street lighting in the second half of the 17th Century helped transform the parochial watch, making them more attentive.[588] Some London parishes had been setting an example to others for some time on how an efficient watch could be operated. The parish of St. John's, Hackney, for example, was situated some five miles from Bow Street and had operated an efficient watch system since 1764, with mounted and foot Constables together with watchmen walking in pairs. There were 92 officers and watchmen of the night watch in 1822, and by 1829 they felt so confident in their system that they opposed, in their evidence to the Government Select Committee, the introduction of the Metropolitan Police.[589] The same level of sustained patrol was very rare, however, in virtually any other London parish.

The issue of security in making the streets and avenues of the metropolis safer became a priority. By the 1780s the notion of the single mounted highwayman, footpad or street robber was disappearing, as Bow Streets Patroles cleared them from the streets of London itself. Instead, a new phenomenon presented itself, another more dangerous problem: gangs. They were sometimes

586 Ascoli, D. (1979) *The Queen's Peace*. Hamish Hamilton, London, p. 48.
587 Moylan, J. (1929) *Scotland Yard*, G. P. Putnam London, p. 14.
588 Beattie, J. M. (2012) *The First English Detectives*. Oxford University Press, Oxford, p. 141.
589 Home Department (1822) *Report for the Select committee of the Police of the Metropolis*, Appendix 1.

groups of six to ten, who confidently roamed the metropolis at night with impunity, often getting away with their crimes and providing a new challenge to the Bow Street police establishment. Bow Street Chief Magistrate Sir Sampson Wright knew he had to fight like with like, and that grouping his men together in teams was the answer. In other words, the disorganised and inefficient parochial watch was supplanted by the effective, structured and professional Bow Street establishment.

From Madness to Method

Before the 1780s, like his brother Henry before him John Fielding formed his various Patroles by enlisting a variety of volunteers, serving Constables, ex–parish Constables, and turnkeys etc., who later became his detectives. These men were of proven aptitude, skill, bravery and honesty, and remained at Bow Street Court to be sent out at any given moment.

The myth of the Bow Street Runners as "all seeing and hearing" had begun to develop amongst the criminal fraternity into what soon became legendary status, and not only in London. This small number of specially selected unpaid Constables formed patrols which were sent out when there was a crime problem or other nuisance. For this they received "an expense", but not a salary. Accordingly they were not official, although John Fielding requested a subsidy from Government for their use which he often successfully received. The Duke of Newcastle provided resources for John Fielding to combat not only the threat to property but also to the person as well, since many of the robberies resulted in injuries to the victim and, on occasion, even death.[590] The accounts held at Bow Street show that there was no place the early Bow Street forces would not go, venturing into Kent, Surrey, Bedfordshire and Hertfordshire.

It is worth re-iterating how the Fieldings saw the existing parochial system as being outdated. It was, in their eyes, a disjointed,

590 Beattie, J. M. (2012) *The First English Detectives*. Oxford University Press, Oxford, p. 34.

fragmented and un-coordinated system in need of reform. They wished to do this through proper regulation, organisation and control in what they said was moving from "madness to method".[591] This could only be achieved by proper supervisory control over men who were appointed as Constables and then worked together, gathering information, developing knowledge and shared expertise – working jointly for a common purpose. Today we call this an occupational culture, which has the same benefits now as it did for the Bow Street police establishment in Georgian London.

In theory, the role of the early 1750s parish Constable then was the detecting (investigation) of crimes against people and property, apprehending suspects and bringing them before the court for examination. Other functions included dealing with riots, prostitutes, brothels, disorderly houses and licensing matters. In practice, however, the system was ad hoc and chaotic. Whilst some parishes gradually improved their parochial watches over time, there was no uniform consistency or control across the metropolis. It was some of the more respectable characters that became his "Real Thief Takers", and they ran in parallel until 1792 when the majority of the London-based parish Constable system was abolished.

Original documents and accounts from Bow Street show that from the 1750s to 1839, expenses were paid to a variety of police who journeyed around on foot. Like the Horse Patrole this was an evolving organisation, and its role and function changed by degrees over time, subject not only to the time of day, the geography of London and criminal opportunity, but also to social and political demands, and exigencies of the magistrates.

"Ad hoc" foot patrols operated as early as 1755, since John Fielding's yearly accounts in 1756 submitted to the Secretary of State included payments "for men patrolling the Westminster Squares and for two officers patrolling the great roads to prevent robberies".[592] Some

---

591 Leslie–Melville, R. (1934) *The Life and Work of Sir John Fielding.* Lincoln Williams, London, p. 55.
592 TNA: T38/671, f.4 and Beattie, J. M. (2012) T*he First English Detectives.* Oxford University Press, Oxford, p. 141.

parochial watches, especially in the City of London, had watchmen who were sent out to patrol a given area in pairs during the night but they were not always Constables as such. In August 1757 Justice John Fielding sent out eighteen Constables to search the fields for a gang of seven men, who were all later apprehended and taken before the courts.[593] Sometimes private patrols were introduced in an instance not entirely made up of Bow Street detectives or attached to the office. These initiatives were reported in the newspapers and involved the clerk of the court equipping them with whatever they needed.[594] This involved coach and horse hire for quick pursuit, or issuing them "with cutlasses, hangers and short swords to arm his protectors in pursuit of the robbers".[595]

In addition to regularly guarding the roads around London, armed Bow Street patrols were watching the squares of Westminster in early 1757 from time to time.[596] By the 1760s Fielding had learnt the value of surveillance, particularly of the roads, avenues and thoroughfares of Westminster and its environs. This was especially relevant as the metropolis grew in size. He proposed a plan, one of many he submitted to the Government in 1761, which included "foot patrols within the City" of Westminster to be placed under the control of magistrates. This idea received a cool response and only had the effect of strengthening the local parochial watch.[597] Their perceived fears were that the foot patrols would effectively become a Government-controlled army of occupation as seen in France, which threatened the very liberty of its subjects. Implementation of routine Bow Street foot patrols would take a little more time.

The effectiveness of foot patrols was demonstrated by how the

---

593 Leslie–Melville, R. (1934) *The Life and Work of Sir John Fielding*. Lincoln Williams, London, p. 82.

594 *Public Advertiser*, 30th August 1757 and Beattie, J. M. (2012) *The First English Detectives*. Oxford University Press, Oxford, p. 35.

595 TNA: T38/671, f.4 and Beattie, J. M. (2012) *The First English Detectives*. Oxford University Press, Oxford, p. 35.

596 *Public Advertiser*, 20th January 1757.

597 Beattie, J. M. (2012) *The First English Detectives*. Oxford University Press, Oxford, p. 142.

authorities used them to cope with troublesome local problems, and this only helped to strengthen Fielding's resolve. St. James's Park was a very busy place which acted as a focal point for the gathering of all sorts of people from different backgrounds. The rich and the poor gathered together, often in such numbers that people came into close physical contact with each other which provided a convenient means for criminal opportunity. The trouble in the Park brought mutual co-operation, as seen in February 1773 when John Fielding helped gather together the largest foot patrol ever sent from Bow Street as part of a joint venture between his forces and the Westminster parish Constables. The problem was that St. James's Park was being overrun by gamblers, pickpockets, prostitutes, beggars and other nuisances, and something had to be done. Repeated warnings in the *Public Advertiser* and action by small patrols had been ineffective. A show of force was needed, and twenty Constables were assembled together who included "four persons belonging to Sir John Fielding" under the directions of the High Constable of Westminster. They were equipped for the purpose with truncheons, which were to remain concealed until needed.

The patrols were assigned to the park at 11.00am and were to sweep through, with Sir John Fielding's men pointing out any known thieves or pickpockets they identified.[598] Once they had completed their sweep through the park, the group were split into four parties of five with a detective (one of Sir John Fielding's men) - a Principal Officer - being assigned to each group. By 3.00pm they were instructed to have a two-hour lunch break and dine together at The Horse and Groom, Mr Rix's public house in Buckingham Gate. At 5.00pm they continued their patrol, apprehending gamblers, beggars, nosegay women and sellers of goods.[599] During the day the sellers were not prosecuted, but were to be moved on out of the

---

598 Leslie–Melville, R. (1934) *The Life and Work of Sir John Fielding.* Lincoln Williams, London, p. 165.
599 Nosegay women were young flower sellers usually accompanied by a small child or dog, who would sell small posies of flowers to well dressed women which they held or pinned to their clothes.

park and then released. At night the same treatment was afforded to both common prostitutes and off duty soldiers not on guard duty.[600]

Fielding was happy to boast of his great success to Under Secretary William Eden, and ask for the scheme to be installed permanently at £120 a year. Allowing the request, the papers from Eden expressed a cautious note over whose authority the police officers operated when he stated that:

> "Orders should be given regularly to the soldiers or to the Gold Stick in Waiting that the Peace officers in the Park are under proper directions... and it is his Majesty's pleasure that they have every countenance and protection in the execution of their duty".[601]

Fielding was wise to gather his men together over a meal, heeding the advice of his lieutenant Saunders Welch, since they would then have exchanged information and learnt about the art of policing, while at the same time reinforcing a spirit of camaraderie and union amongst them. This comradeship and solidarity made his civil power a formidable force that was often much feared by the criminal classes into what was to become the myth of the Bow Street Runners. Good police work leading to a good arrest was often rewarded directly from the court.

In 1776, members of the Islington Foot Patrole were given a guinea each by Sir John Fielding as a reward for apprehending some highway robbers. They were:

> "Thomas Ward, Thomas Tapsell, and Thomas Tracey [who] deposed that they took the 'prisoners under suspicious circumstances;' that upon Charles Parsons they found a loaded pistol."[602]

For the first time, foot patrols were becoming a regular feature on

---

600 SP 37/10, f. 86/8A.
601 Ibid.
602 George Charles Parsons, Charles Davis, Violent Theft > highway robbery, 15th January 1777. t17770115–14 accessed 20th March 2017.

the streets of London and producing results. A "private Foot Patrole" operated in the Kentish Town, Highgate area in 1776.[603] As it was making its way up Highgate Hill towards the turnpike they noticed a man leading his horse who called out to the patrole, suggesting that he himself was one of Sir John Fielding's men looking out for a highway robber on the road. The patrole became suspicious, since they themselves were Fielding's men, so they immediately apprehended and placed him in the local cage. Next morning he was taken to Bow Street, where he was found to be the son of a Yorkshire farmer who was employed by a Clerkenwell gentleman and suspected of robbing a linen draper named Eyre in his coach at Highgate.[604]

A description of the Bow Street Office in 1777 demonstrated that a Foot Patrole like this was immediately available, with supervisors, to be sent out to a given road or locality where active footpads or highwaymen operated.[605] These patroles could not be sustained for long periods, as resources and funds were in short supply. At Bow Street, Sir Sampson Wright introduced his Foot Patroles in 1782 as an armed body of men who patrolled the streets of London from dusk until midnight. These patroles were not officially recognised by the Government at the time since they might have attracted criticism for instituting a central Government-approved body of men.[606] Not until 1790, when another crimewave threatened the safety of Londoners, did the Government feel secure enough to approve of this idea. The difference now was that they were funded officially out of the Treasury budget and not from a secret account. By placing them on an official footing, the Government had more operational control over these forces.

603 Sir John Fielding put together private foot patrols which consisted of a number of ordinary (unpaid) Constables under the guidance but not command of one of "Sir John Fielding's Men" and went out whenever the occasion arose.
604 *Leeds Intelligencer*, Tuesday 16th December 1766.
605 NLI 15929 (3).
606 Babington, A. (1969) *A House in Bow Street*. Macdonald and Co., London, p. 169.

Learning Police Work

The local parish of Bow Street - St. Paul's Covent Garden - was regulated by appointed Constables and 22 watchmen who were not a patrole. These watchmen were often old and infirm, and on low wages, performing their duties at night according to vestry instructions. This meant standing in their sentry boxes or walking the streets with a lantern calling the time every hour. Very little crime prevention or law enforcement was carried out by the majority of these men. This small number of parochial Constables were chosen by the court leet held at Westminster annually to supervise the watch, but they coexisted with the Bow Street men with their differing selection, organisational processes and methods.[607] At times both systems would collide through jealously, argument or dispute, often with serious consequences. London, however, was becoming a cosmopolitan place, attracting foreign visitors to what was the largest conurbation in the world with over one million inhabitants, which brought its own problems. Previously we noted how, from 1750 onwards, a small number of officers were selected by Saunders Welch and Henry Fielding to become Constables for Bow Street duty, having impressed both men. We know little about their attributes but they were chosen because they had certain very rare skills and qualities, very much as Constables are selected today and something we deal with in the next section.

Payments

Initially these men were selected as unpaid Constables by Henry Fielding although later, as they evolved, a weekly retaining fee was paid. There was also an opportunity to perform a wide variety of other court duties where expenses were paid according to a scale of charges. These included the service of warrants for

---

607 The use of the word "leet", denoting a territorial and a jurisdictional area, spread throughout England in the 14th century, and the term "court leet" came to mean a court in which a private lord assumed, for his own profit, jurisdiction that had previously been exercised by the sheriff. www.britannica.com/topic/court–lee accessed 16th August 2017.

assaults, felonies and misdemeanours; or for an indictment, the service of a summons; for the endorsement of a warrant (to show its execution); for examination for bastardy warrants; and for examination, information and execution of a warrant for leaving a family chargeable to the Parish. An additional shilling was paid to a Constable who had to travel an extra mile in pursuit of the parties.[608] Only successful service of documents and apprehension of the parties concerned would bring financial remuneration.

These men must have been streetwise to have shown aptitude and had commonsense, since they had to know where to find the people described in the paperwork. Of course, once brought before Henry Fielding additional expenses were paid for a prisoner to be escorted to a prison, to search for evidence and for attendance at any of the courts to give evidence. Additional duties requiring proactive or preventative police work was also on offer to Bow Street men, often paid for by a private person or organisation. These duties included deterring pickpockets at the theatres, or patrolling the busy parks or thoroughfares to apprehend felons, robbers and burglars. All these methods were performed in plain clothes, since no uniform was worn by the Constables until the Horse Patrole was instituted in 1805.

In sum, specially-selected men formed Foot Patroles from the mid 1750s onwards to go out and deal with particular crime problems and any social unrest. This situation carried on until the early 1780s, when the Gordon Riots revealed the helplessness of the police of the metropolis. The patrols were regularised following these riots in London, although they were not officially recognised by Government until 1790. After this, more Foot Patroles were introduced into different areas as London expanded, but in 1821 another plain clothes Foot Patrole was introduced at Bow Street – the curiously named Dismounted Horse Patrole.

608 HO 42/155 dated 27th November 1816.

Supervising and Regulating the Foot Patrole

The Chief Clerk at Bow Street, John Stafford, had control of the Foot Patrole from the date of his appointment in 1802.[609] The swearing in of the Bow Street Foot Patroles as Constables by the magistrates was formalised by Act of Parliament, 54th Act of George III, called the Police Magistrates, Metropolis Act in 1813. Prior to that there was no officially recognised swearing-in process, but this Act extended the jurisdiction of the Bow Street Constables into Essex, Kent and Surrey.

Strict instructions were published for the Patrole. Foot Patrole rules, orders and regulations were produced in 1816 and directed its members to strictly obey the instructions. These instructions had been formulated since early Bow Street days, designed to avoid mistakes, errors of judgement or omissions. In other words, these were lessons learned from previous experience. The commands were read over to the men on the first day of each month and also on the Saturday before any inspection. The magistrates could see who was allocated to any Patrole at a given time in what was deemed a "duty state". Their beats, names of the Conductors, their respective meeting places, duration of duty according to circumstances and the season were recorded each week in the Orderly Book retained at Bow Street.[610]

The supervisors of the Foot Patrole were given the title of Conductor. They attended Bow Street at 10.00am each Monday morning, producing their Occurrence Book in which all incidents over the previous week had been recorded. Any noteworthy incident or piece of important information was communicated at these meetings and passed on to the magistrates. A duty sheet

---

609 Report from the select Committee of the Police of the Metropolis 17th July 1822, p. 21.

610 *Dictionary of the English Language* (1785) by Samuel Johnson states that "a Conductor is a leader who shows others the way by accompanying him" used by Dryden. Conductors were therefore leaders of the Foot Patrole whereas Inspectors were used for the Horse and Dismounted Horse Patroles.

showing the effective strength of each party, including any names of sick officers or those absent without leave, or employed in the duty office and with a list of appointments (pistols, cutlasses, belts and truncheons) and their condition, was handed in. The Conductors would read the Orderly Book for any fresh orders or instructions, and promulgate these to the men later at the point of parade. The pay for each party, paid in arrears, was prepared each Monday morning, and it was the duty of the Conductor to sign for, collect and distribute this money to the men during the course of that day. The details of the next two men to do duty in the orderly office was also recorded and communicated to them.

Two nominated men from the Foot Patrole also had a duty to staff Bow Street's watch office, commencing at 9.00pm and finishing at 9.00am. One of the men was to remain awake at all times and record the details of any occurrence during the night to the duty officer (a Conductor) in waiting, who would be summoned, review the circumstances or take charge of the incident. By rotation, the parties of the Foot Patrole and their Conductor attended Bow Street as a reserve for one night in thirteen and would report to the sitting magistrate, who later dismissed them. They also remained on call from 6.45pm until 9.00pm, when any deficient party would be supplemented from the reserve party. This party also provided the door keeper for the day, who would relieve the night duty at the watch office and whose duty commenced at 9.00am until relieved at 9.00pm. On Sundays the Conductors attended Bow Street by rotation during the day to complete four-hour periods as duty officer. Out on the ground the Foot Patrole were also required to assist the Horse Patrole at all times on any matter. They were also required to communicate any duty matter of mutual interest to them, and also to receive any instructions in return.

The exact detail of the skills needed to become an early officer at Bow Street eludes us, but perhaps an insight might be gained by our research of Bow Street Foot Patrole applications taken from a much later period, 1823-1829. Teams of Patroles were quickly established and from here these groups helped each other and learnt their trade as they went along - as we say, "on the job".[611] When Constables for the Foot Patroles were being selected in the 1770s, a party system of five Constables was developed which suited this method of training and would give an inexperienced man a better grounding in practical police work. The research undertaken from the register of applicants provides some very interesting and revealing original detail regarding recruitment, with a recruitment profile not very dissimilar to today's police service candidate.

Some 174 applicants successfully applied in the six years 1823-29, indicating the need for about twenty new men annually. We do not know how and by whom these applications were processed or accepted, nor do we have sight of any refused submissions. Interpretation of these and other qualities which follow are, of course, open to modern-day understanding and explanations which may of course be contextually inaccurate; nevertheless, it provides an indication of organisation and arrangement.

What surprised the authors was the fact that the Metropolitan Police Commissioners, with the consent of the Home Secretary, also sent some of their own recently-appointed officers to join the Bow Street Foot Patrole (and Horse Patrole) on duty. There were seventeen in total, who were recruited en masse to Bow Street as Foot Patroles on 11th October 1829 from the Metropolitan Police. The officers were distributed amongst the various parties 6–11, mainly being disbursed in Southwark south of the River Thames. These were William Clifford (Party Number Six), James Gracy (Party Number Seven), William James (Party Number Seven), John Green (Party Number Seven), William Griffith (Party Number Nine), Robert Crowne (Party Number Nine), John Ducker (Party Number Ten), John Fair (Party Number Eleven), William Jennings (Party Number Eleven), Robert White (Party Number Eleven), Robert Hind (Party Number Six), Matthew Noone (Party Number Nine), Thomas Wray (Party Number Seven), James Simmons (Party Number Ten),

---

611 British police officers have for a long time called their work – "the job" as if to singularise this specialism as the only profession of any importance to them and even naming a newspaper with this title.

William Dennington (Party Number Six) and William Hook (Party Number Ten).

The purpose or reason for this move is not entirely clear. Likely scenarios could have been fourfold. Firstly, the development of officers who could learn the art of patrolling a beat with a view of returning to the Metropolitan Police and sharing their experiences. Secondly, experience gained in the development of detectives operating in plainclothes who could stop and search people or investigate crimes. The Commissioners were not of the opinion at the start that they needed a detective force, although the Bow Street Runners were still in existence. Their own police were by nature to be a 24-hour-a-day uniformed professional and preventative force. Each Metropolitan Police officer was allocated to patrol a particular beat on his own, guarding the houses and premises. This was a marked contrast between the uniformed Metropolitan force and Bow Street Foot Patrole. The Bow Street men were well armed with cutlass and pistols, wore plain-clothes and were distributed to a district in groups of five at the discretion of their Conductor. Also, unlike their uniformed counterparts, they were not to be seen in the same place at the same time each day, and they sought out offenders and arrested them to be taken before a magistrate.

Thirdly, there is a possibility that these men were sent to Bow Street for a short period in response to a particular crime problem in Southwark and to supplement the beleaguered Foot Patrole, especially given the massive expansion of London's population, streets and roads etc. Another common feature of these transfers was on their return to the Met force they were all allocated to P or Camberwell Division.[612] Lastly, we know that the Metropolitan Police sent Constables to supplement the Bow Street Horse Patrole because of a shortfall in applicants with mounted experience, and it is perhaps most likely that during the transition period they did the same with the Foot Patrole and the Dismounted Foot Patrole.

612 Camberwell was an area which saw massive house building during the 1820–1840s which caused the local population to expand threefold in that time.

The research tends to show that most men had left the Foot Patrole or resigned to return to the Metropolitan Police by the end of 1830. Therefore it is perhaps best to conclude that since Bow Street could no longer recruit to its Patroles who had resigned or left to join the Metropolitan Police, some were returned as officers to the Patroles for short periods when needed.

Recruitment of Patroles: Qualities for Selection

In the early 19th Century, potential recruits wishing to join Bow Street applied directly to join any of the Patroles, not just the Foot Patrole. The authorities were keen to engage candidates as police officers who were better skilled than the officers employed at the other Public Offices. They felt that the reputation of Bow Street was important to maintain. The potential recruits needed to be of a higher class than the average person, and be of good sound habits, have preliminary education and to have good references. Bow Street looked into the background of each individual and interviewed each candidate. Firstly they joined the Foot Patrole, and senior figures could gauge if a certain officer showed better-than-average initiative and aptitude that might result in promotion to Conductor, to the Horse Patrole or elevation to Principal Officer (Runner).[613] In other words, good police officers, through sound reputation and industry, could gain advancement.

The applications to Bow Street reveal a profile relating to age, address, place of birth, height, build, family profile and previous or current occupation, together with any named recommendations in support.[614] A wide range of skills and qualities were needed for the job, and some of these were highlighted by Saunders Welch in his 1754 *Police Constables Instruction Manual*. Whilst the skills needed were very high, there appears to have been no problem selecting suitable candidates.

---

613 *Report from the Select Committee on Police of the Metropolis* (1816) House of Commons, London, p. 75.
614 As a member of the patroles you were not limited to this occupation and you could work and earn money outside of your patrol hours.

The qualities required in candidates were not only physical, but mental as well. Also essential was a sound reputation, especially important for any sort of enforcement work, for an officer must be truthful, honest and trustworthy. An applicant needed a good character reference from a referee as an essential part of any application to join Bow Street, since this confirmed and validated a sound reputation. A strong reference was often accepted from the upper classes, lords, ladies, gentlemen or people of fashion.[615]

The candidate was required to be mature, so age, physique and strength were important. This was necessary since many of the tasks performed were arduous and demanding, and applicants needed to be disciplined. An applicant had generally to be between the ages of 20 and 39, and be responsible; married family men with on average three children or less were more often chosen. They were of above average height, strong, fit and able. The officer had to have a good bearing so short men were often not taken on, although the Horse Patrole were perhaps an exception, as large men would have found it difficult to secure a suitably-sized horse for themselves. Bow Street applications have described this as being "well made", a term which seemed to sum up acceptable size. To have sound and sober habits, be moral and fair were also required, since drunkenness was an issue in Georgian England. Without exception, dishonesty was harshly punished. This supports the notion that size and presence were very important in the role of the Foot Patrole. Other virtues included strength of character, above average intelligence with good interactive skills such as the ability to be able to speak clearly, read and write. Sound judgement, aptitude and discretion were also essential qualities, although liable to be tested only in the role of Constable. Yet all of this comes to nothing if the person selected did not have an ability to be both suspicious and perceptive. These

---

615 "People of fashion" was a common term in use at the time and referred to those who were Highborn upper classes as opposed to low people of no fashion. In *The Adventures of Joseph Andrews* (Chapter XIII), Henry Fielding discusses the nature of these people who whilst highborn could misbehave in certain circumstances making them difficult to discriminate from the people of no fashion.

are the attributes of an inquiring mind in what today we sum up as "detective ability".

The Ideal Policeman: the Research

Applicants in the main were born in London and aged between 20 and 35 years old. Their height ranged from 5ft 3in to 6ft 1½in, and the majority had a build recorded as "well made", although "stout made" was also used. At the other end of the scale, "rather slim" and "middling" were also used albeit very rarely. The average height for a Foot Patrole officer was 5ft 7in to 5ft 8in tall, representing a quarter of all applicants. The majority of men (60 percent) were married, and (40 percent) had between one and five children.

Some 17 percent, or just under one fifth, had been attached to the army as foot guards or local militia, whilst the next largest groups were servants (12 percent) and shoemakers (11 percent), followed by labourers (seven percent) and porters (five percent). The majority (97 percent) were from the lower classes who worked with their hands, whilst the remaining three percent were from the aspiring middle classes, describing themselves as clerks.

The typical profile of the Foot Patrole applicant was a Londoner, 24-years-old, 5ft 7in, well-made and married with two children. By comparison, the Horse Patroles differed in that they tended to select Constables based on their horsemanship and previous occupation in a cavalry regiment. Very few Londoners were selected in the mounted Patrole, a similarity to later recruitment by the Metropolitan Police who chose non-Londoners, generally considering them to be of better habits and character.

The men were expected to behave appropriately, and neglect of duty, drunkenness or misconduct was punished with dismissal. Just nine percent of Bow Street men were dismissed for these reasons, a far better average than the first 3,000 Metropolitan Police recruits. There is evidence in the records that warnings for misconduct and drunkenness were given by Conductors.

Our research shows that Bow Street Magistrates, the Home

Secretary, senior figures in the Home Department and other members of the establishment made recommendations for applicants to join the Foot Patrole. Fathers would put forward their sons; for example, Samuel Taunton, George Herring, Thomas Mayhew, John Lewis, Daniel Dawkins and William Bond successfully joined the Foot Patrole in this way. Townsend, Vickery, Jealous, Goddard and many more Principal Officers mentioned earlier in this book also commenced their careers as members of the Foot Patrole. For example, Fredrick Thomas Avery, aged 23 years, a shoemaker born in London, applied to join the Foot Patrole in November 1825 and his application was supported by his father, who was a Conductor of the Night Patrole posted to Party Number Seven.[616] Those that showed no promise were replaced. As with later police recruiting, natural wastage was a constant problem, amounting to annual turnover of nearly 15 percent. The breakdown within the Foot Patrole shows that one percent died, six percent resigned, five percent were promoted or transferred to the Day Patrole and two percent were declared unfit by the surgeon and dismissed. This was in addition to the nine percent of dismissals.

The recruiting profile introduced by Robert Peel for the New Police in 1829, according to Reith (1948), was that:

> Requirements for recruits were that they should be under the age of 35 and not less than 5 feet seven inches in height, they should be healthy and strong, physically and mentally; able to read and write and to produce in support of their applications, recommendations from one or more individuals of good social standing to whom they were personally known.[617]

Peel understood from his own experience as Chief Secretary for Ireland, where he introduced the Royal Irish Constabulary in 1813, and also as Home Secretary from 1822 onwards, what worked in the

---

616 Copy original Public Office, Bow Street Foot Patrole No. 67 for Fredrick Thomas Avery. Documents held by the Metropolitan Police at the Heritage Centre Empress State Building, West Brompton, West London.

617 Reith, C. (1948) *A Short History of the British Police*. Oxford University Press, p. 35.

recruitment of Constables. Peel had worked closely with the Bow Street establishment and was able to see for himself the usefulness of their methods of organisation and recruitment. What is obvious from our research is that both methods of recruitment appear the same. Peel seemingly did not develop a separate one for New Police Commissioners Rowan and Mayne to follow, instead adopting the Bow Street recruitment methods and profile used successfully for many years. What Peel knew was that being a police Constable was a difficult and arduous task, and that employing suitable and above-average candidates depended on merit and fitness.

Being Skilled and Brave

From 1800 onwards, large numbers of disbanded soldiers were sent home with their weapons and placed on reserve in case the war with France continued. The availability of firearms, swords and other weapons became a great problem for Bow Street's forces. This meant that being skilled in the art of hand-to-hand combat with fists, knives, cutlasses and swords was a definite pre-requisite. Great experience in the use and preservation of weapons including pistols and muskets was also a distinct advantage. Many felons were armed and would "not be taken", meaning that as the offence was a capital one and conviction meant execution anyway, nothing would be lost in fighting it out rather than being arrested. For this reason the Patroles routinely carried a truncheon and a cutlass, which was sometimes supplemented by a concealed loaded pistol as a means of defence. Those with previous experience, especially of military or naval combat, were prized applicants. Being a good horseman and understanding the needs and abilities of his mount were necessary advantages to the Horse Patrole. On arrival at any crime scene a Bow Street officer needed to be courageous, have a sense of purpose, be skilful in identification, have a suspicious nature and have good detection skills.

The introduction of a Bow Street Foot Patrole was announced in the *London Packet* in August 1782 as a group of "Stout men, who are to go armed, and patrole in different parts from dusk in the evening until 12 o'clock at night".[618] Given that this initiative was introduced by Sir Sampson Wright in response to a particularly violent crime wave, funding this enterprise was Bow Street's obligation; however the Government, appreciating their responsibility, commenced six-weekly payments to Bow Street in early 1783.[619] Realising that this initiative was a six-weekly rolling programme the bankrupt Treasury resisted commitment for longer periods, since the costs were a not insignificant £2,600 per year – funds that Bow Street also could not sustain on their own. Government and the Treasury were at odds over funding, but lessons were being learnt. The robberies had dried up by June 1783, but a few arrests were still being made. As a result, funding was continued as the benefits of prevention were bearing fruit.[620] The Foot Patrole was continued for the next five decades.

Wright had originally asked for thirty men, to be divided into three parties; however, when Government funds became available he increased his force to 46 men and split them into eight groups of five or six, placing a Conductor or Captain in charge of each party.[621] These positions appear to be the equivalent to a Sergeant in the Metropolitan Police rank structure. These parties were allocated as follows: to the Balls Pond Road (Islington to Dalston), to Shoreditch and City Road, to Kentish Town and Hampstead, and to Holloway from Islington (Turnpike). Three parties were sent west to cover the road to Acton and Kilburn, another to Fulham and Chelsea, concluding with a patrol along the Hammersmith Road. The last two parties were sent south of the Thames, one to Deptford and Greenwich and the other along the Clapham and Wandsworth Roads west from Southwark.[622] Sworn in by magistrates as peace officers for the first time, this was a preventive patrol – a central theme of Sir

---

618 *The London Packet*, 28th–30th August 1782.
619 NLI 15929 (3).
620 The six weekly Treasury funds were recorded in the 'Special Service book' TNA; T38/741, 11, 15, 16. For more detail see Beattie, J. M. (2012) *The First English Detectives*. Oxford University Press, Oxford, p. 144.
621 TNA; T1/598. 315–24.
622 TNA; T1/598. 315–24.

John Fielding's original notions had come to fruition. Working seven days a week, the patrole Constable was paid 2s 6d a night, with the captains being paid double that. Their pay would be supplemented by rewards made by private citizens or a court for apprehending convicted felons. Additional fees could be earned for service of warrants or summonses issued by Bow Street and executed by the patroles.

Later this establishment was increased to 68 men and split into thirteen parties, although over time, and as London expanded, additional parties were added to the establishment. The Bow Street Foot Patrole was placed under the superintendence of the Chief Magistrate; however, the Chief Clerk was the Inspector responsible for their pay and expenses.[623] Originally these men were divided into parties of four or five, who patrolled during the hours of darkness.[624] As London grew so did the patrols, with five parties covering the City of Westminster with a further eight parties working the outskirts of the metropolis to a distance of four miles from Charing Cross.[625] In 1798 the annual cost of the patrol was a little under £4,000, and their duties included keeping "the peace on all public occasions".[626]

Bow Street occasionally experienced a shocking outrage when a member of the Patrole was killed, or died on duty. Duncan Grant, one of Bow Street's Constables, was assisting other members of the Patrole to execute a privy warrant on 26th December 1799 at a disorderly house in Maynard Street, St. Giles when they were violently attacked by a mob of Irish men and women armed with cutlasses and bludgeons. Grant was badly cut and injured but survived, lingering on until 22nd January 1800 when he died. Other members of the Patrole were also badly injured during the melee. The King gave a reward of £100 for information as to the assailants

623 *Dictionary of the English Language* (1785) by Samuel Johnson states that an Inspector was a Superintendent and was taken from the Latin.
624 Ibid. The name Captain according to Dryden was a commander of a company in a regiment.
625 Ascoli, D. (1979) *The Queen's Peace*. Hamish Hamilton, London, pp. 48–49.
626 *Report from the Select Committee on the Police of the Metropolis* (1798) House of Commons.

and perpetrators of this crime, although it appears that no-one was caught or faced justice over this matter. Grant was not the only Bow Street Constable to die in the line of duty: others included Hind (1755), Atwood (1771), Wilkinson (1798) and Smithers (1820).

A re–organisation of the Patrole had occurred by 1814. London had been divided into sixteen districts, exclusive of the City of London, to be patrolled in parties of five with one in charge. Each Patrole was allocated to a district and covered by a Conductor and four Patroles, with one party held in reserve.[627] They were regulated by the exigencies of the demand placed on them by daily circumstances rather than the time of year.

A small printed book was produced, containing the rules under which the Foot Patrole operated. These instructions were strictly adhered to and any breach was punished harshly. When an infringement of these rules was discovered the particular Patrole would be either suspended from pay or dismissed.[628] Whilst discipline was strict there was also sympathy and compassion. The magistrates looked after their staff and understood the often dangerous and precarious nature of the Bow Street establishment. In this way, by 1814 any members of the Patrole who were sick, infirm or injured received sick pay, as we would term it today. There was no system of criminal injuries compensation for men who could no longer work, but Bow Street did offer a superannuation scheme for retirement. Records from 1814 show that Christopher Cridland (formally a Foot Patrole Captain) had been on sick pay for 91 days at 3s and 4d a day. By 1814, superannuation payments were also given for certain pensioned officers: for example, Archibald Ruthven Sr, a Captain of the Foot Patrole, received half pay of 2s 6d a day whilst eleven former Constables were paid 1s 6d a day each.[629] Also on the list at the time was William Black, formally Captain

---

627 *Report from the Select Committee on Police of the Metropolis* (1822) House of Commons, London, p. 8.
628 *Report from the Select Committee on Police of the Metropolis* (1816) House of Commons, London, p. 75.
629 Accounts of the establishment of the Public Office Bow Street 1814 and 1815.

of the Foot Patrole, who had been superannuated since April 1812.[630] Others included Henry Crocker, another Captain of the Patrole who had covered the Kentish Town and Hampstead Road areas, Samuel Gyde, Donald McGillivreay (superannuated in 1812), John McGregor, John Holland, Anthony Browne, William Edwards, Alexander Stuart, Thomas Edwards and Ephraim Wood.[631] Sick pay and superannuation was not an automatic right for any worn out, injured or disabled officer, but one agreed with Government, who funded the costs.

Observation, Investigation and the Art of Detection

Since Elizabethan times it had been the law that a victim's family had to commence an investigation and to find evidence to detect a suspect. The financial cost of the investigation and prosecution rested with the victim's family, but an impecunious relative may not have had recourse to justice. If a suspect was identified, the family would present information to the magistrate who might issue a warrant of arrest – directing a Constable to apprehend the accused. Once an arrest had been made, the Constable would search for evidence and take possession of items which he would remove to the court. During the seventeenth century the court permitted and favoured witnesses, hearsay evidence, and any depositions presenting physical evidence to the court. Occasionally, a piece of physical evidence such as a weapon or incriminating personal article belonging to the alleged felon found at the scene of the crime was presented to the judge and jury.[632] Beyond the family, the common law required that the Sheriff investigate any felony and misdemeanour, apprehend, bring to court and prosecute all felons.

While this system had worked well for many years in rural England where people had not strayed far from their birthplace, the same was not true for an expanding metropolis where concentrations

630 Bow Street Accounts T38.674.
631 The Third Report from the Committee on the State of the Police of the Metropolis House of Commons (1818), p. 188.
632 Baker, J.H. (1977) 'Criminal Courts and Procedure at Common Law, 1550–1800' in *Crime in England, 1550–1800*, ed. J.S. Cockburn. Princeton, New Jersey, pp. 15–48.

of the poor, destitute and feckless gathered together, creating opportunities for crime. Sheer numbers of felonies overwhelmed the parochial system of London, rendering the post of Sheriff also as ineffectual. The idea of uniting together trusted Constables, not restraining them to a particular area and allowing them to develop and work together as a group, acquire knowledge of crime and gain experience of felons, was the brainchild of a perceptive Henry Fielding. Fielding was changing the role and function of the Constable, developing a more professional organisation, but also creating a new science of policing.

The Middlesex Justices Act of 1792 was introduced to reform and cleanse a corrupt London magistracy. The Act only marginally attempted to provide a more effective system of policing; however, a controversial clause subsequently added to the Bill increased the discretion of the police. It authorised the Constables to arrest a suspect "on suspicion" and not necessarily as a result of a Justice's warrant.[633] Whilst the notion of crime detection had allowed for constabulary discretion, this clause sought to legitimise a crucial tool in the armoury against criminal behaviour.

In the world of the Regency Constable, suspiciousness meant the same as it does for an officer today – the ability for one to have the idea or impression that someone or something is questionable, dishonest, or dangerous.[634] When this notion is applied to a set of circumstances or a situation, a person, or in answer to a question, it appears to the enquirer as abnormal, odd, out of place, unusual, strange, different, uncharacteristic or wrong, and likely to lead to a heightened sense of suspicion. At this point further questioning might be required to substantiate the suspicion. This is the very essence of policing, since questioning of people is central to every Constable's role no matter whether they are a Detective, Foot Patrole or Mounted Officer. In a sense, this skill needs a certain spatial awareness as well. Not having

---

633 Critchley, T. A. (1967) *The History of the Police of England and Wales*. Constable, London, p. 37.
634 www.google.co.uk/search?q=what+does+suspicousness+mean&ie=utf–8&oe=utf–8&client=firefox–b&gfe_rd=cr&ei=nugNWemiDcPO8gfmybCoBQ accessed 6th May 2017.

a sense or understanding of what is going on around you, or failing to appreciate the environment, would not satisfy selection to Bow Street. Understanding geography and the built environment was needed in order to follow and catch an identified offender, mounted or on foot, and most often travelling into dangerous hiding places, woods and out of the way locations. A good example of suspicious behaviour was observed by members of the Foot Patrole in 1783, when a group of men were behaving furtively. Noticing something unusual, Hugh O'Donnel and James Allen, the Captain of the Patrole, arrested and detained Christopher Trusty and Thomas Howard, who were armed and in the process of preparing to rob a man on the King's highway. Both were apprehended, convicted and sentenced to be transported for seven years, earning the officers a share in the £40 Government reward.[635]

Crime investigation is composed of many elements, and dependent from the outset on observation coupled with an ability to listen, together with the knowledge taken from experiential learning of previous cases. The skills include good recall of events, people, their descriptions and dress. Good communication, questioning and investigation skills and the need to sum up scenarios quickly but perceptively are great skills, although these were often learned "on the job". Learning and understanding the rules of evidence, making the right notes and gathering the relevant evidence were also necessary. These are all difficult matters to comprehend at the time, but Bow Street officers, especially the Runners, soon became very adept at these requirements.

Arrival at a crime scene, or walking the streets of London, requires good observational ability in an officer. The finding of clues, processing information, preserving evidence, and linking it to an identified individual provides reasonable suspicion, which in Georgian London was necessary in order to arrest them. Once the suspect had been arrested and charged with the crime, the officer would need to prepare the evidence for court and present any case papers for prosecution. Instructions for the preparation of case

635 PRO HO 61/1.

papers at court were given in Welch's instruction book and are shown at Appendix 1. These are basic tenets, and have not changed the role of police since Regency times. Police work today is more sophisticated, technological and scientific, but it is also true to say that while the art of police work in Regency Britain was very basic indeed, ultimately the same rules applied.

To prove a case in court, the investigator needs to comply with the notion of "the continuity of evidence" – meaning that the point is proved if the chain of evidence remains continuous and has not been broken. What is the officer looking for? How does an officer become suspicious about an individual or scene? The first steps at the scene of a crime rely on the officer surveying the surroundings and taking stock in looking for clues which may be linked to a suspect. When discovered, any physical evidence is thoroughly explained, examined as to its location and described. The physical evidence can become an exhibit which is properly accounted for, kept safe and sealed into an envelope or other container, and then removed from the scene to a police office where it can be locked securely.

This is what was expected by the Bow Street Principal Officers who were sent out to deal with serious crimes. In another famous murder, that of Mr Weare at Aldenham in 1823, George Ruthven, the Bow Street officer assigned to arrest the suspect Thurtell, secured incriminating evidence in the form of exhibits for the coroner and court when he seized a pistol from the suspect's coat – one of a pair, the other being found near the scene of the murder. Increasing his suspicions, Ruthven seized a neckerchief from Thurtell's lodgings that was heavily bloodstained with Thurtell's name on it. These were produced by Ruthven in evidence before the court even though, in the matter of bloodied items, they could not distinguish between human and animal blood at that time.

Cox (2010, pp.177–185) pointed out some of the early forensic skills of the Principal Officers which were brought to light in a murder in Stourbridge. Just before Christmas 1812 a gentleman farmer named Benjamin Robins of Dunsley Hall was on his way back from market when he met a man on the way. Just short of where

Robins lived, the man produced a pistol and shot Robins in the back. Robins staggered home severely injured and died ten days later. He was 57-years-old. With the family of the victim investigating the circumstances and paying for the prosecution at this time, as mentioned above, a reward of £100 was put up by Robins' brother, who was a local practising attorney. Handbills were posted with details of the reward and an accurate description of the culprit. The sum of £40, a Government–funded incentive, could be added to the reward. The inhabitants of Stourbridge collected a further £50 for the capture of the felon responsible, in addition to a further £100 augmented by the Government. This eventually totalled £290 just in rewards. Bow Street Runners Harry Adkins and Samuel Taunton were sent to investigate at the request of the local magistrate. Adkins and Taunton knew that they had to bring all of their skills together, detective or otherwise, to be able to successfully resolve this case. Given the size of the rewards on this investigation, this was an extremely important and lucrative case for the Bow Street officers to solve.

They started by speaking to family members and witnesses to establish what was already known. They recorded these details in their Occurrence Books which they carried with them. These enquiries quickly ascertained that a stranger had been seen in the area acting suspiciously on the day of the murder, and he was identified by a witness as William Howe, a 32-year-old journeyman joiner from Ombersley, Worcestershire. Adkins and Taunton had to make connections in order to successfully resolve the case.

If Howe was the prime suspect then the link between him and Robins needed to be made. In today's world this is made very much easier with the use of forensic science, in entomology, DNA connections, mobile phone signals and the use of fingerprints. Those officers had none of that since their investigation was very basic, but probably more thorough in some respects than in today's world which arguably creates evidential over-reliance on closed circuit television and not the police officer's word.

The Bow Street officers' approach could have taken one of two avenues. The most difficult and time-consuming course from Bow Street's view was where no suspect had been identified and one needed to be found, whilst the far easier method was to build further incriminating evidence against an already recognised accused. In this case, the Bow Street officers opted for the latter. Here another influence was also at play, and this was the officer's sixth sense, later called "the copper's nose"; the ability to be able to sense things about another who they do not even know. This notion is often found to be correct. Again this is part of the officer's perceptual blueprint, informed from years of experience – a collective psyche – the ability to be able to sum up a person quickly without any tangible evidence or even knowing them. As a police officer, this is a gift which not all of them have. Adkins and Taunton were two of Bow Street's most experienced and respected detectives, and both had the gift.

If Howe was eliminated from their inquiries their task would have been made infinitely more difficult. This meant they focused on finding the gun and establishing this link, although in 1812 forensic ballistics was in its infancy and its expertise still a great many years away. Today's detective commences inquiries with a search of the crime scene, because experience has taught the officer as part of the perceptual blueprint that culprits discard incriminating evidence near the scene to avoid detection. A search of the crime scene and surrounding area is usually carried out, moving out in concentric circles from the scene so as not to miss anything. Here the officers would have been looking for anything, from items dropped to any marks left, including those footprints left by both Robins and Howe. They would have noted the boots both were wearing at the time of the attack. Their problems were time and the weather. Over the intervening period, those footprints would have been erased by other travellers or even washed away by the rain. But the officers had been fortunate from the start, since much of the legwork had been done by the Robins' family, who had collaborated with the principal officers and shared their own inquiries. But the officers had further luck, since an inmate of Stafford jail who had shared a cell with Howe was interviewed by the nephew of the victim and claimed that not only had Howe been the murderer, but that he had pawned Robins' watch. This would have been another line of inquiry but it seems not to have been pursued.

On the issue of the gun, Howe had written to his new wife who was living nearby, telling her that he had hidden the gun and bullets in a hayrick near Stourbridge. Not really knowing her well enough he did not appreciate she could not read so she had asked her landlady to read the letter aloud to her. This unintentionally incriminated Howe, and the prosecuting family were quickly informed of these facts. William Robins, the nephew, found the gun on a farm near the murder scene, a very distinctive square screw barrelled flintlock pistol together with three unfired lead balls. The lead balls had a distinctive groove in them, suggesting there was a fault in the mould from which they were made. But no-one knew at this stage if this was the gun that had killed Robins. In modern day parlance this is called "collecting physical evidence", and so the lead balls and the pistol were not only described in detail but the location they were found at was vital evidence too. The officers took custody of the physical evidence and stored them securely, retaining the exhibits as they are now called for the court hearing later. It was not uncommon before the advent of photography for the officer who found the exhibit to draw a map in his Occurrence Book, detailing its location in relation to the place it was found.

The report from the surgeon who carried out the examination of Robins's body revealed the recovery of a lead ball from the deceased's torso with a distinctive groove in it, matching the bullets found with the gun. This proved the link between the gun, lead shot and the body. The officers established that Howe possessed a trunk that he kept in Bishopsgate, which the officers found and, with a search warrant, opened it. Inside they found a matching screw barrelled pistol, often made as a pair, and a lead mould with a distinctive groove in it. Their task was to identify a maker and either contact them or ask the opinion of a gunsmith. It was established that these guns were effectively unique and were indeed a matching pair, thereby linking them evidentially. The officers made inquiries about Howe's character, which established he was well known and had four aliases. Another part of the officer's perceptual blueprint would have told him that a person usually uses an alias to avoid revealing his proper identity. This would have raised the level of suspicion. Howe was convicted, although there were several gaps in evidence which today would have been exploited by a keen defence barrister. He was sentenced to death and executed, his body being exhibited near the scene of the murder afterwards.

This shows that both Bow Street officers successfully managed to arrest a suspect who had been identified to them, including discovering and acting on the evidence which was needed to convict him. Their knowledge, coupled with a stroke of luck in finding the trunk containing the lead ball mould, was a good piece of basic detective work that made them very wealthy. Adkins and Taunton had learnt the art of policing, not only by experience but also from other officers who had gone before.

Foot Patrole Discipline

Like the rest of the Bow Street police establishment, discipline in the Foot Patrole was strict, and conduct on or off duty was always under scrutiny. From their introduction the leaders – the Superintendent (Chief Magistrate), the Inspector (Chief Clerk) and Conductors exercised a power of control over their men which meant sanctioning them when necessary, using verbal warnings and maintaining official records of the misconduct. More serious matters were brought to the attention of the Chief Magistrate. For example, Sir Richard Birnie found out that a Conductor of the Bedford Square Division of the Night Patrole, Francis Holyland, was attempting to procure Christmas boxes from householders by posting pre-printed leaflets through letterboxes and calling at their houses later. An angry Birnie called an apologetic Holyland before him and said:

> "You called upon the Hanoverian Consul with a pre-printed paper beginning with 'We the undersigned' and at the head of the list appeared your name. You must have known as I am sure you did know, that such a practice was contrary to the orders of the

magistrates and you are suspended from your office"[636]

This effectively would have lost Holyland his responsible job, and as a Conductor and senior member of the Foot Patrole he should have set a better example to his patrole. We are unenlightened as to his punishment but he did not lose his job, as in 1819 he was operating against poachers in the provinces having been promoted, deputising for a Principal Officer in several matters.[637]

Excessive alcohol use by members of the Foot Patrole was a problem for the Bow Street establishment. Barry Conway, an Irishman nearly six feet tall, was appointed in September 1823 and posted to Party Number Three where William Morris was the Conductor. In December the same year Conway was found drunk and had assaulted two women, which led to him being discharged from the Foot Patrole.[638] John Greenway, Patrole Number 55, was discharged for intoxication.[639] Daniel Thomas, Patrole Number 49, was discharged at the end of March 1825 for intoxication and neglect of duty.[640] George Harding, Patrole Number 44, attached to Party Number Nine in August 1824, was deemed unfit by the surgeon and dismissed.[641] The surgeon attached to Bow Street would certify an officer's fitness for duty, and a Conductor would refer a man to him for his opinion. Whilst we are unaware of the nature of Harding's condition, alcohol abuse was often the reason for dismissal. Other punishments were available for excessive drinking, such as in the

636 Fitzgerald, P. (1888) *Chronicles of Bow Street Police-office*. Gilbert and Rivington, London, p. 173.
637 *Annual Register Vol. 60*. (1818), p. 154.
638 Copy original Public Office, Bow Street Foot Patrole No. 10 for Barry Conway. Documents held by the Metropolitan Police at the Heritage Centre Empress State Building, West Brompton, West London.
639 Copy original Public Office, Bow Street Foot Patrole No. 55 for John Greenway. Documents held by the Metropolitan Police at the Heritage Centre Empress State Building, West Brompton, West London.
640 Copy original Public Office, Bow Street Foot Patrole No. 49 for Daniel Thomas. Documents held by the Metropolitan Police at the Heritage Centre Empress State Building, West Brompton, West London.
641 Copy original Public Office, Bow Street Foot Patrole No. 44 for George Harding. Documents held by the Metropolitan Police at the Heritage Centre Empress State Building, West Brompton, West London.

case of James Holyland who was suspended for eight days without pay by Peter Perry, his Conductor, for coming on duty intoxicated in September 1823.[642] Perry took notice of the circumstances, but also the fact that Holyland's uncle and sponsor was a senior Bow Street officer as we have already seen above. While nepotism cannot be ruled out here, in another case David Herring, Patrole Number Two whose father was William Herring, an Inspector with the Day Patrole, was dismissed in July 1823 for coming on duty whilst intoxicated.[643]

Benjamin Johnson, a Bow Street Patrole, was involved with others allegedly in the commission of robbery and in return for £1 let a known thief go. He was also implicated by a respectable man named Baxter, who asserted that his son and Johnson were involved in the burglary of a house in the City of London where cash was known to be. When Johnson went with the younger Baxter they broke into the house, and only when the cash was found did Johnson reveal himself as a Constable and to arrest Baxter.[644] Johnson was subsequently arrested, charged and convicted for his dishonesty. Scotsman John Donaldson, Foot Patrole Number 37, who was appointed in June 1824, was dismissed for neglect of duty.[645] William Swift, an engraver with seven months' service attached to Party Number One, was discharged in December 1825 for misconduct whilst on duty.[646]

Drunkenness, violence and dishonesty on the part of Bow Street Constables was not tolerated, and punished with dismissal.

642 Copy original Public Office, Bow Street Foot Patrole No. 3 for James Holyland. Documents held by the Metropolitan Police at the Heritage Centre Empress State Building, West Brompton, West London.
643 Copy original Public Office, Bow Street Foot Patrole No. 2 for David Herring. Documents held by the Metropolitan Police at the Heritage Centre Empress State Building, West Brompton, West London.
644 *Manchester Mercury*, 13th August 1816.
645 Copy original Public Office, Bow Street Foot Patrole No. 10 for John Donaldson. Documents held by the Metropolitan Police at the Heritage Centre Empress State Building, West Brompton, West London.
646 Copy original Public Office, Bow Street Foot Patrole No. 64 for William Swift. Documents held by the Metropolitan Police at the Heritage Centre Empress State Building, West Brompton, West London.

Operational Matters

The daily working of the Foot Patrole changed little except for an increase in parties and numbers into new neighbourhoods as London expanded. Targeted and focussed Foot Patroles had been operating on an ad hoc basis since the 1750s, paid for out of Bow Street accounts. A regular Government funded Foot Patrole had commenced in 1782, when Sir Sampson Wright established the Patrole originally consisting of 65 men split into thirteen parties (later fifteen) of five men (75 in total), one in each party being the Conductor as supervisor. They operated in the districts of London working during the hours of darkness.[647] They patrolled at uncertain hours which were fixed at Bow Street and not advertised outside of the Patroles. They wore no uniform.

They patrolled to a distance of between three and four miles from London in the immediate vicinity of the metropolis along the principal streets, lanes and alleys of the area, according to the direction of the Patrole Conductor. Each Conductor would ensure that regular patrols would not pass at the same time and in the same place each day. Establishing a meeting point was an important feature of the Foot Patrole system, where the Constables would liaise in the middle of the night and discuss what they had seen and witnessed. In doing this, the Patroles reinforced their authority as a unified group but also provided a check on their personal safety. In the event that a pair of the Foot Patrole failed to rendezvous, the remaining officers would go in search of them in their district until they were found.

Bow Street did not pay for the patrol Constables' lodgings, since it was more expensive to rent at the London end and considered unfair given that some men were single, some married and others had large families.[648] The Conductors would attend Bow Street each

---

647 Brown, R. (2011) The problem in policing London to 1829 richardjohnbr.blogspot.co.uk/2011/04/problem-in-policing-london-to-1829.html accessed 25th January 2016.

648 Report from the select Committee of the Police of the Metropolis 17th July 1822, p. 25.

week and report back to the magistrates about their weekly duties and what had happened. By rota, three of the parties were examined at Bow Street each week and their appointments produced for inspection. Once inspected, if found absent or defective in any way then directions were given for replacement equipment to be obtained at the patrol Constable's expense.[649]

The duties of the Foot Patrole did not impose upon the local parochial watch in any way, nor did they have any control over them, although the watch despised the Bow Street men, thinking that they spied on them.[650] John Stafford, Chief Clerk at Bow Street, re-organised the Patrole in the early 1800s as there were no inspection facilities nor much in the way of any supervision. He split the Foot Patrole into two and sent out half of them to the four mile point where they were stationed and resided. They were nominally called "the country party" and patrolled into London at a given hour, whilst the others – "the London party" – patrolled from the Stones End (where the pavements finished) towards the country party, meeting them half way.[651] While at their furthest extreme – at the four mile point – the Foot Patrole liaised and met with the Horse Patrole, communicating any necessary information with them before returning home. As a result the main roads were well covered and protected from robberies.

In 1821 Home Secretary Lord Sidmouth changed the operating practice of the Foot Patrole. They were withdrawn into London and the officers restricted to only the local area and to the streets of the metropolis, in a move designed to combat street robbery and footpads. Some, if not all, were added to the Dismounted Horse Patrole, which is the subject of the next chapter. The Dismounted Horse Patrole were instructed to cover policing the country duty, formerly carried out by the Foot Patrole, taking up their position between the Foot Patrole in London and the Horse Patrole in the

---

649 Report from the select Committee of the Police of the Metropolis 17th July 1822, p. 23.
650 Ibid, p. 25.
651 Ibid, p. 23.

country.[652]

The Foot Patrole hours of duty were regulated by the season or time of year. They performed their duty from dusk and remained on the streets until 1.00am. Sometimes their duty would start very early, at 3.00 or 4.00pm, and finish at midnight (in winter time) with the object of protecting the public whilst they were generally out and about. The Conductors were still being paid 5s a night and the patrol 2s 6d each in 1812; however, there were increments in pay according to the amount of years' service.

There were other ways for the Foot Patrole to earn money, and six of them attended the two Royal theatres and dealt with pickpockets whilst also keeping the peace. For this they were paid 2s a night, and as they were then unable to perform their night duty they were brought on early and split into pairs to patrol in three parties in the Strand, Holborn and Oxford Street, and Bond Street and Piccadilly.[653] When not on duty, the Foot Patrole was allowed to earn extra monies by carrying out other jobs provided it did not infringe upon their Bow Street duties. In fact, many of the Patrole had their own businesses selling wares such as shoes, which they made, groceries or hardware. Some were workmen who could supplement their income by working as labourers.

Any members of the Foot Patrole who became ineffective were removed or replaced and, if worn out, the unfit or injured were superannuated. The Foot Patrole recruits were young in age, and were not to be over 35-years-old. Advancement to Conductor was achieved through industry and hard work, and each supervisor was drawn from the ranks of the Constables of the Foot Patrole. It was expected that good Constables needed to be of a certain character; honest, active and intelligent. Stafford, in evidence to the Select Committee of 1822, was encouraged by the fact that his Bow Street Foot Patrole had driven away the pickpockets, street robbers and burglars from London itself, but they were forced into

652 Report from the select Committee of the Police of the Metropolis 17th July 1822, p. 23.
653 Ibid, p. 24.

the surrounding villages and were committing crime there instead.

Whilst some of the parochial watch in some wards had a patrol during the night they were often only two in number, and not as effective as the Bow Street Foot Patroles. The parties of the Foot Patrole would look out for suspicious persons and in 1822, since street robberies were in decline, the biggest nuisance was the smashing of shop windows. The Patroles would look out for young boys lurking near shop windows where valuable items were on display and move them on or stop and search them for stolen items, especially youths they knew well. They dealt with lesser offences, including the preparation and conspiracy to commit crimes like pickpocketing, shoplifting or any offence of a public nature (against property).

Details of the Foot Patrole beats are rare; however, we are given an insight in how they covered their allocated beat in Westminster. They consisted of five in number and would:

> "Come on duty.....at half past six in the evening; they patrol down by the House of Lords to Millbank; from thence to Vauxhall Road; then they go to Pimlico; and from Pimlico to Buckingham Gate and James Street, to Vincent Square and the bye streets and go off at half past 12."[654]

Even though the Conductors varied their times and beats, the Foot Patroles became well known and familiar to the local people, since their daily circuits, beats and refreshment times were regular. Those who had nothing to hide conversed with the Patroles, while the "old hands" recognised them as they approached and made off. To know where and when the Patroles took their refreshment, usually in a tavern of their district, was of great value to the rogues and villains of the area, since they could break into houses and steal property with less risk of detection by the local Foot Patrole.

The eight country parties were brought into Westminster on the instructions of Lord Sidmouth in 1821 and the Foot Patrole

654 Report from the Select Committee of the Police of the Metropolis 17th July 1822, p. 45.

reconstituted which is the subject of the next chapter. When the New Police were being formed in 1829, the new Commissioners wished to take as many of the Bow Street establishment as they could. Being a Patrole was an arduous job, undertaken seven days a week, 365 days a year. In patrolling the streets of London the Patroles gained vast experience, which the New Police would benefit from. For many of the younger Patroles this was an option; however, the older men would be disadvantaged and the magistrates at Bow Street realised that quite quickly. During the transition period the Bow Street magistrates publically commented on the disadvantage, especially in one particular case, that of Bow Street Patrole Conductor, John Birchall. Such was the esteem in which he was held that when called in to give evidence at Bow Street in February 1830 Sir Richard Birnie made comment to his fellow magistrates that he feared that this "active and deserving officer would be a material sufferer under the new arrangements."[655]

Birchall had been offered a position as an Inspector in the New Police but had declined it because of his constitution following long service in the army and at Bow Street had left him "worn out".[656] Aged 39 years, Birchall, of Norfolk Street, Strand was a well-built man, 5ft 11in tall, with eight years' Bow Street police service. In his short service he had not only established an unblemished reputation, but had risen to the rank of Conductor, a position to which only responsible officers could aspire to. He had gained hugely valuable policing experience which was going to waste under the new policing arrangements and there was nothing the magistrates felt they could do for him, since their offices were being disbanded. The magistrates recommended Birchall to the New Police, suggesting to the Commissioners that "He was well behaved and trusty, rather hasty (noted as unfit)".[657] The magistrates could superannuate other members of the Foot Patrole who had over ten years' service, but with Birchall this was not possible. Birchall carried on at Bow Street

655 *Morning Chronicle*, 3rd February 1830.
656 Ibid.
657 MEPO 2/25.

"as an officer", having been promoted from the Patrole to become a Principal Officer. In July 1830 he was involved in the arrest of Captain Helsham, who had taken part in a duel in Boulogne and killed his opponent, Lieutenant Crowther.[658] In January the following year Birchall was charged with others at Bow Street for declining to take action in a matter of felony, and appeared at Marlborough Street Court.[659] He was still present there in December 1831, and by 1833 he was a messenger and also gaoler at the office – a position usually taken up by a responsible senior Principal Officer.[660] Birchall was still at Bow Street in June 1834, but by December 1835 he had moved on to the Office of the Commissioners of Stamps and had become an enforcement officer, detecting street vendors who distributed untaxed (unstamped) newspapers.[661]

Having experience gained through being part of the Bow Street Patrole could be turned to nefarious purposes as well. John Purton had been a Patrole at Bow Street but had left when he was arrested for defrauding a coffee house proprietor of a guinea. Purton had for some time been operating as "a cad to informers and others". In other words, he was a go-between who, because of his experience in the shady London underworld, could help to make matters good where there was a dispute. This scam involved approaching the coffee house owner and exclaiming he was aware that a friend had taken out several summonses against him for selling coffee at unlawful hours. However, he could make matters "go away" if both the coffee house owner and his friend came together to make an arrangement. Following this meeting the coffee house owner agreed to pay the complainant and his colleague a fee of 30s each, and also hand over 2s 6d to Purton for his efforts. Not happy, the coffee house owner went to the local police who waited in uniform at the establishment where the monies were to be paid over. Seeing the uniform spooked the two men. Purton, however, was arrested, charged with fraud and

658 *Leeds Patriot and Yorkshire Advertiser*, Saturday 24th July 1830.
659 *Morning Post*, Monday 24th January 1831.
660 *Public Ledger and Daily Advertiser*, Wednesday 21st December 1831.
661 *London Evening Standard*, Tuesday 22nd December 1835.

detained.[662]

On the introduction of the New Police in 1829 the Commissioners sought to recruit members of the Bow Street Foot and the Dismounted Horse Patroles with middling success. Their problem was the weekly pay of the new Constables at one guinea a week, which was far less than what was being paid to Bow Street officers. Also, the system of Government rewards for the conviction of felons altered for officers of the New Police, thereby reducing any further incentive to join. The Commissioners got round this by paying former Bow Street men extra in recognition of their seniority in the Patrole up until July 1831, otherwise they promoted them.

What contributed to the success (and myth) of the Bow Street establishment, and moreover to the Foot Patrole, was their system of discipline and organisation. Information on all significant issues, and not only serious criminal matters, would flow from the Patroles to the Conductors to be passed to Bow Street as a central point for gathering. This information, including any orders or instructions, would pass up and down the chain of command, ensuring promulgation to everyone.

The Patroles would perform duty by rotation at Bow Street, the Conductors were posted there regularly as duty officers to be called to deal with situations necessitating their attention. They were in constant contact with the magistrates, who were informed on a range of topics, not only crimes and criminals, but also on other social problems such traffic matters, disorderly houses, drunkenness, prostitution, brothels, problem taverns and licensing of public houses.

In other words, these co-ordinated, experienced, dedicated professional Patroles were the eyes and ears of Bow Street that allowed for an informed magistracy, who in turn would pass on this valuable knowledge to Governments.

662 *Morning Advertiser*, 9th April 1830.

6

Bow Street
Dismounted Horse Patrole

The Horse Patrole was formed in 1805 by Sir Richard Ford, Bow Street Chief Magistrate, in response to the great increase in both highway and street robberies in the metropolis. The new Patrole was formed in the same manner as the Foot Patrole.

In 1821, the Dismounted Horse Patrol was formed at the time that the Foot Patrole was being withdrawn into central London.[663] This was also a Foot Patrole which acted as a kind of reserve for replacing any mounted Horse Patroles who died, resigned, or were pensioned or considered unfit for further duty. Some 102 Dismounted Horse Patroles were appointed, and supervised by two Inspectors, two Ordinary or Deputy Inspectors and 21 leaders (today we would call these Sergeants) supervising the 77 Constables.

To differentiate between the two Patroles, Conductors of the Horse Patroles were replaced with Inspectors. Each leader was in charge of a party of four and allocated a particular district for seven days a week. The recruits were under 40 years of age. An example of their beat was two of the dismounted men stationed at Highgate and two at Battlesbridge (Islington/Kings Cross), with the leader being at the London end of the road.[664] Again, the main reason for this was in consequence to the alarming increase of street robberies in the metropolis during the night time. Bringing the Foot Patrole

663 Howard. G. (1953) *Guardians of the Queen's Peace*. Odhams, London, p. 101.
664 Report from the select Committee of the Police of the Metropolis 17th July 1822, p. 35.

into London to within narrower limits, it was felt, would make a beneficial change in the establishment of both the Horse and Foot Patroles.

The Dismounted Horse Patroles were stationed along the principal roads to a distance of three or four miles in the suburban areas at night.[665] The times of their duty were regulated by the seasons, and commenced between five and seven in the evening, depending on the time of year, and finished at midnight or 1.00am. Occasionally, they are brought on earlier in the afternoon in winter and started duty at dusk, terminating at 12 midnight.

The Dismounted Horse Patrole was placed under the superintendence of the Chief Magistrate, Sir Richard Birnie. Mr Stafford, the Chief Clerk operated as Inspector, although Mr Day as the Principal Conductor was responsible for the daily operational supervision. Mr Day received a salary of £100 per year.[666] Appointed to the Dismounted Patrole were men under 40 years of age who had served with credit in a cavalry regiment, and they provided a system of promotion to the Bow Street Horse Patrole as replacements when vacancies arose. Dismounted Patroles usually had another occupation for when they were not on duty to help support their families.

The leaders received 4s a day, whilst the Patrole wages were 3s a day, amounting to one guinea a week. They were required to be available for duty at all times, which made it difficult to have any other job, although no extra remuneration was given, not even for the service of warrants.[667] In 1822 their pay consisted of one guinea a week, with an additional 6d a night for those living outside the metropolis.[668] It was felt that the additional money would compensate those who would find it more difficult obtaining

---

665 Report from the Select Committee on Police of the Metropolis (1822) House of Commons, London, p. 8.

666 Ibid.

667 Report from the select Committee of the Police of the Metropolis 17th July 1822, p. 33.

668 Report from the Select Committee on Police of the Metropolis (1822) House of Commons, London, p. 81.

additional day work in the environs rather than the centre of London.[669] The leaders were answerable for the conduct of the men and also compiled quarterly returns of persons arrested. These would be passed on to the Inspectors together with their weekly reports which were passed on to Bow Street's magistrates. In effect, the Conductors were Sergeants and the Inspector was the Head Conductor and the Chief Clerk's deputy.

The Dismounted Horse Patrole were sworn in by the magistrates as Constables, and contrary to any speculation would not call out "Bow Street Patrole", unlike their (mounted) Horse Patrole colleagues.

The Dismounted Horse Patrole were highly-organised and strictly disciplined. They were required to be uniformed only occasionally, during a formal inspection, riot control or ceremonial event, otherwise they remained in their plain clothes when out on duty patrolling. Their uniform, when needed, was like that of the Horse Patrole and consisted of a blue double-breasted coat with yellow buttons, a red waistcoat, blue trousers, black felt hat. They also wore Wellington boots and a white neckcloth. They carried handcuffs, a truncheon, and a cutlass, whilst the Horse Patrol carried a sword. They were armed with a pistol and a heavy sabre or cutlass, with 'Dismounted Patrole' inscribed on the blade, and also on their truncheon staffs. They also carried tin cases for their order books.[670]

Intricate operations involving conference points had been worked out where the unmounted police met up with their mounted colleagues, often at tollgates and bars, to exchange vital information and intelligence.

Crimes of violence and robbery were increasing in the metropolis, and so in the same year Lord Sidmouth ordered that the "Night Patrole" (Dismounted Horse Patrole) or Foot Patroles should be withdrawn into London from the environs. These Foot Patroles were later increased into sixteen districts, each with a Conductor – totalling some eighty men – and confined entirely to the City (of

---

669 Report from the Select Committee on Police of the Metropolis (1822) House of Commons, London, p. 82.

670 *The Morning Post*, 29th July 1822.

Westminster).[671]

By 20th July 1822 the Dismounted Horse Patrole consisted of 100 men who were mustered for their annual inspection in the Privy Gardens Westminster by the Chief Magistrate Sir Richard Birnie, Mr Hobhouse and Mr Dawson, Under Secretaries of the Home Department. Once inspected, they, like their Foot Patrole colleagues, were sworn in as Constables under the new Police Act by the Chief Bow Street Magistrate, which gave them new and wider powers to operate as Constables in the counties of Kent, Surrey, Middlesex and Essex without the need to obtain a sworn warrant from a local magistrate in that jurisdiction.[672]

The numbers of the Dismounted Horse Patrole remained fairly constant, and in 1828 still comprised 89 men and twelve officers.[673]

Hours of Duty

The Dismounted Horse Patrole and the Horse Patroles were instructed to use their discretion and look out for suspicious individuals and movements. Stopping and searching carts, carriages and wagons were a particular difficulty as stolen property was being spirited out of London. The problems were twofold – timing and intelligence. It was believed that empty carts entered London during the day when there was no active patrol on duty, thereby exploiting the gap in policing. It would take a few days for both the Horse and Dismounted Horse Patroles to receive notice of a burglary and a list of property stolen. By then the property would be long gone. The magistrates were helpless at dealing with this problem, although they continued to expect each officer to examine any carts etc. as a matter for each Patrole, notwithstanding that to date they had not found anything stolen.[674]

---

671 Not to be confused with the City of London.
672 *The Morning Post*, 29th July 1822.
673 Critchley, T. A. (1967) *A History of the Police of England and Wales*. Constable, London, pp. 43–44.
674 Report from the select Committee of the Police of the Metropolis 17th July 1822, p. 35.

In appointing the Horse Patroles, the Secretary of State had a call on their time and duty. They could be called upon as a body of men (in uniform) to keep the peace during civil unrest and demonstrations, also for royalty protection, duty lining a royal progress route, State funerals and inspections. A number of fairs took place in and around London during the course of the year, and these were challenges to policing since they attracted thieves, pickpockets and people of bad character. Edmonton Fair, Barnet Fair and Black Horse Fair were three favourites, often attracting 40,000 people at times and the Patroles were expected to do duty at these events. Young apprentices would gather at these locations and freely indulge in drinking, causing drunkenness and bad behaviour.[675]

In August 1829 a Mr Dowling at the Home Office required the Chief Clerk, John Stafford at Bow Street, to remove all the short men on the Dismounted Horse Patrole stationed in the eastern area of Surrey and replace them with men who were taller. The order was immediate, and within a day the Patroles One to Five and Twelve to Sixteen had some 12 men replaced.[676] The height requirements for new police officers applying to the Metropolitan Police conflicted with Bow Street's standards; however, this did not stop the Commissioners from recruiting short Bow Street men. With the notion that a new uniformed professional police was being formed in 1829, members of the Dismounted Horse Patrole and Day Patrole were encouraged to join, and many made application to do so. Those recommended by Bow Street as being fit, well and the right height were enlisted to join the Metropolitan Police. Many Dismounted and Foot Patrole men were put forward to the new Commissioners with comments about their fitness and ability. In fact, one of the replaced so-called "short men", Thomas Mothersell, was a successful applicant, being appointed as the 930th Metropolitan Constable, who had within a

675 Report from the select Committee of the Police of the Metropolis 17th July 1822, p. 58.
676 Copy Letter dated 26th August 1829 from J. Stafford at Bow Street to Mr Dowling at the Home Office. Document held by the Metropolitan Police at the Heritage Centre Empress State Building, West Brompton, West London.

year won promotion to Sergeant.

Many of the Bow Street Patroles on joining were paid 27s 6d, whereas the new Constable received 19s a week, but because of their previous experience and ability many were rewarded with the seniority bonus according to their length of service which was added to their pay.[677] As a result of their background, promotion with its increase in salary was also an incentive for them.

Appendix Four shows 87 men of the Dismounted Horse and Foot Patroles joining the Metropolitan Police between September 1829 and early 1830. From the figures, there were problems with retention and wastage of these experienced men which was a common feature in terms of general recruiting. Of the 87, some 33 (38 percent) were dismissed, 12 (14 percent) resigned within the first year, and eight (nine percent) resigned between their second and fifth year. Three died, leaving 29 (33 percent) still serving in the Metropolitan Police by 1843. Only one third of these applicants continued on to serve six years or more. Also interesting to note is the number of these joiners who were appointed as Sergeants and above. From the figures, 46 (52 percent) were appointed as Constables, six of whom later being promoted to Sergeant during their service, whilst the remainder 41 (48 percent) joined direct to the ranks of Sergeant to Superintendent. The wastage was mainly Constables, whilst those appointed to Sergeant, Inspector or Superintendent were more likely to have remained.

677   The Report from the Committee on the police of the Metropolis 1834, p. 45.

7

Bow Street Day Patrole

Following a recommendation of a Parliamentary Committee under the chairmanship of Sir Robert Peel, a special group of police officers were introduced in 1822 to act as a preventive force together with the Night Patroles so as to provide some consistency and continuous presence by police on the streets of London. The Head Constable (Inspector) and 27 men were recruited from the military, and were to patrol from 9.00am until 7.00pm when they were replaced by the night parties. They were required to distribute themselves judiciously, meaning they should do so in a sensible and wise manner.[678]

The Day Patrole had three Inspectors and they operated to combat daylight burglaries and robberies in the immediate area around the City of Westminster and the environs.[679] They wore the same uniform as the Bow Street Horse Patrole with their distinctive red waistcoats, which Peel thought would make them proud.[680] In 1828 there was a re-organisation and their numbers were reduced to 24 men, with three officers as Inspectors.[681]

678 Fitzgerald, P. (1888) *Chronicles of Bow Street Police–office*. Gilbert and Rivington, London, p. 91.
679 Critchley, T. A. (1967) *A History of the Police of England and Wales*. Constable, London, p. 44.
680 Phillips, D. (1980) 'A new engine of power and authority – the institutionalisation of law enforcement in England 1780–1830' in V. A. C. Gatrell, Bruce, Lenman and Geoffrey Parker (eds) *Crime and Law, the Social History of Crime in Western Europe since 1500*, Europa, London, p. 181.
681 Armitage, G. (1932) *The History of the Bow Street Runners*. Wisehart and Co., London, p. 128.

The Day Patrole were managed, conducted and inspected by Chief Clerk Mr Stafford on behalf of the Chief Magistrate, although he received no extra salary for this increase in workload. The 24 men were subdivided into three divisions, with the first division consisting of one Inspector and eight men meeting at Bow Street every morning at 9.00am. The other two divisions met at other locations according to the directions. They were to patrol the principal streets during the daytime and would cease when the Night Patrole came on duty. Their duty on a Sunday did not commence until after Sunday service. The Inspectors were paid 5s 6d per day, whilst the men received 3s 6d, including Sunday. Seniority was rewarded at seven years' service, when an extra 6d per day was paid, whilst after 14 years this became 1s extra a day. This additional remuneration was granted in 1826.[682]

When vacancies occurred, these were back-filled using men from the Night Patrole. This was a preventive police, so they had to be highly visible and their uniform consequently consisted of a blue coat, red waistcoat and blue trousers, with the Inspectors wearing the same except their waistcoat was blue.[683] What the instructions failed to mention, however, was that each man wore a top hat as well.

The blue uniform seems to become a consistent feature, especially when Peel considered the formation of his New Police in 1829. In August 1829, when the new Metropolitan Police Act came into force, the Principal Officers, the Horse, Dismounted Horse and Day Patroles all continued to operate under the authority of the Bow Street magistrates.

In essence, the two systems ran for a while side-by-side, and some like the Principal Officers lasted nearly a further ten years.

---

682 Armitage, G. (1932) *The History of the Bow Street Runners.* Wisehart and Co., London, p. 128.
683 Ibid.

–8–

Equipment and Uniform

When Henry Fielding set about creating his team of detectives they had no official standing and like their predecessor, the Parish Constable, they wore no uniform. They would have dressed in what is referred to today as plain-clothes. A common belief is that they wore red or scarlet waistcoats and were given the nickname "Robin Redbreasts", when in fact this phrase was generally the preserve of the post-1805 Bow Street Horse Patrole who, as we have seen earlier, only wore the waistcoat when as a group on official functions in London. It also appears that officers who were members of the Foot Patrole from Bow Street, and Runners who performed duty at the theatres from time to time, also wore their distinctive red waistcoats as a sign of their office as a warning to pickpockets etc.[684] Any suggestion of pre-1805 officers or Patroles wearing red waistcoats appears erroneous. Few images exist which relate to the individuals associated with Bow Street, and there are no contemporary pictures of the Patroles. On rare occasions individual descriptions are given, with Townsend receiving this treatment on more than one occasion. An undated article describes his dress as "characteristic", and states "he wore a blue coat, gilt buttons, red waistcoat, drab breeches and gaiters".[685] Principal Officers performed detective duties, and to have operated in any form of uniform would have rendered them ineffective. When engaging in crime-related matters it was

684 Fitzgerald, P. (1888) *Chronicles of Bow Street Police–office.* Gilbert and Rivington, London, pp. 174–175.
685 *Dundee Evening Telegraph,* 14th February 1891 (article based on undated material from *Temple Bar Magazine*).

important for an individual to be able to identify themselves, not least for self-protection, and demonstrate to the wider public under what authority they were acting.

Establishing details of what Principal Officers or members of the Patroles would have been issued with is difficult to determine. Few genuine items relating to the Bow Street office have survived, and as its officials were self-regulating and financially independent there appears to be no standard pattern of uniform and equipment. This meant they were able to approach whichever supplier they wished, and while some items were engraved or decorated with identifiable markings, this was not always the case.

Constables are appointed by the Crown having taken an Oath, which varied from place to place, but generally included service to the Sovereign and a promise to uphold the law. The Oath would have been sworn in front of a magistrate and details generally recorded on a warrant of appointment. This was not discrete and durable like a modern day Constables' warrant card, which started to be routinely issued towards the end of the nineteenth century; rather, early warrants were recorded on pre-printed forms, often of foolscap folio size (8½ x 13½ inches). Producing a large sheet of paper and presenting it to individuals or groups, many of whom were probably illiterate, was not practical and could be dangerous in a fast-moving and developing situation. A sensible solution, which already existed, was to carry something more tangible than a piece of paper, and which came in the form of a badge of office called a tipstaff or tipstave. While tipstaves are found in many shapes and sizes and are made from a variety of materials, the most common had tubular brass bodies affixed to a wooden handle and surmounted by a cast crown. A common myth is that they were formed hollow in order to act as a repository for a warrant. While the hollow body, if one existed, may have be useful for this purpose it is unlikely this would have proved very practical.

The feature of the crown gave a clear indication on where the officer gained their authority, and in some cases the piece was engraved with further details such as a place name or the holder

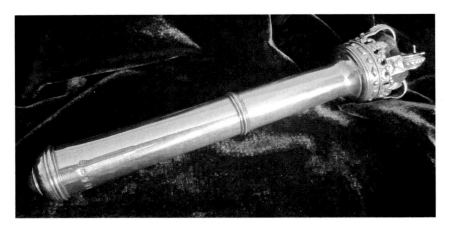

Fig. 37: John Townsend's silver tipstaff

of the office. Between 1953 and 2015 a national Police Staff College existed at Bramshill House near Hook in Hampshire.[686] From its earliest times Bramshill was the home of what was hoped to become a national police historical reference collection, which included a large collection of decorated truncheons and tipstaves. The collection, now cared for by The College of Policing, contains one item which can only be described as a plain and unexceptional tipstaff, with a solid brass crown set on a plain cylindrical body with a turned wood handle.[687] The significance of the piece rests in its attribution of having been carried by the colourful and renowned Principal Officer, John Townsend.

There is another tipstaff, also said to have belonged to Townsend, which has been passed down through generations of Townsend's direct descendants. This tipstaff is a fine quality item made from silver, but like the former example lacks any inscription. It probably dates from the time when Townsend had achieved royal patronage. Beattie records that when on duty with the King at official occasions such as attending Parliament the officers would be in procession,

686 In 2015 the Home Office sold Bramshill and moved The College of Policing (established 2012) to Sunningdale Park, Berkshire.
687 Mitton, M. (1985) *The Policeman's Lot*, p. 69.

"carrying silver staffs".[688]

As we have previously noted, John Birchall was a well-respected and experienced Conductor of the Foot Patrole, working from Bow Street during the reign of George IV. His tipstaff was made of brass, with an openwork crown and a turned wood handle. The tubular body is engraved "J. Birchall / P.O / Bow Street".[689] The fact that his tipstaff was engraved with his name suggests items such as this were personal issue, or possibly purchased privately. In the case of Townsend's silver tipstaff, this was possibly a presentation piece and kept only for his special duties, while he may have retained his ordinary piece for day work. Speculation suggests that he in fact purchased it for himself, which could account for the lack of an inscription. Financing public bodies has always been an issue and one of the biggest obstacles faced by the early Bow Street magistrates. It seems improbable they would have the capacity to spend their budget on luxury or personalised items. When the initials "P.O." are seen it is commonly understood they stand for Public, or Police, Office. In this instance we do know he did become a Principal Officer and retired from Bow Street in 1834 when the Foot Patrole was absorbed into the Metropolitan Police.

The work of John Birchall appears regularly in the records at the Old Bailey. All of his cases occurred between 1823 and 1828. In each he is referred to as either an "Officer" or "Constable". The type of cases he was involved with included embezzlement, theft, pickpocketing, bigamy and grand larceny. These records serve us as a reminder of the harsh punishments imposed at the time. For the above crimes, the many sanctions ranged from six months in prison, transportation from seven years to life, or death. In one particular case where a juvenile aged 14 years was found guilty of larceny, he

688 Beattie, J. (2012) *The First English Detectives*. Oxford University Press, Oxford, p.194.
689 Bow Street tipstaff purchased at auction in 2004 having been in the collection of George Chapman Carmichael QC, MC, MA. Carmichael was a collector of items relating to the criminal justice system. He was born in 1924 and won the Military Cross for bravery at Nijmegen during the Second World War.

was whipped before being discharged.[690]

While the tipstaff was usually, but not exclusively, the item of choice for the detective, it was the more humble truncheon which was the standard issue for the Constable. The tipstaff was, comparatively speaking, an expensive item, whereas a truncheon could be easily produced in greater numbers at less cost, and also offered a degree of protection as a defensive weapon. With the addition of applied decoration it was possible to give it the identification and authoritative qualities conferred by the tipstaff. In certain cases it is possible to narrow the date of issue due to the use of royal ciphers and coats of arms. A cipher is a combination of interwoven initials and in the case of monarchs comprises the first initial followed by the letter "R", standing for Rex, or Regina (King or Queen), and often a numeral appropriate to the reign. Throughout its history the Bow Street Office operated under four monarchs:

George II	1727–1760
George III	1760–1820
George IV	1820–1830
William IV	1830–1837

It is not known what early Bow Street truncheons would have looked like as the only surviving examples come from the period of George IV and bear his cipher and arms. Unlike the cipher, the arms represent the full achievement and display of armorial bearings granted to the individual by the College of Arms, which has acted as the regulating body for grants of arms since the 15th Century. In the 18th Century the royal arms was quartered to include those of England and Scotland, France, Ireland and Hanover. In 1801 George III renounced his title, King of France, and the French quartering was removed. New arms were created, with England occupying the first and fourth quarter, Scotland in the second and Ireland in the third. The escutcheon for Hanover was placed in the centre and

---

690 Proceedings of the Old Bailey references t18230910–229, t18240218–82, t18240916–212, t18251208–42, t18270405–43, t18270405–209, t18271025–214, t18280703–115 and t18281204–203 (available online, accessed January 2007).

Fig. 38: John Birchall's tipstaff

was surmounted by a red "electoral cap" with white ermine fur trimming. A further change was made to these arms in 1816, when the cap was changed to a crown when Hanover became a kingdom. It is these arms which are most commonly found on Bow Street truncheons. Truncheons were issued by the various Patroles, with most surviving examples relating to the Horse Patrole.

One style of Bow Street truncheon is recorded as being 13 inches in length, decorated with a large lion surmounting a crown, over a "G IV R" cipher and "Bow Street" below. Another is 14 inches in length, decorated with a crown over a "GR" cipher and the post-1801 royal arms within a Garter. In this example there is no electoral cap or crown over the central Hanoverian arms, meaning it is not possible to date precisely. The truncheon is the inscribed "BOW STREET" and is also decorated with a coronet from which three white feathers are issuing forth.[691]

The various Bow Street Patrole truncheons can be subdivided between those of the Horse, Dismounted and Night Patroles.

The length of the Horse Patrole truncheons varied between

---

691 The heraldic device comprising three white feathers emerging from a gold coronet is commonly referred to as the Prince of Wales's Feathers. Technically this badge is the badge of the Heir Apparent and the badge of the Prince of Wales a dragon gules gorged by a label of three points argent.

Fig. 39: Left: Three Horse Patrole truncheons.
Right: Dismounted and Night Patrole truncheons

19½ and 21 inches, and was probably carried in a tubular leather scabbard which formed part of the tack. In order they could not be grabbed and torn away from the officer, the end of the handle would be drilled to take some form of leather thong. The Patrole truncheons can normally be distinguished by the use of initials "HP", "DHP" or "NP". In addition to the other decoration it is normal for items to bear a number. The exact use of these numbers is not known, but they were probably a stock or armoury number where the item could be returned at the end of each tour of duty, or retained by the officer and taken home. Officers have always been responsible for equipment allocated to them, and the addition of this number would allow an audit in the event of any loss or damage. Occasionally pieces were made which contained a reference to the rank of the holder. In the case of the Night Patrole, equipment is recorded as bearing the rank of Conductor. The various Bow Street Patroles used the term to refer to an officer in charge of a small group, or party of men, and it was their job to acquaint themselves with their respective patrol areas and keep an Occurrence Book of any accidents, crimes or other events that happened during their tour of duty. It was also their job to inspect and report details of damage to any equipment such as pistols, truncheons, cutlasses and handcuffs, and hand out on a weekly basis pay to the men under their command.

While a truncheon may have been adequate for routine patrol duties, swords and firearms were also carried. Given the irregular nature of those serving at Bow Street in its formative years it is difficult to establish if officials were routinely armed, or if they only drew weapons for specific hazardous duties. Records for the Public Offices formed as the result of the 1792 Middlesex Justices Act do confirm the purchase of tipstaves, truncheons and firearms was standard practice from this time.

The dangers faced by the officers and Patroles can be clearly seen in one example of a robbery, which took place on 10th November 1798 at Hounslow Heath.[692] In September 1799 highwayman

---

692 Proceedings of the Old Bailey references t17990109–11 t17990911–2 (available online, accessed 2015).

Thomas Clark stood trial at the Old Bailey for his involvement in this robbery, although his accomplice, a 29-year-old named John Haines, had already been tried and hanged earlier in the year. In giving his evidence, Henry Edwards, who had been in company with Thomas Dowsett (Bow Street Officer) and Thomas Jones (Conductor of the Patrole), along with two other officers, described how he returned fire having already been shot at by the robbers. Edwards described himself as a "Bow–street officer" and explained how he had been ordered by the magistrate to attend Bedfont, a district of Hounslow, to stop the depredations that had been occurring in the area. Travelling in a post-chaise the group arrived at their destination around nine o'clock in the evening. As they passed through Bedfont Heath near Hounslow they witnessed two men drinking on horseback, although due to the speed they was travelling at did not get a chance to observe their faces. Some minutes later two riders came at speed up the near side of the chaise, and while one threatened the driver to stop or have his brains blown out the other went to the chaise door to confront the occupants. No doubt in an attempt to ensure those inside knew his intention, the rider tapped on the chaise-window with his pistol. In his own words, Edwards describes what happened next:

> "He swore a bitter oath, and demanded my money; I desired him not to be in a hurry, nor use me ill, and I would give it him; I sat on the near side of the chaise, the same side that the person was that demanded my money; the man that was at the horses' heads then said, d–n [sic] your eyes, Jack, give it to them; I had my hand to the window to pull it down, and had a shot fired under my arm; I instantly returned the fire, broke the glass, and fired in an oblique direction at that person, and at the same moment, before I recovered my hand, the person at the horses' heads fired at the chaise, which came in at the front of the chaise, between Jones and me; we afterwards cut the ball out of the lining of the chaise, Dowsett has the ball."[693]

693 Old Bailey Proceedings Online (www.oldbaileyonline.org, version 8.0, 20 July 2018), September 1799, trial of Thomas Clark (t17990911-2).

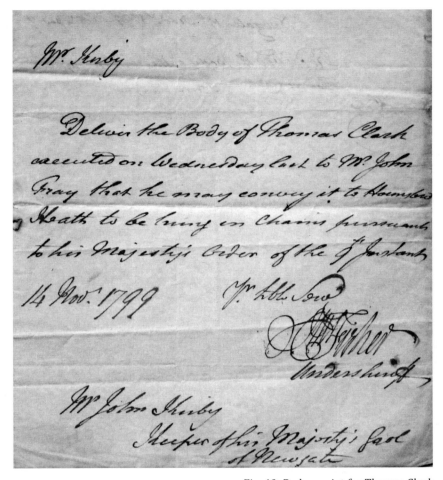

Fig. 40: Body receipt for Thomas Clark

This case clearly shows the easy manner with which criminals were prepared to offer violence to meet their ends. It also highlights that many encounters resulting in the use of firearms took place at close quarters and not over long distances. This is an important factor when considering the type of weapons the Bow Street officers used to protect themselves. Following his execution, the body of Thomas Clark was returned to Newgate Prison, where on 14th November 1799 it was handed over to an official to be taken back to Hounslow

Heath to be hung in chains.[694] There were so many gibbets on the Heath at this time they became landmarks, and even featured on maps of the period. It is difficult to determine a standard level of equipment for Bow Street and the other public offices as they all used a variety of independent manufacturers and suppliers. One name which is particularly associated with the Bow Street office is that of William Parker, who was a gun maker who operated from premises at 233 High Holborn.

The fact that William Parker's name was so synonymous with Bow Street is perhaps not a surprise when it is realised his father-in-law was in fact the Principal Officer, John Clarke. For many years the name William Parker was only known in relation to the manufacture and supply of police-related equipment starting around the last decade of the eighteenth century. Nothing is known of his early years, except that he was born to Thomas and Elizabeth in 1772, at Croscombe in Somerset. By the age of 20 he had made his way to London and in 1792 his name appears in a Holborn rate book for the address of 233 High Holborn. His name is written in pencil alongside that of "Wid'w Field", a jeweller. This address had until this time been occupied by John Clarke and his son–in–law John Field. The pretext by which he came to be there is not understood, but it is likely he was working as an apprentice silversmith. A business operated there under the title "Field & Clarke, silversmiths" between the years 1784 and 1793. Details are also recorded of a "John Field, goldsmith", at the adjacent premises of 232 High Holborn between 1790 and 1793, as well as 322 High Holborn for the same period.

The Field and Clarke partnership came to an end when John Field died around 1790. Entries with his name are recorded in the Holborn rate books from 1783 and continue until 1790. In 1791 his name is still listed, but underlined and the word "Widw" inserted. The union between John Field and John Clarke's daughter, Sarah, resulted in one surviving child, also called John, born circa 1779. Sarah was

---

694 Body receipt for highwayman Thomas Clark dated 14th November 1799, private collection.

remarried on 1st July 1792 to William Parker, at which point he assumed responsibility for raising her son John. No doubt this was a profitable union for William, as it would provide a basis for him developing his own business. It is not unusual for a new business to trade under an established name, and this probably accounts for the name "Field" surviving in various forms for a few more years. Entries in trade directories confirm that by 1796/97 William was operating under his own name as a sole trader, a situation that would continue until his death in 1841. John Clarke survived until at least May 1793, but it is probable he died around this time. Sarah's son, John Field, is often referred to as William's son–in–law, but he was in fact his stepson. In the nineteenth century the term "in-law" meant related by marriage, but also extended to children, which is not the case now. William and Sarah appear to have had no further issue.

Kent's Directory of 1794 and 1795 for the Cities of London and Westminster and Borough of Southwark records the following details; "Field and Parker, Goldsmiths and Gunsmiths, 233 High Holborn". Not only are these some of the last entries to reference a joint company, but they are also the first to mention gun making. That William Parker first trained as a silversmith is established through other work he was engaged in, which started under Sarah's father John Clarke, and a role he later passed to his own stepson John Field. At different times each of them worked on behalf of the Royal Mint as an Inspector of counterfeit coins. The earliest recorded example of William Parker giving sworn evidence in a case of coining was on 30th October 1793 in R v Elizabeth Shirley.[695] One of the next trials he attended was that of R v Michael Green, held on 4th December that year. Having taken the Oath and confirmed that he was employed by the Mint to give evidence, he stated: "I succeeded my father-in-law Mr Clarke". Records show a John Clarke had been employed regularly from about 1768 until his last recorded case on

---

695 Examples of the cases involving the Royal Mint are recorded in the proceedings of the Old Bailey, references t17931030–87, t17931204–49 and t18230115–1(available online, accessed March 2013).

29th May 1793, the same year that William appears to have started giving evidence. The role performed for the Mint by William and later by stepson John was generally as an expert witness giving opinion on coins being officially produced by the Royal Mint, which at this time was based at the Tower of London. Many of the pieces they examined were items cast in Plaster of Paris moulds, and to the expert eye easy to detect. This is in contrast to John Clarke's role as a Principal Officer, when he would actively seek out counterfeiters and attend with other officers. In 1788 he described his position as follows: "I have been employed by the Mint for many years for the discovery of coiners."

It becomes clear how many of those engaged in the work of Bow Street had numerous income streams. William Parker was a well-known gun maker, producing a range of weapons from standard issue items to fine duelling pistols. He later went on to produce truncheons, handcuffs, swords and rattles. Parker survived just long enough to be included in the 1841 census, where he is recorded as a "Gun Maker" living in High Holborn.[696] It was his desire that his business should continue under the control of this stepson John and grandchildren John William Parker Field and William Shakespeare Field. They traded successfully under the name Parker Field and Sons until well into the latter part of the nineteenth century.

The flintlock was the standard firing mechanism for firearms from the mid-eighteenth century and remained in universal use until the 1830s. Previous mechanisms were too complicated in design and difficult to manufacture in great quantity for them to be used in the mass production of weapons. Pistols were generally a close-quarter weapon, and their accuracy depended on a number of things, not least being the fit of the lead ball in the barrel. As the charge of powder sitting behind the projectile burnt the gas, pressure built up thus sending the ball along the barrel. Any gap between ball and barrel allowed for gasses to escape and for the ball to wobble as it

---

696 Census night in 1841 was on the 6th June the same month in which William Parker died.

travelled. At the point of leaving the muzzle this wobble could cause the ball to be deflected, and while deviation might only be slight at this point it could cause the pistol to be wildly inaccurate, even over short distances. In order to ensure a firm fit, the ball could be wrapped in a patch of paper or some other thin material. The tight fit required meant the ball had to be loaded with the aid of a ramrod, which was housed in a slot cut into the stock beneath the barrel.

The flintlock mechanism provided the means for igniting the charge. A weapon was primed by placing a small amount of powder in an external pan and an "L" shaped piece of metal called the frizzen closed over it to keep the powder dry. The cock is a pivoting arm with a jaw-like clamp which holds a piece of knapped flint. When the cock was drawn fully back and the frizzen closed, the weapon was ready to fire. To prevent an accidental discharge, most locks were fitted with some sort of safety catch. On firing the cock was released, causing the flint to scrape down the steel face of the frizzen thereby lifting the covered section and sending a shower of sparks into the pan to ignite the powder. This then set off the internal charge, thus firing the ball.

Pistols are generally classified by size with the smallest being the muff or boxlock pistol at only a few inches in length. This was especially made to be carried in the "muff" or pocket, and the mechanism was designed so as not to snag against clothing. The next size is the pocket pistol, which was approximately six inches in length. The largest type could range from ten to twelve inches and were known as holster or horse pistols. Examples falling somewhere between the pocket and holster sizes were sometimes described as overcoat pistols. While many of the other public offices seemed to favour the smaller boxlock pistols, surviving examples would suggest Bow Street favoured the intermediate pocket or overcoat pistol. While long-barrelled weapons would not have been practical for general use, in 1757 it is recorded they had at least one blunderbuss.[697] Like the pistol, the blunderbuss is a muzzle-loading

697 Beattie, J. (2012) *The First English Detectives*. Oxford University Press, Oxford, p. 38.

*Fig. 41 Reconstruction of the attack made of
Bow Street Principal Officer William Pentlow in 1761*

firearm with a short but large-calibre barrel flared at the muzzle. Loaded with a variety of shot, it was effective at short ranges, but lacked accuracy over distance. In 1761 Bow Street officer William Pentlow had to use a blunderbuss to defend himself and another officer after their post-chaise was held up by a highwayman.

The pocket pistols were marked "W. PARKER" on the side plate, and for those issued for general use engraved on one side of the barrel was "PUBLIC OFFICE" and on the other "BOW STREET". The top flattened section of the barrel was inscribed "MAKER TO HIS MAJESTY, HOLBORN". The trigger guards were numbered, and in the case of the example illustrated in Figure 42 overleaf (top), it bears the number "25". This model has a ramrod contained within a swivel mechanism to prevent loss. Pocket pistols used by the Dismounted Horse Patrole were not engraved on the barrel, but were engraved on the trigger guard with "DISMD HORSE / PATROLE", each is then numbered adjacent to the trigger guard. Where possible, items were repaired rather than replaced and if possible upgraded. This includes conversion from a flintlock to percussion-firing mechanism, as seen in the example shown in Figure 42 (bottom).

Swords, like other equipment, can be categorised into those carried by the different officers and Patroles. The most common style of police sword is called a cutlass or hanger. This is a short sword, generally about 24 inches in length with a curved fullered blade, double-edged towards the point.[698] It was designed as a cutting weapon for use when on foot. When carried it was housed in a leather scabbard fitted with steel or brass mounts. The top of the scabbard fits to a leather "frog", which was fitted to a cross belt allowing the sword to hang at the hip. The blades were etched in a skilled and complex process, with the maker's name on one side and Bow Street details on the other. Contemporary records generally refer to this style of sword as a cutlass rather than a hanger. Examples of etching found on Bow Street cutlasses are as follows:

W, PARKER. Holborn Maker to his Majesty.
BOW STREET OFFICE, 78

~~~~~

W, PARKER Maker to his Majesty HOLBORN LONDON.
DISMOUNTED HORSE PATROL. No. 103.

~~~~

W, PARKER. Holborn, Maker to his Majesty
BOW STREET OFFICE, CONDR N. P. No. 15.

In addition to the numbering on the blade, the corresponding number is sometimes found on the hilt and always on the locket-part of scabbard (metal fitting at the mouth of the scabbard). This style of sword was also used by other civilian services such as prisons and customs officers. William Parker supplied many of these groups, including turnpike trusts. Blades on examples for the Hackney Turnpike Trust are etched "HACKNEY TRUST".

When mounted, officers of the Horse Patrole required a weapon with greater reach, and were issued with the 1796-pattern light cavalry sabre. One of the qualifications for appointment was having

698 The fuller is a groove running along the length of a blade. This lightens the blade and makes it faster without losing any structural integrity.

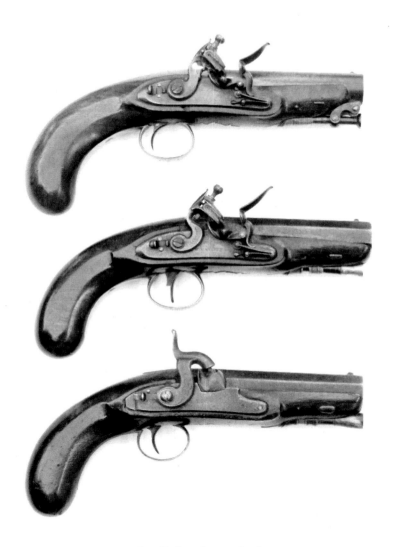

Fig. 42: Bow Street pistols.
Top: Bow Street Public Office.
Middle and Bottom: Bow Street Dismounted Horse Patrole

Above:
Fig. 43: Bow Street hangers.
Top: Bow Street Public Office
Middle: Bow Street Dismounted Horse Patrole
Bottom: Bow Street Night Patrole

Below:
Fig. 44: Bow Street Horse Patrole 1796 pattern light cavalry sabre

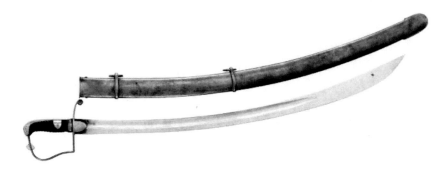

had previous horse experience, which was often gained in the cavalry, meaning they would have been familiar with this weapon and trained in its use. With its pronounced curve, the blade, which widened near the point, was designed for slashing and considered a brutal weapon. Blades were approximately 32½ inches in length and had a single broad fuller on each side. The hilt was of the simple stirrup form, with a single iron knuckle-bow and quillon, so as to be free of unnecessary weight. The iron backpiece of the grip had ears which were riveted through the tang of the blade to give the hilt and blade a very secure connection. It was carried in an iron scabbard and hung from the waist via sword-belt slings attached to two loose suspension rings. The blade would have been etched with the maker's details on one side and the Patrole number on the other. The example in Figure 44 is etched as follows:

W. PARKER Maker to His Majesty HOLBORN LONDON.
HORSE PATROLE No. 55.

Detailed accounts were kept for all expenditure incurred by the office, with Parker's costs generally found under "incidental charges", along with other tradesmen's accounts allowed by the magistrates. Listed under the quarter ending 5th April 1814 is a Mr Mayhew, who supplied belts for cutlasses and pistols at a cost of £8.

Entries for William Parker are included in the following quarter's accounts:

5th October 1814
Item 50 – Parker, for Cutlasses, repairing
Fire Arms, &c. £23 8s 6d
Item 51 – Lewis, for Constable's Truncheons £12 8s 0d

5th January 1816
Item 40 – Parker, for repairing Fire
Arms, Cutlasses, &c. £10 3s 6d

5th January 1817
Item 45 – Parker, for cutlasses, handcuffs, &c.

and repairing fire arms £24 12s 0d

An invoice surviving in the Bow Street accounts dated 1793 is made out to Thomas Gill for the supply of "brass mounted hangers". The Gill family were well-known sword makers from Birmingham in the eighteenth century. In 1816 William Day, Principal Conductor of the Horse Patrole, produced as part of his evidence to a Select Committee a list of appointments used by each Patrole. The items were listed as follows:

> "Headstall with chain-rein, bridle complete, saddle, with holsters and flounces, girths, stirrup leathers and irons, surcingle, crupper, cloak, pad and straps, and breast-plate, horsecloth, cloak, sabre and belt, pair of pistols, turnscrew, picker and worm, pair of handcuffs and key, book of orders and warrant.

> The above appointments, excepting the headstall, chain–rein, and horsecloth, to be brought by each man with his horse, at every monthly inspection; and the whole of the appointments to be brought at the quarterly inspection in January, April, July and October." [699]

The work of the Committee did not finish in 1816 and further reported in 1817, 1818 and 1822. By 1822 the Committee was being chaired by The Right Honourable Robert Peel, and Day was called to give further evidence. He gave a very detailed account of the work of the Horse Patrole, including details on uniform and equipment. With the exception of a cloak, provided at Government expense, the officers had to supply their own uniform dress, which was paid for by the cost being deducted from their salary. Accoutrements were described as being the same as those issued to cavalry regiments, which included pistols in holsters and sabres. He stated they were "given" a truncheon and handcuffs. Although the pistol was supplied, no officially sanctioned means of carrying spare ammunition was available until pouches were added to the saddles from December

---

[699] British Parliamentary Papers – Police of the Metropolis, Crime and Punishment, Vol 1, p. 196.

1852.[700]

While no contract for the supply of the cloaks and arms existed, Day confirmed that the supplier of the cloaks in 1822 was still the original supplier, Praters of Charing Cross (although no date is given to say when cloaks were first issued). The provider of arms was confirmed as Parker in Holborn Hill, who was declared to have supplied the police for some years. Despite the lack of a formal contract, Day confirmed he believed the charges were below what they might be.

The uniform was first proposed by Sir Richard Ford when he re-formed the Patrole in 1805, and it had never been discontinued. The reason for its introduction was to ensure the men would look a "little respectable" when assembled as a body, and they would only wear it at that time. The uniform comprised a blue coat and red waistcoat, and each officer was told on appointment of the requirement for it to be worn. The wearing of the red or scarlet waistcoat led to the nickname "Robin Redbreasts", which has ever since been a source of contention with historians as to its correct application. Many early writers applied the term to the Runners, while more recent authors have tried to correct this by noting the name only applied to the officers of the Patroles. Records show the Horse Patrole would parade annually to be inspected in central London with the Bow Street Magistrates leading out their men. A good example of this occurred when the Patrole united for Royal Ceremonial events in London and it was reported that, "Townsend, Macmanus and Sawyer [sic] assisted by the whole of the Bow Street Patrole attended the investiture at Westminster Abbey of the installation of the Knights of the Bath".[701] These clear attempts to unify the Patroles when together as a body ensured their place in history as the first uniformed police. It also opens the debate to question if, after 1805, the Runners would also have also donned similar attire when operating together as a unit.

---

700 www.eppingforestdc.gov.uk/Library/Leisure/MUSEUM/collections/
     PEELERSPROGRESS.pdf accessed on 9th February 2012.
701 *Morning Post*, 20th May 1803.

Fig. 45: Horse Patrole armband

More detailed descriptions of the Patrole uniform exist, which describe the wearing of scarlet waistcoats, blue double-breasted overcoats with yellow metal buttons and blue trousers, a black leather hat, white leather gloves and black Wellington boots with spurs. To complete the uniform, protective leather stocks were available as a guard against garrotting.[702]

In 1813 the Horse Patrole were required to have their appointments with them in proper condition at all times.[703] Their pistols must be loaded and their sword was to be displayed on the outside of their coat. Under no circumstances were they allowed to enter any public house or other house during their time on duty.[704] In 1822 both the Horse Patrole and the Dismounted Horse Patrole wore the same uniform, except the latter had a black felt hat and wore a white neckcloth.[705] The Conductors were not given a cloak or sword.[706]

While a formal uniform complying to a strict pattern with use of badges or other insignia was some years off, the Horse Patrole appear to have made use of armbands.

While no contemporary account of their issue, exists an armband printed with the initials "HP" either side of the royal arms, and numbered "2", is a rare survivor of this period. Horse Patrole No. 2 was shown to be located on Shooters Hill (see Appendix 8). It was probably worn for general duties, when the Patrole would also call out in a distinct voice, "Bow Street Patrole" to any person travelling along the road no matter if they were walking or riding.

---

702 www.met.police.uk/mountedbranch/history.htm accessed on 22nd February 2012.
703 Report of the Committee of the State of the Police of the Metropolis (1816) House of Commons.
704 Ibid.
705 Wilkinson, F. (2002) *Those Entrusted with Arms*. Greenhill, Pennsylvania, p. 145.
706 Ibid, p. 144.

9

Bow Street Administration

Criminal investigation is a process, and the back office function of running a court or police office is often as important as the ability to apprehend the criminal in the first instance. Considering the hours during which Bow Street operated and the number of cases handled, there was a need to have properly-trained administrative staff working side-by-side with the sitting magistrates. Not only was there a need to administer the court proceedings, which were processed by the Chief Clerk, clerks and administrators, but also there was the supervision, management and direction of the Principal Officers and other various Patroles to contend with.

From the early times at Bow Street anyone who had a grievance could attend the court and, on payment of a fixed fee, swear information before the magistrate which led to a warrant being issued. The warrant would be given to a Constable (often a member of the Patrole) to execute, which meant the named person was arrested and brought before the court to be examined. The allegation would be put to the arrested person, who was either kept in custody, often to be detained at Newgate, or released on bail, providing there was a surety paid which was determined by the magistrate and in some cases was a substantial amount of money. Once a magistrate had issued a warrant the details were entered into a register at court and showed who had signed for it, or to whom the warrant had been given, or its current location. Once executed it would be endorsed to that effect and the prisoner either detained or released pending a further court appearance. On behalf of the issuing magistrate, the court administrative clerks would write to the person who had taken out the warrant, providing information of the next court appearance where both parties needed to attend. It would be for the clerks to write out each letter in long hand, sign it and have posted by the Bow Street Orderly.

Few examples of Bow Street related papers exist outside of national museums and archives. One such piece is a letter written by (John) William Nichols, a clerk and John Upson, a Constable or Principal Officer. The letter was written on 1st July 1823 and sent to Brighton at a cost of eight pence. The uniform Penny Post was not introduced until 1840, so this illustrates that it was costly to post a letter at this time, even for an official body. While at Bow Street, John Upson often worked with Ruthven on a number of high-profile cases. In this letter they informed the recipient of the arrest of a male called Charlton. Upson has countersigned, underneath the signature of William Nichols, who as clerk was presumably the writer.[707]

Nichols was employed at Bow Street from 1831 as Summoning Officer or Signing Officer.[708] The letter informed Mr George Chassereau (who was a Toy Dealer by trade), the Brighton Overseer of the Poor, that on the directions of Mr Thomas Halls, Magistrate of Bow Street, the warrant against Edmund Lechmere Charlton of Down House, Epsom had been executed. He had been bailed on sureties of £25 and £50 to attend for a future court hearing. Charlton not only had a house in Epsom but also resided, when he was in town, at his house in Curzon Street. During the summer holidays he would retire to Brighton where he had purchased another residence.[709] In England, overseers of the poor administered poor relief such as money, food and clothing as part of the Poor Law system. The position was created by the Act for the Relief of the Poor of 1597. Overseers were often reluctant appointees who were

---

707 Egan, P. (1824) The Trial of John Thurtell and Joseph Hunt. Knight and Lacey, London.
708 T38/674 and HO59.10.
709 It was reported that "Mr E. Lechmere Charlton left his house in Curzon Street for his residence in Brighton". Morning Post, 24th August 1829.

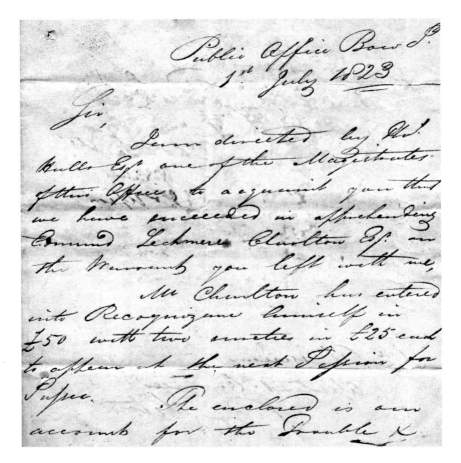

Fig. 46: 1823 letter to the Brighton overseer

unpaid, but for Chassereau this was not the case, as he worked under the supervision of a Justice of the Peace. The law required two overseers, one likely to be the assistant, to be elected every Easter, and churchwardens or landowners were often selected.

Chassereau was responsible for the supervision of the workhouse and the collection of the poor rate from named individuals and householders. Charlton was a well-known radical from Ludlow who often came in contact with the law. Although later he became an MP, he was no stranger to the courts and was at one time sued, committed to prison and later appeared at the Law Courts in the

Strand. He claimed a member's privilege and asked the Speaker of the House to prevent his incarceration. We can only surmise that Charlton had declined or overlooked to pay the poor rate, which supported the workhouse in Brighton. Chassereau (whose not insignificant Parish remuneration amounted to £200 per year) travelled to London having obtained the warrant in Brighton, and deposited it at Bow Street to be executed by an officer. A fee was charged for this service, usually one shilling to execute the warrant. Chassereau held the position for a further two years and resigned to concentrate on his toy business. He died in 1836.

Today there is a distinction made between criminal and civil matters, however back in the early days of trading justices there were no civil courts to hear petty grievances and disputes.

Patrole Administration

The Conductors of the Patrole were required by order to attend Bow Street on Monday mornings. There were a number of reasons for this. The weekly Occurrence Books and forms were required at the court to enable Mr Day to see what had happened and whether to issue further instructions or pass on the relevant information back to the court. The Conductors collected the pay for their Patrole on a Monday, which they were then to distribute to the men, although there is evidence to suggest that the men's pay was periodical and dependant on the Government paying Bow Street. A John Reeves appears to have been the paymaster, described as the "Commissioner of the Metropolis" in 1794, at the Treasury responsible for paying individual bills separately, no matter which public office the application for payment was made from. Reeves would pay the "Keeper of the Publick office" at Bow Street, William Hudson, who would further distribute the monies to be paid to the recipients. A receipt signed by Patrole Captain John De La Fontaine was issued in 1793 for monies to be paid to Lavender and Miller for going to Clapham and other places allowed for by Chief Magistrate, William Addington.

Reeves would pay all the bills submitted including those

for stationery, cleaning chimneys, mops and buckets, buying newspapers, paying for the sending of letters, paying messengers to personally deliver letters, advertisements in the *True Britain* and wine for Mr Bond – the most expensive commodity on the list.[710] George Downing was paid to provide brass lamps for Bow Street, not only for the court but for individual Patroles, as significant numbers of them were required in 1793. Ink stands, ink, pens, pen knives, receipt books, tape, sealing wax paper, books of various sorts, paper sticks, paper cases, bodkins etc. were obtained from Mr J. Downes, "Printer to the Police" in the Strand.

Another of the regular documents created at Bow Street were warrants. These official documents could only be issued by competent persons such as magistrates or judges, as they gave instructions to officials, such as Constables, to carry out functions which had the power to remove an individual's liberties through acts such as detention and arrest. Warrants were drafted using a pre-printed pro forma. A rare surviving example relates to a bastardy case emanating in the Parish of Basing and is dated 9th August 1775. This parish lies north east of Basingstoke in the modern-day county of Hampshire. Previously the county was called Southamptonshire or, as in the case of this warrant, Southton. The warrant is a clear instruction to the Constables, and others of his Majesty's Officers of the Peace for that county alone. The warrant was made out at the request of one of the local Overseers of the Poor, Charles Bargent, against Thomas Taplin, a labourer from Basing who was charged with getting one Rebecca Hall pregnant.

The warrant was issued not for any issues of social morality, but rather a fear the baby could become chargeable to the parish if the father failed to marry Miss Hall or face up to his responsibilities and support the mother and child. Where such cases were suspected the local authorities could cause an examination of the mother where she would be questioned on Oath to establish the identity of the father. This investigation would fall to the Overseer or the

710 HO 42/32.

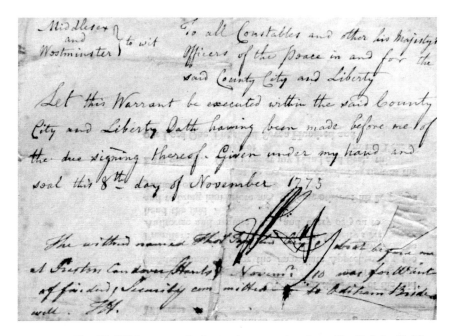

Fig. 47: 1775 reverse of a bastardy warrant endorsed by Sir John Fielding

Churchwarden, who gained their powers from the Bastardy Act of 1575. Once the identity of the father was established he would normally be made to enter into a bond whereby he agreed to pay for the child's maintenance until they were old enough to be apprenticed out. In cases where the father tried to abscond, a warrant was issued to bring him before the court.

In this instance Thomas Taplin appears to have made his way to London, as the powers of the warrant have been transferred to the Constables and officers of the County Middlesex and City of Westminster. This is achieved by an endorsement by Sir John Fielding dated 8th November 1775. The warrant would have been conveyed to London in person, in order for an Oath to be sworn regarding the request for assistance. The Constables of Bow Street appeared to have acted with zeal and efficiency because the warrant is further endorsed to say that on 10th November Thomas Taplin appeared at Preston Candover, Hampshire where for the want of being able to

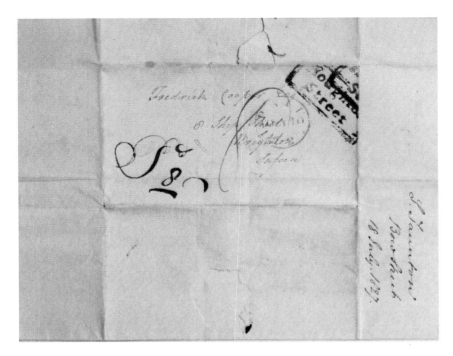

Fig. 48: Letter to solicitor Fredrick Cooper

provide security was committed to the Odiham Bridewell.

Almost no private correspondence written by Principal Officers or Runners is known to survive. One of the few examples is a short letter sent by Samuel Taunton to Fredrick Cooper at 8 Ship Street, Brighton in July 1837. It cost 8d to send and its message was contained inside. The letter was folded at the edges into the centre and sealed with wax, and would bear a Bow Street impression in the seal. Mr Fredrick Cooper was a partner in the firm of Solicitors Atreet and Cooper, who represented the owners of the Brighton Race Course situated on Whitehawk Hill. Taunton had been previously employed at the races by Cooper to prevent and detect pickpockets, gamers and other crime. Taunton knew that when the races were on in Brighton large crowds gathered, and were attended by the royal entourage and nobility. Accordingly, there were opportunities for crime and since he had knowledge of the offenders and their acquaintances he was well placed to identify and apprehend them.

He would, of course, be well paid for his attendance, if required, which he probably was.

There is a paucity of such documents from Bow Street, but these few examples help us add meaning and understanding of events at the time.

10

Concluding Themes

By the 1750s Georgian London was emerging from a state of stagnation and austerity; a place where crime was rife. London was made up of two cities – London and Westminster – together with an assortment of parishes and outlying villages which were gradually being absorbed into the metropolis, soon to create the world's largest city. The existing medieval system of watch and ward designed to police the masses was breaking down. Societal change and urban growth were destabilising the fabric of society. Weak, independent local Government added another layer of complexity and ineffectiveness. A further weakness in the law enforcement system inevitably bred public corruption and led to deterioration in public morals. Unscrupulous and dishonest individuals found themselves in positions of power as Trading Justices, dispensing the law to a fee-paying public. Public disorder became a problem; religious, political and social grievances expressed themselves in public scenes of dissatisfaction. Life on the Hogarthian margins was laid bare, with rampant prostitution, drunkenness, hooliganism, bawdy houses and civil disorder. Something had to be done.

Many of these issues had been going on for years, and whilst change was needed no-one seemed to have a plan. Henry Fielding was desperate to change the system of watch and ward, moving the practice from what he called "madness to method". Fielding needed to be innovative, clever and insightful in helping to resolve many of these problems.

He saw the "method", as his Plan presented in 1749, which he entitled "Charge to the Grand Jury". He was determined to take control of the problem and causes of crime. His methods, though unique at the time, are ones we still recognise and understand today. Fielding was not a well man and frequently suffered from a number of ailments, and after a few short years he died in 1754. His place was taken by his blind half-brother John Fielding, who continued for the next 26 years developing, modifying and improving on his brother's plan. When John died in 1780, other incumbent magistrates continued to follow Bow Street's systems, with occasional modifications and improvements.

Central to Henry's plan was the need to overcome the issue of law enforcement, which was the duty of the parish Constables. They were part of the watch and ward system which was weak, disjointed disparate and ineffective. There were many other problems to overcome too.

Henry Fielding's plan dealt with a number of issues:

- A reluctant public not taking their civic responsibility seriously in helping the police to overcome crime.
- A flawed yearly selection system for parochial Constables – nominated not volunteers.
- No continuity of Constables doing their parochial duty for a year.
- Parish boundaries and court jurisdictions limited the ability of Constables to operate in pursuit of felons and offenders.
- No proper wide geographic understanding of public mobility, which created opportunities for crime.
- No proper co-ordinated or central control over crime reporting and recording system.
- No suitable method of broadcasting to the public details of victims' losses.
- No appropriate initiative that sought to reduce the rewards of criminal enterprise, eg recovery of stolen property.
- No real effective method to deal with mass civil disturbance and public disorder.
- A general lack of understanding of poverty, housing conditions

and social problems on the causes of crime.

- An unfair and over-harsh criminal justice system reliant on execution and transportation.

All these issues and many more worked against bringing offenders to justice. Even with a harsh punishment practice, there was no real effective deterrence to prevent crime. The founding principles originally laid down as part of Henry Fielding's plan remained consistent at Bow Street for the next 80 years.

Getting the citizens onside was his starting point. Henry Fielding realised that the most powerful antidote to crime was action by the people themselves. In trying to persuade active public co-operation, Henry reminded them of the available £40 Government reward, the Tyburn Ticket (worth £20-30), which exonerated them from parochial duty and the personal possessions of the convicted felon, as incentives. In appealing to them he pointed out the advantages of collective public action – working together with the police. Acting as one with the civil authorities was not only their responsibility, it was their duty. Today, public participation with the police is a fundamental part of neighbourhood community safety which perhaps we often take for granted. What Fielding had understood then (exactly 270 years ago) was how helpless the police would be without active public support and co-operation. In fact, Robert Peel felt this aspect was so important he enshrined this as part of his principles of law enforcement in 1829.[711]

Next, Fielding realised that he needed a stronger, more flexible system of police; so he developed his own. He understood that the wrong types of people were pressed into doing their civic duty as Constables for a year. He required specially-selected public-spirited expert citizens who volunteered, not pressed men. The men must have particular skills and qualities too, such as shared values and an ability to work together for the common good, and become a unified

---

711 Principle 2 – The ability of the police to perform their duties is dependent upon public approval of police existence, actions, behaviour and the ability of the police to secure and maintain public respect.

body of men. Police duty though must be consistent and continuous – lasting more than just one year. With help from Welch, he selected six able volunteers that fitted these requirements. What he could not do was abolish the watch and ward system completely; but he could create his own court constabulary to run parallel.

Fielding and Welch concentrated on working methods, organisation and control of their group of Constables. Police instructions and rules were developed. Welch's *Observations on the Office of Constable* (1754) provided a framework for the men on how to avoid the pitfalls and problems of being a Constable. Many of the features and advice given then has helped provide a blueprint of policing practice since that time. The guidance helped unite and professionalise their role as Constables, aiding their development into an effective united group of disciplined officers. They became successful in their duty. The success of these thief-takers also rested on their actions, not as individuals but as a group. A level of trust developed in effect re-enforcing their bond of loyalty through their comradeship and co-operation. This helped cement their culture of solidarity; acting together remains a cornerstone of today's British policing.

Henry Fielding unfettered them from parochial boundaries by making them Constables of Bow Street, which had a wider jurisdictional area within which to operate. The Fieldings knew that in considering the shape of crime a great knowledge of place and time was needed, a lesson they learnt from managing the Universal Registry Office. Copying principles introduced there helped them understand the geography of crime through developed knowledge on transport means, methods and systems. This revealed where people congregated, all transport routes, links, roadways and pinch points, and created a map of likely crime spots. The Fieldings' experience with the spatial world helped them better understand crime.

Co-ordinating and bringing together in one place victims reporting their crimes was his next objective. He created a "centre" or "centre office" at Bow Street for reporting serious crimes no matter where they happened, and recorded for the first time in the criminal registers. Fielding even offered to pay victims' expenses to facilitate them reporting the crime. The Register Clerk, like a modern collator later intelligence officer, maintained the criminal registers. This enabled Fielding not only to make a note of crimes in one place and to provide an immediate response by his real thief-takers, but also to be able to link crimes together by analysing trends, patterns and descriptions. "Quick notice and sudden pursuit" was key to apprehending a suspect before they had a chance to escape and before the trail went cold. Descriptions of the assailants were noted and the registers consulted for further information before venturing in pursuit. Experience taught the pursuers to also consult with fellow officers first. Fielding only selected those of his officers for the job if they were highly-skilled as good horsemen, often brave battle-hardened ex-cavalry soldiers who had served the army with credit. The men were well-trained, properly armed and good marksmen. The Constables appreciated the dangers of violence towards them under these circumstances and often went in sufficient numbers. His methods of sudden pursuit paid dividends, since many highwaymen were swiftly caught and brought back to court to face examination. With an added confidence, soon more witnesses and victims of crime attended the court to make their reports, with each case being investigated and acted on quickly. Quick response has become a useful police strategy. And so the concept of a modern day police station at Bow Street commenced as we know it today. It became a place for reporting, administrative hub, housed police officers and detained prisoners for court. Unwittingly, this became the model for police stations when Robert Peel formed the New Police in 1829.

Broadcasting information and descriptions of stolen goods to citizens was a useful technique, since its object was to make people aware of criminal enterprise and reduce the rewards to offenders. Posters and handbills with descriptions offering a reward for information of wanted felons were distributed near the crime scene and to pawnbrokers, innkeepers, stable owners and turnpike keepers among others. This was also another means of gathering useful crime information.

This local advertising of crime later became a national scheme; news from the registers was distributed and exchanged over long distances between the boroughs and counties. Leaders, officials and magistrates were encouraged by the Fieldings to receive and exchange information, and much of it was printed in the *Quarterly Review* and *Hue and Cry*, later the *Police Gazette*; this is still published today and distributed bi-monthly by the College of Policing. By advertising criminal deeds countrywide in this way, Bow Street became more proactive; operating as a collection point in what was a central Criminal Investigation Bureau. Fielding used the newspapers to identify offences, highlight suspects and wanted persons, including court results. He encouraged positive reporting especially of successes by any of his Constables, plus their heroic and brave deeds in tracking down persistent criminals. The Fieldings alerted people to criminal offences but also to new enterprises and methods. Warning of sky farming (fraud), false coinage and extortion were advertised not only in London but also into the environs and beyond. Henry Fielding's occasional essays often advised his audience on the detail of the criminal law, thereby also cautioning them to the dangers of violence. Exchanging and recording crime information led to more arrests and felons being caught years later, since consulting the criminal registers showed their names, descriptions, methods and haunts too.

Fielding felt that the barbarity of the death penalty as a punishment for up to 200 offences worked against natural justice. He felt the punishment did not fit the crime. Juries and some judges might determine that stolen goods were over-priced and bring their value down below the five shilling threshold, where other lenient sentence options were available.

Henry Fielding highlighted the ease with which juries acquitted against the weight of evidence because the punishment was so severe. This was problematic for two reasons; it released the accused back on the street to carry out more crimes, whilst not rewarding those who had done their civic duty in prosecuting the offender.

This nullified the whole system. While both Fieldings were lenient, they often downgraded punishments themselves in place of the death penalty whilst advocating a less severe system. John Fielding was charitable, working tirelessly towards the common good, even setting up three philanthropic societies in an effort to remove young boys and girls from the criminal equation. This included the Marine Society (1756), where young boys were given an opportunity to break from their criminal past by going to sea with the Royal Navy; the Magdalen Hospital (1758), which took in and cared for penitent prostitutes; and the Royal Female Orphanage (1762), to house and school orphaned girls while training them for a productive life in service or marriage. These societies gave Fielding and other Bow Street Magistrates sentencing options for young boys and girls. In this way, he was giving young people not only better conditions, a more productive future and a worthwhile existence, but also removing them from the streets and opportunities for crime.

Crime investigation was also an art which was learnt by the whole Bow Street establishment. Crime investigation is reliant on learning to spot the abnormal, uncharacteristic, or out of place. Being able to read, write, learn criminal law and evidential procedures required a higher-than-average applicant. The Bow Street authorities had always maintained a high standard, ensuring their officers had good references and a sound reputation before they were selected. Bow Street continually selected the right men for the job as Constables. The art and science of policing practice was enhanced by successful working practices, especially that of crime investigation, contributing not only to the perceptive blueprint of policemanship, but adding to the myth of Bow Street.

The Fieldings appreciated the importance of non-uniformed foot patrols. Specially-selected men were sent out on an ad hoc basis, often comprising of some Bow Street Constables and a mix of other volunteers to deal with particular crime problems. These patrols were neither regular, routine, uniformed nor professional patrols. Coterminously, many of the parishes also had roving patrols of watchmen operating independently from Bow Street and often in co-operation with each other. A regular Foot Patrole was introduced following the disastrous Gordon Riots of 1780, as these revealed the weakness and helplessness of the London police system due to insufficient numbers of available officers. Armed foot patrols took control of the streets of London following the riots of 1780 in London, although they were not officially recognised by the Government until 1790. Core Foot Patrole men kept the peace at ceremonial events, royal engagements, public occasions, meetings and where necessary to combat public disorder. Men from the Foot Patroles supplemented Principal Officers during house searches, raids on gaming establishments and executing dangerous arrest warrants. Duties were becoming more complex, and included deterring pickpockets at the theatres, or patrolling the busy parks or thoroughfares to apprehend felons, robbers and burglars. Of course their duties not only involved dealing with criminal matters, but as time went on these included a wide variety of other social problems as well. Their craft as members of the Foot Patrole also included crime investigation. Bow Street's role in this has often been understated, but recognised more recently by scholars (See Beattie, 2012 and Cox, 2010). Peel introduced his Detective Department in 1842, but perhaps the art and science of crime investigation predates this initiative by up to 80 years.

Particular crime problems have changed, yet the underlying principles have never altered; crime today is the same as it was in Georgian times, that is to say, crimes against people and property. Its detection also follows similar lines too, with the same questioning skills, albeit perhaps enhanced by computerisation which replaced the criminal registers.

The overarching Bow Street strategy was multi-dimensional and a many-faceted plan. Included were the principles of Fielding's original plan – grounded in a proper understanding and complexities of the social problems of the day. The role of Bow Street's Georgian Constables was a transformative one, being developed and improved on as time went by. Fundamentally, the right men – volunteers – were chosen for their skills and moral character, and moulded through proper organisation and discipline. From the earliest times this rested on common principles, practices and features. From the police cultural perspective, this included good fellowship and friendship that supported the public good. Sharing their collective knowledge, disclosing experiences and proficiency jointly in this way enhanced their expertise and further galvanised the men. Divided they became ineffective, but collectively they were a formidable body. These men developed into a disciplined, unified, cohesive group with an "esprit de corps". Strong leadership also developed, with the supply of information and instructions up and down the chain of command which kept everyone vitally informed. Organisationally the system was strict, and bound with regulation and self-control. The police became disciplined and well-organised, rapidly learning fresh tactics and new methods of their craft. All this created an image of them as professional, strong and brave, adding to the misplaced perception they were everywhere. Bow Street's methods moved with the times, developing new systems with which to enhance the role of the police officer. As time moved from the Fieldings to Sampson Wright and beyond, changes were introduced as other social problems involved the Runners and Patroles. Policing moved from being reactive in the early days to becoming more proactive by the time the Foot Patroles were introduced.

Sir Robert Peel was an experienced Chief Secretary for Ireland and as Home Secretary had learnt the processes and procedures of police work, understanding the types and qualities needed as a police recruit. In working closely with the Bow Street establishment over many years he appreciated and understood the merits and defects of their methods and principles. It seems that Peel wasted no time re-inventing structures, styles and methods. He adopted and improved their employment practice, instructions to Constables, unifying methods, investigation processes and the general principles of law enforcement successfully used by Bow Street in Georgian London – many of which are still basic tenets of policing today. Organisationally, he discarded the practices that had not be quite so satisfactory.

Not everything at Bow Street was rosy, as its character was being questioned. The notorious McDaniel case (1816) saw six police officers, one a Bow Street Patrole, involved in framing innocent people in crime. Most of the Runners were openly accepting bribes from criminals, even acting as middlemen for the return of stolen artefacts. The Bow Street reputation was becoming tarnished, with allegations of corruption. Perhaps Peel declined to allow any of them to become Constables of his New Police for this reason.

The early police sub-culture was an absolute necessity in Georgian times and greatly aided their success. These methods and practices helped to inform Peel's Nine Principles of Law Enforcement published in 1829. Since those early times of policing, what was learnt then has informed the way we police today – our history is closer to us than we think.

Observations on
the Office of Constable[712]

SAUNDERS WELCH (1754)

On the Office in General

Laws were made by the legislature, the process is issued by the magistrates but the execution belonged to the Constable alone. Any intimidation which undermined the Constable also reduced the effective power of the magistrates.

To the Constables

- In executing your office serve the public with credit.
- Keep yourself safe.
- Exercise your office by doing good.
- Protect the innocent from the hands of violence.
- Protect and preserve the [public] peace and to bring those who disturb the peace [offenders] to justice.
- Do not make yourself officious, use wanton acts of power [violence] and prevent your own prejudices from becoming involved in your duty.

---

712 We need to express a note of caution on the issue of translation in reviewing and transcribing this book published some 265 years ago. Certain words appear, which were in common usage at the time and need further elucidation and explanation in today's context. This translation has relied on the twin lenses of literal clarity and our own interpretation of current language. This runs the risk of perhaps not properly giving its true explanation in today's context so that any error in this regard is ours as authors.

- Ensure people are not falsely imprisoned.
- By doing these you will become a person of esteem, prisoners will respect you, have public acclaim as the reward in the faithful execution of your office.

The Advantage of union in the officers

- Ensure proper union [teamwork] and cheerful assistance to one another [properly united and acting together], connected, corresponding, at times and places for fixed meetings – not for drinking or sotting [drink alcohol habitually] but for consulting. Gangs of villains will not last a week given this successful union.
- Good temper and sobriety in the execution of his office. Being in liquor [drunk] will lead to contempt and ridicule.
- Don't be provoked or take insult yourselves. [The modern day police instructions on which this warning was built suggested that "Idle and silly remarks were unworthy of notice and should be disregarded."]
- Do not listen to vexatious talk by someone close on whom you may be executing a warrant.
- Don't be diverted in your duty by arresting the fool [the bystander causing a disturbance or trying to distract you or secure themselves instead of the person you are trying to arrest] rather than the real prisoner who by your action goes free.

Your powers without a warrant namely, as conservators of the peace to quell affrays, riots, &c.

- In a riot pick out a person you know call on them to desist and should they not do so then arrest them.
- If your safety was threatened and assistance is not readily available and the person(s) still fail to take your advice or escape then indict them for their contempt and the court will support you.
- That a Constable had the power to apprehend without warrant but should be mindful that this was a found committing power

and actionable only in the first instance.

- Do not to take action when the affray, riot etc. has finished since the Constable could be indicted himself for false imprisonment. Advise any assaulted person following a riot to apply for a magistrates warrant, however, if the victim is dangerously or partly wounded and the accused is still present the Constable should detain him as the delay in obtaining a warrant may allow a murderer to escape.
- Where there has been a dangerous blow or wound applied or there is an immediate danger of further riot etc, surrender your prisoner, to a justice of the peace.
- Intervening to break up an affray where blows have been struck separate both parties and make no arrest.

Not to intervene in Alehouse Brawls

- Constables should refrain from breaking up Alehouse brawls. Constables who have intervened in such a way have often been in receipt of a writ by the very people to whose assistance they came.
- The danger of your striking in the execution of office.
- The Constable in seeking to preserve the King's peace may on resistance be justified in beating and putting the persons in the stocks.
- However, if the Constable in beating should kill it is to him justifiable but it is murder if the Constable is killed by the rioter.
- **Never strike a person except in absolute defence but striking should be avoided at all if possible and the sword of justice not the arm of the Constable should be the punishment.**
- Carry the maxim in all you do; "do not do all you may do but always do what you ought to do."

Concerning the Watch

- Your immediate duty is to provide sufficient and able watch.
- Do not to collect money to pay hired men, the law only says he

shall warn able bodied men, in their turn, station them properly, and present such as neglect or refuse to their duty therein; Constables may be hired from amongst the people to help in preventing a breach of the peace or response to the level of violence.

- The watch to be honest able bodied men.
- The hired Constable or watchman should not only be able, active and honest but also to arrive regularly and devote the whole time to their duty.
- Do not allow them to spend their Duty time "sotting" in night cellars and regularly inspect your men when on duty to ensure against drinking or sleeping in the watch house or leaving their place to go somewhere else or before the time.

Objects of the night

- Be aware of people that present problems for the Constable such as rogues, vagabonds and disturbers of the peace at night and whores who frequent the corners of the streets.

Care in searching suspicious prisoners

- On arrest of any person to ensure that they are properly searched.
- Remove from them anything uncommon like firearms or offensive weapon.
- Detain them securely.
- Take their account and record exactly what they say because this leads to useful discoveries.
- Be sure to give a charge to the keeper of the roundhouse into whose care you leave the prisoner.
- Ensure that no one has access to your prisoner, or
  allow a message to be sent to anyone (about the prisoner), or
- To make any alteration to their (prisoners) habits before they are brought to the justices by a change of clothes so that their dress may help them evade justice.
- Do not allow prisoners to put on wigs change clothes to evade

identification under the guise of being seen as clean in front of the justices.[713]

- Do not take men of credit and imprison them over minor street squabbles.
- If you or members of the watch did not see a breach of the peace then do not be too officious making sure the watchmen are not impertinent nor squabble with those they should protect – the people of credit when heated by liquor. There should not be attempts to raise contributions [rewards] from the public and passers–by in the morning when the streets are clear of rogues and whores.

On imprisoning a person of credit in the night

Anyone may approach a justice of the peace and obtain a warrant only providing very loose and general description of the culprit (and need to supply no name) for some misdemeanour or other. Motivated by resentment they may have obtained a warrant against a person of fashion (gentleman or man of credit) which means any gentleman may be subject to arrest and detention. Be extremely cautious in this event; and instead return the warrant and have the matter served by a summons instead unless a felony has been committed.[714]

On your conduct in the watch house

- Supervise the watch house properly and do not allow the "absurd behaviour of many officers either for gross ignorance, passion and drunkenness".

---

713 When a person is taken before a magistrate the victim will be asked to identify that the prisoner at the bar is the same person who committed the felony, misdemeanour etc. Should the person charging be in any doubt as to the identification of the prisoner then he will be acquitted. Changing the appearance of an accused before an initial court appearance lessens the context under which the prisoner was detained.

714 A Constable would have received one shilling for executing a warrant so sometimes arresting the gentleman would ensure he was paid.

- Calmly enquire into the offence complained of and don't lose sight of this fact from any improper behaviour or manner of the parties giving you the information.
- Beware of bringing friends to a "watch–night". This situation gives rise to drunkenness and "showing off" by the officer who wishes to demonstrate the absolute power he possesses. This folly gives rise to ridicule and he will also have to account for himself later.
- Remove people from the watch house who have no business there. "Dirty Solicitors" have often mixed with complainants before the Constable keen to see an error made by the officer who later will receive a court action against him.

Apprehending of Felons

- The apprehension and bringing to justice a felon is one of your greatest responsibilities.
- The law has given you power to raise a "hue and cry".
- Search all suspected places and break open doors in the pursuit of felons.
- Should the Constable or headborough not raise the hue and cry in the case of a robbery or refuse or neglect to do so he renders himself liable to a fine of £5.
- Raising a hue and cry renders their escape next to impossible.
- If this statute was executed with vigilance equal to the wisdom if its construction, highway robberies, the depredation of footpads and burglaries in the county would cease.
- A warrant is unnecessary when a delay in obtaining a warrant would allow the felon to escape so the Constable had to be sure that a robbery had really been committed and that the person arrested is properly suspected of the crime.
- Investigate properly when a robbery is brought to your notice. The law will punish you for refusal to do your duty and pursue and apprehend a felon.
- Having arrested the felon do not allow him to escape. It is inexcusable for a Constable to allow a prisoner to escape since

the law has given you the power of calling in help enough to secure and bind the felon.

- Search the fellow for your own safety so that he has taken from him anything that may cause mischief (that may injure you and/ or aid him in escaping) and evidence may be secured.
- Once secure take him before a magistrate and keep him in your sight at all times.
- Do not remove to a less secure temporary prison in their own houses so as to take a few dirty shillings which allows gangs to assemble and try and effect [sic] a rescue of the prisoner and if not to effect an artful defence (or alibi).
- Be sure to see your prisoner is safely in the hands of the gaoler and do not trust the care of your prisoner to a runner to a prison.
- Any property taken from felons should not be left out of your sight unless you have put some private mark on them so as to be able to identify them.
- Do not forget to bring the property before the court in evidence. [Failure to do this often led to a dispute of ownership by both the felon and the victim.]
- On the felons acquittal any property subject of the charge reverts back to the prisoner.

Other responsibilities of Constable

- The preservation of good order in the public streets.
- The safety of all public carriages and the repair of holes in the pavement by householders since the latter is responsible for the repair of any such damage.
- Another nuisance is rubbish which obstructs the free passage of the town.
- Carman travelling too fast cause danger not only to coaches but to the lives of infirm persons and children. A recent Act of Parliament empowered you to apprehend any driver or other person riding on the carriages having no one on foot to guide the horses, carry them before the Justices of the Peace.

- Orange Box drivers [illegal gaming by trickery]. This nuisance is about gamblers and the use of orange box barrows on the streets. These wretches first teach the art of gaming and with this the foundation of ruin is already laid to thousands.
- Profane swearing is the next nuisance and the Constable should banish the swearing and horrid imprecation [swear words] from the streets.
- Another nuisance are the swarms of beggars who frequent the streets and artful wretches to prey upon the compassion of the weak minded.
- Some necessary hints for your behaviour to those from whom you derive the rest of your power. Those are the Sessions, the Sherriff and coroner, the justice of the peace and your High Constable. Warrants under their hand or seals (except if the justice is with you) it is wise to read over the warrant and this part of your duty is less liable to error than if you act on your own discretion.
- The justices of the peace assembled in their sessions may with great propriety be deemed the counsel of the country for the preservation of the peace and good order of it and it is your duty to pay strict attention to orders and warrants of every magistrate and how much more is it incumbent on you to exert yourselves in the execution of such warrants and orders as comes from them.

Of the Common Fairs about Town

Another problem was the numerous fairs about town with excesses of debauchery and immoralities that attracted not only the youth of both sexes but the increase in robberies.

Cock throwing

Cock throwing was a barbarous custom developed over time reflects a character of cruelty on the nation.

Gaming upon the Lord's Day

The suppression of gaming and other disorders on the Lord's day carried on in the fields adjoining the town in the summer season and during divine service so the problem for the parents and the employers of the youth you should be aware that they are associated with gamblers, pickpockets and other abandoned wretches.

Obedience to the Sheriff

It is also your duty to execute the warrants from the Sheriff punctually since it demonstrates to the public the strength of the civil power. Let your behaviour at public executions do credit to yourselves and your office, obey the Sherriff or his substitute, preserve the King's Peace and ensure the public do not extend their punishment beyond the just sentence of the law.

To the Coroner

You are also obliged to execute the warrants of the coroner which summons juries, apprehend persons charged with or suspected of murder. In your summoning of the juries I am sorry to say that very indifferent people both of character and worth have been called upon them; and this I am told arises from the resentment of the Constables, for is a troublesome worthless fellow affront them he is reserved by way of punishment to attend a coroner's jury. As this is the first inquisition for the discovery of murderers and of the highest consequence of society, men of ability and character should constitute the jury. Please on these occasions do not show your resentment instead leaving matters to the public good.

Presentments to Sessions and Grand Jury
[prosecution papers to the court]

Respect the orders from the High Constable in your dealings with the sessions;

- distinguish between Christian and surnames of offenders,
- their occupations and

- places of abode;
- If women whether single, married or widowed.

If you present on your own knowledge either bawdy or gaming houses;
- mention the time they have been kept and
- Let your presentation [court papers] be complete and absolute.
- If only upon report of others then mention only as reputed so.

The keeper (and proprietor) of the notorious bawdy house whose iniquitous practices have for some years since produced a riot by artful means (concern amongst the honest people). He would do this by shifting the names of the occupiers of his house and at other times by entering an appearance in the crown office [the whole charge did not amount to a sum of more than £8 for the year, did still openly carry on a bawdy house for years unpunished even though it was presented each year before the Grand Jury. Here Welch infers that to create fictitious names which have been put forward as occupiers of these places creates a situation where summonses cannot be served on people who do not exist and the powers of the Constables do not necessarily extend to investigating who or finding the whereabouts of these people.]

Where such persons of notoriety endanger the public peace it should be that such prosecutions should be presented at the public expense. Let me conjure you to do your duty as honest men bound by solemn oath and whether defects there may afterwards be, exert yourself in the first instance for your prosecution sentiment as this is the foundation to proceed.

Respectful behaviour to the magistrates
- You should at all times be respectful and obedient to the magistrates.
- Teach the common people subordination by setting an example for others to follow including to your superiors.
- Never make yourselves officially parties in any complaint you bring before the magistrates and unless called upon by the

magistrate you should remain silent.
- When you are required to speak do so impartially.
- Officious behaviour in interesting yourselves in the disputes of others must bring the resentment of one party upon you.

Expedition in executing warrants

Be sure to execute all warrants as quickly as possible; and bring the offenders as soon as you can, to answer the complaint properly.

Minor offence warrants produced by people who harbour resentment against others are the most troublesome part of your office – be gentle and kind and through persuasion you may moderate matters and get feuding parties to reconcile themselves again as friends.

How safe in executing warrants

As the law formally stood the Constable was answerable for false imprisonment if he executed a warrant in cases where the justice, had no jurisdiction, and yet at the same time, was indictable for refusing to obey.

Care in preserving warrants

You are only concerned in the execution of warrants, and if they be illegal, for the defendant, has a right to demand a copy and perusal of such warrant which if you refuse, may result in an action for false imprisonment, or if the warrant is illegal it will lie against you, whereas once you have given such a copy, or permit the perusal the Justice, he must abide by the consequence of the warrant and you are discharged.

Distinguishing people of credit from vagabonds in executing warrants.

In warrants of common assaults amongst neighbours of credit and fortune, your own sense will tell you a different conduct is necessary than when they are against vagabonds.

Search warrants

- Great prudence is necessary in executing of search warrants. This must be done; between the rising and the setting of the sun, at most by visible day-light.
- With good nature acquaint the parties upon whom the warrant is to be executed, and of the felony committed.
- Indicate that suspicion has arisen that part of the goods are lodged with them, for which reason you are obliged by the warrant to search, advising them, if any of the things stolen are in their custody, to produce them voluntarily, and you give evidence accordingly.
- If they deny knowledge of them, and such things upon a search should be found, or evidence afterwards appears that they were in their custody, the law will construe their denial and secreting the goods, into a felonious intent, the consequence of which is, transportation for 14 years.
- Your warrant tells you if you find the things stolen or any part of them, you are to bring them and the parties, in whose custody they were found, nor break open locks until parties have first refused to open them.

Powers in breaking open doors

Where the law prescribes that power to your office, you are upon finding the doors fast to call with an audible voice to the persons within, demanding entrance there, in the kings name, as a Constable, and if upon this the parties refuse to answer or answering, refuse to open the door, then you are justifiable in using force.

Caution not to act out of your divisions

Be careful not to execute warrants, or to do any act as a Constable, out of your respective parishes or places except when you are especially appointed by a warrant or in aiding your high Constable in the discharge of his duty. Magistrates may empower any person to execute their warrants within their jurisdiction and the high

Constable has the same authority in every parish in each division as you have in your separate parishes and you partake of that authority when you are with him.

Warrants generally and specially directed

If you have had any dispute or prior problem with any person on whom you have a warrant I would advise you to decline serving it, but refer it to a brother officer.

Warrants of distress

- In the execution of warrants of distress first demand; the sum to be levied.
- If that is denied, then you will have to seize so many of the goods as would be sufficient to pay the contents of your warrant and the necessary expense consequent thereupon; do this, with as little hurt to the parties as possible.
- Let your seizure be rather of superfluities than necessaries, and take a broker with you, who can judge of the value of the goods and will direct you in respect of the quantity and
- Which goods should be immediately disposed of.
- Any surplus if any arising be paid back to the parties on whom the seizure was made.

Landlords seizing goods

On being called upon by landlords at the seizure of goods, your duty there is only to preserve the peace, with intermeddling otherwise, except when violence has been offered and the peace broke [sic], then you are to apprehend the parties striking the first blow.

Quartering of soldiers

Quartering of soldiers both married and single can cause a little trouble at first. It will be of great benefit to them and utility to your publicans; so as the guards consist of married and single men; to put single soldiers with spaces to lodge them and married men in the smaller dwellings. To quarter a married soldier in a lodging house, is taking from him 3s a month; and sending single men to both money quarters is distressing both him and his landlord. I therefore recommend to you to consult the Sergeants of the respective companies upon the general remove and they will inform you of the condition of their men, and by placing them properly in quarters, according to their wants, you will preserve peace in your respective divisions, and should any disputes arise between the landlord and the soldier, endeavour to friendly reconcile them. If this fails to prevent worse consequence remove them to other quarter's and avoid if possible all imputation of particularity, than which nothing can be more odious in the public trust.

Behaviour of soldiers to landlords and landlords to soldiers

The Kings commands are that soldiers behave peaceably in their quarters and their officers do severely punish such as do not conform

Duty in assisting at fires

- The law required on notice given to you that you should;
- Attend the fire and assist in extinguishing it.
- Compelling person present to work the engines including other methods to prevent the flames spreading.
- Apprehend pilferers and idle persons supposed to attend for the barbarous purpose of robbing the distressed.
- Note that thieves will abscond when you are present and the idle and curious will, by your means, be made useful.
- Direct your watchmen if it be in the night, to call you even though not in your immediate division.

Avoid passion resentment and imperious conduct in office

I have already cautioned you against passion and refinement in the execution of your office; also avoid that impertinent, imperiousness of conduct too frequently seen in Constables and called the drunkenness of power. The cruel execution of the law, creates an implacable enemy in every prisoner, and makes the apprehender, in many cases, the greater criminal. Do every–thing you can to secure them but let the law punish them.

Duty to your High Constable

In deed by virtue of his office, your High Constable has no positive authority over you, and is only authorised to command you, by virtue of warrants and orders he received from the sessions, sheriff and judges. For if we go no further than the letter of the law obliges us, the public will be ill served. In fine, union secrecy and bravery are the great points in the joint execution of our office. These will answer the intention of the institution and truly denominate us protectors to the innocent preservers of the public peace and a terror of the sons of violence.

Conclusion

I have shown you what has been useful in your office, and I hope you take notice as I have in my humble station, to the duty of my office, in service of the public, and the protection of those who have been united with and acted under me. But if heaven spare a life, invaluable to his friends and family, hazarded I may say with truth, sacrificed to the public welfare, I mean a magistrate whose good heart, and great abilities, justly entitles him to the affection of every worthy mind, he will give you a perfect directory in your office, both of law and prudence.

In excuse for myself, in this imperfect sketch, I shall only say, that men enjoy the faint light of stars, when the sun is absent. If there be the least degree of merit in this honest intention to serve you and the public, it is derived from the friendly cautions and prudent advice, I have at all times received from Mr Fielding, and to him I most humbly beg leave to inscribe this most imperfect essay.

FINIS

APPENDIX 2

Patrole Orders

Police Horse Patrole

Orders for the Government of the Police Horse Patrole, under the direction of Sir Nathaniel Conant, Chief Magistrate at the Public Office Bow–street, November 1813; Mr Day, conductor.

1   All orders given by Mr Day, to the patrole, or to the Inspectors, and delivered by them to the patrole, are to be strictly obeyed.

2   The patrole are to obey with the strictest punctuality, all orders they shall receive as to the time of their going and continuing on duty; and they are to proceed on the road as such a pace as will bring them to the extreme end of their journey at the time they are directed; they are there to halt ten minutes, before they begin their journey back.

3   The patrole stationed on the same road, are to meet and communicate together, both going and returning, halting for each other at some given spot half way on the journey. They are to be attentive to any information they may receive of any robbery having been committed or attempted, or of any suspicious persons having been seen on the road, and to endeavour to get a description of them and the road they have taken; and if any robbery be committed or attempted, the patrole first receiving information of it, is to join his companion if he can conveniently do it, and use every exertion to take the offenders; or if he cannot conveniently join his companion, he is to make an immediate pursuit with such other assistance as he can get, and if the party

should be apprehended, to lodge them in some place of security until he can bring them to Bow–street, which he is to do by eleven o'clock the following morning, and to warn the witnesses against them, to appear there at the same time.

4   Every patrole when on duty, is to have all his appointments with him in proper condition, his pistols loaded, and his sword worn on the outside of his coat; and no patrole under any pretence whatsoever, is to go into any public or other house during the time of his duty; and they are to make themselves known to all persons, as well in carriages as on horseback, by calling out to them as they pass, in a loud and distinct tone of voice "Bow–street Patrole."

5   If any patrole shall lose any part of his appointments, it is to be replaced at his expense.

6   No patrole whilst he is on duty, is to deliver his horse to the care of any other person, or suffer him to be out of his sight, for the purpose of being put into a stable, or otherwise.

7   If any patrole shall be taken ill, or his horse shall become lame or unfit for duty, he is to report it immediately to Mr Day; and in the case of his horse being unfit for duty, he is to do duty on foot (taking his pistols with him) and to go not less than half the distance he would on horseback.

8   If any patrole shall not be met by his companion, on the road, in the manner directed, he is to report the same on the following morning to Mr Day; and not any excuse will be admitted for neglecting to make such a report.

9   No patrole is to use his horse for any other purpose than his regular duty, nor keep his horse at grass without leave for that purpose; nor is he, except in case of illness, to entrust his horse to the care of any other person.

10 Each patrole will be allowed for his horse per week, a bushel and a half of oats, three bushels of chaff, a truss and a half of hay, and a truss of straw.

11 Every patrole is to feed his horse regularly three times a day;

namely, at eight o'clock in the morning, one o'clock in the afternoon, and when he gets home from his duty at night : he is to remain at his stable one hour at least from eight o'clock in the morning, to dress his horse and clean his appointments; from one o'clock in the afternoon he is also to remain there half an hour at least, to dress his horse; and when he returns at night from his duty, he is to be sure to let his horse be clean and dry before he leaves the stable.

12 No patrole is to be absent at any time more than two miles from the place he is stationed at, except on duty, without leave for that purpose; nor is he to change his lodgings without first giving notice of it to Mr Day.

13 Mr Day, with the Inspectors, will inspect the patrole once every month, in the several districts appointed for that purpose, when the men are to appear in the uniform of the establishment, with their arms and all their appointments, which their horses will be expected to be found in perfect order, and fit for service.

14 The Inspectors in their respective districts, are to visit the patrole on their night–duty, and to report to Mr Day any particular occurrence or neglect of their duty, on the following morning. The Inspectors are also to report their own duty to him in writing every week, and to specify in such report what has been the general conduct and behaviour of the patrole during that period.

15 The Inspectors are also frequently to visit the stables of the patrole, at the hours they are directed by the 11th order to be there, and report to Mr Day any neglect or disobedience of such order.

Police Horse Patrole Dismounted

Orders for the Government of the Police Horse Patrole Dismounted, under the direction of Sir Nathaniel Conant, Chief Magistrate at the Public Office Bow–street; Mr Day, conductor.

1   All orders given by Mr Day, to the patrole, or to the Inspectors,

and delivered by them to the patrole, are to be strictly obeyed.

2 The patrole stationed on the same road, dismounted and mounted, are to meet and communicate together, both going and returning. They are to take notice of any suspicious persons they may see on the road, and to attend to any information they may receive of any highway or footpad robbery having been committed or attempted; and if any such robbery has been committed or attempted, they are to use every exertion to take the offenders; and if the party should be apprehended, to lodge them in some place of security until he can bring them to Bow–street Office, which he is to do by eleven o'clock the following morning, and to warn the witnesses against them, to appear there at the same time, and to apprise Mr Day thereof.

3 Every patrole, when on duty, is to have his warrant, truncheon, and cutlass with him, and he is not to go into any public or other house during the time of his duty.

4 If any patrole shall lose any either his truncheon or cutlass, they are to be replaced at his expense.

5 If any patrole shall be taken ill, or become lame, or unfit for duty, he is to report it immediately to Mr Day.

6 If any patrole shall not be met by his companions, on the road, either mounted or dismounted, in the manner directed, he is to report the same on the following morning to Mr Day; and not any excuse will be admitted for neglecting to make such a report.

7 No patrole is to be absent at any time more than two miles from the place he is stationed at, except on duty, without leave for that purpose; nor is he to change his lodgings without first giving notice of it to Mr Day.

8 Mr Day, with the Inspectors, will inspect the patrole once every month, in the several districts appointed for that purpose; when the patrole are to appear in the uniform of the establishment, with their truncheon and cutlass.

9 The Inspectors in their respective districts, are to visit the patrole on their night–duty, and to report to Mr Day any

particular occurrence or neglect of their duty, on the following morning. The Inspectors are also to report their own duty to him in writing every week, and to specify in such report what has been the general conduct and behaviour of the patrole during that period.

No 1 – 1816
Rules, Orders, and Regulations,
For the Government and Observance of the Foot Patrole Establishment, at the Police Office, Bow–street. – London, printed by J. Downes, 240, Strand, 1816.

1   The Foot Patrol Establishment is under the direction of Sir Nathaniel Conant, the Chief Magistrate, whose orders, when not personally given, will be communicated by Mr Stafford, Chief Clerk, to the respective conductors of parties, who are strictly to obey all such orders and directions, and be responsible for carrying them into effect : the men are to be attentive and obedient to their conductors, and if they are not so, or commit any irregularity, or in any way neglect their duty, the conductors are to report them with the particulars of their misconduct; and they will be punished by suspension from pay or discharged. Any neglect of duty or improper conduct on the part of the conductors, will be punished in like manner.

2   [*Contains the names of the 13 conductors, with their respective places of meeting.*]

3   The time of meeting, and the duration of duty, will be regulated by circumstances and the seasons of the year; and will be given out, and entered weekly in the Orderly Book, at Bow–street.

4   When each party assemble at the appointed place of meeting, the conductor, pursuant to his instructions, will divide them into two or more divisions, according to the effective strength of the party; and before he proceeds on his duty with the first division, he will select and place proper and experienced men at the head of the other division, and give them directions as to the particular part of the district they are to patrole, and when

and where to meet again or communicate with each other; and in the whole party will assemble together at the usual place of meeting when the time of duty shall expire, and then, if nothing shall have happened to require their further services, they shall be discharged by the conductor.

5   Should the conductor be prevented by sickness or any other cause, from meeting the party at the appointed time, the senior man present is to take the direction of the party for the evening, and report the occurrence in writing, the next morning, at the office.

6   Should the party hear of any murder, burglary, robbery, or other atrocious offence being committed, they are to procure every particular they can relative to the same, and the number of offenders, and their description, and use every exertion in their power to apprehend them; and the conductor to report the circumstances at the office the next morning.

7   The conductors are to attend every Monday morning, at Bow-street, at 10 o'clock, and each to produce an occurrence book, to be kept by the conductor, in which he shall enter a journal of the duty of the party during the week, and report every particular occurrence that may have taken place; the conductors shall, at the same time, deliver in a printed report with the blanks filled up, of the effective strength of the party, the names of any that may be sick or absent without leave, and of such as may have had leave of absence, or been employed on office–duty; the number of pistols, cutlasses, belts, truncheons, &c. in the use of the party, and whether fit for service; the conductors will also peruse the Orderly Book, and any fresh orders they may find; they are to communicate to the men at the meeting place in the evening, or sooner if requisite; they are also to take from the book the names of men who shall be entered for night duty at the office during the ensuing week, and for the orderly duty in the day–time, and they are to acquaint the men therewith, and will be considered responsible for their attendance accordingly: the conductors will also receive every Monday morning, the amount

of the pay for the party for the preceding week, and are to pay the men in the course of the same day.

8   Two of the parties of patrole in rotation to attend every Monday morning, at half past nine o'clock, with their pistols, cutlasses, belts, and truncheons, which will be inspected, and, if found in any way damaged or injured from negligence or carelessness of the persons entrusted with them, the necessary repair shall be done, and the expense stopped from the pay of the person by whose default the damage shall be occasioned.

9   Two men of the nightly watch at the office, are to be taken from the respective parties to patrole in succession, according to their number; but only one man is to be taken from the same party on the same night; they are to come on duty at nine o'clock in the evening, and remain until nine o'clock in the morning; one of them to be always up and on the watch; they are to keep themselves within the watch–room and remain perfectly quiet; and are not to suffer any person to come in, or remain with them, nor are they to leave the office, except on duty, until relieved by the door–keeper, in the morning; and in case of any particular occurrence taking place during the night, one of them is to call the officer in waiting for the week, whose name will be hung up in the watch–room, who will act according to the best of his judgement, and if he thinks necessary he is to acquaint the Chief Clerk or one of the Magistrates thereof, as the exigency may require.

10 Any misconduct on the night duty, arising from drunkenness, negligence, or any other cause, will be attended with the immediate discharge of the person who shall be found to have offended; and no man whose turn it is for the night duty, will be suffered to send another to do the duty for him, without leave first obtained.

11 The parties of patrole in rotation, will be excused from the road duty one night in thirteen, but on that night they are to be on duty at the office, in Bow–street, at a quarter before seven; and at seven, the conductor is to report to the Sitting Magistrate,

whether the whole of his party are present; and they are to attend from seven o'clock until nine, when they will be dismissed, if their further attendance is not required; but if both or either of the men for the night duty should not be in attendance at the time, the conductor is to order one or two of his men, as the case may be, to take the night duty, and remain until relieved; and the conductor is to report the absence of the men who ought to have attended. The two men on the night duty will be relived at nine in the morning by the door–keeper and the orderly man. An orderly man is to be furnished daily from the parties in rotation, and is to attend at the main office from nine in the morning until nine in the evening, unless otherwise directed by the Sitting Magistrate.

12 One of the conductors in rotation shall attend at the office, in Bow–street, every Sunday, from nine in the morning until one in the afternoon; and another conductor also in rotation, from one in the afternoon until five in the afternoon; and at five, one of the conductors, with his party, is to come on duty at the office, and not depart until nine, nor until the night duty is provided for, in the manner directed by the last regulation (No.11.)

13 When any party of the Foot Patrole meet any of the Horse Patrole, attached to the office, on duty on the roads, the conductor of the party of foot is to communicate to the Horse Patrole, any matters that may have occurred concerning their mutual duty, and receive his communications in return, and at all times to aid and assist the Horse Patrole in furtherance of his duty, when occasion may require.

14 A printed Copy of the Rules and Regulations will be delivered to each of the conductors, who are to read them over to their men on the first day of every month, and on the Saturday preceding the inspections.

15 All persons belonging to the establishment, when on duty at the office, are strictly to obey the orders of the Sitting Magistrate.

APPENDIX 3

Dismounted Horse Patrole
1829–1830

Appointed	Name	Rank	Warrant No.	Promotion	Removal	Div
04.02.1830	William Adamson	Ps	690	Insp 01.07.1830		A
21.09.1829	Edwin Alewood	Pc	932		Dismissed 24.01.1831	
21.09.1829	John Brundly	Ps	1331	Insp 13.03.1832	Resigned 03.05.1842	C
21.09.1829	James Birch	Pc	482		Resigned 07.12.1829	
08.02.1830	William Brown	Pc	2403 763 (sic)	Insp 12.12.1848		L
21.09.1830	James Barton	Pc	1475		Dismissed 20.08.1832	
06.02.1830	William Bartlett	Pc	1766		Resigned 10.05.1836	G
03.02.1830	John Blayney	Pc	2040		Resigned 05.04.1830	
08.02.1830	Richard Beckett	Pc	2416			V
21.09.1829	William Beck	Pc	732		Resigned 14.11.1830	
08.02.1829	James Cheeseman	Pc	2316		Died 15.09.1830	L
21.09.1829	Samuel Chambers	Pc	1048		Dismissed 27.08.1830	
21.09.1829	James Covington	Ps	958			C
22.05.1830	John Cain	Pc	4292		Resigned 02.10.1830	
09.02.1830	James Dawkins	Ps	3012	Insp 25.10.1832	Died 17.12.1844	S

365

Appointed	Name	Rank	Warrant No.	Promotion	Removal	Div
21.09.1829	William Davis	Pc	695		Resigned 29.08.1831	
04.02.1830	Charles Dawson	Pc	710		Dismissed 27.10.1830	
04.02.1830	John Dixon	Pc	2740		Resigned 09.01.1843	S
29.09.1829	William Eckett	Pc	137 6847		Dismissed 09.12.1829 Re-joined 29.09.1831	
01.02.1830	George Feltam	Insp				T
01.02.1830	William Fryer	Ps	2765	Insp 02.12.1831	Resigned as Supt 27.08.1841	H
01.02.1830	William Featherston	Pc	2668	Ps 29.09.1830		M
21.02.1829	Charles Freeman	Pc	1020		Dismissed 13.04.1833	C
21.02.1829	Thomas Franklin	Pc	540		Resigned 21.09.1829	
21.02.1829	Thomas Fletcher	Pc	1067		Dismissed 15.04.1830	
05.04.1830	Philip Froud	Pc	3405	Ps 17.09.1830	Resigned as Insp 20.03.1841	L
01.02.1830	Geo. Allen Greening	Insp			Resigned 28.02.1831	
01.02.1829	Samuel Greening	Pc	549		Resigned 06.10.1829	A
01.02.1829	William Hooker	Ps	761	Supt 18.05.1830	Died 27.031849	D
21.09.1829	Abraham Howell	Pc	1043	Ps 19.10.1831	Resigned 17.04.1834	P
04.02.1830	William Holton	Ps	2966		Dismissed 13.07.1835	R
08.02.1830	Charles Hayes	Pc	2556		Dismissed 09.02.1831	
09.02.1830	Abraham Howton	Ps	2773		Dismissed 24.03.1830	
08.02.1830	Francis Howell	Pc	2949		Resigned 19.11.1831	

Dismounted Horse Patrole 1829-1830

Appointed	Name	Rank	Warrant No.	Promotion	Removal	Div
08.02.1830	George Huntley	Pc	2967	Reduced 06.07.1830 Promoted 20.04.1831	Resigned 02.04.1832	
01.02.1830	James Joslen	Pc	1771	Ps 23.01.1835		G
01.02.1829	Hy Robert Jervis	Ps	224		Dismissed 01.01.1830	
		Pc	2495		Reapplied 04.02.1830 Dismissed 03.08.1830	
01.02.1829	Edward Leader	Pc	253		Dismissed 07.03.1830	
04.02.1830	William Lodwick	Pc	2042		Resigned 29.09.1836	B
21.09.1829	James Lillywhite	Pc	699		Resigned 07.10.1830	
21.09.1829	Geo Patrick McKee	Ps	665	Insp 12.10.1829	Resigned 30.08.1832	
21.09.1829	John Manning	Ps	672	Insp 29.12.1829	Dismissed 28.09.1831	
21.09.1829	Henry Mumford	Pc	700		Resigned 01.04.1836	
21.09.1829	William Morris	Ps	1327		Dismissed 30.04.1830	
04.02.1830	Richard Meadowcroft	Ps	3016		Resigned 28.10.1840	K
10.02.1830	Mathew Noon	Pc	3056		Dismissed 05.09.1830	
21.09.1829	Edward O'Kill	Pc	1355		Dismissed 19.07.1830	
29.09.1829	Wm Fitzmaurice Peirse	Ps	1887	Insp 28.04.1830		H
29.09.1829	Richard Purcell	Pc	608		Resigned 30.09.1829	
29.09.1829	William Pooley	Pc	322		Dismissed 25.12.1829	
21.09.1829	Jno Wildman Paine	Pc	1330	Ps 29.12.1830	Dismissed 31.05.1830	B
		Pc	4520		Reapplied 04.07.1830 Died 01.07.1833	

Appointed	Name	Rank	Warrant No.	Promotion	Removal	Div
08.02.1830	Stephen Parkes	Pc	2428			L
08.02.1830	Thomas Parslow	Pc	3245		Resigned 08.09.1831	
10.02.1830	Thomas Peake	Ps	3009	Reduced 03.01.1832	Dismissed 13.03.1834	S
10.02.1829	George Smith	Pc	636		Resigned 02.11.1829	
10.02.1829	Daniel Smith	Pc	637		Dismissed 14.11.1829 Reapplied as Pc 4540 Dismissed 22.08.1830 Reapplied 27.11.1830 as Pc 5497 Resigned 16.09.1835	
21.09.1829	James Stringer	Pc	702		Dismissed 22.08.1830	
01.02.1830	John Sheppard	Pc	1835	Ps 14.12.1831		G
04.02.1830	James Sheppard	Pc	1968	Ps 17.03.1830		H
21.09.1829	William Southey	Pc	1054			P
21.09.1829	Jno Phillip Scurr	Pc	931	Ps 18.05.1830	Reduced 13.08.1830 Dismissed 07.03.1831	
21.09.1829	James Stace	Pc	1608	Ps 11.08.1830	Resigned 05.08.1833	F
01.02.1830	Jno James Smith	Pc	1711		Dismissed 09.07.1835	K
08.02.1830	Wm Sidney Smith	Ps	2447	17.05.1830		L
09.02.1830	John Stevenson	Ps	2770			V
08.02.1830	Joseph Smithers	Ps	2965		Resigned 11.05.1833	R
08.02.1830	Richard Sendell	Pc	3246		Dismissed 27.04.1830	
21.09.1829	Robert Taylor	Pc	1539	Ps 10.02.1831		F
21.09.1829	Richard Stripp	Pc	1581			T

Appointed	Name	Rank	Warrant No.	Promotion	Removal	Div
04.02.1830	William Thomas	Insp	2738		Resigned 15.08.1839	N
09.02.1830	John Taylor	Ps	3018		Resigned 11.10.1841	S
10.02.1830	Thomas Thompson	Pc	3111		Dismissed 12.04.1830	
08.02.1830	Thomas Turner	Pc	3247		Reappointed twice: Pc 5889 Resigned 16.03.1830 Pc 12104 Re-joined 18.02.1831 Resigned 28.11.1831	
09.02.1830	Richard Walters	Ps	2766	Insp 15.12.1830		P
09.02.1829	Joseph Wilkins	Pc	423		Dismissed 24.09.1829	
21.09.1829	Thos Henry Westcott	Pc	1654		Died 27.11.1834	F
10.02.1830	Robert Woolley	Ps	3007		Died 09.10.1838	S
08.02.1830	Thomas Wallace	Pc	2582	Ps 29.12.1830	Dismissed 14.05.1831	
04.02.1830	Charles Waller	Ps	2672	Reduced 23.10.1831	Resigned 26.03.1832	
21.09.1829	Martin Whealen	Pc	1345		Dismissed 05.06.1830	
08.02.1830	John Wright	Ps	2480		Resigned 16.11.1836	R
01.02.1830	Nicholas Pearce	Ps	189	Re-appointed as Ps 21.02.1831 Insp 16.07.1833	Resigned 05.10.1830	

Dismounted Horse and Foot Patrole Who Joined the Metropolitan Police up to 1833

Appointed	Name	Rank	Warrant No.	Promotion	Removal	Div
10.02.1830	William Ashford	Pc	3057		Resigned 26.07.1830	
21.09.1829	Edward Allen	Pc	871	Ps 11.01.1832		B
07.09.1829	George Blackman	Insp			Resigned 16.02.1830	
07.08.1829	William Bond	Ps	670	Insp 29.12.1829		L
21.09.1829	Charles Baker	Ps	965	Insp 30.03.1832		C
21.09.1829	Henry Brown	Pc	475		Resigned 23.09.1829	
21.09.1829	George Bower	Pc	476		Resigned 23.09.1829	
21.09.1829	Edward Bell	Ps	1319		Resigned 11.06.1845	E
21.09.1829	William Ball	Ps	2289		Resigned 24.08.1840	T
21.09.1829	James Brown	Pc	773		Dismissed 13.05.1830	
21.09.1829	John Bann	Pc	18		Dismissed 09.1829	
14.02.1830	Joseph Collard	Ps	3013	Insp 04.09.1832		
12.02.1830	Thomas Current	Pc	2763		Resigned 17.06.1833	
09.1829	Thomas Currend	Pc	63		Dismissed 13.10.1829	

Appointed	Name	Rank	Warrant No.	Promotion	Removal	Div
09.1829	William Craig	Pc	503		Resigned 03.10.1829	
21.09.1829	William Cale	Pc	706		Dismissed 12.04.1830	
21.09.1829	Charles Cook	Pc	1295		Dismissed 19.09. 1830	
21.09.1829	James Cormick	Ps	2676		Dismissed 13.05.1831	
21.09.1829	Thomas Cruttenden	Ps	2279		Died 29.03.1836	L
22.02.1830	Thomas Drew	Insp				K
29.09.1829	William Dickenson	Ps	895		Resigned 05.01.1831	H
21.09.1829	James Dodd	Ps	1501	Insp 28.04.1830		P
21.09.1829	Michael Doran	Pc	117		Dismissed 27.12.1829	
21.09.1829	Thomas Donolan	Ps	2843		Dismissed 30.03.1830	
21.09.1829	William Dove	Ps	2093		Resigned 13.12.1832	
21.09.1829	Fredk Dorrington	Pc	987		Dismissed 02.06.1831	
21.09.1829	Francis Fagan	Ps	670	Insp 23.12.1829		
21.09.1829	George Furlong	Ps	2294		Resigned 18.05.1833	
21.09.1829	James Fowler	Pc	539		Resigned 21.09.1829	
07.08.1829	William Edgar Grimwood	Insp		Supt 31.08.1832		
07.08.1829	Samuel Giles	Insp	164 1579		Dismissed 23.10.1829 To Pc 03.11.1829 Resigned 03.10.1830	
07.08.1829	Frederick Grossmith	Ps	668	Insp 29.12.1829		B
21.09.1829	William Gillett	Ps	999		Resigned 15.07.1835	N

Appointed	Name	Rank	Warrant No.	Promotion	Removal	Div
10.02.1830	Robert Glasgow	Ps	3058 10970	Returned to Ps 02.02.1832 Ps 04.06.1836	Reduced 07.05.1831 Resigned 07.03.1832 Rejoined as Pc 29.09.1835	P
01.08.1829	David Herring	Insp		Supt 19.12.1829	Died 15.06.1831	H
21.09.1829	Joseph Hammond	Pc	713	Ps 21.06.1830		L
21.09.1829	John Hughes	Pc	1051		Dismissed 18.11.1831	
21.09.1829	James Hall	Ps	2090		Dismissed 23.11.1830	
21.09.1829	Edward Huggleston	Ps	2476		Resigned 20.03.1834	E
21.09.1829	James Hackwell	Pc	201		Dismissed 16.11.1830	
21.09.1829	Benjamin Ibberson	Pc	214		Dismissed 15.12.1829	
21.09.1829	William Jones	Ps	1147		Resigned 17.11.1834	N
21.09.1829	William Augustus Jones	Pc	222		Dismissed 06.12.1829	
21.09.1829	John James	Ps	1141		Dismissed 18.06.1830	
30.01.1830	William Jones	Pc	1000		Resigned 15.08.1832	
1829	Francis Keys	Pc	576		Resigned 21.09.1829	
06.08.1829	John Lincoln	Insp			Resigned 22.04.1844	E
1829	James Medlecot	Pc	261		Dismissed 02.10.1829	
1829	Edward Moore	Pc	281		Dismissed 30.12.1829	
1829	William Merry	Ps	590		Resigned 09.10.1829	
21.09.1829	John Mason	Ps	1322	Insp 17.10.1834	Resigned 13.10.1843	E
21.09.1829	Daniel Mobbs	Pc	1336	Ps 04.09.1832	Resigned 23.12.1843	E

Appointed	Name	Rank	Warrant No.	Promotion	Removal	Div
21.09.1829	George MacGregor	Pc	1346		Dismissed 08.10.1832	
21.09.1829	Thomas Mothersell	Pc	930	Ps 29.04.1830	Resigned 07.06.1838	B
29.09.1829	John McWilliams	Ps	1885	Reduced to Pc 22.09.1830 Ps 03.11.1831	Resigned 23.12.1837	H
20.02.1830	Richard Mills	Pc	3059			S
20.02.1830	Joseph Mobbs	Pc	3060		Dismissed 23.05.1830	
21.09.1829	John Miles	Pc	697	Ps 23.02.1831	Resigned 18.03.1833	A
21.09.1829	William Mitchell	Pc	2132	Ps 16.07.1830	Resigned 14.03.1833	H
21.09.1829	William Osborn	Pc	1353	Ps 31.07.1835	Reduced 10.09.1836 Dismissed	
01.08.1829	Thomas Prosser	Insp			Resigned 01.11.1832	
01.08.1829	Joseph Priece	Insp				P
29.09.1829	Thos Bradley Pollington	Ps	1902	Insp 20.10.1831	Died 25.11.1831	H
29.09.1829	Joseph Pine	Pc	625			
29.09.1829	Phillip Parish	Pc	315			
21.09.1829	Matthew Pattison	Pc	1388			
21.09.1829	Jason Osmond Philpott	Pc	983			
21.09.1829	William Pritchard	Pc	1436	Ps 14.04.1831		
21.09.1829	Thomas Plume	Ps	2479	Reduced 23.09.1830	Resigned 22.12.1830	
21.09.1829	William Rayner	Pc	345 689		Dismissed 17.11.1829 Re–joined 01.02.1830 Resigned 12.09.1836	A
29.09.1829	George Russell	Ps	2095		Resigned 20.01.1838	K

Dismounted Horse and Foot Patrole Who Joined the Metropolitan Police

Appointed	Name	Rank	Warrant No.	Promotion	Removal	Div
21.09.1829	Joseph Robinson	Pc	1516		Resigned 21.03.1830	
21.09.1829	Daniel Rierdon	Ps	786		Dismissed 05.01.1832	
21.09.1829	Thomas Smee	Pc	367		Dismissed 26.09.1832	
21.09.1829	Robert Stride	Ps	360		Dismissed 24.09.1829	
21.09.1829	Samuel Sloman	Pc	1526		Dismissed 08.04.1830	
21.09.1829	Phillip Swingler	Pc	1575		Dismissed 29.09.1831	
21.09.1829	Robert Tyrrell	Ps	625		Resigned 10.12.1829	
21.09.1829	Richard Tuckerbridge	Pc	1537		Dismissed 08.04.1830	
21.09.1829	Thomas Thompson	Pc	1022 8489		Resigned 10.01.1831 Rejoined 06.06.1833 Resigned 20.07.1833	
29.09.1829	Chas James Topper	Ps	397 3213		Dismissed 22.09.1829 Re-joined 1829 Resigned 20.07.1835	
29.09.1829	Will John Wright	Pc	444		Dismissed 19.11.1829	
02.02.1830	James Wells	Pc	2653		Dismissed 27.03.1830	
1829	Henry Wilson	Pc	429		Dismissed 13.10.1829	
21.09.1829	William Wheatley	Ps	1512		Dismissed 06.10.1831	
08.10.1829	Joseph Wormald	Ps	789		Resigned 15.10.1841	
21.09.1829	Joseph Wilkins	Pc	888		Resigned 10.04.1835	

Statement of the number of men, transferred from the Foot Patrole and the Dismounted Horse Patrole to the Metropolitan Police since the commencement.

Originally joined	166
Dismissed	53
Resigned	33
Died	3
Total remaining	77

NB Of the whole number, 33 had been promoted above the rank of their first appointment.

APPENDIX 5

Horse Patrole Establishment 1836

Bow Street Horse Patrole establishment with ages as of 28th September 1836:

Chas Allan	49	Samuel Dunner	44
John Aris	40	Thomas Duggin	36
John Argust	30	George Drake	30
John Barnett	41	John Emerson	46
William Bassett	47	William Fair (Snr)	44
William Biggs	49	William Fryer	35
Richard Boucher	59	Thomas Garrard	42
George Bristol	44	James George	37
Thomas Bray	46	Richard Glendenning	49
Martin Burton	45	Thomas Gregson	41
Tomas Butler	35	Samuel Guttridge	42
Robert Buffham	32	Joseph Higgs	49
Samuel Collard	44	William Higgins	30
David Cornwell	41	Thomas Jacques	44
William Cook	32	John Jenkinson	39
William Davis	46	David Johnson	43
William Davidson	46	Thomas Jones	36
John Denton	39	Moses Lander	27
Robert Dick	34	William Lawrence	37
Thomas Dow	55	William Mason	44
Primrose Douglas	40	John Marlow	32

Charles May	55	**Inspectors**	
James Mew	36	James Carter	60
Thomas Morton	51	James Beswick	50
James Othen	46	Samuel Bonton	62
Edward Palmer	39	Richard Dowsett	47
John Parnel	35	Benjamin Pritchard	40
Jas Prile	46		
Thos Purchase	52		
John Rainsley	43		
William Richardson	45		
Richard Shepherd	32		
James Simpson	54		
Samuel Simmons	39		
Richard Skidmore	46		
John Smith (Jnr)	47		
John Smith (Snr)	49		
Joseph Spillman	42		
Robert Stewart	36		
William Thompson	41		
Thomas Thompson	39		
Richard Watkin	43		
George Weston	42		
Thomas Whitbread	52		
Henry Williams	36		
Charles Whitman	n/k		
William Wright	30		

APPENDIX 6

Bow Street Patroles Transferring to the Metropolitan Police 1837

Appointed	Name	Age	Warrant No.	Horse or Foot	Removal
04.06.1821	John Argust	31	15488	Horse	Resigned 01.02.1852
15.01.1823	Charles Allen	50		Horse	Resigned 21.01.1839
26.01.1822	John Aris	41	15537	Horse	Resigned 24.08.1840
05.01.1815	James Beswick	51	Insp	Horse	Resigned 24.08.1840
08.03.1815	Samuel Bonton	63	Insp	Horse	Resigned 24.08.1840
25.04.1824	William Biggs	50	Insp	Horse	Died 06.09.1838
16.07.1823	George Bristol	45	15487	Horse	Resigned 20.12.1847
10.10.1821	Thomas Bray	46	15504	Horse	Resigned 03.12.1854
05.01.1823	William Bassett	48	15503	Horse	Resigned 24.08.1840
13.09.1821	John Barnett	42	15491	Horse	Resigned 24.08.1840
17.09.1821	Martin Burton	46	15531	Horse	Resigned 24.08.1840
20.05.1823	Charles Baker		965	Foot	Insp still serving
15.04.1825	Edward Bell		1319	Foot	Resigned 11.06.1845
Autmn. 1817	William Ball		2289	Foot	Resigned 24.08.1840

Appointed	Name	Age	Warrant No.	Horse or Foot	Removal
11.06.1823	John Brundley		1331 Insp	Dismounted	Resigned 03.05.1842
18.09.1822	David Cornwall	42	15498	Horse	Resigned 14.10.1852
11.09.1821	Samuel Collard	45	15521	Horse	Resigned 24.08.1840
05.01.1829	James Covington		Ps 958	Dismounted	Died 21.06.1841
06.02.1821	Primrose Douglas	41	15484	Horse	Resigned 24.08.1840
05.01.1814	Richard Dowsett	48	Insp	Horse	Remained on V Div.
21.06.1826	William Davidson	47	Insp	Horse	Died 10.08.1831
11.09.1821	William Davis	47	695	Dismounted	Resigned 29.08.1831
12.02.1823	James Dawkins		3012 Insp	Dismounted	Died 16.12.1844
25.01.1826	John Dixon		2740	Dismounted	Resigned 09.01.1843
20.05.1817	William Dickenson		1895	Foot	Resigned 05.01.1841
05.07.1824	George Feltham		Insp	Dismounted	Remained on R Div.
01.12.1817	William Fryer		2765 Insp	Dismounted	Resigned 27.08.1841 (Supt)
31.01.1827	Phillip Froud		Ps 3405	Dismounted	Insp on L Div. (Resigned 20.03.1841)
03.02.1825	W. E. Grimwood		Insp	Foot	Insp on L Div.
07.12.1825	Joseph Higgs	50	15578	Horse	Resigned 13.04.1857
05.01.1829	William Hooker		Ps 761	Dismounted	Pc on D Div. (Promoted 18.05.1830)
27.02.1826	Joseph Hammond		713	Foot	Ps on K Div.
01.08.1826	Thomas Jacques	45	15530	Horse	Resigned 10.05.1842
02.02.1821	David Johnson	44	15534	Horse	Resigned 24.08.1840

Appointed	Name	Age	Warrant No.	Horse or Foot	Removal
05.02.1825	John Jenkinson	40	15507	Horse	Resigned 25.04.1846
08.02.1827	James Joselin		1770	Horse	Ps on G Div.
10.10.1820	William Lawrence	38	Insp	Horse	Insp on T Div.
01.01.1834	Moses Lander	28	15528	Horse	Resigned 01.04.1857
19.10.1820	John Lincoln		Insp	Foot	Resigned 22.04.1844
20.01.1834	James Mew	37	15476	Horse	Resigned 20.06.1849
10.10.1829	William Mason	45	–	Horse	Dismissed 29.12.1838
30.10.1828	Daniel Mobbs		1336	Foot	Resigned 23.12.1843
23.04.1829	Thomas Mothersell		930	Foot	Resigned 07.06.1838
29.05.1826	John McWilliam		1885	Foot	Resigned 23.12.1837
10.07.1823	Richard Mills			Foot	Resigned 02.04.1845
05.03.1823	Richard Meadowcroft		3016	Horse	Resigned 28.10.1840
02.02.1821	Thomas Morton		15520	Horse	Resigned 24.08.1840
17.07.1823	John Mason		Insp	Foot	Resigned 13.10.1843
22.02.1821	Benjamin Pritchard	41	Insp	Horse	Resigned 19.01.1844
13.02.1826	Edward Palmer	40	15475	Horse	Resigned 29.03.1847
27.11.1823	James Price	47	15497	Horse	Resigned 12.05.1849
12.05.1825	Nicholas Pearce		Insp	Foot	Still serving on F Div.
20.01.1823	William Pritchard		1436	Foot	Still serving on S Div.
05.06.1829	William Fitzmaurice		1887	Foot	Supt on H Div.
16.09.1824	Stephen Parker		2428	Horse	Resigned 05.12.1837
07.02.1821	John Rainsley	44	15482	Horse	Resigned 12.03.1837

Appointed	Name	Age	Warrant No.	Horse or Foot	Removal
09.02.1826	William Richardson	46	Insp	Horse	Serving on K Div.
17.10.1825	George Russell		2095	Foot	Resigned 20.01.1838
07.07.1824	Richard Skidmore	47		Horse	Died 23.02.1838
22.11.1821	James Simpson	55	15481	Horse	Resigned 24.08.1840
11.10.1824	Robert Stewart	37		Horse	Resigned 08.07.1839
24.03.1825	James Shepherd	33	1968	Dismounted	Insp on V Div.
19.06.1822	Joseph Spelman	43	15508	Horse	Resigned 24.08.1840
02.02.1821	John Stephenson		2770	Horse	Resigned 30.09.1841
20.11.1822	John Smith	48	15522	Dismounted	Resigned 24.08.1840
14.05.1828	William Teatherton		2668	Horse	Died 25.04.1841
23.04.1827	Thomas Thompson	40	3111	Horse	Dismissed 12.04.1830
07.05.1829	Robert Taylor		1539	Dismounted	Ps on R Div.
29.01.1821	John Taylor		3018	Horse	Resigned 11.10.1841
05.01.1829	Richard Tripp		1581	Horse	Pc on T Div.
14.04.1828	William Thomas			Dismounted	Resigned 15.08.1839
30.03.1821	Thomas Whitbread	53	15477	Horse	Resigned 24.08.1840
04.06.1821	George Weston	43	15538	Horse	Resigned 24.08.1840
21.04.1820	Charles Whitman	51	15532	Horse	Resigned 24.08.1840
03.03.1821	Richard Watkin	44	15525	Horse	Resigned 24.08.1840
14.11.1823	William Wight		444	Horse	Dismissed 29.11.1829
11.06.1823	Robert Wooley		3007	Horse	Died 19.10.1838
24.08.1825	Richard Walter		Insp	Horse	Resigned 13.05.1843
07.05.1822	Joseph Wormald		789	Foot	Resigned 15.10.1851
02.01.1837	James Ligham		7727	Horse	

Appointed	Name	Age	Warrant No.	Horse or Foot	Removal
02.01.1837	John Beach		9752	Horse	Joined 01.02.1830 Resigned 22.03.1830 Re–joined 22.05.1830 Resigned 22.01.1833 Re–joined 13.08.1834
22.07.1829	Clarke Nichols		14297	Horse	

Bow Street Horse Patrole Transferring to the Metropolitan Police 1839

Bow Street Horse Patrole transferring to the Metropolitan Police on 31st October 1839:[715]

Appointed	Name	Warrant No.	Removal	Service in the saddle
02.01.1837	John Beeche	15478	Resigned 30.10.1847	10 years
16.07.1823	Geo Bristol	15487	Resigned 28.12.1847	23 years
09.09.1839	John Brooks	15489	Resigned 28.12.1847	8 years
26.05.1838	James Balls	15490	Resigned 09.03.1840	1 yr 10 months
27.02.1839	John Barnett	15491	Resigned 24.08.1840	1 yr 6 months
02.01.1837	Thos Barnes	15495	Resigned 07.07.1845	7 years
04.01.1823	William Bassett	15503	Resigned 24.08.1840	17 years
10.101821	Thos Bray	15504	Resigned 03.12.1854	33 years
05.01.1832	Thos Baker	15514	Resigned 25.03.1847	15 years
02.01.1837	Peter Baker	15524	Resigned 03.01.1846	9 years
23.05.1838	Thos Brunt	15526	Resigned 10.03.1855	16 years
17.09.1821	Martin Burton	15531	Resigned 24.08.1846	24 years
12.02.1819	John Bartlett	15540	Resigned 04.01.1840	20 years
27.07.1801	James Bolas	15546	Resigned 04.01.1840	39 years
02.1804	Leonard Barginall	15584	Resigned 09.05.1854	50 years
05.02.1821	Primrose Douglas	15484	Resigned 24.08.1840	19 years
28.02.1836	Geo Drake	15492	Resigned 20.11.1852	16 years

715 MEPO 4/333.

Appointed	Name	Warrant No.	Removal	Service in the saddle
20.10.1834	Robert Dick	15506	Resigned 18.04.1850	15 years
25.02.1836	John Denton	15509	Resigned 09.04.1850	14 years
05.01.1832	Thos Duggan	15512	Resigned 19.06.1852	20 years
11.09.1821	William Davis	15516	Resigned 24.08.1840	19 years
29.03.1825	John Dailey	15567	Resigned 04.01.1840	14 years
26.03.1831	William Dewey	15573	Resigned 22.06.1839	8 years
26.12.1838	William Dyson	15606	Resigned 08.11.1841	2 years
20.09.1833	William Cook	15493	Dismissed 22.01.1841	7 years
02.01.1831	Charles Churchill	15494	Resigned 15.03.1865	34 years
18.09.1832	David Cornwell	15498	Resigned 14.10.1852	20 years
12.12.1838	Simon Croker	15515	Resigned 31.04.1843	4 years
11.09.1821	Samuel Collard	15521	Resigned 24.08.1840	18 years
08.08.1833	Thos Garrard	15501	Resigned 04.06.1846	12 years
29.01.1834	Thomas Jones	15496	Resigned 07.05.1840	6 years
05.07.1825	John Jenkinson	15507	Resigned 25.04.1846	20 years
01.08.1826	Daniel Johnson	15534	Resigned 24.08.1840	14 years
01.01.1839	Joseph Hindhaugh	15499	Resigned 07.09.1840	8 months
02.01.1837	James Hall	15517	Resigned 01.10.1854	17 years
07.12.1825	Joseph Higgs	15518	Resigned 13.01.1857	31 years
02.01.1837	William Hogg	15535	Resigned 05.09.1837	8 months
02.01.1837	James Langham	15474	Resigned 21.01.1841	4 years
14.10.1839	William Lynes	15484	Resigned 28.04.1863	23 years
11.09.1839	Hugh Latimer	15486	Resigned 19.06.1853	13 years
01.01.1834	Moses Lander	15528	Resigned 01.04.1857	23 years
16.03.1838	Patrick Kelly	15510	Resigned 07.08.1845	7 years
12.07.1826	Ed Palmer	15475	Resigned 29.04.1847	20 years
19.11.1823	James Price	15497	Resigned 12.05.1849	26 years
22.05.1825	James Pitchford	15500	Resigned 11.02.1840	14 years
28.05.1836	John Parnel	15513	Resigned 30.11.1840	4 years
20.01.1834	James Mew	15476	Resigned 20.06.1839	5 years
20.11.1837	Thos Milsing	15511	Resigned 17.05.1841	3 years
02.02.1821	Thos Morton	15520	Resigned 24.08.1840	19 years
20.08.1838	Thos May	15523	Resigned 25.04.1857 (Promoted to Inspector)	19 years
20.11.1837	Thos Meredith	15527	Resigned 20.07.1841	3 years
22.11.1821	James Simpson	15481	Resigned 24.08.1840	19 years

Bow Street Patroles Transferring to the Metropolitan Police 1839

Appointed	Name	Warrant No.	Removal	Service in the saddle
22.07.1839	Hugh Sandilawns	15502	Resigned 09.05.1846	6 years
19.06.1822	Joseph Spillman	15508	Resigned 24.08.1840	18 years
20.11.1822	John Smith	15522	Resigned 24.08.1840	17 years
28.10.1839	Charles Geo Schurr	15529	Dismissed 29.06.1840	1 year
30.08.1833	Richard Shepherd	15533	Resigned 23.11.1850	17 years
06.02.1821	John Rainsley	15482	Resigned 12.03.1847	26 years
31.03.1821	Thomas Whitbread	15477	Resigned 24.08.1840	19 years
20.08.1833	Henry Williams	15519	Resigned 24.10.1857	24 years
03.03.1821	Richard Watkin	15525	Resigned 24.08.1840	19 years
21.04.1840	Charles Whitman	15532	Resigned 24.08.1840	4 months
04.06.1821	George Weston	15538	Resigned 24.08.1840	19 years

Distribution of Horse Patroles 1836

Distribution of First Division Horse Patroles dated 1st October 1836:

No.	Name	Pay	Station	Road Patrolled	From and to (milestones)	Miles	Times	Remarks
1	James Lingham	3/6d	Shooters Hill	Dartford	To the 5th, 8th and back to the 7th	6	Twice	1 mile twice over
2	Edward Palmer	4/–	Shooters Hill	Dartford	Top of Shooters Hill to the 5th and back to the 7th	6½	Twice	½ mile twice over
3	James Mew	3/6d	Welling	Dartford	To near the 7th milestone and to near the 11th	7	Twice	
4	Thomas Whitbread	4/–	Welling	Dartford	To Dartford Turnpike	5	Twice	¾ mile twice over
5	John Beech	3/6d	Bexley Heath	Dartford	To Dartford Turnpike and to near the 11th	7	Twice	
6	William Mason	3/6d	Bexley Heath	Dartford	To the 5th	6¾	Twice	
9	John Rainsley	4/6d	Eltham	Dartford	Near to the 10th	4½	Twice	2 miles twice over
8	James Simpson	4/6d	Lee Green	Maidstone	To Foots Cray turnpike	6	Twice	1 mile twice over
10	Thomas Thompson	3/6d	Sidcup	Maidstone	To between the 4th and 5th	6½	Twice	½ mile twice over

No.	Name	Pay	Station	Road Patrolled	From and to (milestones)	Miles	Times	Remarks
11	Prim. Douglas	4/6d	Sidcup	Maidstone	To the 15th	4	Twice	3 miles twice over
12	Henry Williams	3/6d	Lewisham	Maidstone	To near the 8th	4	Twice	1½ miles twice over
7	Richard Skidmore	3/6d	Lee Green	Seven Oaks	To Bromley Common	5½	Twice	1½ miles twice over
13	William Biggs	4/-	Lewisham	Seven Oaks	To Farnborough Turnpike	7	Twice	
14	George Bristol	4/6d	Bromley Common	Seven Oaks	To Pratts Bottom Turnpike	4	Twice	3 miles twice over
15	John Argust	4/6d	Bromley Common	Seven Oaks	To near the 5th milestone	7	Twice	
16	William Lawrence	4/6d	Thornton Heath	Croydon	To Hermitage Bridge and Bread Green	2	Twice	1½ miles once
	Daniel Costello dismounted				Thomas Bray Orderly Rams Mews Kings Street Westminster			James Carter Principal Inspector
	Jason Beswick Inspector		Lee Green Kent					

Distribution of Second Division Horse Patroles dated 1st October 1836:

No.	Name	Pay	Station	Road Patrolled	From and to (milestones)	Miles	Times	Remarks
17	Henry Boucher	3/6d	Sutton	Sutton and Epsom	Sutton to Mitcham and Stone Bridge Border Morden	6	Twice	
18	William Wright	3/6d	Merton	Epsom and Sutton	Merton to Mitcham and Sutton	4	3 times	

No.	Name	Pay	Station	Road Patrolled	From and to (milestones)	Miles	Times	Remarks
19	George Drake	3/6d	Merton	Epsom	Merton to Ewell turnpike	6¼	Twice	
20	William Richardson	4/–	North Cheam	Epsom	Cheam to Ewell Turnpike and Merton gate	6½	Twice	
21	Charles Churchill	3/6d	Wimbledon	Wimbledon to Kingston	Wimbledon to Kingston Road Robin Hood Hill	4¼	3 times	
22	Thomas Barnes	3/6d	Robin Hood Hill Kingston	Kingston	Robin Hood Hill to Wandsworth side of Wimbledon Common	3	4 times	
23	Thomas Jones	3/6d	Robin Hood Hill	Kingston Esher	Robin Hood Hill to Esher	6½	Twice	
24	James Price	4/–	Kingston	Kingston	Kingston to Robin Hood turnpike	2	6 times	
25	David Cornwell	4/–	Esher	Esher	Ditton Marsh to Esher and Kingston	6½	Twice	
26	John Jenkinson	4/–	Hounslow Heath	Staines	Hounslow Heath to Stanwell and Hounslow	7½	Twice	
27	Charles Allen	4/6d	Hounslow Heath	Staines and Colnbrook	Hounslow Heath to Staines and Colnbrook	7½	Twice	
28	William Cook	3/6d	Bedfont	Staines and Windsor	Bedfont to Egham and Frogmore Lodge near Windsor	8	Twice	
29	Thomas Garrard	3/6d	Bedfont	Staines and Windsor	Bedfont to Hounslow and Cranford Bridge	7½	Twice	
30	Robert Stewart	3/6d	Hounslow	Colnbrook	Hounslow to Colnbrook Turnpike	6½	Twice	
31	William Bassett	4/6d	Hounslow	Staines	Hounslow to Staines Turnpike	6½	Twice	

No.	Name	Pay	Station	Road Patrolled	From and to (milestones)	Miles	Times	Remarks
32	Thomas Bray	4/6d	Harlington	Colnbrook & Staines	Harlington to Hounslow and Bedfont	6½	Twice	Still serving in 1839
33	William Thompson	4/–	Harlington	Colnbrook and Slough	Harlington to the 20 mile-stone at Slough	7	Twice	
34	Robert Dick	3/6d	Colnbrook	Slough & Eaton	Colnbrook to Slough Turnpike nr Eaton and Salt Hill	4	4 times	
	John Dunton (dismounted)	3/6						
	Richard Dowsett Inspector		Kingston Surrey					

Distribution of Third Division Horse Patroles dated 1st October 1836:

No.	Name	Pay	Station	Road Patrolled	From and to (milestones)	Miles	Times	Remarks
35	Joseph Spillman	4/6d	Hanwell	Uxbridge	Old Hats Ealing to Hillingdon Gate	7	Twice	
36	John Denton	3/6d	Hanwell	Uxbridge	Old Hats Ealing to Hillingdon Gate	7	Twice	
37	Moses Lander	3/6d	Hayes	Uxbridge	Hillingdon Gate to Old Hats Ealing	7	Twice	
38	William Fair (Sr)	4/6d	Hayes	Uxbridge	Hillingdon Gate to Old Hats Ealing	7	Twice	

Distribution of Horse Patroles 1836

No.	Name	Pay	Station	Road Patrolled	From and to (milestones)	Miles	Times	Remarks
39	Thomas Duggan	4/–	Stonebridge	Harrow Road, Harrow	4th milestone to the 9th	5	3 times	
40	John Parnel	3/6d	Stonebridge Road, Harrow	Harrow	4th milestone to the 9th	5	3 times	
41	Thomas Butler	3/6d	Edgware	Edgware	8th milestone to the 3rd	5	Twice	4th to 7th x 4
42	John Barnett	4/6d	Edgware	Edgware	8th milestone to the 3rd	5	Twice	3rd to 5th x 4
43	Martin Burton	4/–	Edgware	St. Albans & Watford	8th milestone to the 10th then to 12th at Watford	6	Twice	9th to 10th x 4
44	William Davidson	4/–	Mill Hill	Hendon	9th milestone to the North End Hampstead	5	Twice	5th to 7th x4
45	Joseph Higgs	4/–	Finchley New Road	Finchley New Road	Barnet Road to Grand Junction Gate	5½	Twice	4th to 5th x 4
46	Robert Buffham	3/6d	Finchley New Road	Finchley New Road	Barnet Road to Grand Junction Gate	5½	Twice	2nd to 3rd x 4
47	Thomas Norton	4/6d	Finchley	Barnet	Wellington Bar to Whetstone Gate	4	Twice	6th to 8th x4
48	Samuel Collard	4/6d	Finchley	Barnet	Wellington Bar to Barnet	5½	Twice	9th to 10th x 4
49	John Smith	4/6d	Whetstone	Barnet	Barnet to Archway Highgate	6 4	Twice	8th to 9th x
50	William Davis	4/–	Whetstone	Finchley New Road	Station to Grand Junction gate	6	Twice	3rd to 4th x 4
	Samuel Bonton Inspector		Kilburn Middlesex					

Distribution of Fourth Division Horse Patroles dated 1st October 1836:

No.	Name	Pay	Station	Road Patrolled	From and to (milestones)	Miles	Times	Remarks
51	James George	3/6d	Green Lanes, Enfield	Enfield	6th to 4th and return to 10th milestone	8	Twice	
52	Richard Watkin	4/6d	Enfield	Enfield	Enfield to 4th milestone	7	Twice	
53	Richard Glendenning	4/6d	Lea Bridge	Lea Bridge and Forest	Lea Bridge to Leytonstone	6½	Twice	
54	John Emerson	4/-	Woodford	New Woodford	Woodford to Walthamstow	2½	4 times	
55	Thomas Marlow	3/6d	Woodford	New Woodford	Woodford to Walthamstow	2½	4 times	
56	William Fair	3/6d	Woodford to Snakes Lane	Woodford Bridge	Woodford to 13th milestone Abridge	8	Twice	
57	Thomas Jacques	4/-	Loughton	Epping	Loughton to Woodford return to 15th Milestone	6½	Twice	
58	William Higgins	3/6d	Epping	Epping	Epping to Woodford	7	Twice	
59	Charles Witman	4/6d	Leytonstone	Forest and Lea Bridge	Leytonstone to Lea Bridge	7	Twice	
60	Samuel Simmons	3/6d	Chigwell	Abridge & Woodford Bridge	Chigwell to Abridge to Leytonstone	7	Twice	
61	David Johnson	4/6d	Stratford	Epping	Stratford to Woodford Turnpike	6½	Twice	
62	Samuel Gutteridge	4/6d	Stratford	Ilford	Stratford to Ilford	3½	3 times	
63	James Othen	4/6d	Ilford	Ilford	Ilford to Stratford	3½	3 times	1832
64	John Aris	4/6d	Ilford	Romford	Woodford to 10th milestone	3	4 times	
65	George Weston	4/6d	Romford	Romford	Romford to Ilford	3	4 times	

Distribution of Horse Patroles 1836

No.	Name	Pay	Station	Road Patrolled	From and to (milestones)	Miles	Times	Remarks
R*	Richard Shepherd	3/6d	Leyton	Woodford to Walthamstow	Woodford to Walthamstow	2½	4	May be substitute for No. 54 or 59
	William Hogg Dismounted	3/6d						
	James Carter Principle Inspector Millbank		54 Holywell Street					

R* = Reserve

Timeline

1729   Thomas de Veil sets up his first office as a Justice of the Peace in Leicester Fields (now Leicester Square).

1740   Thomas de Veil establishes a Magistrates' court at 4 Bow Street.

1744   Thomas de Veil became Sir Thomas de Veil after being knighted in recognition of his work.

1746   Death of Sir Thomas de Veil.

1748   Henry Fielding appointed Justice of the Peace for Westminster.

1749   Crime Reporting began, where victims of crime were encouraged to report their losses to Bow Street and the Fieldings began to compile a register in which they recorded all house breakings and robberies with a list of items stolen, names and descriptions of suspects and particulars of the arrests and trials of suspects.

1750   A small group of non-uniformed men is formed by Henry Fielding to help detect highway robbery on the roads into the metropolis.

1751   Henry Fielding publishes his Enquiry into the causes of the late increase in robberies.

1753/54   The robber gangs causing many violent offences in the metropolis had been largely broken up.

1754   The death of Henry Fielding on 8th October in Lisbon, Portugal aged 48 years. Buried in the British Cemetery in Lisbon.

1763   First Horse Patrole introduced of eight men (later increased to ten) on 17th October.

1764   Despite its success, the Horse Patrole ends in October due to a lack of Government funding.

1772   John Fielding issues *The Weekly or Extraordinary Pursuit*, a bulletin listing wanted offenders who had escaped London, in the autumn. This was to become *The Public Hue and Cry* and then *The Hue and Cry*. In 1829 this became *The Police Gazette*.

1780   Death of Sir John Fielding on 4th September at Brompton after a long illness, aged 58 years.

1780   The Gordon Riots.

1782   Sampson Wright appointed Senior Magistrate at Bow Street.

1782   The Government secretly sanctions the introduction of the Bow Street Foot Patrole.

1792   Seven new Public Offices modelled on Bow Street opened across London.

1805   Due to the increase of highway robbery the Horse Patrole reintroduced to patrol the roads leading into the metropolis. Two Inspectors, four deputy Inspectors and 54 Horse Patroles were appointed.

1822   The Bow Street Horse Patrole establishment was increased to 72.

1822   The non-uniformed Horse Patrole was introduced, with the appointment of 100 men to patrol on foot.

1822   A uniformed Day Patrole was introduced by Robert Peel numbering 27 men with a Head Constable (Inspector) in charge to distribute themselves judiciously between 9.00am until 7.00pm, when they would be relieved by the night parties. These men wore the blue and red uniform of the Horse Patrole and were a preventive police.

1829	The Metropolitan Police were inaugurated.
1829/30	Selected members of the Bow Street Foot Patrole join the Metropolitan Police and the remainder disbanded.
1837	The Bow Street Horse Patrole absorbed by the Metropolitan Police.
1839	The Bow Street Runners were disbanded.

Abbreviations

Div	Division
Insp	Inspector
JP	Justice of the Peace
MEPO	Files held by the National Archives originating from records submitted by the Metropolitan Police.
MPD	Metropolitan Police District
Pc	Police Constable
Ps	Police Sergeant
Supt	Superintendent
£	Pounds
s	Shillings
d	Pence

Bibliography

Adam, Hargrave, L. (1920) *The Police Encyclopedia, Vol. 1*.
Blackfriars Publishing Co., London

Ainsworth, W. H. Cruikshank, G. and Browne, H. K. (1849)
*Ainsworth's Magazine: A Miscellany of Romance, General
Literature, Volume 7*.
Published by John Mortimer, London, Southampton

Anon, (1748) *Memoirs of the life and times of Sir Thomas de Veil*

Anon, (1748) *London Magazine* (December)

Armitage, G. (1932) *The History of the Bow Street Runners*.
Wisehart and Co., London

Ascoli, D. (1979) *The Queen's Peace*. Hamish Hamilton, London

Babington, A., (1969) *A House in Bow Street*.
MacDonald and Co., London

Battestin, M. C. (2000) *A Henry Fielding Companion*.
Greenwood Press, Westport

Beattie, J. (2012) *The First English Detectives*.
Oxford University Press, Oxford

Bevan, F. (2006) *Criminals and Conspirators
in Ancestors*, November, p. 33

Black, J. (2015) *British Politics and Foreign Policy, 1744–57:
Mid–Century Crisis*. Ashgate, Farnham

Brown, B. (1990) *Romford Police: The Anniversary of a Change
in the Romford Record*. Romford and District Historical Society

Brown, J. (1757) *Estimate of the Manner and Principles of the
Times*. Davis, L. and Reymers C. Holborn

Browne, D., (1956) *The Rise of Scotland Yard.*
George Harrap and Co., London

Buchanan, B (1992) *The Great Bath Road 1700–1830.*
Bath History Vol. 4. Millsteam

Colquhoun, P., (1796) *A Treatise On The Police Of The Metropolis,
Explaining The Various Crimes And Misdemeanours Which
At Present Are Felt As A Pressure Upon The Community; And
Suggesting Remedies For Their Prevention.* H. Fry, London

Cook, A. C. (2014) *Truncheons – An Unequal Match.*
Alan Cook, Essex

Cox, D. (2010) 'Ruthven, George, Thomas Joseph (1792/3–1844),
Police Officer.' *Oxford Dictionary of National Biography,*
Oxford University Press

Cox, D. (2010) *A Certain Share of Low Cunning – A History Of
The Bow Street Runners 1792–1839.*
Willan, Cullumpton

Critchley, T. A. (1967) *The History of Police in England and Wales.*
Constable and Company

Dilnot, G. (1926) *The Story of Scotland Yard – Its History and
Associations.* G. Bles, London

Directors of the Bank of England (1823) *The names and
descriptions of the proprietors of unclaimed dividends
on Bank stock and on all Government Funds and Securities
transferable at the Bank of England.* Teape and Jones, London

Elliott, B. (2001) *Peelers Progress.*
www.eppingforestdc.gov.uk/phocadownload/Museum/
peelers%20progress.pdf accessed on 22nd June 2016

Fielding, J. (1755) *A Plan of the universal register office,
opposite Cecil Street, and that in Bishopsgate Street,
the corner of Cornhill 8th ed.* London

Fielding, J. (1758) *An Account of the origin and the effects of a
police set on foot by his grace the Duke of Newcastle in the year
1753, upon a plan presented to his grace the Duke of Newcastle
by the late Henry Fielding.* London

Fenn Clark, E. (1935) *Truncheons*. Herbert Jenkins, London

Fitzgerald, P. (1888) *Chronicles of Bow Street Police-office*. Gilbert and Rivington, London

Goddard, H. (1956) *Memoirs of a Bow Street Runner*. Museum Press Ltd.

Griffiths, A. G. (1898) *Mysteries of Police and Crime*. Cassell and Comp, London

Gronov. (1889) *The Reminiscences and Recollections of Capt. Gronov*, 2 vols

Haggard, J., Scott, W. (Baron Stowell) (1822) *London Reports of Cases Argued and Determined in the Consistory Court of London* Volume 1 by Church of England, Diocese of London

Hartley, J. (1785) *History of the Westminster Election*. Debrett, J. London

Highfill, P. H., Burnim, K. A., Langhans, E. A. *A Biographical Dictionary of Actors, Actresses, Musicians, Dancers, Managers and others Stage Personnel in London*, vol. 8

Home Department (1772) *Report from the Committee of the House of Commons into the Burglaries and Robberies committed in the Cities of London and Westminster*

Home Department (1797) *The Report of the Select Committee on the Police of the Metropolis*

Hotten, J. C. (1859) *The Slang Dictionary* John Hotton, Piccadilly, London

House of Commons *The Report of the Committee on the Police of the Metropolis 1816*

House of Commons *The Committee on the State of the Police of the Metropolis 1817*

House of Commons (1818) *The Third Report from the Committee on the State of the Police of the Metropolis*

House of Commons (1822) *Report of the Committee of the State of the Police of the Metropolis*

Howard. G. (1953) *Guardians of the Queen's Peace*.

Odhams, London

Howell, T. and Cobett, W. (1818) *A Complete Collection of State Trials and Proceedings for High Treason and Misdemeanours.* Hansard, London

Kennison, P., Swinden, D. and Moss, A. (2013) *Discovering More Behind the Blue Lamp.* Coppermill Press, Essex

Kesselman, B. (2015) *Paddington Pollakey, Private Detective. The Mysterious Life and Times of the Real Sherlock Holmes.* The History Press, London.

King, P. (2000) *Crime, Justice and Discretion in England 1740–1820.* Oxford University Press, Oxford

Lambert, T. (2011) *A Brief History of Kingston upon Thames*

Leslie–Melville, R. (1934) *The Life and Work of Sir John Fielding.* Lincoln Williams, London

Martin, S. (1970) *The Policing of Finchley Through the Ages.* MPS Historic Collection ESB

Melville–Lee, W. L. (1901) *The History of Police in England.* Methuen and Co.

Mitton, M. (1985) *The Policeman's Lot* Quiller Press, London

Moylan, J. F. (1929) *Scotland Yard and the Metropolitan Police.* Putnam's London

Moylan, I. F. (1929) 'The Blue Army' in *Country Life*, May edition

Newcomb, T. M. (1960). 'Varieties of Interpersonal Attraction' in D. Cartwright and A. Zander (Eds.), *Group Dynamics: Research and Theory* (2nd ed.)

Newman, G. (1997) *Bow Street Runners. Britain in the Hanoverian Age, 1714–1837: An Encyclopaedia.* Taylor & Francis, London

Ogborn, M. (1998) *Spaces of Modernity – London Geographies 1680–1780.* Guilford Press

Paley, R. (1983) 'The Middlesex Justices Act of 1792; its origins and effects', Ph.D. thesis (University of Reading)

Phillips, D. (1980) 'A new engine of power and authority – the institutionalisation of law enforcement in England 1780–1830' in Gatrell, V. A. C; Bruce; Lenman and Parker, G. (Eds) *Crime and Law, the social history of crime in Western Europe since 1500.* Europa, London

Pringle, P. (1955) *Hue and Cry – The Story of Henry and John Fielding and their Bow Street Runners.* Morrow and Co., London

Pringle, P. (1968) *Henry and John Fielding – The Thief Catchers.* Dennis Dobson, London

Protheroe, M. (1931) *The History of the Criminal Investigation Department at Scotland Yard.* Herbert Jenkins, London

Reith, C. (1938) *The Police idea.* Oxford University Press, London

Robson, W. (1993) *Britain– Access to History 1750–1900.* Oxford University Press

Rubenstein, J. (1977) 'Henry and John Fielding – Police Philosophy and Police Technique' in *Pioneers in Policing.* Philip Stead (ed). McGraw-Hill, London

Searle, M. (1930) *Turnpikes and Toll Bars.* Limited Edition, Hutchinson & Co.

Sibley, M. (1794) *The Genuine Trial of Thomas Hardy for Treason.* Vol. 2. J. S. Jordon, London

Stead, P. (Eds) (1977) *Pioneers in Policing.* McGraw-Hill

Stockdale, J. (1820) *The Royal Kalender, and court and City register for England Scotland Ireland and the Colonies.* Galabin and Marchant, London

Tobias, J. J. (1972) *Nineteenth Century Crime: Prevention and Punishment.* David and Charles, Newton Abbot

Toynbee, P. (1903–5) *The Letters of Horace Walpole.* 16 volumes Oxford, Clarendon Press, and supplemented by 3 further volumes (1918–1925)

Walpole, H. (1859) *Journal of the reign of King George*

Webb, S. and Webb, B. (1922) *English Local Government: Statutory Authorities for Special Purpose.* Longmans, Green and Co., London

Webb, S. and Webb, B. (1906) *English Local Government (Vol. 1) – The Parish and the County.* Longmans, London

Welch, S. (1754) *Observations on the Office of Constable.* Millar, A., Strand, London.

Wilkinson, F. (2002) *Those Entrusted with Arms.* Greenhill. Pennsylvania

Wilkinson, F. (2010) *A History of Handguns.* Wiltshire. The Crowood Press Ltd

Zirker, M. R., (1998) *Henry Fielding – An Inquiry into the causes of the late increase of Robbers and related writings.* Oxford University Press, Oxford

Index

Page numbers in *italics* denote illustrations